This monograph challenges the increasingly accepted notion that Galatians is either a sample of classical rhetoric or should be interpreted in light of Graeco-Roman rhetorical handbooks. It demonstrates that the handbooks of Aristotle, Cicero and other such writers, discuss a form of oratory which was limited with respect to subject, venue and style of communication, and that Galatians falls outside such boundaries. The inapplicability of ancient canons of rhetoric is reinforced by a detailed comparison of Galations with the handbooks, a survey of patristic attitudes towards Paul's communicative technique, and interaction with twentieth-century discussions of the nature of New Testament Greek. Dr Kern concludes that rhetorical handbooks were never a tool of literary criticism and that they cannot assist the search for a distinctly Pauline rhetoric. Thus this study has implications not only for Galatians but also for other New Testament epistles.

PHILIP H. KERN is Lecturer in New Testament at Moore Theological College, Sydney.

SOCIETY FOR NEW TESTAMENT STUDIES
MONOGRAPH SERIES
General Editor: Richard Bauckham

101

RHETORIC AND GALATIANS

Rhetoric and Galatians

Assessing an approach to Paul's epistle

PHILIP H. KERN

CAMBRIDGE
UNIVERSITY PRESS

PUBLISHED BY THE PRESS SYNDICATE OF THE UNIVERSITY OF CAMBRIDGE
The Pitt Building, Trumpington Street, Cambridge CB2 1RP, United Kingdom

CAMBRIDGE UNIVERSITY PRESS
The Edinburgh Building, Cambridge CB2 2RU, United Kingdom
40 West 20th Street, New York, NY 10011–4211, USA
10 Stamford Road, Oakleigh, Melbourne 3166, Australia

First published 1998

Printed and bound in Great Britain by Biddles Ltd, Guildford and King's Lynn

Typeset in Times Roman 10/12pt [CE]

A catalogue record for this book is available from the British Library

Library of Congress cataloguing in publication data

Kern, Philip H.
Rhetoric and Galatians: assessing an approach to Paul's epistle / Philip H. Kern.
    p.   cm. – (Society for New Testament Studies monograph series; 101)
Includes bibliographical references and index.
ISBN 0 521 63117 3 (hardback)
1. Bible. N.T. Galatians – Language, style. 2. Rhetoric, Ancient.
I. Title. II. Series: Monograph series (Society for New Testament Studies); 101.
BS2685.2.K47   1998
227'.4066 – dc21   98-12098 CIP

ISBN 0 521 63117 3 hardback

For Amy

CONTENTS

Preface   *page* xi
List of abbreviations   xiii

1   Introduction   1

√ **2   Towards a definition of rhetoric**   7
           Rhetoric   7
           Rhetor   34
           Rhetorician   34
           Species   34
           Taxis   36
           Topoi   37

3   Methods of rhetorical analysis and Galatians   39
           Sources   39
           History of rhetorical approaches to Galatians   43
           Analytical presuppositions   56
           Intrinsic and extrinsic approaches   69
           Methods of analysis   86

4   Rhetorical structure and Galatians   90
           Galatians 1–2   92
           Galatians 3–4   109
           Galatians 5–6   112
           Conclusion   118

5   Rhetorical species and Galatians   120
           The limits of forensic rhetoric   125
           The limits of deliberative rhetoric   125
           The limits of epideictic rhetoric   126
           The limits of rhetoric and Galatians   129
           Galatians as a forensic speech   131

	Galatians as deliberative rhetoric	136
	Subsequent solutions to the question of species	156
	Conclusion	164
6	**The language of Paul's letters: 1. As evaluated by early Christian writers**	**167**
	The church fathers	169
	Post-patristic 'rhetoricians'	198
	Conclusion	203
7	**The language of Paul's letters: 2. The contribution of modern studies**	**204**
	Acts 24: a courtroom analogy	204
	Orientation to Paul's background	210
	The level of Paul's language	215
	Alternative explanations of Paul's language	230
	Excursus: the activities of the orator	245
	Language levels were steeply graduated	247
	Paul's mode of discourse	249
	Conclusions	254
8	**Conclusions**	**256**
	Summary	258
	Implications and significance	259
	Further study	260
Select bibliography		262
Index of subjects		297
Index of modern authors		302

PREFACE

I set out for Sheffield in late summer of 1990 to do an exegetical study of Galatians, especially 2.15–21. It became apparent, however, that much ground-clearing work was required before exegesis could begin. In the end, and because of the skilful prodding and questioning of my supervisor, Dr Loveday Alexander, these preliminary matters became the thesis, and the exegesis still lies just beyond the horizon. I thank Dr Alexander for broadening my perspective and introducing me to a world about which I knew little.

There are others without whom this work would have been impossible. Friends at Tyndale House who have encouraged and provoked me include Gerald Peterman, Andrew Warren (who constantly pointed out my abuse of the English language, and occasionally assisted with German too), Peter Bolt and Bruce and Lyn Winter. The church family at Lansdowne Chapel, Sheffield, made our two years there wonderful. Thanks also for warm friendship at Wauwatosa and Norwood. Stanley Porter, Philip Satterthwaite and Janet Fairweather of the Classics Faculty at Cambridge have interacted with the content of the book, been fine friends and fountains of information. Thanks go to Jack Fish and David MacLeod for drawing me to Pauline studies, and to Scot McKnight, Doug Moo and D. A. Carson for endeavouring to elevate me to the next level. The careful, critical reading offered by my examiners, Andrew Lincoln and Ian McDonald, has been much appreciated, as has the help of librarians at the universities of Sheffield and Cambridge, Trinity International University (Deerfield), Northwestern (Evanston), Macquarie (Sydney) and Tyndale House. Special thanks to Andrew Clarke for help both in the library and over tea – and again to Bruce Winter for too many things to mention.

This research was funded in part by a Tyndale Council Research

Grant, and was much facilitated by opportunities afforded at 'the House'. My thanks go to them for their assistance. The project would have been impossible without the support of my family, especially my wife to whom I dedicate this book.

ABBREVIATIONS

Abbreviations have been largely restricted to works directly related
to biblical studies and follow the *NTS* (38.1, Jan. 1992) conventions. For papyri see E. G. Turner, *Greek Papyri: An Introduction*,
Oxford: Clarendon Press, 156–71. The following is a supplement.

ANF	*Ante-Nicene Fathers*, ed. Alexander Roberts and James Donaldson, Grand Rapids: Eerdmans, 1989
ANRW	*Aufstieg und Niedergang der Römischen Welt*, ed. H. Temporini and W. Haase, Berlin: De Gruyter, 1972–92.
BAGD	*A Greek-English Lexicon of the New Testament and Other Early Christian Literature*, 4th edn., ed. W. Bauer, W. Arndt, T. Gingrich, and P. Danker, Chicago: University of Chicago Press, 1957
BETL	Bibliotheca ephemeridum theologicarum lovaniensium
DDC	*De Doctrina Christiana*
EB	*Encyclopaedia Britannica*
ET	English Translation
JAC	*Jahrbuch für Antike und Christentum*
JSNT	*Journal for the Study of the New Testament*
JSNTS	Journal for the Study of the New Testament Supplements
JSOT	*Journal for the Study of the Old Testament*
JSOTS	Journal for the Study of the Old Testament Supplements
LCL	Loeb Classical Library
LCM	*Liverpool Classical Monthly*
LSJ	*Greek–English Lexicon*. Liddell, Scott, Jones
LXX	Septuagint

NABPRDS	National Association of Baptist Professors of Religion Dissertation Series
NovT	*Novum Testamentum*
NPNF	*Nicene and Post-Nicene Fathers*, ed. Philip Schaff and Henry Wace, Grand Rapids: Eerdmans, 1991
OCD²	*Oxford Classical Dictionary*, ed. N. G. L. Hammond and H. H. Scullard, Oxford: Clarendon Press, ²1970.
PEQ	*Palestinean Exploration Quarterly*
PG	Patrologiae cursus completus, ed. Jacques-Paul Migne, Series Graeca
PL	Patrologiae cursus completus, ed. Jacques-Paul Migne, Series Latina
repr.	reprint
SBLDS	Society of Biblical Literature Dissertation Series

1

INTRODUCTION

This inquiry concerns itself with the intersection of two interpretative methodologies. On the one hand we may speak of 'rhetorical criticism' as used in biblical studies to describe a text-centred approach, the purpose being to determine how the shape of that text, its innate strategic impulse, affects the reader. This in turn, depending on the stance of the practitioner, breaks down into two more channels. Either those impulses may inform the analyst's recreation of the text's tradition, travelling back to questions of the intent and strategy of the writer, or such questions may be bracketed off to allow the analyst to locate a text-immanent intent,[1] strategy and world of discourse. Either way this stream of scholarship attempts to deal with the text at hand and take its shape and content as primary.

On the other hand – and we will see that this approach is commonly identified with studies of Galatians – 'rhetorical analysis' may be a new and improved approach to form criticism, attempting to describe textual shape and content by measuring its conformity to classical handbooks on rhetoric. This approach is concerned with neither the shape nor prehistory of the text merely for their own sake; thus it side-steps some of the weaknesses of form criticism. But the question of what it can add to the discovery of meaning remains open, for it often addresses only matters peripheral to the text with any great effectiveness,[2] and even regarding these matters (primarily linked to sociology), it does little more than open new questions. Unfortunately, these questions often receive troubling answers because both the literary-critical and classical backgrounds of the interpretative scheme have been ignored.[3]

---

[1] That is, the intent of the text as opposed to that of its creator.
[2] Clines, *Pentateuch*, 7–15.
[3] It will become clear that I do not question the use of Galatians as an artefact –

The educational system of the ancient world at once found its centre and pinnacle in rhetoric. Thus to credit Paul with producing a piece of refined oratory imputes certain qualities to him; for example, the rhetor necessarily depended upon a particular linguistic register reflecting the 'oratorical domain', discussed in this thesis in terms of levels of language. This use of language, as remains the case to some degree, reveals the speaker's level of *paideia*.

Rhetoric has thus been used of late to refine our understanding of Paul's backgrounds, providing the data to work back from a rhetorical discourse embedded within an epistle to the source of Paul's ability.[4] Manifold explanations for Paul's oratorical prowess are proffered, ranging from prolonged higher education in the manner of his day to a rejection of the question altogether as irrelevant to the matter of his background. But conclusions concerning Paul's backgrounds – social, educational, financial – affect too much of NT studies to be determined by excessively hypothetical propositions; it is imperative that we build on a solid foundation.

For evidence that literary conclusions control wide-ranging discussions, consult David Aune's article in which he treats 'Romans as a *Logos Protreptikos* in the context of Ancient Religious and Philosophical Propaganda'.[5] He has five questions relating to (1) Jewish literary history; (2) Paul's education and what it tells of Jewish proselytism; and (3) Paul's view of leadership over against philosophical schools – all of which arise from Paul's supposed employment of a particular letter/speech form. Joop Smit and C. K. Barrett feel that Paul's writing permits us to speak of his 'professional skill as a rhetorician';[6] while John Fitzgerald, also allowing the implications of his work to run their course, more cautiously observes: 'Inasmuch as this instruction in epistolary style was provided by teachers of rhetoric, the correspondence of Paul's letters to the styles and letter types given by Ps.-Demetrius and Ps.-Libanius

---

i.e. as a tool useful for understanding Paul's social world. But wrongly identifying the epistle as a piece of classical rhetoric is as misleading as, say, confusing a first-century Jewish potsherd with a Greek one from four hundred years earlier.

[4] The fault lies not with the logic of this move but with the inherent weakness of an edifice built without a foundation. Since the evidence opposes the suggestion that Paul wrote classical orations, it cannot support the conclusion that Paul reveals the *paideia* behind rhetoric.

[5] Aune, 'Romans as *Logos Protreptikos*', 91–124.

[6] Smit, 'Deliberative Speech', 24; Barrett, *Freedom and Obligation*, 32. Cf. also Fitzgerald 'Ancient Epistolary Theorists', 193; Marshall, *Enmity in Corinth*, especially 400.

is highly significant. It provides another piece of evidence that Paul's educational level was high and that he received training in rhetoric'.[7] Christopher Forbes moves from 1 Corinthians via reference to Paul's tertiary education to 'a certain social standing'. Though his logic is sound, and his conclusions held tentatively, he builds, like the others, on the premise that Paul's means of expression are those of classical oratory.[8] Thus certain elements coalesce, permitting a direct flow of logic from employment of rhetoric to the appropriate education (i.e. tertiary) to social standing.

For the second position, that the question holds little relevance, one may begin with the influential reflections of Kennedy:

> It is not a necessary premise of this study that the evangelists or Saint Paul had formally studied Greek rhetoric. In the case of Paul the evidence is somewhat ambivalent . . . Even if he had not studied in a Greek school, there were many handbooks of rhetoric in common circulation which he could have seen. He and the evangelists as well would, indeed, have been hard put to escape an awareness of rhetoric as practised in the culture around them, for the rhetorical theory of the schools found its immediate application in almost every form of oral and written communication: in official documents and public letters, in private correspondence, in the lawcourts and assemblies, in speeches at festivals and commemorations, and in literary composition in both prose and verse.[9]

These words are heavy with implications for NT studies. While to Kennedy Paul's rhetorical awareness says more about his literary milieu than about his education, it is surely significant that, at least at some level, Paul and the evangelists are thought to stand in a similar relationship to rhetoric.

Burton Mack, occupying a middle ground, maintains (though undoubtedly he does not intend his absolute claims to be taken literally) that '*all* people, whether formally trained or not, were *fully schooled* in the wily ways of the sophists, the eloquence required at civic festivals'.[10] Hence he concludes that 'To be

---

[7] Fitzgerald, 'Ancient Epistolary Theorists', 193. Fitzgerald then cites Betz, 'Problem'. Cf. Marshall, *Enmity in Corinth*, 400; Malherbe, *Social Aspects*, 59.

[8] Forbes, 'Comparison, Self-Praise and Irony', 22–4.

[9] Kennedy, *New Testament Interpretation*, 9–10.

[10] Mack, *Rhetoric and the New Testament*, 31; emphasis added.

engulfed in the culture of Hellenism meant to have ears trained for the rhetoric of speech'.[11] Lest one think that Mack simply refers to a high gloss on one's natural ability to argue well – without implying a system of rhetoric – he goes on to label what was learned by these means 'the rules of discourse' and describes them as 'firm'.[12]

Perhaps the clearest expression of this position comes from Douglas Campbell, who explains that because Graeco-Roman society was so thoroughly immersed in it, rhetoric maintained some degree of influence over everyone. Paul would have been no different: his general education, continual travel and innate intelligence were sufficient for rhetoric to infuse his patterns of speech and thought.[13]

Betz avoids the question of Paul's status in his commentary – though he does betray an awareness of sociological implications when he refers to 'the myth of Paul the non-thinker' and the inseparable falsehood that 'he cannot have received a decent education'. His commentary attempts to show that Paul's carefully constructed epistle reflects his 'literary skills',[14] undermining disparaging views of Paul by highlighting his sophistication.

Rhetoric relates more directly to Paul's background in the argument of Robert G. Hall, who insists that those who favour the biographical evidence of Galatians over that of Acts have a misplaced faith: rhetorical conventions allow for details in the narrative which, though not altogether reliable, pose no threat to the educated listener. Hence Paul presents no more reliable biographical data in Galatians than does Acts – meaning that we have very little evidence for his life except what we infer from the less direct statements of his letters.[15] Gerd Lüdemann similarly argues that in a forensic dispute the most useful account of events is preferable to the most accurate, so Paul's narrative need not supply historical detail.[16]

Another question which rhetoric may help answer concerns the nature of the Galatian churches. To the tired discussion of who received the epistle Betz adds a fresh insight: 'The sophisticated

[11] Ibid.
[12] Ibid.
[13] D. S. Campbell, *Rhetoric of Righteousness*, 75–6.
[14] Betz, *Galatians*, xiv.
[15] Hall, 'Historical Inference', 308–20.
[16] Lüdemann, *Paul*, 57–62.

character of Galatians as a literary and rhetorical product suggests that the Galatian churches were composed primarily of Hellenized and Romanized city dwellers, rather than the uneducated and the poor'.[17] It is unclear how this observation correlates with his remark that 'The effectiveness of rhetoric depends primarily upon the naiveté of the hearer, rather than upon the soundness of the case',[18] but such an assessment clearly opposes the tenor of Lightfoot's discussion: he described the Galatians as barbaric Celts who never completely gave up their rude and fiery ways, and found Paul's language to accord well with such a readership.[19]

Thus the concern underlying this thesis is significant because Paul's rhetorical abilities are being asked to enlighten our understanding of Paul the man, his background, and the churches to whom he writes. Bruce Winter, Duane Litfin and others, moreover, demonstrate that Paul's attitude towards rhetoric also says much about his theology.[20]

At least some readers of the NT feel that we ought to combine the awareness of our inability to read as a member of Paul's society with the goal of trying to overcome whatever anachronism and displacement we *can* successfully identify. While this may not yield the only valid reading of the text, it does seem to such scholars a necessary exercise, and in light of methodological advances is thought to be overlooked at scholarship's peril. An example of such a path forward is the anthropological approach undertaken by, among others, Bruce Malina and Jerome Neyrey.[21] Another approach, one that at times aims for the very heart of Paul's world of discourse, is rhetorical criticism.

This latter method claims a long history, and of late, a growing popularity. I aim to define and evaluate 'rhetorical criticism' in order to determine what it can contribute to understanding Galatians. Chapter 2 will therefore provide a mini-lexicon of the terminology heard in the world of rhetorical studies, though in the end one might conclude that this entire project is nothing more than an attempt to define an analytical mode.

Following matters of definition, chapter 3 will present and

---

[17] Betz, *Galatians*, 2; cf. Aune, 'Review of Betz', 323–4.
[18] Betz, *Galatians*, 24.
[19] Lightfoot, *Galatians*, especially 13–14.
[20] Betz, 'Problem', 16–48; Winter, *Philo and Paul*; Kennedy, '"Truth" and "Rhetoric"', 195–202; Litfin, *Theology of Proclamation*.
[21] See especially Malina, *Christian Origins*; Neyrey, *Paul*.

analyse the various methodologies which use rhetoric to explain Galatians. By overlooking the restrictions inherent within Graeco-Roman rhetoric, some scholars have applied categories which properly describe material from another sphere altogether. Chapters 4 and 5 will then test the claim that Galatians is a classical speech, arguing first that it does not conform to the structure of the classical oration. Often the sources depended upon to support a rhetorical approach are read in questionable ways. It is then argued that with regard to species, Galatians again conflicts with expectations created by readings of the oratorical handbooks. Chapters 6 and 7 will discuss Paul's language: first, by surveying the attitude of the church fathers and some later writers towards Paul's writing, it is shown that he was not thought to have produced Graeco-Roman oratory. This finds confirmation in the ongoing debate concerning NT Greek. Each attempt to classify Paul's language solidifies the position that he did not use the language of oratory. A brief conclusion reviews the argument that with regard to structure, species and level of language, Paul does not conform to Graeco-Roman oratory. Furthermore, to wrongly attribute such a procedure to him interferes with the attempt to understand the apostle's social and educational background.

2

TOWARDS A DEFINITION OF RHETORIC

Rhetoric

Rhetoric, the first and most difficult term to be defined, loses precision due to its broad cluster of meanings and its complex history. We will isolate four levels of rhetoric – though each, in the appropriate sphere, could be understood as the only necessary referent of the term. Our definition will endeavour to explain the following chart:

Level 1: strategic communication
↓
Level 2: painting *oratory* statuary etc.
↓
Level 3: classical Ch'an rhetoric *Graeco-Roman rhetoric* etc.
↓
Level 4: diatribe market language classroom language *handbook rhetoric* etc.

These levels constitute a schema which grows out of the classical rhetorical handbooks – meaning that the order has been reversed. The handbooks discuss the narrowest level of rhetoric, while we begin with the broadest.

Universal rhetoric or strategic communication

Level 1 rhetoric is persuasion, i.e. effective communication, summed up as 'strategy'. To speak only in terms of discourse is to impose unnecessary restrictions on the discussion, since a painting or a sculpture can have rhetorical force, that is, it may be effective. And clearly the effect of a painting is the result of neither reading nor hearing, so it must be accomplished through something broader – something we will call participation. Much investigation has gone into the question of what happens in a participatory event; for example, Chaim Perelman and L. Olbrechts-Tyteca, in their now standard text, *The New Rhetoric*, attempt to describe how persuasion comes about in a communicative encounter.[1]

But they represent only one way to approach persuasion, and while their effort is wide-ranging, it must admit as one of its antecedents the work of Aristotle, who attempted to describe how to persuade in a more restricted sphere: the courts and council of Athens. Much that he says would be true of arguments conducted in other spheres, for it is inconceivable that the courts employ a method of argumentation and a language that has no place outside the halls of justice. For example, Perelman and Olbrechts-Tyteca discuss at some length the limits of rational forces as persuasive, and the necessity of various non-rational appeals for the generation of conviction. This non-rationality, now often associated with Perelman and Kenneth Burke, was already recognized by the ancients, as revealed by the handbook identification of three persuasive forces: ethos, the personal appeal of the orator; pathos, the emotions of the audience; and logos, the rational arguments. Thus non-rational appeals are seen to have loomed large in classical theory, even as in modern. But this observation does not suggest that Aristotle ever envisaged an expansion of rhetoric to other persuasive spheres.

Our first level of rhetoric is thus established at least partially by contrast with classical oratory and represents the larger group of which classical rhetoric is only a subset. To isolate points of overlap should not be difficult, and it should not lead to the equating of the subset with its superset. But precisely this confusion appears in several studies which apply rhetorical theory to Galatians for analysis. We need continually to ask if the analyst is speaking of rhetoric as universal strategic communication, or as one of its many subsets.

Oratory

One type of strategic communication is that which employs words – thus 'persuasive speech'.[2] Politicians, lawyers, preachers and scholars all employ particular modes of speech with which they try to accomplish their purposes. Very often, it is assumed, their

[1] Perelman and Olbrechts-Tyteca, *The New Rhetoric*.
[2] Kennedy, *New Testament Interpretation*, 158.

primary strategy is rational argument – but such is not necessarily the case. Although the television advertisement and the politician often seem to use different techniques to manipulate the participant into buying the goods on offer, we again see the relevance of Perelman and others who have attempted to show that much persuasive discourse is effective outside the sphere of the rational.[3] Perelman's explanation is that other forces intervene to convince; similarly, Kenneth Burke argues that rhetoric is about identification – that is, the rhetor's goal is to lure the participants into identifying with the rhetor or with a foundational aspect of the argument so that they can then be transported to a new position.[4]

A further observation concerning this particular level 2 rhetoric may prove helpful: by calling it a rhetoric which employs words we mean simply that they are the material of this rhetorical subset. Thus, in contrast to other forms of rhetoric on the second level, the rhetoric of our concern does not use paint and canvas or stone.

Graeco-Roman rhetoric[5]

The third level of rhetoric is a subset of larger groups of rhetoric, the particular type with which we are concerned being Graeco-Roman. We must recognize that each example (1) is a form of verbal discourse; and (2) conforms to specific patterns of expression determined by the group of which the speaker is part. Thus after dividing universal rhetoric into various material classes, we split our particular material class (verbal discourse) into cultural groups. The source of the patterns exhibited in many rhetorics is linked to conventions appropriate to particular communities, meaning that we move from persuasive discourse employing words (level 2) to their employment within a particular milieu (level 3).[6]

---

[3] Cf. Skinner, *Beyond Freedom and Dignity*, especially chapter 5 ('Alternatives to Punishment'). He argues that reason is a weak tool for persuasion – that conditioning is actually the operative element.

[4] Burke, *Rhetoric of Motives*. Cf. Koptak's use of this rhetoric of identification in Galatians ('Rhetorical Identification', 97–113).

[5] Only this once will we use the label 'Graeco-Roman' rhetoric to mean level 3 because our purpose here is to highlight its cultural origin. Henceforth, in conformity with standard usage, we will use the designations Graeco-Roman, classical, and level 4 rhetoric to speak of the specific oratory of the handbooks and the public civil oratory of the Graeco-Roman world.

[6] This milieu could be based on, for example, cultural, social or educational conventions, so that we would understand the rhetoric of Aristotle to be linked to his Greek culture (and some might even link it more particularly to Athens: cf. E. Black,

Perhaps considering a rhetoric which diverges from Graeco-Roman at level 3 might assist our understanding; and some of the relevant points may be reinforced if we choose a remote, non-Western, rhetoric. Such a rhetoric is introduced in Dale Wright's article on the rhetorical practices of classical Ch'an Buddhism. He describes four 'rhetorics' found in that tradition, including the rhetorics of strangeness, of direct pointing, of silence, and of disruption.

The 'rhetoric of strangeness' is employed when the enlightened one adopts a mode of discourse characterized at least in part by a movement away from didactic conventions and representational language. This non-representational language, free of propositional statements, is then used to present arguments that do not have persuasion as their goal; so the 'ungraspability' of the subject-matter – enlightenment – becomes embodied in and characteristic of the text. Since persuasion is not a goal, the speaker is free to engage in discourse that abuses the conventions of the listener,[7] thus the rhetoric of strangeness.[8]

With 'the rhetoric of direct pointing',[9] gestures form an indispensable part of communication in the Ch'an tradition. It should be noted, however, that these also conform to the rhetoric of strangeness. In one instance a monk queried: 'What is the meaning of Bodhidharma coming from the West?' Without speaking his 'master came down from his elevated lecture seat and stood beside it. The monk asked: "Is that your answer?"'[10]

The absence of discourse, a 'rhetoric of silence', became an

Rhetorical Criticism, 126), though one could envisage the linking of his rhetoric to status enjoyed as an intellectual with an Athenian education, or to the fact that he was not native to Athens, or to any other group-classification which fits. With regard to Galatians, we could attempt to describe the rhetorics of economic, social or gender groups without regard to 'cultural boundaries'; our concern, however, is with the rhetoric which has been pulled into the study of Galatians, and that has tended to be rhetoric associated with Graeco-Roman society. (Thus we are not interacting with those who have done a Marxist or feminist reading of Galatians, but rather with those who have done a Graeco-Roman rhetorical reading.) Furthermore, the rhetoric with which we must interact has usually been understood to be that of the classical handbooks. The handbooks represent a source for a rhetoric which cuts a reasonably unified path across the diversity of that culture, indeed a narrower one than has often been assumed, as we will suggest at level 4.

[7] Though this too can become conventional, and in fact does create a rhetoric of its own. See Wright, 'Discourse of Awakening', 27.
[8] Ibid., 24–7.
[9] Ibid., 27–30.
[10] Ibid., 28; citing T. 51:277c (where T. 51 = *Ching-te ch'uan-ten lu (Transmission of the Lamp, Ching-te era)*). Taisho 51, Number 2076.

important signifier in itself.[11] Wright details an encounter that ends: 'He answered merely by sitting silently in his seat'.[12] But silence is eloquent only when foregrounded 'and supported by a discourse that articulates its profundity. Lacking that, silence isn't much of anything'.[13] Silence furthermore does not represent surrender to an opponent, but rather has an unsettling effect in that it bespeaks the non-speaker's power to 'disrupt all talk that derives from conventional awareness'. The truly awakened, those who fully comprehend the 'emptiness' and 'selflessness' of silence, 'can "hear" it without fear and loss of bearing'.[14]

This discussion of the rhetoric of silence ought to point to the links between a culture and its rhetoric, for silence also has a powerful but different effect in the West. Even today, a Chinese person's exercising a rhetoric of silence may be recognized by the Westerner, but is it often understood?

A fourth example is the 'rhetoric of disruption'. Disruption and disorientation are goals of Ch'an rhetoric, for one cannot catch a glimpse of where they are until dislocated from that place.[15] In a culture which invites the relinquishing of self as subject, and the realization of 'the groundlessness of all things',

> the Ch'an master is the one who no longer seeks solid ground, who realizes that all things and situations are supported not by firm ground and solid self-nature but rather by shifting and contingent relations. Having passed through this experience of the void at the heart of everything, he no longer fears change and relativity. The master is undaunted by the negativity in every situation and every conversation. He no longer needs to hold his ground in dialogue and therefore does not falter when all grounds give way.[16]

In this 'discourse of awakening' we find a rhetoric which shares little with the kinds we normally come across in biblical studies or in our actual experience, yet one can imagine this rhetoric being turned into an analytical tool in two ways. First, an awareness of

---

[11] Ibid., 30.
[12] Ibid.; citing T. 51:327c.
[13] Ibid., 31.
[14] Ibid.
[15] Wright, 'Discourse of Awakening', 32.
[16] Ibid., 35.

these 'conventions' and the way they illuminate the universe of their adherents would help us understand texts produced by Ch'an Buddhists. This runs parallel to the conversion of Graeco-Roman rhetoric into a kind of analytical filter to be applied to a text produced within that milieu, such as Cicero's murder-trial orations. A second way of 'using' the rhetoric described by Wright would be to adopt the persona of one who reads texts from that perspective and then apply it to the text of our interest.[17] The question that arises is: What can such an undertaking contribute to texts produced in another sphere? If the enlightened ones, or for that matter Aristotle or Cicero, possessed an unsurpassable insight into the workings of texts and the mind this would be an attractive task, but in the past two millennia we have certainly gained some new insights into the workings of the mind and emotions, and even into the forces which move them – forces which we will call persuasion or argument, and which some prefer to call manipulation or brainwashing.[18] We thus ask: What can it matter to us how the classical Buddhist or Aristotle would have read a text with which they had no real points of contact – whether philosophical, literary or historical?

Graeco-Roman handbook rhetoric

Level 4 rhetoric is the discourse employed by Graeco-Roman society in various venues. The language of the diatribe takes on stereotypical forms which differ from market-place conventions, which in turn differ from the conventions of the court. The discourse of the court is the concern of the classical handbooks,[19] along with the rhetoric of speeches for Graeco-Roman political councils and public *polis*-related gatherings. Thus (and in keeping with classical categories), the level 4 rhetoric we will consider is the one appropriate to Graeco-Roman society as manifested in these specific venues.

Aristotle defines the rhetoric of his concern as 'the faculty of discovering the possible means of persuasion in reference to any

---

[17] This comes close to the goal of reader-response criticism, though the humility we ought to display when donning the Buddhist monk's attire hints at some of the dangers of such an approach. When falling so far short of even self-understanding, how far can we enter into the persona of other classes, sexes and cultures?

[18] Cf. E. Black, *Rhetorical Criticism*, 147.

[19] Sources will be treated in the next chapter.

subject whatever'.[20] Despite the fact of Aristotle's *Rhetoric* going largely unnoticed in the Hellenistic world, his definition has become widely known. What is less often appreciated is that though his vision of rhetoric may relate to any subject, it does not therefore include discourse for any and every venue, nor does it take an unrestricted view of its subjects but allows for this diversity of discussion in the sphere and subject of *politics*: 'Thus it appears that Rhetoric is as it were an offshoot of Dialectic and of the science of Ethics, which may be reasonably called *Politics*'.[21] This lack of clarity concerning the definition is typical of the *Rhetoric*: it is often unsystematic and is thought to represent Aristotle's after-noon lectures on rhetoric rather than a treatise.[22]

Quintilian recites various definitions of rhetoric, including the following: Ariston claims that 'Rhetoric is the science of seeing and uttering what ought to be said on political questions in language that is likely to prove persuasive to the people'.[23] Theodorus of Gadara suggests: 'Rhetoric is the art which discovers and judges and expresses with an elegance duly proportional to the importance of all such elements of persuasion as may exist in any subject in the field of politics';[24] and Cornelius Celsus: 'To speak persuasively on any doubtful subject within the field of politics'.[25] Quintilian also cites but does not attribute: 'rhetoric is the power of judging and holding forth on such political questions as come before it with a certain persuasiveness, a certain action of the body, and delivery of the word'.[26] Cicero considers rhetoric 'a department of the science of politics'.[27] Alburtius confines rhetoric to political themes.[28] Plato, no friend of rhetoric, calls it 'a dishonest counterfeit of justice'.[29] Quintilian himself seems to open out the subject of rhetoric to an all-encompassing mode of discourse,[30] but this is only an illusion, for he soon reveals that this broadening applies to

[20] Aristotle, *Rhetoric* 1.2.1.
[21] Ibid., 1.2.7.
[22] Quintilian, *Institutio* 3.1.14. Cf. Kennedy, *Classical Rhetoric*, 61–2; Litfin, *Theology of Proclamation*, 75.
[23] Quintilian, *Institutio* 2.15.19.
[24] Ibid., 2.15.21.
[25] Ibid., 2.15.22.
[26] Ibid., 2.15.21. Cicero's term for what the handbooks discuss is anglicized to 'oratory'.
[27] Quintilian, *Institutio* 2.15.33, citing Cicero, *De Inventione* 1.5.6.
[28] Quintilian, *Institutio* 2.15.36.
[29] Ibid., 2.15.25, referring to Plato's *Gorgias*.
[30] Quintilian, *Institutio* 2.21.18–19.

any subject – so long as the discourse is delivered in court. Thus, the rhetor may speak of the science of chemistry, but only in so far as, for example, it touches on a trial related to murder by poisoning.

The *Rhetorica ad Alexandrum* offers no definition since the work is framed as a private treatise responding to a request. It opens: 'You write to me that you have again and again sent people to me to speak about my composing for you a treatise on the principles of political oratory';[31] the goal of the treatise is then stated as instruction in 'political and forensic oratory'.[32] The *Rhetorica ad Herennium* states: 'The task of the public speaker (*oratoris officium*) is to discuss capably those matters law and custom have fixed for the uses of citizenship, and to secure as far as possible the agreement of his hearers'. Each definition adds to the evidence that rhetoricians regarded rhetoric as restricted. It did not embrace all persuasive communication but constituted the discourse of legal and political persuasion and was heard in the court or in the political assembly.[33]

Although other forms of discourse – for example, the diatribe or first-century letter writing – touch upon our discussion in that they are (1) products of the Graeco-Roman era; and (2) rhetoric when understood as purposive discourse[34] – thus they are Graeco-Roman rhetoric – the forms of classical rhetoric as taken up in rhetorical analysis are more narrowly restricted. These other varieties co-exist with the rhetoric of our concern at levels 1, 2 and 3, but split off and are situated elsewhere on the horizontal line that comprises level 4. A useful description of the Graeco-Roman rhetoric most often employed in Galatians studies can be deduced from the procedure of Betz and Kennedy: it is the rhetoric of the handbooks (i.e. those instructional texts that have been handed down from Aristotle, Cicero, Quintilian and other ancient writers on rhetoric). An investigation of definitions of rhetoric found in work on Galatians, and the actual practice of those who claim methodological links to classical rhetoric, would reveal that these handbooks inform their understanding.

The handbooks assert repeatedly, however, that their concern is for oratory, and where it is not stated it is assumed. Examples are

---

[31] *Rhetorica ad Alexandrum* 1420a.1–3.
[32] Ibid., 1421b.1–4.
[33] Kennedy, *New Testament Interpretation*, 6.
[34] Ibid., 158.

too many to cite, but the *Rhetorica ad Alexandrum*[35] is typical when it reads: 'Public speeches are . . .' and '. . . the species to which public speeches belong'.[36] Indeed, until the modern era theorists defined rhetoric consistently, though the stress often shifted away from the specific subject-matter while maintaining the emphasis on orality. Bishop Whately, author of *The Elements of Rhetoric*, hesitated to use the term rhetoric in his title because 'it is rather the more commonly employed with reference to public speaking alone'.[37]

Nor does this tradition of rhetoric's oral nature escape modern specialists. Perelman and Olbrechts-Tyteca, in addressing the relationship between dialectic and rhetoric, assert that 'Rhetoric confined itself to the technique of the long, sustained speech'. They then speak of 'speech with all the oratorical action involved in it.'[38] Elsewhere we read that 'rhetoric took its point of departure from the direct and oral encounters of classical civic life, and even . . . into the first phase of modern print culture, it inevitably referred back to a face-to-face rhetorical situation'.[39]

Indeed Demosthenes, when asked what he considered to be the most important part of rhetoric, replied, 'Delivery, delivery, delivery'.[40] Cicero states 'We are therefore almost justified in concluding that [Demosthenes] regarded [delivery] not merely as the first, but as the only virtue of oratory'.[41] A similar assertion Cicero places on the lips of Crassus: 'But the effect of all those oratorical devices depends on how they are delivered. Delivery, I assert, is the dominant factor in oratory'.[42] In fact, Cicero in the same place has his favoured speaker argue that a speech, when delivered by another, 'would be a different thing'.[43] All of this is meaningless to a non-oral conception of rhetoric.

Handbook rhetoric was not, however, restricted only with regard

---

[35] *Rhetorica ad Alexandrum* 1421b.7–13.

[36] Cf. Lambrecht ('Rhetorical Criticism and the New Testament', 246), 'Rhetoric originally deals with the spoken word'. H. Rackham, in his Introduction to *Rhetorica ad Alexandrum* describes the work as 'a practical handbook for public speakers. It merely considers the problem of how to carry conviction with an audience' (in LCL: *Rhetorica ad Alexandrum*, 258).

[37] Whately, *Elements*, cited in Hudson, 'The Field of Rhetoric', 7.

[38] Perelman and Olbrechts-Tyteca, *The New Rhetoric*, 35.

[39] Bender and Wellbery, 'Rhetoricality', 15.

[40] Cicero, *De Oratore* 3.56.213.

[41] Quintilian, *Institutio* 11.3.6; Cf. Burke, *Rhetoric of Motives*, 65.

[42] Cicero, *De Oratore* 3.56.213.

[43] Ibid.

to speeches, for the speeches were themselves restricted to specific venues. A quotation from Quintilian pulls rhetoric back from an all-encompassing nature into the sphere in which orations are delivered:

> What, say some, has the knowledge of the way to describe an equilateral triangle on a given straight line got to do with pleading in the law-courts or speaking in the senate? Will an acquaintance with the names and intervals of the notes of the lyre help an orator to defend a criminal or direct the policy of his country? They will perhaps produce a long list of orators who are most effective in the courts but have never sat under a geometrician and whose understanding of music is confined to the pleasure which their ears, like those of other men, derive from it.[44]

Quintilian and those to whom these words respond know that their type of rhetoric is restricted to these venues. His imaginary opponent thus cannot fathom how geometry or music can assist the speaker, and leaves it to Quintilian to defend such views. The important fact for us is that they agree on the venues and purpose of oratory.

Cicero describes the ideal orator as 'the political leader of the nation, guiding the government and pre-eminent for wisdom and eloquence in the Senate, in the assembly of the people and in public causes', adding, somewhat antagonistically, that philosophy 'appeals to us to abandon the platform and the courts and parliaments'.[45]

We learn that 'much of [Cicero's] treatise is written out of his experiences in the Senate and the law courts';[46] and reading his *De Oratore* reveals that speeches are again assumed to be delivered from 'the well of the court or the floor of the house or from the bench or rostrum'.[47] The handbooks, as well as subsequent treatments of rhetoric outside the study of Paul, almost universally accepted this restriction of level 4 rhetoric to specific venues.[48] Even

---

[44] Quintilian, *Institutio* 1.10.3–4. These other skills are introduced not because rhetoric expands infinitely, but because Quintilian's concern is with the (hypothetical) perfect orator who is master of all things (*Institutio* 1.10.4).

[45] Cicero, *De Oratore* 3.17.63.

[46] Burke, *Rhetoric of Motives*, 52–3.

[47] Cicero, *De Oratore* 3.6.23.

[48] Cf. Leeman ('Variety of Classical Rhetoric', 44), who cites Aristotle, *Rhetoric* 1.3 on this point. Also significant is the fact that Isaeus, Lysias and Dinarchus – of

the exercises performed in the rhetorical schools envisaged specific spheres; they were intended – though with time they went astray – for the imminent careers of the educated class: that is 'for the oratory of the law courts and of politics'.[49] This is further reinforced by the widely circulated notion that 'rhetoric was a mere knack, to be picked up by experience in the courts'.[50] Thus, in response to Richard Longenecker's suggestion that rhetoric was 'in the air',[51] we find that if it was, it seems to have been the air of the courts, and was inhaled through the ears.[52]

Tacitus' *Dialogue on Orators* reveals Aper imploring Maternus thus: 'Otherwise you would not turn your back on your profession of speaker and pleader (*orationum et causarum*) . . . all the while you are being summoned to the forum by the long list of your friends' cases, and the equally long list of colonies and country towns for which you ought to act'.[53] Alluding to the rewards of rhetoric in contrast to poetry he adds: 'Such are the honours and distinctions and resources which we find to repletion in the houses of those who from youth up have dedicated themselves to the practice of law and the profession of oratory'.[54] Aper pleads: 'I am trying to get you . . . to the forum and to the real contests of actions-at-law' for the task of being 'the public speaker'.[55] The public speaker, at least according to Tacitus' dialogue characters, conducts business in the courts and the forum.[56]

Rhetoric's restriction to particular venues appears in some NT studies which describe the historical basis underlying their method. Burton Mack identifies the three venues for the use of rhetoric:

the Ten Attic Orators – had limited opportunity because their 'non-Athenian status . . . debarred them from full participation in political and judicial life'. So Worthington, 'Canon of Attic Orators', 244, 260, n. 6.

[49] M. L. Clarke 'Quintilian on Education', 102. Hudson ('The Field of Rhetoric', 8) informs: 'The pupils of Isocrates were the great orators, generals, and statesmen of their time . . . I suppose that when, at the present time, we combine work in Americanization or studies in patriotism with Public Speaking, preparing students to speak on principles of Americanism, we are doing somewhat as Isocrates did in his time'.

[50] Winterbottom, 'Quintilian and the *Vir Bonus*', 96.

[51] Longenecker, *Galatians*, cxii–cxiii.

[52] Similarly, opera's mass popularity in Italy, and the fact that many would have an ear attuned to it, does not imply that the listening public would be able either to perform or create it.

[53] Tacitus, *Dialogue on Orators* 3.4.

[54] Ibid., 7.1.

[55] Ibid., 8.4, 10.5.

[56] See also Ibid., 12.3–4, where the court is again assumed.

'The forum for the practice of rhetoric was the assembly (*ekklesia*) or the council (*boule*) gathered for deliberation and litigation, or the public gathering for celebration of civic-religious occasions'.[57] The classicist George Kennedy is also aware of the venues of handbook rhetoric.[58]

One can restrict the handbooks even further, for a casual reading of the handbooks – especially the Hellenistic sources – is sufficient to detect the degree to which they emphasize forensic matters.[59] In fact, *Institutio Oratoria* has been described as 'a kind of politician's and pleader's encyclopaedia . . . by the lawyer and laureate rhetorician Quintilian'.[60] The bulk of the handbook material pertains to those headed for the courtroom.

Another important facet of handbook rhetoric is its exclusivity with respect to content and purpose. Considering content first, not all ancient persuasive discourse was 'rhetoric'. Level 4 rhetoric is a sub-species of level 2, and as such must be recognized as only one of many level 4 discourses. Its theorists have appropriately been described as 'a plethora of technicians of rhetoric, whittling away at a limited enough theory of expression'.[61] We need properly to assess the scope of the rhetorical handbooks, for one frequently reads that since Paul was a creature of the first century he must have engaged in 'classical rhetoric'; but if level 4 rhetoric is meant, then this is only true when he appears in those venues for which rhetoric was designed.[62] Thus it is equally necessary to specify in some detail what is not included under the rubric 'handbook rhetoric'. If we proceed with the working definition of Graeco-Roman rhetoric as that which is discussed in the handbooks (the definition assumed in many current studies of Galatians) then logically other forms of rhetoric fall outside this sphere of interest.[63]

---

[57] Mack, *Rhetoric and the New Testament*, 28.

[58] Kennedy, *New Testament Interpretation*, 6. See also Betz, *Galatians*, 24.

[59] Russell and Wilson, ed. and trans. *Menander Rhetor*, xxii.

[60] Wimsatt and Brooks, *Literary Criticism I*, 103.

[61] Reardon, *Form of Greek Romance*, 7–8.

[62] As Luke realizes. See Acts 24 (and our discussion in chapter 7) for Paul and Tertullus in court.

[63] It is difficult to use this language precisely. Our classification draws on the observation that when various studies attempt to define classical rhetoric, they often use only the handbooks or speeches as their source and allow historical inferences to be drawn. We thus use their term 'Graeco-Roman rhetoric' in this thesis, though only after arguing that it actually modifies only one particular form of 'Graeco-Roman rhetoric'. We will see that the handbooks occasionally allude to matters

So, positively, we see that in the classical world 'rhetoric' implied to those who discussed it a public discourse of the courts or the political sphere. Negatively, rhetoric was often set apart from other modes of discourse on level 4 – the most important being the discourse of philosophy. This has perhaps not been properly appreciated: the handbooks offer neither help in analysing all manner of texts, nor even a description of the general epistemological conventions pertinent to persuasive techniques; they only teach how to craft speeches for specific contexts. Cicero in his *De Inventione* describes rhetoric as a branch of politics – and he rebukes Hermogenes for bringing matters into oratory that properly belong to philosophy. In fact, the history of rhetoric almost from the beginning reveals that rhetoric and philosophy were hostile to one another.[64] Thus we must make clear from the outset that rhetoric was not a tool for analysis but for the construction of speeches, that it never attempted to handle discourse in general but only the needs of civic discourse, and that even philosophy was excluded from rhetoric.[65]

These contrasts are assumed in Plato's *Gorgias*: in this dialogue Socrates and Gorgias agree that all teaching aims at conviction;[66] 'hence rhetoric is not the only producer of conviction'.[67] Socrates then asks, 'What kind of persuasion, and of persuasion dealing with what, is rhetoric the art?'; and Gorgias responds: 'That kind of persuasion, Socrates, which you find in the law-courts and in any public gatherings . . . and it deals with what is just and unjust'.[68] Thus we see not only that handbook oratory is distinct from another level 4 rhetoric, namely teaching, but also that ancient

outside their specific sphere, but not, despite assertions to the contrary, in any systematic way.

[64] Cicero, *De Oratore* Book 1: Socrates severed rhetoric and philosophy, which inevitably led to the separation of wisdom and eloquence. Betz writes that in 'philosophical literature, especially . . . the diatribes of the Hellenistic period . . . "rhetoric" is denounced with regularity as nothing but concoctions of lifeless syllogisms': cf. 'Composition and Function of Galatians', 376. Aune cites Epictetus 3.23.33–5 ('Romans as *Logos Protreptikos*', 94–5).

[65] Cf. Quintilian, *Institutio* 12.2.6–8; 11.1.70; Cicero, *De Oratore* 3.20.76. See also *De Partitione Oratoria* 23.78. The standard discussion is in Marrou, *History of Education*, especially 71–91. Philosophy did of course possess its own rhetoric when understood as modes and conventions of discourse: it did not, however, conform to the techniques of the handbooks.

[66] Plato, *Gorgias* 453d–e.

[67] Ibid., 454a.

[68] Ibid., 454b.

writers saw the branching out of their shared level 3 rhetoric into a plethora of shoots.

But philosophy and teaching are not alone in being excluded from classical rhetoric: Kenneth Burke severs Aristotelian rhetoric from any specific subject-matter apart from oratory itself with his observation that 'in proportion as the rhetorician deals with special subject matter, his proofs move away from the rhetorical and towards the scientific'.[69] This is no more than we should expect of an art intended to defend or accuse, or to persuade the senate to undertake some course of action. The orator must be able to discuss all topics in such situations, though a detailed scientific understanding of any subject will contribute very little to persuasion – other factors are often more persuasive.[70] Hoyt Hudson, in a now classic essay, agrees:

> Aristotle, in discussing deliberative rhetoric, says that the subjects embraced are finance, war and peace, defence of the country, imports and exports, and legislation. Yet the rhetorician does not necessarily become an expert in those fields. He attempts to learn the authorities and sources of information in each, what questions to ask – and to answer. The peculiar contribution of the rhetorician is the discovery and use, to the common good, of those things which move men to action.[71]

We have not, however, exhausted the different forms of discourse with which handbook rhetoric was contrasted in the ancient world. Quintilian tells us that oratory was different from 'dialogues and dialectical controversies' in both content and style.[72] Stanley Porter also illustrates the narrowness of rhetoric when he tells us that 'Demetrius makes a clear distinction between conversation and oratory. After citing Aristotle writing to Antipater, [Demetrius] states, "A man who conversed in that fashion would seem not to be talking but to be making an oratorical display"'.[73] Porter aptly quotes from Seneca's *Moral Epistles*:

> I prefer that my letters should be just what my conversa-

---

[69] Burke, *Rhetoric of Motives*, 51.
[70] Thus television advertisements have rejected the technician in a lab-coat in favour of a housewife who presumably uses the product being promoted.
[71] Hudson, 'Field of Rhetoric', 12.
[72] Quintilian, *Institutio* 5.14.27.
[73] Porter, 'Theoretical Justification', 112; citing Demetrius, *On Style*, 225.

tion would be if you and I were sitting in another's
company . . . Even if I were arguing a point, I should not
stamp my foot, or toss my arms about, or raise my voice;
but I should leave that sort of thing to the orator, and
should be content to have conveyed my feelings toward
you without having either embellished them or lowered
their dignity.[74]

David Aune, adding further to our list, suggests that Romans is a
'*Logos Protreptikos*',[75] a form of (non-handbook) rhetoric used by
philosophers to win potential adherents to their system or way of
life. He remarks that 'Romans is a speech of exhortation in written
form',[76] and then proceeds to discuss a whole range of philosophical discourse which stands alongside that of the handbooks and
is aware of the existence of the other.[77]

Oratory which grows out of handbook rhetoric (level 4) is thus
seen to be only a subset of Graeco-Roman (level 3), for the
Hellenistic age obviously contained modes of speaking besides
those discussed in the handbooks. The diatribe, the synagogue
homily, and everyday conversation are other examples of competing rhetorics. Furthermore, if defined as a structural strategy
employed in the first century, epistolary conventions constitute
another rhetoric too. No warrant exists for equating the handbooks
with the totality of first-century discursive strategies.

This, to be sure, begs the question of Paul's use of classical
rhetoric; and we will argue from several lines of evidence that he
did not employ it – forcing the conclusion that some scholars
impose handbook categories upon texts which result from other
types of rhetoric. In other words, the boundaries distinguishing
various levels of rhetoric, and segregating rhetorics of the same
level, are being overlooked or ignored. What can readings based on
such oversight offer other than a distorted and anachronistic
reading?

Complementing handbook rhetoric's exclusivity with regard to
content is its exclusivity of purpose. This limitation of rhetoric
requires defence, for it opposes Kennedy's assertion that 'There are
three *species* of rhetoric . . . . Although these categories specifically

---

[74] Porter, 'Theoretical Justification', 113, quoting Seneca, *Moral Epistles* 75.1–2.
[75] Aune, 'Romans as *Logos Protreptikos*', 91–124.
[76] Ibid., 91.
[77] Ibid., especially 95.

refer to the circumstances of classical oratory, they are in fact applicable to all kinds of discourse'.[78]

One easily loses sight of classical rhetoric's real purpose when the air is filled with the term 'rhetoric' to describe alternative approaches to the text. Jan Lambrecht's introductory remarks afford a good starting point for discussing shifts implicit in the use of rhetoric as an analytical tool. He writes: 'Rhetoric is the art of persuasive speaking. Since all biblical texts are to some degree persuasive texts, a knowledge of rhetoric is part of the equipment of the exegete. Rhetorical analysis, then, constitutes one of the exegetical tools'.[79] Thus, having defined rhetoric as persuasive speaking, Lambrecht abruptly shifts to discussion of persuasive texts, which soon yields to discussion of analysis. But in so doing, Lambrecht has identified Galatians as an example of level 2 rhetoric which he will understand through the tools of level 4. If he had argued that level 4 rhetoric applies to every text we would merely request evidence for the assertion and ask what benefit the approach offers; but since Lambrecht sets out to argue that Galatians is an example of one level of rhetoric, we question the 'application' of another.

Rhetorical critics must not overlook the fact that 'As originally conceived, rhetoric was primarily a synthetic act – an art for "building up," for "composing" something': so says Corbett in *Classical Rhetoric for the Modern Student*.[80] Another modern approach to rhetoric is that of William Brandt, articulated in his *Rhetoric of Argumentation*, though he too realizes that rhetoric was originally for creation and not analysis.[81] Brandt works backwards – but in full awareness of having reversed the process. His helpful monograph contains a glossary of terms not as they apply to the creation of a text but as employed for analysis.

So a tool intended for the construction of speeches is called upon to assist in the analysis of texts, with a defence of the transitions absent from most NT studies. Furthermore, one could in part defend rhetorical analysis as the breaking down of that which the handbooks teach how to construct, but even this defence fails because the analysis is seldom applied to Graeco-Roman orations

[78] Kennedy, *New Testament Interpretation*, 19.
[79] Lambrecht, 'Rhetorical Criticism and the New Testament', 239. Cf. Hester, 'Use and Influence of Rhetoric', 389, n. 12.
[80] Corbett in *Classical Rhetoric*, 30.
[81] Brandt, *Rhetoric of Argumentation*, 117–20.

(the indisputable goal of the handbooks' instruction), but instead to a wide variety of *texts*.[82]

As a fundamental, then, one must see that the handbooks train their readers in the crafting of speeches.[83] Kennedy recognizes this, and also that the rules for analysis must accommodate the fact that all that remains of the speech is a text, when he writes that 'rhetoric originates in speech and its primary product is a speech act, not a text, but the rhetoric of historical periods can only be studied through texts'.[84] This coheres with his earlier statement that 'the primacy of speech is clear. To cite a few of the most important signs, the study of rhetoric in Greece originally emerged as a way to learn how to speak in courts and assemblies. The goal of the influential schools of declamation of the Roman Empire was the training of public speakers'.[85]

Kennedy subsequently tells us that though the handbooks were 'primarily intended to train a student to speak in a court of law' with only a little effort they could be converted into the 'basis of analysis of other forms of discourse; this was in fact done by ancient critics like Demetrius, Dionysius of Halicarnassus, and Longinus, who even illustrates his theory of sublimity by citing the first chapter of Genesis (*On Sublimity* 9.9)'.[86] He further speaks of the expansion of rhetoric's role into other spheres, suggesting that while it was taught for the purpose of developing public speakers, and 'found its fullest development in formal oratory, it was also utilized to teach and to analyze literary composition'.[87] But we must again hesitate, for what exactly did the ancients mean by

[82] We will see that this is true of Kennedy. Betz represents the rare scholar who attempts to provide a foundation for the examination by first linking Galatians with a speech-setting, namely the court.

[83] *Rhetorica ad Alexandrum* 1421b.6 speaks of 'a treatise on the principles of political oratory (πολιτικων λόγων)'. Cf. 1421b.7–10; 1423a.21–5. Aristotle's *Rhetoric* 3.1.4 discussion of style is for 'political contests'. See my chapter 5. Quintilian, *Institutio* 2.20.8: oratory is used to 'urge a policy'; 'plead in law courts'; 'speak in the midst of a crowd of armed soldiers': cf. 3.2.4. Arguments which find rhetorical activity in courts, the forum, and public assemblies also point to the notion that rhetoric is an oral activity, for court cases and public assemblies are not well conducted through the submission of manuscripts but depend on oral activity. Contrast Thucydides, *History of the Peloponnesian War* 1.22.4 – writing is for private possession, not public performance.

[84] Kennedy, *New Testament Interpretation*, 5.

[85] Kennedy, *Classical Rhetoric*, 108. Cf. also 111. See Leeman ('Variety of Classical Rhetoric', 45): 'As far as antiquity is concerned, "the art of persuasive speaking" should be considered the most usable definition'.

[86] Kennedy, *New Testament Interpretation*, 13.

[87] Ibid., 30.

analysis of literary composition? And in what way may this literary criticism be called rhetorical?

In fact, we possess evidence that 'literary criticism' in the Graeco-Roman world shared little with the rhetorical-critical methodology presented in *New Testament Interpretation*. Kennedy himself writes elsewhere that, historically, 'the most striking developments' in literary criticism 'are the establishment of the great Museum and Library at Alexandria, which became a centre for *textual criticism* and exegesis of texts based on *literary, historical, biographical, and linguistic* scholarship'.[88] To understand these forms of exegesis more completely let us consider the activities undertaken by those who handled texts in the ancient world.

The 'critics' of the Graeco-Roman period proceeded in a manner quite different from today as they pursued different sorts of information. Kennedy writes concerning Aristophanes of Byzantium: 'Although he did not write commentaries on the texts, he composed monographs on literary subjects, collected proverbs, and provided *hypotheses*, or simple introductions to tragedies and comedies'. These *hypotheses* discussed the play's production, 'identified other treatments of the story' and provided an outline of the play's plot.[89] One finds neither interpretative efforts in this description, nor neglect of the orality and performance-orientation of the text. Kennedy further adds that Aristophanes and his successor, Aristarchus, judged the quality and the authenticity of the text.[90] These two features were the special concern of the times, quality usually being associated with the store of ideas and the style of the text, and the question of authenticity being valid for its own sake.

Such literary criticism Kennedy characterizes thus:

> The chief critical positions advanced are that the themes of the Classic poets are now sterile and should be avoided and that the characteristic excellence of poetry, corresponding to the 'virtue' of style in rhetoric, should be slimness, avoiding epic or inflated language, seeking to be thin (*leptos*), precise, disciplined, not fat, coarse, and gross (*pachus*).[91]

---

[88] Kennedy, 'Hellenistic Scholarship', 200; emphasis added.
[89] Ibid., 207; emphasis added.
[90] Ibid.
[91] Ibid., 203. Secondary 'critical positions' relate to plots, other versions of the story and historical references.

This kind of analysis shares nothing with modern rhetorical studies of Galatians; but such distancing is not to our advantage: the handbooks speak of the style appropriate to each of the species of orations, and so, should we regard Galatians as belonging to classical oratory, the ability to discern the level of style employed by the text would be invaluable. Unfortunately, few modern rhetorical critics have been interested in identifying slimness, fatness, coarseness, and such like, in Paul.

So much for Kennedy's 'chief critical positions'. Secondary interests relate to plot, other versions of the story being examined, and historical references in the text. All of this implies a limited range of interests, which supports Kennedy's assertion that 'literary criticism[92] was slow to develop in antiquity and was never fully conceptualized'.[93]

The rhetoricians, however, had prescribed uses for literature; in Quintilian's scheme its study makes a twofold contribution: it assists in the art of speaking and in the interpretation of poets.[94] Thus the task of the teacher of literature is to 'speak of style or expound disputed passages, explain stories or paraphrase poems.'[95] Literature was studied to uncover the author's intent, to assist with elocution, and to contribute in other practical ways.[96] These activities fit nicely with the benefits Quintilian hopes to derive from such study: they aid the orator by enriching the store of both vocabulary and ideas from which to draw.[97] Three qualifications are placed on this study of literature in school: (1) it should be devoted primarily to poetry; (2) the material should be read aloud; (3) the reading should develop in a 'manly' way.[98] Cicero similarly writes that the study of literature includes 'the study of poets, the learning of histories, the explanations and proper intonation in

---

[92] In Cicero (*De Oratore* 3.19–35) oratory is treated 'as one of several literary genres and [Cicero] takes as his starting point the whole field of literature'. So Fantham, 'Literature and Criticism at Rome', 232. In the passage from Cicero we again see that the concern is with style and structure – though not the sort found in Galatians.

[93] Kennedy, *Classical Rhetoric*, 111. See also Reardon, *Form of Greek Romance*.

[94] Quintilian, *Institutio* 1.4.2–4. Bender and Wellbery (*The Ends of Rhetoric*, 17) tell us that classical authors were translated, memorized, and imitated. Interpretation entered with the beginnings of philology.

[95] Quintilian, *Institutio* 1.2.14.

[96] Ibid., 2.5.1–6.

[97] Ibid., 1.4.2–4.

[98] Ibid., 1.8.1–2. Other arts can assist the rhetor as well; for example, music can aid the development of rhythm and metre (1.4.4).

speaking them'. But even these practices, with their self-evident aid to the public speaker, are by the remarks that follow completely isolated from the art of oratory (as well as from music, geometry and astronomy).[99] He maintains the boundary that separates literary criticism, even as defined in his own day, from rhetoric (therefore, we might add, from 'rhetorical analysis'). Thus, as in Quintilian, most attention focuses on style, tropes and figures of speech/thought, but little or none on extracting meaning.[100] In fact, rather than finding in rhetoric a tool for the analysis of literature (as Kennedy implies), we again find the situation turned upside-down so that literature is a tool for the development of the orator. While the latter may not exclude the possibility of the former, one cannot be inferred from the other.

In a section entitled 'Manifestations of Literary Rhetoric' Kennedy refers to Demetrius' *On Style*; Dionysius of Halicarnassus' *On Composition*; Longinus' *On the Sublime*; and Hermagoras' *On Ideas of Style*. The earliest, Dionysius, 'considers how words are put together into sentences, the various styles of composition and poetical elements in prose, and prose elements in poetry'.[101] Clearly this work relates to composition, not analysis of rhetoric as literature. Furthermore, the features addressed relate to word choice and composition (treating figures, sentence structure and variety).[102] Longinus' *On the Sublime*, it is explicitly stated, is 'intended to be a practical aid to composition'.[103] Although Kennedy describes the categories used to create 'sublimity' as rhetorical, a reading of the work reveals that the chief concern is with one department of rhetoric: style – a department which is almost universally overlooked in rhetorical studies of Galatians. Indeed we will see that ancient writers considered Paul to fall short of the *literati*,[104] and a great classicist of the last century called Paul

---

[99] Cicero, *De Oratore* 1.42.187. Cicero's meaning is difficult to grasp apart from the larger context. The argument is that various elements of different arts and sciences floated around independently until unifying principles were found. Thus various elements combined to form different branches of the arts, though for our purposes, the point is that limits to the combining were reached while there still remained distinct branches, namely music, geometry, astronomy, literature and oratory.

[100] Quintilian, *Institutio* 1.18.16. Kennedy, 'Hellenistic Scholarship', 219.

[101] Kennedy, *Classical Rhetoric*, 112–13; the title of the work of Hermagoras reveals that it lies outside the sphere of discussion for the same reason.

[102] Kennedy, Ibid., 118.

[103] Ibid., 113.

[104] This is the issue addressed in chapter 6.

'most unhellenic'.[105] When Kennedy turns from the above texts to Roman literature he is less specific about which ones to consider 'manifestations of literary rhetoric', but seems now by 'rhetorical' to mean 'political writings'.[106] In the end, we agree with Kennedy only if 'rhetorical' does not imply handbook rhetoric, but remains at level 2 and acknowledges a 'rhetoric' which is the power of words to accomplish their purpose.[107] Surprisingly, when he moves away from discussion of style, he shows how the NT writers *do not* conform to classical models, concluding: 'In general, identification of genre is not a crucial factor in understanding how rhetoric actually works in units of the New Testament'.[108] This provides further evidence that Kennedy's concern is not with level 4 but with level 2 rhetoric.

As we have implied, the handbooks do not introduce literary works when treating *taxis, inventio* or species.[109] Not until discussion turns to an area rather more neglected in rhetorical studies of Galatians, *figures*, do the handbooks themselves draw *illustrations* more heavily from literature; such discussion treats the ability of words to create emphasis and amplification[110] – but this does not imply the validity of analysis for its own sake; nor should we infer a sort of 'rhetorical' analysis of literature. Instead, writers of literature, in their level 2 rhetoric, use devices that overlap with oratory;[111] and when illustrating such devices, literature is more accessible than speeches. We will return to this matter of figures, having got ahead of ourselves for the moment. We note only that with the displacement of rhetoric from the realm of

---

[105] Norden, 'Patristischen Literatur', 417–72.

[106] Kennedy, *Classical Rhetoric*, 113–14.

[107] This restriction of rhetoric can lead one far from classical rhetoric. At Harvard 'rhetoric was taught, not for eloquence, but in order to teach the young seminarian how to rub off the cosmetic tropes of Scripture before going to work on the doctrine with dialectical dichotomies'. Rhetoric was equated so tightly with ornamentation that they felt it was external, something to be removed so that the bare ideas would become accessible. Wimsatt and Brooks, *Literary Criticism*, 74 (quoting McLuhan, 'Edgar Poe's Tradition', 28). The notion of a neat separability of form from meaning has also been demolished.

[108] Kennedy, *New Testament Interpretation*, 33.

[109] After works such as the writings of Homer put *speeches* into the mouths of characters in the text, the handbooks often treat illustrative material drawn from those speeches as if taken from oratory. They do not, however, even in these cases (which clearly describe oratory), teach or encourage the *analysis* of the fictitious oration into structural parts or isolation of the species.

[110] Quintilian, *Institutio* Book 9 deals with figures.

[111] Cicero, *De Oratore* 2.9.38.

oratory into that of literary analysis, a significant portion of the handbooks becomes irrelevant. Of the five departments of oratory (invention, arrangement, style, memory, delivery),[112] the final two help only with oral performance – they contribute nothing to written texts (by way of creation or analysis). Omitting them, as already noted, would represent a severe distortion to Demosthenes or Quintilian.

Also illustrative of the ancient world's use of rhetoric is the observation that little commentary writing on speeches took place. In fact, we possess only one commentary in Latin from the classical period: that of Asconius Pedianus, writing about the middle of the first century of our era. He presents a 'valuable discussion of the historical background and allusions in five orations of Cicero, written about AD 55',[113] further evidence that even analyses of oratory dealt with historical details but did not analyse it through anything akin to Kennedy's well-defined method.

Kennedy also refers to another much later commentator: Servius. In his commentary on the *Aeneid*, Servius describes his interests this way: 'The following must be considered in explicating authors: the poet's life, the title of the work, the quality of the song, the intent of the writer, the number of books, the order of the books, and explanation'.[114] We still find no interest in applying rhetorical categories to literature. Kennedy removes the commentaries of Servius even further from the realm of rhetorical analysis when he declares their aim: to 'teach the proper use of Latin to adolescents'. Furthermore, they treat poetry.[115] We simply do not find, even as the commentary tradition develops, evidence of investigations which analyse texts, even speeches, according to the categories and concerns of the handbooks.

When we *do* find analysis, which reaches its height in Dionysius of Halicarnassus, the basis of value judgements is propriety, not conformity to the structural or topical recommendations of the

[112] Cf. Quintilian *Institutio* 6.4.1; 11.3.1; 11.3.2. He goes on to address physical development (11.3.28–9), how to hold the head (11.3.68–71), the eyebrows (11.3.79), the nostrils (11.3.80), the lips (11.3.81), hands (11.3.97), clothing (11.3.137), how to wear that clothing (11.3.138–9), hair care (11.3.160). Section 12.10.47 offers instruction on how to wear a toga and fix the hair.

[113] Kennedy, 'Hellenistic Scholarship', 209. Kennedy says that this is the only extant Latin text from this period in commentary form.

[114] Kennedy, 'Christianity and Criticism', 342. He dates this work to *c.* 400 ('Christianity and Criticism', 341).

[115] Kennedy, 'Christianity and Criticism', 341–2.

handbooks.[116] In Dionysius, 'appropriateness dominates the discussion'.[117] His treatment of Thucydides is perhaps the most interesting for our purposes, for it recognizes, like students of Acts, that speeches follow the rules of the handbooks because of their setting, not because of some supposed inevitable attraction to rhetorical standards. All of Dionysius' critical essays, in that they represent a 'rhetorical analysis' by a member of the ancient world, ought to be of interest to the modern rhetorical critic. But 'rhetorical analysis' here need imply nothing more than 'analysis of rhetoric'. Thus one might conclude that Dionysius provides a method for those who have already established that Galatians is a rhetorical speech. While many studies of Galatians claim to be an analysis of rhetoric, and some assume that Galatians is a speech dressed as an epistle, only Betz appears intent on showing that Galatians really is a speech appropriate to a rhetorical venue.[118] An additional limit to the use of Dionysius is the question of why we would want to read a discourse in the way he would. Is such a historicist reading defensible?

Norman Petersen reworks the question:

> Exceeding the legitimate historical-critical tasks of establishing and interpreting the written word as evidence, historicism reduced the possible meaning of such evidence to what it meant and construed what it meant as the product of its immediate historical and cultural context, of which authors were more or less representative. In this way the spirit of culture became the primary perspective from which its product could be construed. As the understanding of texts became a matter of understanding the culture that produced them, the critic increasingly worked from the cultural context to the text rather than vice versa, as historical method requires.[119]

Reading through the eyes of Dionysius or, for that matter, Aristotle, implies that classical descriptions of method offer greater control than modern ones, but why then speak of universals, as Kennedy and others who wish to apply Aristotle to Galatians are

---

[116] Propriety is a concern of the handbooks, but it cannot be argued that they held a monopoly on it. It should be part of all formal communication.

[117] Usher, Dionysius of Halicarnassus, *On Thucydides*, LCL 459.

[118] See on Betz in chapters 4 and 5.

[119] Petersen, *Literary Criticism*, 25.

prone to do? This tension between finding the handbooks applicable on the one hand because they address universal aspects of persuasion (level 2), and on the other, because they describe the milieu of which Paul was part (level 4), is telling and has not been properly addressed – much less resolved.

A distinct category of text demands attention at this point. It would seem that speeches within literary texts allow the analyst to escape this tension, and also provide a paradigm for 'applying' rhetoric to the written page. Indeed, when Kennedy speaks of rhetoric within ancient literature he often alludes to speeches embedded within artistic literary texts.[120] But such speeches are not like those thought to constitute Galatians, nor does their existence suggest the rhetorical analysis of literary material per se. He refers to speeches given by fictional orators within the texts, but they are always delivered in the appropriate speech-context. When one views the issue this way, even Acts 24.1–9 enters the discussion, for it begins with the introduction of a rhetor and a context appropriate to a forensic speech.[121] But this does not imply that the whole of Acts is a speech. Similar presentations are found in Homer, Herodotus and Thucydides.[122]

A final category of text which will play a large role in this study and which must be handled judiciously is letters. Letter-writing was not, in fact, a part of level 4 rhetoric:[123] it took on a significant role only during the Middle Ages[124] – and then, importantly, there was no suggestion that a letter ought to conform to one of the three species of speeches or that it should be constructed according to the *taxis* found in the handbooks.[125] One might perhaps add, though it hardly seems necessary, that the handbooks did not discuss how to dissolve letters into the parts of a rhetorical composition. Only later still, after the invention of movable type, was rhetoric applied as a matter of course to printed material. Even then, though, it remained a tool for composition – for synthesis[126] – with limited analytical application.

But compare what Kennedy says: 'The rhetoricians were aware

---

[120] Kennedy, *Classical Rhetoric*, 110.
[121] Winter, 'The *Captatio Benevolentiae*', 505–31. See chapter 7 below.
[122] Kennedy, *Classical Rhetoric*, 110. Westlake, 'Setting of Thucydidean Speeches', 90–108.
[123] More precisely, letter-writing represents a distinct variety of level 4 rhetoric.
[124] Corbett, *Classical Rhetoric*, 20; Sloan, 'Rhetoric', 10: 20; cf. also 26: 803.
[125] Porter, 'Theoretical Justification', 108–16.
[126] Corbett, *Classical Rhetoric*, 30; Booth, *Rhetoric of Fiction*.

of the existence of traditional conventions in other forms of composition (in the epistle, for example) but appear to regard these as either subliterary, or perhaps more accurately as attaining to what literary qualities they have by imitation of one of the three literary genres'.[127] Significantly, the NT epistles *were* considered subliterary by early Christians schooled in rhetoric – but such an evaluation did not cause them to reject the texts;[128] we will see that they allowed other qualities to overcome any disappointment caused by lack of artistry. One thing these rhetors did not do, however, was to confuse *oratory* with the printed page.[129] Kennedy himself elsewhere contrasts rhetorical and literary analysis;[130] and more to the point for the student of Galatians, Duane Watson concedes: 'In the ancient world rhetorical theory and epistolary theory were not integrated, and matters which concerned letter writing were not discussed systematically by rhetors.'[131]

Epistolary conventions certainly do overlap on occasion with rhetorical ones, though not more than one might consider inevitable; for example, both speeches and letters must open, have a body, and close; they must endeavour to use words effectively; and they must consider the recipient in the creation of the discourse. Further evidence for this lack of any significant connection may be drawn from the observation that students of epistolary structure[132] often show little interest in those handbooks which 'rhetorical critics' latch on to for analytical purposes.[133]

Furthermore, while T. O. Sloan does inform us that, 'Inevitably, there were minor shifts of emphasis in so long a tradition, and for a long time even letter writing fell within the purview of rhetoric', one

[127] Kennedy, *New Testament Interpretation*, 31. By 'literary genres' Kennedy means oratory, historiography and the philosophical dialogue. He cites Quintilian, *Institutio* 10.1–2.

[128] See chapter 6 for discussion; so too Wilder, *Early Christian Rhetoric*, 36.

[129] Of course speeches could be, and were, written down, but I know of no instance of a letter being confused with a speech (until the modern era).

[130] Kennedy, *New Testament Interpretation*, 5–6.

[131] Watson, 'Rhetorical Analysis of Philippians', 104; cf. Bouwman, 'De Twee Testamenten', 259–76 (especially 272).

[132] For example, Bahr, 'Paul and Letter Writing', 465–77; Malherbe, 'Ancient Epistolary Theorists', 3–77; Dahl, 'Letter', 538–41; Stowers, *Letter Writing*; White, *Light from Ancient Letters*; White, 'New Testament Epistolary Literature', 1730–56. See Hester, 'Use and Influence of Rhetoric', 386–7 for a select bibliography of this large and growing body of literature.

[133] Contrast Hughes, *Early Christian Rhetoric*, especially 19–30, 47–50. He 'is convinced that ancient letters employ rhetorical style'. So says Lambrecht, 'Rhetorical Criticism and the New Testament', 251, n. 22.

must not abuse such information.[134] Oratory and the epistles of the
NT are not of the same genre. Corbett's more precise description of
this shift of rhetoric towards the inclusion of letter-writing clearly
shows the entire matter to be outside the bounds of NT study when
he writes:

> From its origin in fifth-century Greece through its flour-
> ishing period in Rome and its reign in the medieval *trivium*,
> rhetoric was associated primarily with the art of oratory.
> During the Middle Ages, the precepts of classical rhetoric
> began to be applied to letter-writing, but it was not until
> the Renaissance, after the invention of printing in the
> fifteenth century, that the precepts governing the spoken
> art began to be applied, on any large scale, to written
> discourse.[135]

The distinction is crucial. Our thesis depends in part on the
maintenance of discrete compartments: letter-writing and oratory
were distinct enterprises which did not merge in the classical mind.
Malherbe's work on epistolary theorists,[136] in contrast, seems to
defend the mingling of the two, and even to suggest that a classical
precedent for this merger exists.[137] Stanley Porter, however, disputes such a reading of Malherbe's data; the evidence (to make his
case, Porter surveys the handbooks cited in Malherbe's work)
reveals that letter-writing was not a concern of the rhetoricians but
that epistolary conventions were merely referred to occasionally in
the handbooks, often to highlight the differences, and usually in the
discussion of *style*.[138]

Concerning the parallels Betz offers to defend Galatians' status
as an apologetic letter,[139] and by implication as an epistolary
speech (and very few after Betz feel obliged to support the latter),
Longenecker assaults the credibility of such a claimed relationship
with his insistence that Plato's *Letter 7* is not a real letter; Isocrates'
Antidosis differs from Galatians in shape, content and style;

[134] Sloan, 'Rhetoric', 26: 803.
[135] Corbett, *Classical Rhetoric*, 20; so also Sloan and Perelman, 'Rhetoric', 10: 20;
Hudson, 'Field of Rhetoric', 7.
[136] Malherbe, 'Ancient Epistolary Theorists'.
[137] See Thurén, *Strategy of 1 Peter*, 64.
[138] Porter, 'Theoretical Justification', 110–16.
[139] Betz surveys the response to his Hermeneia commentary in the German
edition, *Der Galaterbrief*, 1–4. He does not, however, offer any significant new
parallels to sway the unconvinced. Cf. also Betz *2 Corinthians 8 and 9*, 130–1.

Demosthenes' *De Corona* was a speech delivered to more than five hundred; and Cicero's *Brutus* is not a letter but a treatise on oratory. 'In fact, none of the claimed precedents for Galatians really illuminates the epistolary structure of Galatians, for none is a real letter.'[140] Despite assertions to the contrary,[141] we still lack examples of the apologetic letter when understood as an epistle crafted around a classical oration.

More compelling is the suggestion of Frank W. Hughes that Demosthenes' Epistle 1 is an example of deliberative rhetoric in epistolary form. This letter was sent from exile to the Athenian assembly, and in structure and conformity to the handbooks, it seems to be a member of the deliberative species.[142] But even with this fascinating text we must proceed critically. This model of an oration was to be delivered to the assembly – the proper venue for deliberative oratory – and was necessarily dispatched because of exile. The shape resembles an oration more than an epistle, so that though the text does represent an imitation, it is not the 'rhetorical fiction' that some consider Galatians to be, but rather an epistolary fiction from exile.

That Epistle 1 is actually an oration is evident, for it (1) is addressed to the council; (2) argues for the taking of a political decision of interest to the city-state; (3) conforms to the shape and structure of a deliberative speech; and (4) employs the language appropriate to the formal public gathering. Upon turning to Galatians, however, we find wide-ranging differences from these criteria. In fact, this thesis will argue that by each canon Galatians does not conform to deliberative speech.

Thus Demosthenes' Epistle 1 is a fascinating anomaly, but is not evidence of a deliberative epistle genre. It is more likely the exception that proves the rule – and exists only because of Demosthenes' exile from the city-state.

From the above collection of evidence we see that rhetoric was for the crafting of speeches,[143] and, as such, was for construction, not analysis. Kennedy himself writes, 'Literary criticism, ancient

---

[140] Longenecker, *Galatians*, civ. See also below for an assessment of the language Paul used.

[141] See Mitchell, *Rhetoric of Reconciliation*, 8, n. 26.

[142] Hughes, *Early Christian Rhetoric*, 47–50, following Goldstein, *Letters of Demosthenes*, 176–81 (for ET see 204–7).

[143] But note the widening of scope by, among others, Robert Jewett, who offers the defining statement: 'Classical rhetoric aimed at training speakers *and writers* to persuade their audiences to make some kind of change in their situation': *Thessalo-*

and modern, has used the system of rhetoric without giving adequate attention to important differences between speech and literature'.[144] Significant shifts are needed before one may conclude otherwise; and such shifts have indeed taken place, resulting in an analysis that is not Graeco-Roman rhetoric, but a 'new rhetoric'. Unfortunately, students of Galatians have sometimes failed to notice the transition.

Rhetor (Latin: *Orator*)

In keeping with his view that handbook rhetoric (oratory) is restricted, Quintilian describes his ideal orator:

> The man who can really play his part as a citizen and is capable of meeting the demands both of public and private business, the man who can guide a state by his counsels, give it a firm basis by his legislation and purge its vices by his decisions as a judge, is assumed to be no other than the orator of our quest.[145]

Quintilian further specifies the orator as a pleader,[146] and one who has mastered the 'science and art of speaking'.[147] The root-words that underlie both rhetor and orator portray the orator as one who speaks. And the handbooks reveal that in level 4 oratory, the orator exists either for the purpose of statesmanship or for functioning in court.

Rhetorician

For the sake of clarity and consistency, we will refer to the one who delivers the speech as the 'rhetor' or the 'orator', and the theorist who describes the art of rhetoric or its effect on the auditor as the 'rhetorician'.

Species

Cicero writes that 'a *genus* is a class that embraces several *species* . . . a *species* is that which is part of a *genus* . . . But often the same

nian *Correspondence*, 63, emphasis added. He cites in support Lausberg, *Elemente*, 15f.; Martin, *Antike Rhetorik*, 2–12.

[144] Kennedy, *Classical Rhetoric*, 109.
[145] Quintilian, *Institutio* 1 Pr. 10.
[146] Ibid., 1 Pr. 12.   [147] Ibid., 1 Pr. 18.

thing is a genus in relation to one thing and a species in relation to another. For example, man is a species of animal, but a genus of which Thebans or Trojans are species'.[148]

Applying this to rhetoric, three species are widely acknowledged to fall under the *genus* or genre 'oratory'. According to Cicero, deliberative, epideictic (and judicial) 'are to be regarded as the genera of oratory',[149] but for our purposes the term 'genera' is replaced with 'species', since Cicero refers to the subsets of hand-book oratory. So we mean by handbook rhetoric what Cicero and Quintilian would call oratory, and diagram it as follows:

Level 3:   *Graeco-Roman rhetoric*
↓
Level 4:   *handbook rhetoric*
↓   ↓   ↓
Level 5:   (species)   1. *judicial*   2. *deliberative*   3. *epideictic*

Judicial speeches are those delivered in courts of law. They concern some past action, in that a trial attempts to arrive at a judgement concerning a crime already committed; the primary concern is with the just and unjust. H. D. Betz and Bernard H. Brinsmead believe that Galatians is judicial rhetoric.

Deliberative speeches are delivered in the Roman forum or the Greek assembly. They attempt to effect a judgement concerning a future course of action; the primary concern is with the expedient. George Kennedy and Joop Smit argue that Galatians is delibera-tive.

Epideictic was understood as the oratory of display, usually delivered at ceremonies such as funerals, to rally the troops, or to show skill in oratorical contests. In the Athenian tradition epi-deictic, which primarily though not exclusively[150] meant funeral oratory, was still transparently linked to civic matters. A speech would praise fallen armies, often mythical, in such a way that it provoked a deeper commitment to a cause. This class of speech eventually became a catch-all for what is neither judicial nor deliberative. James Hester and John L. White have recently suggested that Galatians is epideictic.[151]

---

[148] Cicero, *De Inventione* 1.22.32.
[149] Ibid., 1.10.14.
[150] A prominent exception is Gorgias' *Helen*, which was not a funeral speech, but rather his 'plaything'.
[151] Hester, 'Placing the Blame', 281–307; White, 'Apostolic Mission and Message', 145–61.

We provide only preliminary information here because chapter 5 is devoted to exploring species as applied to Galatians.

Taxis (Latin: *Dispositio*)

The handbooks discuss at length how to arrange the parts of a classical speech.[152] Generally speaking, a speaker opens with an *exordium* or *prooemium*, the purpose of which is to ingratiate oneself with those who must make a decision. Second comes a *narratio* or statement of facts of the trial. Then comes a statement of the points to be argued in the body of the speech – the *propositio*, which if enumerated is called the *enumeratio*; this is followed by the *probatio*, the attempt to prove the point. Finally, the *peroratio* sums up the argument and makes an emotional appeal to the judge.

But to identify aspects of disposition in an established text is not unlike the attempt to identify species. If a passage conforms precisely to a handbook definition, or to part of an actual speech, the label may have value; but if function alone is depended upon, the value is thrown into doubt. For example, White tells us that the opening (and closing) of an epistle functions to 'convey sentiments which enhance friendly relations . . . whereas the body expresses the more specific occasion of the letter'.[153] This last is defined as the disclosure or pursuit of information and 'making requests of the recipient'. But these functions are performed by many different parts of different genres. Sermons, speeches and television documentaries often attempt similar things in similar parts of the structure, so that a great deal of communication attempts to ingratiate the speaker to the hearer at the outset; surely, though, this does not mean that all discourse which attempts this is an epistle. In the same way, the simple fact that Paul uses narrative in Galatians 1–2 does not mean that he depends on the *narratio* of a classical oration.[154]

By transposing Doty's suggestion that 'generic definitions are best understood as relational terms – they demonstrate how literary works are similar',[155] we have a useful means of understanding how smaller structural units can be understood as well. Such units, in

---

[152] On the five parts of rhetoric see Lausberg, *Handbuch*, §256; Kennedy, *New Testament Interpretation*, 13–14.

[153] White, 'New Testament Epistolary Literature', 1731.

[154] In terms of logic, this appears to be an undistributed middle.

[155] Doty, 'Concept of Genre', 439.

their similarity to one another, may help us by way of analogy to understand how a particular element may function; but one must exercise great caution if the goal is to work back from function to identification of sub-generic particle to identification of genre.

Topoi (Latin: *Topica*)

Wayne Booth informs us concerning *topoi* (also referred to as commonplaces) that their 'original source is Aristotle (especially the *Rhetoric* and *Topics*), but the topics really came into their own, as it were, with Cicero's elaborate developments, especially in his *Topica*.[156] *Topoi* were, as their name implies, standardized 'places' where one looked for assistance in making an argument. Cicero writes that

> It is easy to find things that are hidden if the hiding place is pointed out and marked; similarly if we wish to track down some argument we ought to know the places or topics: for that is the name given by Aristotle to the 'regions', as it were, from which arguments were drawn.[157]

For example, in a legal dispute, one can appeal to definition, or perhaps it is helpful to enumerate the parts of a law, so that one may say: according to the law if a, b or c were performed, my client would be guilty of violating law x – but he did none of the three – therefore he is innocent.[158] Etymology, value and a whole plethora of other 'places' are provided as a checklist for the disputant. The commonplaces of letter and intent remain crucial to law and, in fact, to many kinds of writing. Cicero suggests that when accused of violating the law, one might deny breaking its real intent. Alternatively, if accused of breaking the intent of the law, one response would be: 'perhaps I did, but I obeyed its letter'.[159] The letter/intent issue has as sub-arguments the question of the effect of disobedience on society,[160] the ability of the law-writer[161] and a host of other points. Each of these can be used by the trained

[156] Booth, *Rhetoric of Irony*, 34, n. 1.
[157] Cicero, *Topica* 2.7–8.
[158] Ibid., 2. 9–10.
[159] Ibid., 42.121–48.143.
[160] Ibid., 44.129.
[161] Ibid., 45.130.

person, often regardless of his own stance towards the issue in question.

More recently, Kenneth Burke has written: 'Rhetoric moves from commonly held opinions to matters not held conjointly until the persuasive effect is at work. Thus the movement is from opinion to opinion'. The first originally shared opinion is, according to Burke, a 'commonplace'.[162] Thus they have been identified as the burden-carrying beast of persuasion.

Often overlooked in Pauline studies is the fact that common-places can be identified in texts so that one can detect the sort of rhetorical presuppositions which make up the particular level 4 rhetorics of a given community; that is, Paul certainly depended on 'commonly held opinions' as foundational to arguments which attempted to move the hearer to other positions. So the classical handbooks, as they discuss commonplaces, tell us much about what they consider the accepted 'opinions' of their particular milieu, namely the law-courts and civic oratory; and one may profitably mine the Pauline correspondence to discern what 'opinions' are foundational to his discourse. Although this undertaking is missing from most modern discussions of Pauline rhetoric, it would, were it performed, undoubtedly show the distance of Paul's world from that of the handbooks.[163] This is no claim that Paul necessarily thought in different categories from Cicero (that must be argued elsewhere), but that Paul had different venues and subjects to deal with in his 'rhetoric', and that his mode of expression had been shaped by a different experience of the world.[164]

Having established a preliminary understanding of classical rhetoric, we can now assess the way it has been fashioned into a methodology for reading Galatians. It is to this that we turn in chapter 3.

[162] Burke, *Rhetoric of Motives*, 56. He suggests that today they may be classed as 'attitudes' or 'values'.
[163] An exception is Wuellner's 'Topusforschung und Torahinterpretation', 463–83.
[164] For example, Paul's references to 'the games' or to rural life reflect specific commonplaces used to make his argument.

3

METHODS OF RHETORICAL ANALYSIS
AND GALATIANS

Rhetorical analyses of Galatians are necessarily selective regarding both the data they adapt from the classical world and the methodological avenues they pursue. This chapter will identify the choices made and, at times, question their appropriateness. It will begin with the classical sources which inform the discussion.

Sources

The agenda as set by Betz and reaffirmed by Kennedy is to look to the Graeco-Roman rhetorical handbooks as sources for the material of the discussion.[1] These are as follows: Aristotle's *Ars Rhetorica*; *Rhetorica ad Alexandrum* (pseudonymously attributed to Aristotle);[2] Cicero's *De Inventione, De Optimo Genere Oratorum, Topica, De Oratore, De Partitione Oratoriae, Brutus, Orator*; *De Ratione Dicendi*;[3] pseudo-Cicero's *Rhetorica ad Herennium*, Quintilian's, *Institutio Oratoria*.[4] Of the works of Cicero, only *De Inventione* is a true handbook, the rest being dialogues – but they have all been used to varying degrees by readers of Galatians.

These works are easily misconstrued. Indeed, the melting together of the various rhetorical sources has caused confusion. The

---

[1] For syntheses of the major handbooks see Spengel, *Rhetores Graeci*; Walz, *Rhetores Graeci*; Kroll, 'Rhetorik', 1039–1138 (especially 1096–1100); Solmsen, 'Drei Rekonstruktionen', 133–54; Solmsen, 'Aristotelian Tradition', 35–50, 169–90; Kennedy, 'Earliest Rhetorical Handbooks', 169–78. For more recent handbooks and compendia see Volkmann's *Rhetorik der Griechen und Römer*; Baldwin, *Ancient Rhetoric and Poetic*; Lausberg, *Handbuch*; Kennedy, *Persuasion in Greece*; *Rhetoric in the Roman World*; *Greek Rhetoric under Christian Emperors*; Martin, *Antike Rhetorik*.

[2] Stevens ('Aristotle and Koine', 204) suggests a date during the second half of the fourth century.

[3] In English: *On the Theory of Public Speaking*.

[4] All these are most readily available in the LCL and so references to quotations will follow the scheme provided therein.

classical sources employed to analyse Galatians, while all attempting to describe the same type of rhetoric, are not all of the same cloth; they require critical investigation before they can help us understand Paul.

This has occasionally been recognized in NT studies, as attested by F. W. Hughes:

> It might be easy to come to the false conclusion that Graeco-Roman rhetoric was a single, rather tightly unified system. In order to introduce most New Testament colleagues or others to the complexities of different systems of rhetoric, everyone who attempts to systematize rhetoric (including the present reviewer) runs the risk of making Graeco-Roman rhetoric look more unified or uniform than it really is likely to have been, in actual practice.[5]

He then adds that noted writers on rhetoric of the last hundred years have each adopted 'a major ancient synthesis of rhetoric': Richard Volkmann and Josef Martin discuss rhetoric from a pre-Socratic perspective, while Heinrich Lausberg favours the approach of Quintilian. The practice, therefore, does not originate in NT studies, though it is being perpetuated.

Despite occasional references to handbook inconsistency, discussion rarely centres on it, and just as rarely does it receive satisfactory treatment. Thomas Olbricht seeks to clarify which sources best help us understand Galatians. He writes: 'If Paul was affected by rhetoric, it was Greek rather than Roman. It is interesting that Betz, in his Galatians commentary, cites largely the *Rhetorica ad Herennium*, Cicero, and Quintilian.[6] It seems highly unlikely that Paul was influenced by any of the three'.[7] Douglas Campbell conversely writes that the 'best source for rhetorical theory at this time is Quintilian'.[8] Joop Smit observes that (1) Quintilian is encyclopaedic, 'Eclecticism is therefore a threatening danger'; (2) Betz uses 'incidental remarks by Quintilian which in more than one case are also interpreted in a strange way'; and (3)

---

[5] Hughes, 'Review of Watson', 274.

[6] Martin discusses differences in the handbooks (*Antike Rhetorik*, 219–29).

[7] Olbricht, 'Aristotelian Rhetorical Analysis', 221. It is overlooked that though *Ad Herennium* is bound with Cicero and wears a red jacket in the LCL, it nevertheless reflects *Greek* rhetorical theory. Cf. Mack, *Rhetoric and the New Testament*, 27: Aristotle is valuable within limits, for his work on rhetoric was lost from view until Cicero.

[8] D. Campbell, *Rhetoric of Righteousness*, 78.

Cicero's *De Inventione* and the *Rhetorica ad Herennium* date from about 85 BCE, 'are handbooks without much personal input, are close to a Greek source, and, because of that, reflect Hellenistic rhetoric in a reliable way'.[9]

Thus two watersheds may require attention: first, are Greek and Latin handbooks to be distinguished? And second, does date matter? Should a post-Pauline guide, such as Quintilian's, be rejected, or have we good reasons to accept it?

At least one specialist in rhetoric at Rome agrees with Smit on such questions. M. L. Clarke writes: 'No more need here be said of *De Inventione* than that it shows the elaboration of the scholastic rhetoric by now established at Rome and the thoroughness with which a gifted and zealous student had mastered it'. He then turns to the *Rhetorica ad Herennium*, describes the author as 'entirely dependent on Greek theory',[10] and bases his discussion on it because 'it is the most convenient guide, for it is relatively simple and it best represents the traditional rhetoric of the schools, the sort of thing that was taught by the ordinary rhetorician in Rome'.[11]

The diversity of understanding extended even to rhetoric itself: it is most commonly defined as the pursuit of eloquence – the art of speaking well in the court or assembly. This is not, however, the only definition available.[12] Aristotle, as we have seen, describes the function of rhetoric as the *discovery of arguments*. We have also observed that Aristotle (and most other handbooks follow him in this) can be thought of as providing a template ready to be filled in with the particulars of the speech. In turn, when focusing on word choice, the analogy of a template gives way to a checklist of effective terms. Not surprisingly the amount of instruction concerning memory and the presentation of the speech in a handbook as theoretical as Aristotle's differs considerably from others.

So the differences in rhetorical handbooks must not be underestimated. They extend not just to the theoretical positions taken by their authors, but even to the very elements of rhetoric which they deem worthy of inclusion.

---

[9] Smit, 'Deliberative Speech', 6. But Mitchell insists that Smit has not in fact helped move the discussion forward since his solution still relies on theory and handbooks rather than actual texts (*Rhetoric of Reconciliation*, 8, n. 26).

[10] Clarke, *Rhetoric at Rome*, 14.

[11] Ibid., 24; Clarke further notes that *Partitione Oratoriae* had little influence.

[12] Aristotle, *Rhetoric* 1.1.14.

Sometimes diction is neglected and arrangement alone considered (as in the discussion of rules for composition in different types of genres discussed by the late author known as Menander Rhetor). At other times arrangement is relegated to the status of addendum to *inventio*, a simple indication of what section of a speech – prologue, narrative, proof, epilogue – is most appropriate for a given argument. This classification underlies the method of organization found in the principal Latin authorities on rhetoric: the Auctor ad Herennium and, to a lesser degree, Cicero and Quintilian. Alternatively, both diction and arrangement may be placed under one rubric (Hermagoras's *Oikonomia*, for example).[13]

Aristotle's *Rhetoric* contains statements indicating that his positions differ from more popular ones: 'But the division now generally made is absurd; for narrative only belongs in a manner to forensic speech, but in epideictic or deliberative speech how is it possible that there should be narrative as it is defined, or a refutation; or an epilogue in demonstrative speeches?'[14] We will see presently that later rhetoricians singled out Aristotle for disagreement concerning structure.

Kennedy tells us that, according to Cicero,[15] the first century BCE witnessed the merging of the Isocratean and Aristotelian traditions.[16] Cicero then, 'draws on their separate traditions, relying on Isocrates for the pedagogic and stylistic theories of the first two books and on Aristotle for the theory of invention and expression'.[17] Quintilian speaks of changes in practice through the ages;[18] criticism of contemporary practice;[19] criticism of contemporary theory;[20] and the conflict of theory and

[13] Cole, *Origins of Rhetoric*, 18–19.

[14] Aristotle, *Rhetoric* 3.13.3. Cicero, *De Oratore* 3.141 states that Aristotle began to write in reaction to Isocrates. *The Rhetorica ad Alexandrum* represents the sophistic school of rhetoric that Aristotle opposed. (See *Rhetorica ad Alexandrum*, LCL 258, n. a.) It must also be observed that a variety of now lost handbooks existed before Aristotle's. Plato wrote the *Phaedrus* in reaction to these books and the practices of their authors (*Phaedrus* 266d).

[15] Cicero, *De Inventione* 2.8.

[16] Kennedy, 'Theory of Artistic Prose', 190.

[17] Fantham, 'Literature and Criticism at Rome', 231.

[18] Quintilian, *Institutio* 4.1.9; 5.14.5; 8.3.35; 8.5.38.

[19] Ibid., 4.1.11; 4.2.2.

[20] Ibid., 4.1.28; 4.1.50; 4.1.70; 4.2.32; 5.11.2 (where Quintilian disagrees with Cicero); 5.14.5.

practice.[21] Quintilian similarly discusses widespread disagreement over style: he distinguishes Attic from Asianic,[22] declares the Rhodian style to be a halfway house,[23] and asserts that the Attic style is best.[24] We learn that in his own day Cicero was criticized as florid and out of control, while by Quintilian's day he was considered 'too jejune and dry'.[25] Quintilian criticizes the best, including Aristotle[26] and Cicero.[27]

Other writers naturally offer different opinions.[28] Perhaps the starkest illustration of the diversity of rhetoric can be found in Cicero's fictitious dialogue, *De Oratore*,[29] in which various rhetors present their views on the breadth of education needed by an orator[30] and the extent of rhetoric's influence on society.[31] Differences run deep among the orators of the dialogue.

Thus any confidence in finding unity among the handbooks is misplaced: they represent a wide range of attitudes and philosophies towards rhetoric.[32]

History of rhetorical approaches to Galatians

Prehistory

Scholarship often recounts the history of biblical rhetorical studies as a stumbling movement – fits and starts mark the way rather than

---

[21] Ibid., 5.13.59; 5.13.60.

[22] Ibid., 12.10.16.

[23] Ibid., 12.10.18.

[24] Ibid., 12.10.20.

[25] Ibid., 12.10.13.

[26] Ibid., 3.9.5: 'I disagree with those who, like Aristotle [*Rhetoric* 2.26], would remove *refutation* from the list [i.e. list of the parts of a case] on the ground that it forms part of the *proof*: for the *proof* is constructive, and the *refutation* destructive. Aristotle also introduces another slight novelty in making *proposition*, not *statement of facts*, follow the *exordium*'.

[27] Ibid., 3.11.18, for inconsistency within various works; cf. also 5.11.2. Other texts in Quintilian that express disagreement include: 3.4.16; 3.11.5; 4.1.9 (on style); 8. prologue 11, 12, 26; 8.5.25; 9.1.10, 22–4; 9.2.65, 2.101, 106; 9.3.3–4, 60; 9.4.16, 38, 53–5, 87–9, 110, 132, 137, 146; 10.1.7, 43–4; 11.2.25–6; 11.3.103, 107, 117, 120, 123, 126, 128, 131, 148, 160; 12.1.14; 12.10.40, 47, 73.

[28] Aristotle, *Rhetoric* 3.13.3–36.

[29] Cicero, vol. 3 (*De Oratore* Book 1–2), p. xiii gives a date of September 91 BCE.

[30] Cicero, *De Oratore* 1.10.41–4; 1.11.45–60; 1.49.213.

[31] Ibid., 1.8.30–10.34, 10.45–13, 57; 1.9.35–10.44.

[32] For a treatment concerned with the philosophical differences see Leeman, 'Variety of Classical Rhetoric', 41–6.

a smooth flow. References to Carl Heinrici,[33] Hans Wendland,[34] Johannes Weiss[35] and Rudolf Bultmann give way to silence concerning more than a half-century.[36] That silence was, according to frequent account,[37] shattered by James Muilenburg, who wished to 'go beyond form criticism' by resorting to rhetorical analysis as an aid to study of the book of Isaiah.[38] Indeed, it is claimed that 'James Muilenburg almost single-handedly introduces the phrase "rhetorical criticism" into twentieth-century interpretation of the Hebrew Bible in North America and the United Kingdom'.[39] With only little variation, his works are alluded to as the forerunners of a new era of study – but Muilenburg in fact applied the label 'rhetoric' to a sort of stylistics,[40] that is, to only one aspect of rhetoric. Of rhetorical criticism, he writes:

> What I am interested in, above all, is understanding the nature of Hebrew literary composition, in exhibiting the structural patterns that are employed for the fashioning of a literary unit, whether in poetry or in prose, and in discerning the many and various devices by which the predicates are formulated and ordered into a unified whole. Such an enterprise I should describe as rhetoric and the methodology as rhetorical criticism.[41]

[33] Heinrici, *Erste Korinther*.

[34] Wendland, *Die Briefe an die Korinther*.

[35] Weiss, 'Beiträge zur paulinischen Rhetorik', 165–247; *Erste Korintherbrief*.

[36] See Mack, *Rhetoric and the New Testament*, 11–16; Jewett, *Thessalonian Correspondence*, 63–4. Another frequently cited work is König, *Stilistik, Rhetorik, Poetik*. Other works, usually overlooked but highly relevant, include Colson, 'μετασχημάτισα 1 Cor. iv.6', 379–84; Callaway, 'Galatians and Plato's *Lysias*', 353–6; older significant works are Bengel, *Gnomon*; Bullinger, *Figures of Speech*.

[37] For example, Wuellner, 'Where is Rhetorical Criticism Taking Us?', 448–63. Kennedy, *New Testament Interpretation*, 4.

[38] See especially Muilenburg, 'Form Criticism and Beyond', 1–18; reprinted in *Beyond Form Criticism*, 46–69.

[39] Robbins and Patton, 'Rhetoric and Biblical Criticism', 327. Eissfeldt (*Introduction*, 57) is listed as a source for precursors to Muilenburg. Cf. also the helpful introduction found in Fleming, *Genesis 2–3*. Works by Muilenburg's devotees are many; see especially Jackson and Kessler, *Rhetorical Criticism*; Trible, *God and the Rhetoric of Sexuality* and *Texts of Terror*. For discussion of the movement see Anderson, 'New Frontier', ix–xviii. A NT work in the same vein as Muilenburg is Dewey, *Markan Public Debate*. Lundblom offers a Muilenburg bibliography with comments (*Jeremiah*, 129, n. 3).

[40] I use 'stylistics' not in its technical sense, but as an attempt to explain the effect of rhetorical devices on the reader. An example of this approach would be to address the ability of a rhetorical question to control the structure of an epistle. Specific examples will arise in our discussion of this sort of stylistics (see pp. 82–6).

[41] Muilenburg, 'Form Criticism and Beyond', 8; see also Clifford, 'Rhetorical

In reality, Muilenburg is very much in line with the German works cited above in that he, like them, focused on style, structure and, perhaps above all, the 'argumentative devices employed by the author'.[42] His concern was not with the pre-textual analysis which dominated studies of both testaments until about 1970 (and continues in many studies of the NT),[43] but with the text itself as conveying plots and themes which must be involved in any truly 'literary reading'. He was motivated at least in part by the realization that texts of a similar literary type often diverge widely in their stylistic and rhetorical dimensions;[44] thus the old way of handling the text, form criticism, was not repudiated, but recognized as inherently limited.[45] He introduced a broader method in order to attend to the individuality of texts – for form criticism, because of its concern with the stereotypical elements of a group of texts, 'applies an external measure to the individual pericopes' and overlooks their distinctiveness.[46]

Muilenburg resists the temptation to bypass the text itself and over-emphasize what lies behind it,[47] Burton Mack describing his goal as 'the analysis of the formal features of a composition that could take account of authorial accomplishment and creativity. His move was calculated to correct both form-critical assumptions about essentially authorless genres and traditions, as well as fend off the tendency by some literary critics (e.g., the school of New Criticism) to bracket all historical considerations when investigating a text'.[48]

Although his goals are readily discernible, Muilenburg did not

Criticism', 21. Kessler ('Methodological Setting', 32–5) also addresses the relationship between form and rhetorical criticism.

[42] Jewett (*Thessalonian Correspondence*, 64, n. 7), who describes works clustered around the passing of the last century such as those of Wilke, Weiss, Koenig, Bultmann and Allo. He thus opposes the position held by Mack (see *Rhetoric and the New Testament*, 11) who sees a direct line from Heinrici to Betz.

[43] His article, 'Form Criticism and Beyond', was originally presented as the presidential address of the Society of Biblical Literature in 1968.

[44] Muilenburg ('Form Criticism and Beyond', 5) points to the literary similarity but obvious differences between Deuteronomy 32 and Micah 6.1–8.

[45] Ibid., 4–5.

[46] Ibid., 5. Cf. Fleming, *Genesis 2–3*, 27, and Anderson, 'New Frontier', xiii for the notion that Muilenburg seeks to go beyond the generalities of form criticism to the specifics of individual texts. For the generality of form criticism as a liability see Greenwood, 'Rhetorical Criticism and Formgeschichte', 418.

[47] House, 'Literary Criticism', 7.

[48] Mack, *Rhetoric and the New Testament*, 12.

provide a detailed methodology.[49] We can, nevertheless, discover much about how he reads the text: first he divides the text and isolates the individual units to be examined; then he observes

> how the single unit moves, 'shifts or breaks in the development in the writer's thought'. Poetic devices and word play are particularly helpful at this stage in the process. Next, how the writer's thought progresses from one unit to the next must be charted. Finally, the data should be assembled to explain the author's intention or intentions for the piece.[50]

Another theorist/practitioner of rhetorical criticism, Isaac M. Kikiwada, willingly applies the label to works that precede Muilenburg.[51] For example, he calls Umberto Cassuto's Genesis commentary rhetorical.[52] He further considers an article by W. F. Albright[53] rhetorical though it was written before the method gained widespread acceptance.[54] Thus 'rhetorical criticism' was not something invented by Muilenburg; instead it was a *literary approach* to the text that needed a voice and found one in his 1968 address and subsequent article. The Bible had traditionally been viewed from the perspective of the seminarian, theologian or cleric until this point, but now the student of literature was becoming prominent. This was Muilenburg's background and he was importing skills learned elsewhere into the guild of which he was now a member, and this at a time when he would not be alone. Northrop Frye was already published[55] and others, such as D. F. Rauber,[56] were getting their turn. But even for Muilenburg this was no new beginning, for he did not launch a new methodology with his address, but clarified the approach he had used in some of his

[49] For method see Kessler, 'Methodological Setting', 22–36; Kikiwada, 'Definition of Rhetorical Criticism', 67–91.

[50] House, 'Literary Criticism', 8; following Muilenburg, 'Form Criticism and Beyond', 10–13.

[51] Kikiwada, 'Shape of Genesis 11:1–9', 18–32; 'Definition of Rhetorical Criticism', 67–91; 'Genesis on Three Levels', 3–15; 'Quantitative Analysis', 195–203.

[52] Cassuto, *Genesis I* and *Genesis II*.

[53] Albright, 'Patriarchs to Moses: I', 22–6; 'Patriarchs to Moses: II', 48–76.

[54] See Kikiwada, 'Quantitative Analysis', 195, n. 1.

[55] See Frye (*Anatomy of Criticism*) for a most important discussion which at times used literary criticism to analyse biblical texts. Chapter 5 especially relates to rhetorical criticism. His later work, *The Great Code*, was equally weighty and influential.

[56] See Rauber, 'Literary Values', 27–37.

earlier works. His 'Literary Form in the Fourth Gospel', written in 1932, and 'The Literary Character of Isaiah 34', from 1940, both stand within the tradition only formally announced some thirty years later.[57] In the former article Muilenburg writes: 'It is a primary canon of ours that form and content are intimately interrelated',[58] and in the latter: 'The literary features of the eschatological poem of Isaiah 34 are so clear and striking, so numerous and varied in character, that they afford a good insight into the methods of Hebrew literary composition and Hebrew literary taste'.[59] Precisely these types of presuppositions infuse with life modern literary readings; and Muilenburg was so engaged earlier than some realize.

Muilenburg and his followers appear to be in line, at least as a precursor, with what David Clines and Cheryl Exum call the '"new" literary criticism', which they describe as 'not a historical discipline, but a strictly literary one, foregrounding the textuality of the biblical literature. Even when it occupies itself with historical dimensions of the texts – their origin or their reception – its primary concern is the text as an object, a product, not as a window upon historical actuality'.[60] Clines and Exum speak of rhetorical criticism as a subset of literary criticism, and in a list of definitions of various methodologies write:

> Rhetorical criticism, sharing the outlook of new criticism about the primacy of the text in itself, and often operating under the banner of 'the final form of the text', concerns itself with the way the language of the texts is deployed to convey meaning. Its interests are in the devices of writing,

[57] Muilenburg, 'Fourth Gospel', 40–53; 'Literary Character of Isaiah 34', 339–65.

[58] Muilenburg, 'Fourth Gospel', 42.

[59] Muilenburg, 'Literary Character of Isaiah 34', 339.

[60] Clines and Exum, 'New Literary Criticism', 11. Adele Berlin (*Poetics and Interpretation*, 13) provides a lucid introduction to literary criticism as intrinsic analysis. She speaks of biblical narrative as a representation to be studied for its own sake (see especially 13–16), and employs the term 'poetics' to describe her approach. She writes: 'Poetics, the science of literature, is what Todorov has called "internal"; it seeks its rules and principles from within literature itself, without recourse to sciences outside of literature, such as psychology, sociology, etc. (and one may add, in the case of Biblical studies, history and archaeology). Now Todorov is not committing the sin of New Criticism by closing off the world of the text from the real world. He is simply and correctly promoting the idea that literary works should be analyzed according to the principles of literary science rather than according to the principles of some other science' (16). Her assertion is that 'if we know *how* texts mean, we are in a better position to discover *what* a particular text means' (17).

in metaphor and parallelism, in narrative and poetic structures, in stylistic features. In principle, but not often in practice in Hebrew Bible studies, it has regard to the rhetorical situation of the composition and promulgation of ancient texts and to their intended effect upon their audience. But, like new criticism, its primary focus is upon the texts and their own internal articulation rather than upon their historical setting.[61]

The method established by Muilenburg has thus proven highly adaptable and useful – even in areas where the questions are not necessarily his. For example, if the unity of a text is revealed by that same structural coherence as Muilenburg discussed,[62] then Ivan Ball is justified in using rhetoric as a means to demonstrate the integrity of Zephaniah through its rhetorical shape.[63] While this conclusion may have been reached by other means or even without a defined approach, the value of a methodology often lies in its providing a set of questions and a terminology to express the answers: in short, efficiency in both reaching conclusions and propounding them often results from a sound method. Thus Muilenburg and those who share his outlook maintain that modern rhetoric 'regards the text as the embodiment of a piece of discourse, a design – not a map . . . [The rhetorician] knows, also, that the structure of a piece of discourse, the way its major parts fit together, is profoundly a result of its intention'.[64] So we find in such efforts an approach to the text which appeals to a great many scholars.

But to understand Muilenburg properly we must observe that he never relates his rhetorical approach to level 4 rhetoric, but instead sees the text as a timeless piece of literature and analyses it accordingly. His analysis relates to level 2 and thus neither provides a precedent for analysts who investigate level 4, nor resurrects classical rhetoric; he seeks to go beyond the search for the general-

---

[61] Clines and Exum, 'New Literary Criticism', 16.

[62] Muilenburg ('Form Criticism and Beyond', 9) writes: 'What I am interested in, above all, is in understanding the nature of Hebrew literary composition, in exhibiting the structural patterns that are employed for the fashioning of a literary unit, whether in poetry or in prose, and in discerning the many and various devices by which the predications are formulated and ordered into a unified whole. Such an enterprise I should describe as rhetoric and the methodology as rhetorical criticism'.

[63] Ball, 'Rhetorical Shape of Zephaniah', 155–65. For NT studies undertaken with the same concern see: Rolland, 'La Structure littéraire', 213–16; Sumney, 'Pauline Rhetorical Pattern', 192–204.

[64] Sloan, 'Restoration of Rhetoric', 26: 803.

ities of a text (as in form criticism) by isolating its more specific setting.[65] Criticism of his work faults the replacing rather than complementing of form criticism, and attacks practice more than theory.[66] Muilenburg, in defending his method, produces a number of examples – but he does not demonstrate conformity to 'classical rhetoric'. He shows the OT employment of a *Hebrew rhetorical technique*, and never loses sight of the individuality of the text.[67]

C. Clifton Black, applying Muilenburg's conclusions to recent works of NT rhetorical analysis, writes that 'those who share Muilenburg's sensitivity to the distinctiveness of specific texts may discern in the studies of Gitay, Betz, Jewett, and Watson, a disquieting tendency to press oracles or letters into elaborate rhetorical schemes of organization (from *proem* to *epilogos*). While rhetorical models function as heuristic guides, particular texts often resist preset patterns'.[68] Further: 'Cicero's *Catilinarian* is a different creature from, say, the first book of Samuel; though they both intend to persuade, they invite different approaches. The adequacy of strictly rhetorical canons for interpreting all texts of all genres with persuasive intent is a debatable premise, which rhetorical critics need to think through'.[69]

Muilenburg's method transfers well at certain points to reading the book of Galatians, for it moves beyond the *Sitz-im-Leben* of a text by emphasizing its particularity.[70] Paul does not craft an epistle addressing a clearly discernible *Sitz-im-Leben* as defined in form criticism, but a crisis for which he combines common episto-lary conventions with any alterations needed to accomplish his purpose. Thus the form we can identify for Galatians is 'epistle', and this particular epistle sometimes breaks the generic boundaries of the vehicle.[71] Galatians does not reveal a setting as understood by the form critics. Instead it hints at a more specific context.

So Muilenburg offers an alternative view of the text, but few exegetes use his sort of rhetoric to understand Galatians; Black, in

[65] Muilenburg, 'Form Criticism and Beyond', 18.
[66] Representative of these critics, and aiming at Muilenburg's Isaiah commentary (which was printed a dozen years before the above-quoted speech), are: Westermann, 'Sprache und Struktur', 106–10; Melugin, *Formation of Isaiah 40–55*, 10.
[67] Clifford, 'Rhetorical Criticism in Exegesis', 21.
[68] C. C. Black, 'Rhetorical Criticism', 255.
[69] Ibid., 257.
[70] Clifford, 'Rhetorical Criticism in Exegesis', 19.
[71] See below on Wilder; Brinsmead, *Galatians*, 37–55.

fact, finds his conclusions hostile to so-called rhetorical studies of Galatians.

The literary critic Amos Wilder appropriated a similar method at roughly the same time. His contributions, like Muilenburg's, however, are more properly described as the prehistory of an approach – and like Muilenburg, Wilder does not deal with level 4 rhetoric. He does, as a literary critic concerned with the forms of authority and power in the NT, take his audience to level 3 and imply that there is a level below that.[72] Not once, though, does Wilder suggest that any NT writer conforms to the particular form of rhetoric with which we are concerned at level 4, namely that of the handbooks.

He begins with the supposition that 'shape and substance are inseparable and mutually determinative'.[73] Thus the shape of Biblical texts, that is, their structures as parables, sayings, and the like, had rhetorical significance, inviting, as Robbins and Patton put it, 'consideration of patterns of consciousness and culture or "the life orientation that produced them" as well as attention to "particular social patterns" which govern and constrain the use of forms'.[74] Thus form reveals 'categories of knowledge and belief' as well as 'the historical conditions or exigencies that generate' discourse.[75]

Wilder is therefore interested in the relationship between early Christian works and the classical literary world from which many suppose they sprang. He writes that 'early Christian literary arts were different from those that ancient paganism produced, and . . . Greek and traditional humanist categories are inadequate as measuring rods'.[76] He explains that when scholarship began to

---

[72] Cf. the title of his monograph *Early Christian Rhetoric: The Language of the Gospel*, first printed in 1964 as *The Language of the Gospel: Early Christian Rhetoric*. See also *New Voice*; *Theopoetic*; *Bible and the Literary Critic*. One way to understand the designation 'Early Christian Rhetoric' (and it would seem to be the way Wilder intends) is as a discussion of the particular rhetoric of the early Christians. Such a rhetoric sits on level 4, though it is certainly distinct from handbook rhetoric. That is, it follows different rules, the apprehension of which requires that one turn not to the rhetorical handbooks (for they describe another sphere of rhetoric altogether), but to the texts that comprise this Christian rhetoric in order to discern what they reveal about early Christian commonplaces, worldviews, etc.

[73] Wilder, *Early Christian Rhetoric*, 25.

[74] Robbins and Patton, 'Rhetoric and Biblical Criticism', 329, citing Wilder, *Early Christian Rhetoric*, 25–6.

[75] Robbins and Patton, 'Rhetoric and Biblical Criticism', 329.

[76] Wilder, *Early Christian Rhetoric*, 36.

attend to the style of early Christian writings, they inevitably compared their texts with contemporary non-Christian material. The failure of such an enterprise, however, was assured, for the 'existing Greek literary forms were almost all sophisticated and artistic. They belonged to a different world. Even much Jewish literature in Greek – Josephus, the Letter of Aristeas, etc. – was consciously artistic and written for a wide public'.[77]

With epistles the Christians adopted the familiar, which is 'all the more interesting in this case because the letter is already such a combination of the conventional and the personal'.[78] 'Paul, as he himself says, is only a minister of the word and not a rhetorician.'[79] So Wilder refuses to link Paul with the sophisticated stylists of his day and rounds out his brief history by referring to Franz Overbeck's demonstration that Christian writings up to and including the apostolic fathers (160 CE) 'fall outside the history of literature properly so called. They were sub-literary products and naive in the best sense'. He concludes that, apart from heretical writings, with Clement of Alexandria Christian writings first appear which resemble the Graeco-Roman literature. He rightly observes therefore that Christian literature must be recognized as distinct and treated as such.[80]

In fact, Wilder opens a fairly sizeable gap between the Bible and classical literature. He denies the terms 'literature', 'poetry', 'biography' and 'history' to the output of early Christianity, and argues that 'oratory' is not 'appropriate to the discourses of the apostles or the prophets. Our usual tools for rhetorical genres and forms are at home in the classical and humanist traditions, but come short when we face our present task'.[81]

In terms of the schema outlined in chapter 2, Wilder is placing Christianity's rhetoric alongside Graeco-Roman oratory at level 3, but then proposing that it diverges at level 4. 'The Christian writings are assigned to the class of *Kleinliteratur* rather than *Hochliteratur*; that is they are popular in the sense of unsophisticated and unliterary', and written for the 'unliterary classes of the Roman empire. It is true that there were in the Mediterranean

[77] Ibid., 44.
[78] Ibid., 31; cf. Brinsmead (*Galatians*, 37–55), who agrees that traditional forms are inadequate to describe Paul's epistle.
[79] Ibid., 34.
[80] Ibid., 36.
[81] Ibid., 28.

world of that period pagan writings of a popular character. But even here real distinctions can be made'.[82]

So then Wilder places the NT texts outside the sphere of Graeco-Roman rhetoric at least in terms of literary level, audience and genre. He correctly sees that Christianity possessed its own code of communication, value structure and shared worldview – all of which were often antithetical to Graeco-Roman oratory. This does not, however, deny that Christian communication possessed a 'rhetorical' idiom.[83] Indeed he describes the qualities of 'Christian Rhetoric' as a 'creative novelty in styles'; a 'dramatic immediacy' enhanced by dialogue; an employment of 'common idiom and media'; an 'addiction to narrative'; and a 'subordination of the personal role or talent to the Spirit in the community'.[84]

Finally, Wilder explicitly identifies the appearance of Christian 'literature . . . in the classical sense' as a second-century event.[85] So he does not link Paul with the works of a Cicero or Quintilian. Rather than upholding a classical rhetorical analysis of the NT, he provides data which oppose such an attempt:[86] he often speaks not of 'rhetoric' but of 'rhetorics', and equates 'rhetorical study' with a particular sort of 'literary study' – not with a classical analysis of the text.[87] That is, he does not engage level 4 rhetoric. And his work spawns no such efforts.

History of use in Galatians

Hans Dieter Betz's articles and commentary on Galatians marked the end of gestation for the new approach; academia now possessed not hesitant beginnings but mature works dependent on a highly developed methodology.[88] His effort centred primarily on the shape of Galatians as compared to an oration, that is, Betz (1) argued

---

[82] Ibid., 28.

[83] Cf. Olbricht, 'Aristotelian Rhetorical Analysis', 226.

[84] Wilder, *Early Christian Rhetoric*, 34–5.

[85] Ibid., 39.

[86] Ibid., 38.

[87] Wilder, *Bible and Literary Critic*, 10–11. Heirs to the thought world of Wilder include Funk, *Language* and Via, *Parables*. These works share Wilder's concern for the shape of a text's flow of thought (cf. Robbins and Patton, 'Rhetoric and Biblical Criticism', 330) but have nothing to say concerning classical rhetorical *dispositio* or species. See also Tannehill, *Sword of His Mouth*; Trible, *God and Rhetoric of Sexuality*.

[88] Betz, 'Literary Composition and Function', 353–79; *Galatians*; *2 Corinthians 8 and 9*. Much can be drawn from the earlier *Paulus und die Sokratische Tradition*.

that Galatians is a particular type of level 4 rhetoric, namely a
classical oration; (2) attempted to specify the type (species) of the
oration as judicial; and (3) explained the epistle in light of that type.
Although his methodology was not explicitly detailed, there was no
great outcry for a way to make the approach widely useful, perhaps
at least in part because of a certain awe inspired by one who
possessed so expert an understanding of classical rhetoric.

The first major response to Betz came in a review by Wayne
Meeks in which he wrote that Betz 'does not really show that [Gal.
5–6] must be conceived primarily as *defensive*. The monitory
element in [Paul's] letter is curiously neglected: only 5:1–6:10 are
hortatory in Betz's scheme. Yet, if he were not so determined to
make "apology" the basic type to which the letter must conform,
would it not appear that the whole argument from 3:1 on is
primarily designed not to defend Paul's position but to exhort the
Galatians to abandon their new mentors?'[89] One should also note
Meeks' reference to Galatians as a letter. Finally, he seems to clear
the way for Kennedy by adding: 'The major question which must
be put to Betz, then, is whether *apologia* is the most appropriate
category to apply to the letter as a whole. It is a question to which
those more expert than I in the literature of rhetoric should
speak'.[90]

The classicist George Kennedy, who promulgated a methodology
to assist those lacking Betz's grasp of the details, is an acknowledged expert in the realm of Greek rhetoric. Indeed, his several
volumes on the topic give us the broader history of rhetoric. He
goes to great lengths to argue that Galatians is not forensic but
deliberative rhetoric. The effect his writing has had on methodology
is highly significant but has rarely been critiqued. When Muilenburg took up the term 'rhetoric', he meant something quite broad –
something like how the text achieves its purpose through stylistic
devices.[91] Betz, however, and then especially the classicist Kennedy,
mean something quite different – at least regarding Galatians.
Muilenburg consciously applied rhetoric to Hebrew poetry, but
with Galatians, the major proponents try to identify exactly what
sort of classical Greek oration Galatians represents: is it a judicial

---

[89] Meeks, 'Review of *Galatians*', 305. In our fourth chapter we will consider the
role chapters 5 to 6 play within the epistle.

[90] Ibid., 306.

[91] One branch of rhetoric had become closely associated with style and with the
identification of devices.

speech or a deliberative speech? Thus the endeavour has shifted from Muilenburg's search for meaning and intention back to a new type of form criticism – complete with implications for Paul's education and preaching strategy. Rhetoric has lost the text-centredness it possessed in Muilenburg's hands, and its practitioners now, at least after Kennedy, and with respect to Galatians, stand firmly in the historical-critical camp once again. And once again, as Muilenburg implicitly predicted, much attention has moved toward generic questions reaching behind the text, rather than to questions concerning the text in its particularity.

Thus we need to assess rhetorical approaches to Galatians. It is unique among all biblical texts in that it is held to be an example of Graeco-Roman rhetoric, that is, not just an epistle that can be analysed with the help of rhetoric but an actual oration. While there is little agreement as to the precise details, exegetes are beginning to accept such conclusions as their starting point.[92]

R. B. Hays, in an article devoted to 'Recent Books on Galatians', faults Betz for relying on 'apologetic letters' for which 'the evidence is scanty, as Betz himself acknowledges'.[93] He adds that 'Betz would have served his readers better if he had applied his magisterial learning to the task of tracing the way in which Paul eclectically adopts and transforms a variety of literary genres and conventions';[94] and then charges that Betz downplays 'the strongly

[92] Lüdemann extracts from Galatians 1–2 its autobiographical detail (in *Paul*). He depends on Betz's analysis of the epistle as a whole (especially singling out 6.11–18 as a *peroratio*: 47), and then moves to a self-described 'form-critical analysis of Gal. 1:6–2:14' which labels these verses the *exordium* and *narratio* (48ff.). The implications of following Betz step to centre-stage when discussing the chronology of 'The Narratio', 2.11–14. Lüdemann uses the relevant passages in Quintilian to demonstrate that the order most helpful to the argument is preferable to the historical order (57–8). He then offers his assessment of the autobiographical section, always with this form-critical assumption before him (see 59–60, and esp 62) and is thus free from the burden of explaining the difficult order implied by Paul's statements. Another adherent to Betz's views is Beaudean, who writes in *Paul's Theology of Preaching*, 63, of the two disadvantages Paul must overcome in Galatia: his presence is mediated through a letter, and 'he is compelled to use the rhetorical devices of the apologetic genre, which among knowledgeable persons was always suspect'. Joop Smit is confident enough in his form-critical conclusion that upon arriving at the passage which troubles Betz the most – the paraenesis of 5.13–6.10 – he argues that it must have been added later (cf. Smit, 'Deliberative Speech', 1–26). Cf. also Smiles, *Gospel and Law in Galatia*. He works with the premise that Galatians 2.15–21 is the *propositio* of an apologetic speech. More examples of scholars who follow Betz are discussed in chapter 4.

[93] Hays, 'Recent Books on Galatians', 97. Hays has also presented an important literary reading of Galatians: *Faith of Jesus Christ*.

[94] Hays, 'Recent Books on Galatians', 97.

Jewish style and content of Paul's argumentation'.[95] Thus Hays
suggests that Galatians conforms to no single genre, but like much
of the NT, takes hold of whatever is needed at a given moment.
This in effect throws the emphasis back on Paul's purpose rather
than his artistry – though not ruling out the latter. Hays further
reminds us that the modern interpretative community often considers Paul's outlook to be determined largely by Jewish constraints
– and we will see in chapters 6 and 7 that linguistically at least,
there is no reason to consider Paul a classical orator.

These objections are significant, for they highlight the move
away from the search for purpose in poetry – but Muilenburg's
approach was most successful where applied to 'more artistic' texts
such as OT poetry and narrative, and the gospels, and less
successful when dealing with didactic texts. Perhaps this is partly
because outwardly propositional texts have different methods of
accomplishing their purpose, or perhaps because the analyst too
easily strays from a purely Muilenburg-type analysis when en-
countering such elements. Whatever the reason, Muilenburg's
approach seems to have worked well with certain text-types – of
which Galatians is not one.

Galatians also suffers from misapplication. If the epistle is
recognized to be a persuasive, purposive text, then it should be
analysed as such, and within the rhetorical world that created it.
The constraints of that world shape the text; and, if the text and its
shape can reveal the intent of the author (as Muilenburg maintained), then that social world with its particular constraints may
be properly brought in. Thus Hays' objections merge: he suggests
that the genre of Galatians must be understood, and that Paul must
be read as a member of his own milieu, both of which in this case
point in the same direction because of the genre's ties to the
author's literary milieu. It is dangerous to force upon Paul a
Graeco-Roman rhetorical standard when his Jewish cultural and
stylistic elements at least appear more relevant. Chapters 6 and 7
will argue that Paul's style of writing differs from that demanded of
oratory, and that it at times points in the direction of a Jewish
rhetoric.

Bernard H. Brinsmead, in *Galatians: Dialogical Response to
Opponents*, pays particular attention to the audience of the letter.[96]

---

[95] Ibid., 97–8.
[96] Brinsmead, *Galatians*.

He concludes, with Betz, that Galatians belongs to the apologetic letter genre. The stress in his study is more on the rhetorical situation and the notion that it demands an apologetic response than on measuring conformity to an external standard. François Vouga in his mini-article proposes that the solution to the Betz versus Kennedy debate is to recognize the great similarity between Galatians and the clearly deliberative speech of Demosthenes, *On the Peace*.[97] He depends almost exclusively on the structure of Galatians to discern its genre (oratory), and its species (deliberative). Richard Longenecker and G. Walter Hansen have advanced the discussion with their suggestion that both rhetorical and epistolary conventions ought to be employed as analytical tools, and that rhetoric furthers not only diachronic, but more importantly, synchronic analysis.[98]

Analytical presuppositions

The assumptions and perspectives of rhetorical approaches are seldom spelled out. We will therefore attempt to categorize some of the major scholars who engage in rhetorical analysis of Galatians according to the following three classes: (A) those who consider the epistle a classical speech; (B) those who propose that rhetoric can decode rhetorical figures found anywhere; and (C) those who maintain that all literature is rhetorical.

Conformity to Graeco-Roman rhetoric

To many rhetorical analysts of Galatians, 'rhetoric' means 'Graeco-Roman speeches' and implies the production of a discourse based on the classical handbooks.[99] Thus Betz can discuss

---

[97] Vouga, 'Rhetorischen Gattung', 291–2.

[98] Longenecker, *Galatians*. Hansen, *Abraham in Galatians*. 'Diachronic' in Saussure's *Course in General Linguistics* (1915), refers to the development of a language through time. 'Synchronic' views language as a system employed in a given moment in time. Applied to rhetorical studies, diachronic has come to mean a focus on what we can know about the texts' history, even prehistory; synchronic relates to what a text means abstracted away from any historical situation – this is often reduced to 'what the text means now', though the real issue is what the present text means intrinsically, regardless of its provenance and history (see Kessler, 'Methodological Setting', 22–36).

[99] Though some would add, at least theoretically, as Mitchell does in practice, that wherever possible the actual speeches of the era ought to inform the analysis (see her *Rhetoric of Reconciliation*).

the structure and species of Galatians with the handbooks as his measure. Furthermore, as Margaret Mitchell says in reflection on Betz's work and in anticipation of her own analysis of 1 Corinthians, 'Rhetorical criticism, as here understood, is one of the panoply of tools which bear the name "historical-critical method"'.[100] Thus they understand rhetoric to be the means of persuasion used by the author, and identify Paul's chosen form of rhetoric as that described in the ancient handbooks and practised in official functions during the days of the Roman empire and, more importantly, during the first century CE. These analysts clearly intend by 'rhetoric' what we call 'level 4': the rhetoric of the handbooks.

A main tenet of this position is that Galatians is a speech. Betz writes that 'the form . . . and the order . . . completely conform to the classical rules of rhetoric for a judicial speech (*genus iudiciale*)'.[101] Joop Smit is even more explicit:[102] he is so persuaded by Betz's detailed use of the handbooks (including their discussion of the sociological settings for the three species) that he accepts that Galatians conforms to the pattern of 'classical speech'. Smit agrees that Galatians is a speech, but prefers the category 'deliberative'. Evidence that he thinks the epistle is a speech abounds. First, in his title he calls Galatians 'A Deliberative Speech'[103] and in his third main heading writes: 'Rhetorical Analysis of Paul's Speech'.[104] Second, Smit constantly refers to Galatians as a speech in his analysis.[105] Third, throughout his analysis, Smit draws comparisons based upon the assumption that the epistle conforms either to classical speeches or to the handbooks: 'In classical rhetoric an exhortative passage such as this is completely unknown as a separate part of a normal speech';[106] 'The speech contained in the letter to the Galatians follows an approved pattern';[107] 'Force of habit was not the only reason for Paul to conform to the familiar model. Everything shows that he thoroughly understood its intention';[108] 'Paul's speech further responds entirely to the norms the

---

[100] Mitchell, *Rhetoric of Reconciliation*, 6; following Betz, *Galatians*, xv.
[101] Betz, 'Literary Composition and Function', 377.
[102] Smit, 'Deliberative Speech', 1–26.
[103] Ibid., 1.
[104] Ibid., 9.
[105] See especially Smit, 'Deliberative Speech', 10; but cf. also 13.
[106] Ibid., 4.
[107] Ibid., 22.
[108] Ibid., 23.

handbooks of rhetoric set for the deliberative genre. The question whether rites of religion should be changed or not, is explicitly listed by the *Rhetorica ad Alexandrum* among the subjects proper for the deliberative genre and, in that context, amply discussed.[109] It is precisely with that question that Paul's speech deals';[110] 'This recommending and dissuading which determines and pervades Paul's entire speech is based, as is customary in the *genus deliberativum*, on two values: advantage (*utilitas*) and honour (*honestas*)'.[111] At this point Smit refers to Paul's 'professional skill as a rhetorician'.

Thus we find that methodologically, Betz and Smit are similar. The latter, acknowledging his debt to the former,[112] considers Galatians a classical speech, and likewise sets out to prove its conformity to the handbooks. He finds fault not with Betz's method but with its execution, insisting that Betz does not demonstrate that Galatians conforms to the handbooks' account of forensic speech. Based on his own reading of those same handbook citations he suggests: 'the speech Paul sent to the Galatians more probably belongs to the *genus deliberativum* than to the *genus iudiciale*'.[113]

François Vouga also argues that Galatians is deliberative, but he reaches this conclusion via a different methodology from that of Kennedy and Smit.[114] Rather than depend on the handbooks as the basis for his comparison, he draws on similarities between Galatians and Demosthenes' *On the Peace*, thus thinking himself to have avoided the pitfalls inherent to comparison of the text with the handbooks.[115] He too sees the text as an example of Graeco-Roman oratory.

James Hester writes: 'As Funk points out, Paul's style is as much oral as it is written.[116] It is as though Paul wrote speeches: not sermons, but speeches. This insight was brought to full expression by H. D. Betz in his commentary on Galatians . . . [Betz] saw the letter as having the form and function of a forensic speech and

---

[109] Ibid., 23, n. 5 citing *Rhetorica ad Alexandrum* 2.
[110] Ibid., 23.
[111] Ibid., 24.
[112] Cf. the use Smit makes of Betz, 'Literary Composition and Function', 353–79. See Smit, 'Deliberative Speech', 1–7 and especially 1, nn. 1–2.
[113] While considering species in chapter 5, we will assess Smit's position.
[114] Vouga, 'Rhetorischen Gattung', 291–2.
[115] Ibid., 291.
[116] Citing Funk, *Language*, 245.

attempted to demonstrate how the letter structure fits into the traditional pattern of that kind of speech'.[117] So Hester also treats Galatians as conforming to an actual speech.

In critiquing an 'analysis of Paul's speech which is built almost exclusively on modern rather than ancient literary theory . . .', Christopher Forbes writes: 'It is to be doubted whether this really brings us any closer to understanding Paul in his own environment'.[118] While it is not explicit, Forbes at least implies that (1) Paul wrote a speech; (2) its analysis should be based on ancient theory; and (3) Paul received a formal rhetorical education.

But every one of these reconstructions fails to resolve certain problems. Representative of these difficulties is the following statement, found in a monograph intended to be a guide to performing rhetorical criticism. Burton Mack writes that:

> Speech and speeches were signs of Hellenistic culture . . . To be engulfed in the culture of Hellenism meant to have ears trained for the rhetoric of speech. Early Christians were not unskilled, either as critics of their cultures of context or as proponents of their own emerging persuasions.[119]

Clearly this statement cannot be taken absolutely, for speech is not the sole possession of the Hellenes, nor, for that matter, is speechmaking. While speeches may characterize Hellenistic culture, they cannot be considered markers of the presence of such culture. Furthermore, were certain species of speeches more widely heard than others? No doubt members of all classes heard the epideictic speeches of the festivals and games, but can we assume that such a high percentage attended trials or listened to the deliberations of the forum? Readings which suggest that Paul has written a classical oration fail to answer such questions.

With Betz, Smit, *et al.*, Galatians is *treated as* a classical speech because they are convinced that it *is* a classical speech. There are, however, other options open to those who hold that Galatians conforms to classical rhetoric. As mentioned already, Mitchell's analysis of 1 Corinthians resembles Betz's analysis of Galatians in

---

[117] Hester, 'Use and Influence', 387. Page 389 refers to speeches; thereafter Hester writes of 'speech writing'.
[118] Forbes, 'Comparison', 1; with reference to Zmijewski, *Paulinischen 'Narren-rede'*.
[119] Mack, *Rhetoric and the New Testament*, 31.

that one of her goals is to demonstrate Paul's conformity to classical rhetoric. She depends on a host of parallels from actual speeches to make her case: she does not, however, in contrast to those cited above, imply that the epistle is a speech or even a 'rhetorical fiction'. Betz attempts to prove that Galatians is a judicial speech: Mitchell simply maintains that Paul's text conforms substantially to her sources without demanding that 1 Corinthians be identified as a speech. It is enough for her to demonstrate the similarities so that she can then argue that oratorical practices should inform one's reading of the text.

It seems that Mitchell moves in the direction of what the rhetorical critic Edwin Black would call a 'Neo-Aristotelian' analysis of Paul. In such an approach the parts of a discourse are viewed according to their function: thus the emphasis is not on the particular form to which one stamps Aristotelian names – for example *narratio* – but on the question of whether or not the role of a *narratio* is fulfilled.[120] This approach outside biblical studies works within certain rather strict confines: 'Because simplicity is a virtue in this instance, many rhetorical critics use the Aristotelian plan of organisation as the criterion for evaluating *disposition*. This would seem to be a defensible standard since the critic is not interested in form for its own sake, but rather for the contribution it makes in eliciting a desired response from the hearers'.[121]

Scholars in our first category need to do more towards articulating their methodology if they wish to demonstrate that their interest is not merely in form for its own sake. Is the goal of rhetorical analysis to demonstrate that the text in question displays a particular structure and thus belongs to a certain sociological milieu? Or is it to discuss how the text's own characteristics work to achieve certain ends?

Handbooks interpret figures found anywhere

A second group of scholars contend that classical rhetoric consists of a host of devices (i.e. stylistic phenomena such as irony or metonymy), situated within a text belonging to one of the three species of rhetoric. Thus everywhere these devices are found they can be analysed with help from the handbooks. It is maintained

---

[120] E. Black, *Rhetorical Criticism*, 71.
[121] See Thonssen and Baird, *Speech Criticism*, 398.

that because it contains rhetorical devices within a particular structural scheme and corresponds to one of the three species, Galatians can be understood with the help of rhetorical analysis at each point where Paul's devices overlap with descriptions found in the handbooks. Kennedy seems to fit into this group; he maintains not that Galatians is a speech but that, since it springs from the first-century world and contains many features discussed in the handbooks, it can be understood with the handbooks' assistance.

This position does not require the epistle's intentional conformity to classical oratory. Bruce Johanson writes that he will employ 'both modern and ancient rhetorical theory' to analyse 1 Thessalonians. He defends this by noting 'a basic or "deep" rhetoric universal to mankind' standing alongside 'the fact that Paul lived in a culture where rhetoric was very much alive and highly conceptualized'.[122]

Kennedy proceeds similarly: 'In understanding how [Jewish pre-Christian] rhetoric worked we have little choice but to employ the concepts and terms of the Greeks'.[123] But it is unclear why this is so. Is it because we do not know enough about second temple Judaism's distinctive rhetorical patterns? This does not seem reason enough to superimpose another rhetoric on their discourse. Is it because all discourse is best understood by the canons of classical rhetoric? This would obviate the need for any subsequent work on rhetoric, yet new works continue to appear, each time by their very existence implying that classical rhetoric did not solve all the problems addressed by the discipline. Have we no better English terms? What exactly does it mean to 'employ the concepts' of the Greeks? One discovers by surveying those rhetorical studies which depend on classical concepts and terms, that they have little predictive value for texts created in other spheres,[124] and they have not shown themselves to be distinct enough to differentiate between even fundamental classifications, as evidenced by the debate over

---

[122] Johanson, *To All the Brethren*, 34.

[123] Kennedy, *New Testament Interpretation*, 11.

[124] 'Predictive value' means (1) recognition of genre (and species) creates expectations which ought to be fulfilled ('knowing' that Galatians is judicial or deliberative never tells us what to expect next); (2) Bultmann (*History of the Synoptic Tradition*, 6) writes: 'the aim of form criticism is to determine the original form of a piece of narrative, a dominical saying or a parable. In the process we learn to distinguish secondary additions and forms, and these in turn lead to important results for the history of the tradition'. With Galatians Paul differs so much from the actual form of a speech that only Smit has suggested an accretion: Galatians 5–6; but for many this is the passage which determines the identity of Galatians.

whether Galatians is judicial or deliberative. Furthermore, and this
will impede our way at many turns, there is a disorienting oscilla-
tion from classical to modern understandings of the terms even
within individual studies – often unacknowledged and sometimes
surely unawares. This has inevitably created a great deal of confusion as the significance of the classical labels has been drastically
altered.

Duane Watson has done much to clarify this methodology. He
writes that 'rhetorical criticism of the New Testament using only
Greco-Roman rhetoric is an historical enterprise' which depends on
a highly developed 'discipline from the Greco-Roman era to
analyze the New Testament'. Like other historical-critical
approaches, this ancient discipline endeavours to uncover the
situation (of author and reader) which led to the text's production.
Thus the modern reader can 'hear and respond to the text in a
fashion akin to the original first century audience. Rhetorical
criticism in this tradition thus stands between ahistorical literary
criticism and historical-criticism'.[125] He is careful to emphasize,
furthermore, that intrinsic to his approach is the assumption that
the NT authors had learned the rules of rhetoric as encoded in
handbooks, speeches, letters and classroom exercises from either
formal education or participation in a culture 'permeated with
rhetorical practice'.[126]

Watson then declares that Kennedy's methodology as detailed in
New Testament Interpretation[127] was the first consciously to build
on such an understanding of rhetoric,[128] that his own study of Jude
and 2 Peter[129] was the first thoroughgoing application of Kennedy's
approach to a NT book, and that the rhetorical endeavour comple-
ments quite nicely 'historical-critical enterprises'.[130]

This position seems to merge historical and literary questions, for
it uses historical categories (i.e. Aristotelian, Ciceronian, etc.), yet,
as applied by Kennedy, does not demand any formal connection
between the writer and rhetoric. Kennedy, as we have seen, first
suggests that the pre-Christian Jewish rhetoric alluded to above is
informed by studying classical handbooks and that such an aware-

[125] Watson, 'Rhetorical Criticism of the New Testament', 110.
[126] Ibid.
[127] Kennedy, *New Testament Interpretation*, 33–8.
[128] Ibid.
[129] See Watson, *Invention, Arrangement and Style*.
[130] Watson, 'Rhetorical Criticism of the New Testament', 111.

ness of rhetoric was widespread throughout Palestine, and then applies his approach even to material that does not connect so cleanly with classical oratory. Thus his assertion in defence of the applicability of rhetorical concepts and terms does not mean that the texts are produced in conformity with the sources, but rather that the handbooks are somehow 'applicable'. The fact that such terms and concepts have been 'applied', at least by Kennedy, declares that they are 'applicable' – but what does this really mean? In fact, what category is not applicable? We once again suggest that any category can answer specific questions about a text (see above on Ch'an Buddhist rhetoric, p. 12) but this does not suggest the value or appropriateness of such an activity.

The solution to these difficulties lies in Kennedy's attempts to extract from the rhetorical handbooks 'universal' categories appropriate to all literature.[131] 'It is perfectly possible to utilize the categories of Aristotelian rhetoric to study speech in China, India, Africa, and elsewhere in the world, cultures much more different from the Greek than was that of Palestine in the time of the Roman Empire'.[132] Thus Galatians, according to Kennedy, must match one of the three species – since all persuasive discourse does – not because it is a classical speech.

With this last observation Kennedy and Watson go beyond the more common forms of what Edwin Black refers to as Neo-Aristotelian analysis. Such an approach finds in Aristotle, the consummate categorizer, a way of thinking about all manner of discourse. Usually ancient terms inform the vocabulary of the Neo-Aristotelian critic and often interest in genre dictates the shape of the study.

The difference between Neo-Aristotelianism and Kennedy, however, relates to the role which direct dependence plays in the latter's approach. To most Neo-Aristotelians, it is enough, for example, to depend on Aristotle as the provider of the notion of genre, commonplaces and the like. The Neo-Aristotelian reader need not demand that the discourse under examination conform to one of the genres Aristotle describes, but simply that a discussion of genre take place. Likewise a discourse need not depend on the particular commonplaces described in ancient rhetorical handbooks intended for the courtroom; the analysis may proceed with an

---

[131] See C. C. Black, 'Rhetorical Criticism and Biblical Interpretation', 257.
[132] Kennedy, *New Testament Interpretation*, 10.

awareness of the function of commonplaces which arises from the
categorizing activity of Aristotle. Thus we can provide examples of
presidential speeches which are labelled deliberative, for a speech
delivered to the nation's representatives to effect a desired course of
action is, by any conception of conformity to the classical texts,
deliberative. That does not mean that a didactic discourse must, or
even can, be identified with one of the three species detailed in
Aristotle's discussion of civic oratory. Melanchthon provides a
truer representation of the Neo-Aristotelian mindset when he
describes Romans not as forensic, deliberative or epideictic, but
rather as a member of the *genos didaktikon*.[133]

In terms of the schema we have been using, Neo-Aristotelianism
depends on Aristotle's discussion of level 4 rhetoric to derive a
methodology – a mindset – that will apply to whatever example of
level 4 rhetoric is being treated. Thus if a text branches off at level 3
to provide a modern American rhetoric, that too can be subdivided
into level 4 rhetorics such as civic oratory, classroom language,
preaching and rap music – each possessed of its own particular
combination of the available store of stylistic devices, commonplaces and generic sub-classifications. The analysis of these discourses would be Neo-Aristotelian because of the search for these
particulars, not because of any suggestion that a particular sermon
(or rap song) is like Aristotle's construction of forensic or deliberative speech.

C. J. Classen, in 'Paulus und die Antike Rhetorik', writes: 'The
question of whether the categories of ancient rhetoric can be
usefully applied in explaining the letters of Paul occasions a
fundamental observation: the tool-kit of Graeco-Roman rhetoric
can profitably be used in the analysis of any written or spoken
text'.[134]

Another practitioner of this approach to rhetoric is Douglas S.
Campbell.[135] Campbell points to Betz,[136] Kennedy[137] and Judge[138]
as three pioneers who offer differing approaches to the text. The
first two he calls 'architectonic', and the third 'sociological'; he then
turns to Malherbe's 'stylistic' analysis.[139] He admits that Mal-

---

[133] See chapter 6's discussion of Melanchthon.
[134] Classen, 'Antike Rhetorik', 2–3. Cf. also p. 6.
[135] D. Campbell, *Rhetoric of Righteousness in Romans*.
[136] Ibid., 73–4.
[137] Ibid., 74–5.
[138] Ibid., 75.
[139] Ibid., 76 and n. 4. Campbell refers to Malherbe's 'Beasts at Ephesus', 71–80;

herbe's is not a rhetorical analysis per se, but finds it a provocative way to exploit the text with the help of the rhetorical handbooks. Campbell will ultimately opt for an analysis which emphasizes ornamentation or *elocutio*[140] – one aspect of rhetoric – and for the most part will ignore the other four: invention, disposition, memory and delivery. He explicitly articulates his approach and its relationship to classical rhetoric:

> Investigation of the rhetorical possibilities available to Paul at the level of style will be primarily through the standard rhetorical manuals and treatises. It is not assumed that he read these directly, but if 'two or more' speak of a given principle or technique, and Paul also uses it, then it may probably be assumed that a rhetorical device is operative in the text that can be used to explain it.[141]

He then turns to the handbooks with the only further explanation being that 'the best source of rhetorical theory at this time is Quintilian'.[142] But this may not be enough explanation for some. All will agree that if there is discussion of a device in the handbooks, and then it appears in Paul, 'then it may probably be assumed that a rhetorical device is operative in the text'. All would probably further acknowledge that understanding that device will help explain the text. But this does not claim enough. What it proves is that some of the same devices appear in Paul and in the handbooks. But should we assume that Paul got those devices from the handbooks? That he got them from society at large? Campbell himself is unwilling to say that Paul read the handbooks, but if he got the device from Graeco-Roman society should we assume that he used it in the same way as a highly educated and introspective theoretician such as Quintilian suggests? It may have even come from the particular rhetoric of another mode of discourse, such as diatribe, popular philosophy or Judaism itself. All of these had a distinct mode of expression, though they would inevitably depend on some of the same devices. For example, irony is a wide-ranging device, as is the one which has so troubled students of Galatians (including the early Christian experts in rhetoric), allegory. Thus we

---

'"Gentle as a Nurse"', 203–17; 'Exhortation in First Thessalonians', 235–56 and *Paul and Popular Philosophers*.
[140] Campbell, *Rhetoric of Righteousness in Romans*, 77.
[141] Ibid., 77–78.
[142] Ibid., 78.

again see that Campbell is attempting to superimpose one type of level 4 rhetoric, that of the handbooks, on what is quite likely a distinct (though not discrete) level 4 rhetoric which has inevitable points of overlap.

Furthermore, the statement of Campbell that claims Quintilian as explicator contains an ambiguity that should not be overlooked. When Campbell writes 'the best source of rhetorical theory at this time is Quintilian', does he mean Paul's day, or ours? While it would seem the former, it is neither clear nor substantially defended. The question's significance derives from the failure of rhetorical critics to explain why the handbooks, or in this case Quintilian, help more than a modern study. Such a conclusion seems warranted only if Paul wrote according to their instructions. Our contention at this point is not with the question of Paul's intent, or with the notion that rhetoric informed much of ancient society's discourse, but rather with the idea that a text that is ancient and persuasive but not the sort discussed in the handbooks can be better understood by a guide to the construction of civil orations than by a modern theoretician's explication of argumentation.

C. Clifton Black II shares our question. He describes rhetorical criticism as the attempt to isolate and understand the 'persuasive purposes' of the writer.[143] But then he adds: 'One wonders if Graeco-Roman standards are as congenial to the Old Testament as to the New . . . we should beware of rhetorical analyses that mask characteristics of Jewish or Christian discourse peculiar to their distinctive cultures'.[144] Black's hesitance is apposite; he should not, however, assume that only the OT uses a rhetoric that depends on 'characteristics . . . peculiar to their distinctive cultures'. The NT has not yet been shown to be more closely allied to classical rhetoric than to the literary and discursive cultures that produced the LXX and other distinctively Jewish texts. This is yet another matter that must be resolved before a 'traditional' approach to rhetoric can satisfy.

All literature is rhetorical

The third perspective views rhetoric as a strategy of persuasion, and is often in line with the major writers on 'rhetoric' outside the field

---

[143] C. C. Black, 'Rhetorical Questions', 62.
[144] C. C. Black, 'Rhetorical Criticism', 257.

of biblical studies. These works attempt to apply the perspective of thinkers such as Chaim Perelman, Kenneth Burke or Wayne Booth, and are really the only one of the three approaches which may unhesitatingly be called synchronic. This approach attempts to discover and interpret the rhetoric, now understood as persuasive effect (even the term 'strategy' may imply too much since it imputes an extrinsic interest), which is at work in a discourse. The source for analysis is whatever is helpful, be that a classical handbook, a manual on the new rhetoric, or a psychological insight which accounts for a device's effectiveness.

This category can again be broken down into various ways of understanding 'rhetorical criticism',[145] though none is in line with analyses informed exclusively by classical works. Thus we sound a cautionary note concerning Pogoloff's assertion in his article 'Isocrates and Contemporary Hermeneutics'.[146] He cites Hans Gadamer as a defender of rhetoric – but he never clarifies whether Gadamer means classical oratory, a technique to analyse persuasive discourse, or something else altogether. Reading Gadamer reveals a concern not with the production of speeches or their analysis, but with the epistemological question of knowledge (philosophy) versus probability (rhetoric), addressing the age-old debate between philosophy and rhetoric. Thus while Gadamer defends rhetoric, he does not defend handbook oratory.[147]

Pogoloff continues: 'Further, since the rhetors claimed that virtually all speech is rhetorical . . .'[148] But who claims this, and where? Does Pogoloff mean 'rhetors' or 'rhetoricians'?[149] His assertion is simply not true of the handbooks, for they envisage only a particular sort of level 4 rhetoric. We have seen that even where the handbooks seem to broaden out, for example, when Quintilian states that rhetoric deals with everything,[150] the context links such statements to forensic settings.[151] Cicero, in *De Inventione*, defines rhetoric as 'a department of the science of politics'.[152]

---

[145] Ibid., 255–57.
[146] Pogoloff, 'Isocrates and Contemporary Hermeneutics', 338–9.
[147] See especially Gadamer, *Truth and Method*, 18–24.
[148] Pogoloff, 'Isocrates and Contemporary Hermeneutics', 342.
[149] The context refers to 'rhetoricians' except for two phrases: one that refers to the speech-setting, clearly envisaging the deliverer of the speech, and the statement we are considering. Unfortunately, no sources are provided in defence of the assertion.
[150] Quintilian, *Institutio* 2.21.4.
[151] Cf. especially ibid., 2.21.19.
[152] See ibid., 2.15.33 for this reference to Cicero, *De Inventione* 1.5.6.

To speak of rhetoric in universal terms is to exceed the bounds of a rather narrow ancient discipline which assumes primarily one method of argumentation (i.e. rational) for the sake of civic oratory.[153]

Vernon Robbins and John Patton avoid the second error of Pogoloff when they state that rhetorical analysis serves 'the purpose of explicating the nature and function of metaphor, form, and structure in the creation of meaning'. The texts in their multiplicity of forms are treated 'as structures of meaning'.[154] They clearly mean a kind of literary criticism when they refer repeatedly to 'rhetorical and literary analysis'. In fact, one could be led to believe that they speak of a single discipline, rhetorical-and-literary-analysis, were it not for the plural form 'disciplines' which modifies their concluding paragraph.[155] While it is not closely tied to Graeco-Roman rhetoric at all, this approach is the one championed by Muilenburg and most other OT critics, though there is considerable variety in the details.

David Rhoads and Donald Michie write in *Mark as Story* that structure and style contribute to producing 'certain effects on the reader'.[156] This relates to a literary criticism consistent with Neo-Aristotelian tendencies but does not depend on Graeco-Roman descriptions to unpack the contents. In fact it is from this perspective not far removed from various other works which are more in line with literary studies, such as Robert Alter's *The Art of Biblical Narrative* and *The Art of Biblical Poetry*; Adele Berlin's *Poetics of Biblical Narrative*; and L. Alonso-Schökel's *The Inspired Word: Scripture in the Light of Language and Literature*.[157]

These examples come from scholars who, like Muilenburg, wish to apprehend the force of features that appear in texts, rather than discuss conformity to the handbooks. In fact, their titles prompt the question: Why do critics wish to use Aristotle's *Rhetoric* for analysis but not his *Poetics*? Such a question would presumably

---

[153] I.e. classical rhetoric does not assume that only rational arguments are effective, but it does assume that the constructor of the argument can proceed logically. Even emotional appeals are discovered rationally. This does not hold for (e.g.) Perelman.

[154] Robbins and Patton, 'Rhetoric and Biblical Criticism', 327. A larger goal seems to be 'meaning beyond the banal, the unambiguous, and the conventional' (335).

[155] Ibid., 'Rhetoric and Biblical Criticism', 337.

[156] Rhoads and Michie, *Mark as Story*, 35.

[157] Alter, *Art of Biblical Narrative*; *Art of Biblical Poetry*; Berlin, *Poetics of Biblical Narrative*; Alonso-Schökel, *Inspired Word*.

pose a challenge to our first two classes of critics, but not to this third group. One might simply ask: Why use Aristotle to understand a text at all?

Thus the analyst in this view would consider the question of a text's relationship to classical rhetoric irrelevant, perhaps even an impertinence. The practitioner redefines many of the most significant terms and often relies on psychology, sociology or linguistics more than the views and proposals of the handbooks. On a continuum, this approach then is at the literary rather than the historical end.[158] But these works rightly claim the label rhetoric for this reason: they address 'questions about *rhetoric*, about "how" the story is told to create certain effects on the reader'.[159] Black finds that 'literary and rhetorical studies [converge] at an important point: both attempt to gauge the persuasive strategies and impact exerted upon their readers'.[160]

Regarding Paul, holders of this third perspective include K. A. Plank, whose monograph, *Paul and the Irony of Affliction*,[161] deals with persuasion in its various forms, and has been recognized as a synchronic analysis by Margaret Mitchell.[162] Folker Siegert's *Argumentation bei Paulus, gezeigt an Röm 9–11* is also synchronic.[163] Regarding Galatians, Paul Koptak provides a Burkean analysis of the 'narrative' part of the epistle: Galatians 1.13–2.14.[164]

Intrinsic and extrinsic approaches

Goals and analytical questions

Daniel Patte, in *What is Structural Exegesis?*, asserts that 'traditional historical exegesis' equals text criticism, philological study, literary criticism, history of traditions, form criticism and redaction criticism.[165] He then asserts that historical effort ought to give way

[158] Cf. Wuellner, who attempts to bring the poles together ('Where is Rhetorical Criticism Taking Us?', 454).

[159] Rhoads and Michie, *Mark as Story*, 35. Others, such as Dietz Moss, see rhetoric as anything dealing with probability and persuasion: cf. 'Galileo's *Letter to Christiana*', 547–76.

[160] Black, 'Rhetorical Criticism', 256.

[161] Plank, *Paul and Affliction*.

[162] Mitchell, *Rhetoric of Reconciliation*, 7, n. 21.

[163] Siegert, *Argumentation bei Paulus*. Pages 5–15 deal with argumentation – he rejects overemphasis on arrangement (p. 16).

[164] Koptak, 'Rhetorical Identification', 97–113.

[165] Patte, in *What is Structural Exegesis?*, 9.

to a 'modern hermeneutic which would reveal the meaning of the biblical text for modern man' – but in this it has failed.[166] This accusation of failure might strike some as a bit harsh. Is the *raison d'être* of reading always 'meaning' as understood by Patte? Judge, Betz and others might find validity in a host of additional questions, including what the structure of the text says about the community that produced it. In light of the variety of methods going by the name 'rhetorical criticism', we must specify the questions being asked, and thus allow the readers to decide what sort of answers they wish to pursue.

At one end of the methodological spectrum lies the work of Betz, whose exegesis is based on the assumption that Paul is using a specific rhetorical model, namely Graeco-Roman rhetoric. He is followed by Margaret Mitchell, who implies that a goal of rhetoric in her approach, in contradistinction to that of Perelman, is not 'expanding the realm of argumentation [but] classifying the particular texts according to genre or arrangement'.[167] Expressing her motivations quite clearly, she sees rhetorical criticism as practised by herself and her mentor as 'one of the panoply of tools which bear the name "historical-critical method"',[168] because the 'resources drawn upon in reconstructing this rhetorical tradition are the ancient Greco-Roman handbooks, speeches and letters themselves.'[169] Thus Mitchell depends on the rhetoric which she believes Paul himself employed in crafting 1 Corinthians. She possesses sufficient clarity of perspective to add:

> Appeals to modern philosophical examinations of the rhetorical force of all texts should not be put at the service of historical arguments. This is not to say that all such investigations are invalid in their own right, but they should not be confused or intertwined with historical arguments about Paul's rhetoric in the light of the Greco-Roman rhetorical tradition, the sources for which are ancient texts. The present study is an historical rhetorical analysis of 1 Corinthians in the light of the literary/rhetorical conventions operative in the first century.[170]

---

[166] Ibid., 10.

[167] Mitchell, *Rhetoric of Reconciliation*, 7, n. 19.

[168] Ibid., 6. Cf. our discussion of Mitchell on pp. 57, 60.

[169] Ibid.

[170] Ibid., 7; she is reacting to such works as Wuellner, 'Where is Rhetorical Criticism Taking Us?', 448–63; 'Greek Rhetoric and Pauline Argumentation',

So Mitchell represents what is in reality rather rare: she wishes to analyse the text in the light of Graeco-Roman rhetoric because she believes that it was formed in that light. This raises the question of whether Paul's letters exhibit the particular characteristics of that rhetorical tradition.[171]

We do not wish to suggest, as may be inferred from both our previous and subsequent statements, that historical concerns are strictly synonymous with extrinsic, and literary with intrinsic. Concerning extrinsic rhetorical studies of Galatians, however, the primary importation is a notion of *literary* form which implies particular *historical* assertions. That is, imposed on the text from outside is the suggestion that Paul wrote according to oratorical conventions, and that those conventions have much to say about the author (e.g. his education, literary sophistication, social standard, and even regard for the truth), the setting of the epistle, the opponents and the readership – as well as a host of other matters. All of these are external to the world embodied by the text itself and thus are properly labelled extrinsic. It just so happens that with respect to Galatians, the extrinsic issues are dominated by historical questions.

While it may appear inevitable that history dominates the study of ancient texts, it is not in fact necessary. Another option relates to the entire range of theological questions which so dominated biblical studies before the relatively recent rise of historical exegesis. For a recent study of the theological implications of Paul's relationship to rhetoric see Duane Litfin's *St Paul's Theology of Proclamation*.[172]

At the other end of the methodological spectrum is the sort of work which we have found in association with OT studies. When it comes to stating the methodological presuppositions at work in the

---

177–88; Jewett, *Thessalonian Correspondence*; Siegert, *Argumentation bei Paulus*. All of these analyse human communication with modern techniques, and would argue that their approach is universal to the extent that persuasion is universal; but with Jewett especially we see a merging (what Mitchell calls a confusion (see *Rhetoric of Reconciliation*, 7, n. 22)) of classical rhetoric and modern analysis.

[171] Mitchell seems to assume that all first-century rhetoric is discussed in her sources: the handbooks and speeches. 1 Corinthians and Galatians, even at just a glance, look little like a speech. In fact it took two thousand years for someone to suggest that Galatians is one. Based on a host of criteria (see the chapters which follow, where we discuss structure (chapter 4), species (5), and language (6–7) to show the distance between Paul and, say, Cicero), we conclude that Galatians is not a classical oration.

[172] Litfin, *Theology of Proclamation*.

latter, we find a consistency in the field and, seemingly, an awareness of engagement in a non-historical enterprise.[173] Clines and
Exum, as we have seen, relate rhetorical criticism to 'the final form
of the text', that is, to 'the way the language of the texts is deployed
to convey meaning'. The 'primary focus is upon the texts and their
own internal articulation rather than upon their historical
setting'.[174]

In practice, this approach adopts presuppositions shared by a
number of disciplines. Joy Fleming, in a rhetorical reading of
Genesis 2–3, insists that while literary criticism will at times focus
on the details, its main concern is generally with the whole of a
work. Rhetorical criticism, a subset of literary, focuses on the
details – texture, irony, word play, etc. – which empower a text.[175]
She claims to have been initially drawn to rhetorical analysis
because it sees the text itself as the primary controller of interpretation.[176] Not only do her desires match those of Muilenburg and his
followers, but she also shares their identification of rhetoric as a
form of literary criticism.[177]

Because of the 'hypothetical nature' of results won by historical
studies, and an ever more refined appreciation of Hebrew literature,
new methods were sought which could at once capitalize on the
fresh insights while transcending the limits of the historical approach.[178] The term 'hypothetical' comes from J. P. Fokkelman[179]
who maintains that reconstructions of a text's prehistory provide a
fragile foundation able only to support hypothetical conclusions.
He proposes that a useful approach is a synchronic reading, but not
before stating that 'Diachronic study needs no justification; the
origin and tradition of texts are in themselves worthwhile and form

[173] At least some of this awareness can be traced back to the ideas articulated by
Wellek and Warren, *Theory of Literature*. See p. 139 for the observation that 'literary
history has been so preoccupied with the setting of a work of literature that its
attempts at an analysis of the works themselves have been slight in comparison with
the enormous efforts expended on the study of environment'.

[174] Clines and Exum, 'New Literary Criticism', 16.

[175] Fleming, *Genesis 2–3*, 40; Porter notes the contrast between this and the sort
of studies that have dominated study of Galatians when he writes: 'Authors nuance
their treatments of these categories, but then usually concentrate upon determining
the species of discourse and suggesting a suitable outline of its organization, while
neglecting style almost entirely (or at least placing it a distant third in importance)'.
Cf. 'Rhetorical Categories', 103–4.

[176] Fleming, *Genesis 2–3*, 25; italics hers.

[177] See also Trible, *God and Rhetoric of Sexuality*, 8.

[178] Fleming, *Genesis 2–3*, 29–30.

[179] Fokkelman, *Narrative Art in Genesis*, 2.

an independent object of research'.[180] The primary caveat is that, as we have seen already, the prehistory of a text is not to be conflated or confused with the text itself.[181] This latter rule, as articulated both within and without the sphere of biblical studies, is too often overlooked in studies of Galatians.

A third approach to rhetoric attempts to merge historical and literary matters while remaining distinct from the two ways of reading already discussed. For example, Elizabeth Castelli claims that her focus is on the 'textual effect rather than on any (fictional) inherent meaning in the text, or in other words, on how the text operates rather than what it means'. She is thus able to speak in terms not of a derived rhetoric, be it Graeco-Roman or otherwise, but instead of a 'rhetoric of social experience' – a testing of the strategic function of the text as informed above all by that text.[182]

But with such an approach we move away from both of the first two models. Although no historical approach to rhetoric controls the exegesis, neither does a purely literary-structural methodology. What we find is a middle position which merges the force inherent to the structure of the text, complete with its effect-producing devices, with a realization that the reader can be brought into the foreground and analysed alongside the text. Thus Castelli's work imports a philosophical model to help unravel the text, which brings us back to the likes of Perelman, who, with his 'New Rhetoric', provides the means to investigate the forces working in all acts of communication.[183] Perelman, while bringing us into the larger realm of epistemology as he discusses argumentation, maintains that rational attempts at persuasion are insufficient, that the human animal also responds to non-rational forces; and so his work is an attempt to describe those forces which cause us to change positions or accept arguments. This attempt to get into one's inner workings has obvious appeal to those who wish to isolate the power of Paul's persuasive discourse – and so serves Castelli well.

Lauri Thurén maintains that reliance on strictly classical

---

[180] Ibid.

[181] This approach Fokkelman labels 'genetic explanation' (ibid., 3).

[182] Castelli, *Imitating Paul*, 18. Cf. also 'Interpretations of Power in 1 Corinthians', 197–222.

[183] Though Castelli's model, at least in 'Interpretations of Power in 1 Corinthians' (see especially 201–4) is not Perelman but Foucault and his discussion of power structures.

categories opposes 'an effective use of rhetorical criticism',[184] and thus modern theory must supplement Graeco-Roman sources.[185] The same position is defended by C. Joachim Classen who, in response to Mitchell's assertion that 'rhetorical criticism as employed here is an historical undertaking', simply asks: 'But why? Why should one restrict oneself in this way and not use modern rhetorical theory as well; no literary critic would confine himself to the categories of ancient literary criticism'.[186] C. Clifton Black also mixes historical and traditional literary concerns:

> Of what benefit, then, is rhetorical criticism? A most attractive feature of the method is its position at the cusp of biblical scholarship's older, historical concerns and its newer, literary interests. The New Testament was nurtured in the womb of Roman Hellenism, and rhetoric was integral to that culture's lifeblood. For that reason, rhetorical studies stand alongside source and form criticism, firmly within historical scholarship.[187] Unlike those older methods, however, rhetorical criticism cares little to dismantle texts and to track their history of composition. Akin to current literary approaches, rhetorical criticism explores the complex relationships that exist between the form and content of unified texts, between the intentions of those who generated such texts and the perceptions of those who received them. [188]

This refusal to let go of historical matters is not necessarily a bad thing, for scholarship, with its evolving methods, has left even the most basic question unanswered: exactly what sort of text is a Pauline epistle? It is not enough to respond with a catalogue of epistolary or rhetorical conventions, for the question is bigger than that. To cast it differently, though in so doing one loses much of the question's force, is Galatians 'literature'? Muilenburg, Fokkel-

---

[184] Thurén, *Strategy of 1 Peter*, 47.

[185] Ibid., 41–78.

[186] See Mitchell, *Rhetoric of Reconciliation*, 6; and Classen, 'St Paul's Epistles', 291, n. 78.

[187] Though cf. the insistence of Hughes ('Review of Watson', 273) that 'like other rhetorical critics, Watson accepts James Muilenburg's critique of form criticism'. We are left to ask if Hughes means by 'other rhetorical critics' all who comprise the class or simply 'some other ones'. It would seem to be true of the majority, though if form criticism is defined to include Betz's work, the number naturally decreases.

[188] Black, 'Rhetorical Questions', 69.

man and others have had great success with their methods in the OT, for a literary approach works with presuppositions which are friendly to certain types of texts. Fokkelman, like others, speaks of the world created by the words of the text, and finds in them an end rather than a mere means to something else.[189] Muilenburg preferred to work with poetic texts, and more specifically, prophetic discourse. At least partly because of the dissociation from any historical provenance inherent to a work like, for example, Genesis, one must read it apart from questions which to many analysts cannot be answered anyway. But what of Galatians? Does the text create a world of its own which will satisfy the reader's desire to apprehend whatever the text is about?

Significantly, Galatians shuts out questions of its prehistory, for the 'history of composition' collapses into the rhetorical situation. But certain inquiries nevertheless remain form-critical, attempting to describe the shape of Galatians not for its own sake but in order to grasp the implications of that shape. If Galatians is like a first-century speech delivered in court then certain things can be gathered concerning its author – though they do not necessarily concern the meaning of the text. It seems that an outside force, at least partly determinative, is at work with respect to Galatians, so that the text ought to be acknowledged as the embodiment of an argumentative agenda aimed at a concrete situation. To bracket off all points of contact with the world extrinsic to the text is certainly possible, but would bar the reader from the questions many of Paul's readers find most interesting. Until this question of the applicability of purely intrinsic techniques to Galatians is answered, external matters will no doubt continue to be addressed.

This questioning does not suggest that we may overlook difficulties with intentionality or ignore the implied author and readers. Such matters remain crucial to any reading, whether they are acknowledged or not; what we are suggesting is that beyond these concerns one might gain much from certain texts by acknowledging that they exist as a product of a concrete rhetorical situation and as such are a conduit into the social world of the text itself. While this raises a host of questions (sparking Fokkelman's use of the term hypothetical), most problems relate to matters of certainty rather

---

[189] Cf. Anderson, 'Analysis to Synthesis', 23–39; see also the work of Hans Frei, who, when dealing with narrative, argues that the story is the meaning – not that it creates a window back into the history behind the story as the locus of meaning (*Eclipse of Biblical Narrative*).

than to constructs of reality. Thus at the outset we are pushing the debate into areas of social history – for, as we will see, some 'rhetorical critics' do not realize the historical implications of their work, considering themselves engaged in a postmodern reading of the text.

Indeed if one chooses to pursue historical questions, Galatians can be thought to relate to two contexts. First, the immediate 'rhetorical situation' of the letter, the exigency which led Paul to write, may be considered. It is difficult, in fact, to imagine how Galatians can be understood apart from the conflict which it addresses.[190] For better or for worse, we possess only the text itself as a source of data concerning this conflict, and so this investigation is text-centred.

Second, the more general social world inhabited by Paul and the Galatians is open to investigation, though it might not contribute much to understanding the text. In fact, Galatians might reveal more about Paul's social world than that social world reveals about Galatians – a prospect which some will find stimulating. This second approach naturally welcomes data from sources outside the text as it attempts to recreate Paul's microcosm.

What is troublesome is the move that some 'rhetorical critics' make (without acknowledgement) from an ahistorical 'rhetorical' reading of Galatians to historical assertions about Paul's education and social standing. Some argue, for instance, that the handbooks describe universal rhetoric, but then insist that the presence of handbook rhetoric in Paul points to an advanced education. But if the handbooks describe 'universal rhetoric', then the existence of handbook rhetoric in Galatians can prove neither Paul's dependence on them nor anything about his education. This argument is, in fact, both illogical and founded on a false premise, for the handbooks do not describe a universal rhetoric.

Another angle from which to approach rhetoric is to define the relationship between intrinsic and extrinsic concerns: foundational to many rhetorical studies is the distinction between diachronic and synchronic analysis. Ahistorical approaches often emerge from the inability of historical approaches to answer questions of meaning and effect; thus 'synchronic' results have flourished in an environment characterized by scepticism concerning the historical-critical

---

[190] Unlike, say, one of the gospels or Acts, which are less clearly directed at a particular problem. The 'Romans debate' also highlights this point.

method. Due to such perceived shortcomings, many have opted for
a text-immanent approach which can supplement or replace previous strategies. We borrow our definition from W. Ross Winterowd as mediated by Martin Kessler.[191]

Winterowd proposes ten 'steps' by which the reader encounters
the text. The points of interest are: (1) the whole unit; (2) authorship; (3) setting; (4) medium (Gattung); (5) stance (stance relates to
the particulars of a text as opposed to that over which the author
possesses less control); (6) form; (7) style; (8) metastyle; (9) ratio;
(10) meaning (especially the consubstantiality (standing together)
of speaker and hearer).[192] Kessler arranges this list to fall under the
headings 'Diachronic' and 'Synchronic', so that they may be
presented as follows:

Diachronic	*Synchronic*
	1. whole unit
2. authorship	
3. setting	
	4. medium
	5. stance
	6. form/structure
	7. style
	8. metastyle
	9. ratio
	10. meaning

Rhetorical criticism is then described as 'dealing with the junc-
ture of the diachronic and synchronic methods'.[193] 'Rhetorical
criticism might include not only the identification and description
of classical rhetorical figures (tropes and schemes), but also the
widened perspective of the new rhetoric. Obviously this calls for an
increasingly interdisciplinary approach and more dialogue with
literary critics in English and other modern literatures.'[194] Kessler
is arguing that really to read a text, the historical matters listed in
the left column are not enough. The items on the right are the
vehicle, and what we possess is that vehicle. Therefore, these items

[191] Kessler, 'Methodological Setting'. He depends heavily on Winterowd,
Rhetoric: A Synthesis.
[192] See Winterowd, ibid., 94. He defines the 'rhetorical motive', like Burke, as
identification. Again the move is away from an Aristotelian (purely rational) view of
persuasion.
[193] Kessler, 'Methodological Setting', 31.
[194] Ibid.

ought to be the goal of study and source of information. They will at times reveal an exigence, and then (and this is what is distinctive about rhetorical studies) broach the question of how the text accomplishes the author's purpose. Understanding rhetorical approaches as the attempt to answer this question highlights the unity of the various studies called rhetorical.

A caution is in order. Misusing a synchronic element can push discussion under the heading 'Diachronic'. That is, if one argues that Galatians is strewn with stylistic features discussed by Cicero or Quintilian and then leaps from that presence to Pauline reliance on forms learned from books or in school, the discussion has reverted to 'authorship' (item 2 above), is no longer strictly stylistic (item 7 above), and thus slips from synchronic to diachronic. It is when the discussion of style contributes immediately to one's understanding of the text that the work is synchronic.[195] And 'rhetorical analysis', it must be remembered, is not concerned with the left or right column but with the space in between, the point at which they merge. Thus in this scheme the identification of 'stance' answers a synchronic question; the relationship of 'stance' to 'setting' a rhetorical one.

This brief treatment of Kessler's programme shows the direction that many rhetorical studies have taken. Muilenburg, Wilder and others operate with such distinctions in mind and emphasize synchronic matters. They, like practitioners of other types of 'literary approaches', incorporate extrinsic data where appropriate, but favour intrinsic matters, sharply contrasting with readers of Galatians who attempt to assess Paul's level 4 rhetoric by (1) importing an outside form of rhetoric, or (2) delving into more appropriate forms of first-century Graeco-Roman rhetoric. Thus the sort of study engendered by Betz is not representative of rhetorical studies outside the circle attached to NT epistles.

A study which betrays a great deal of methodological awareness, and an intentional mingling of both sides of the coin, is the investigation of Hosea by Walter Vogels called 'Diachronic and Synchronic Studies of Hosea 1–3'.[196] This work provides a clear precedent in OT studies for successfully merging synchronic and diachronic matters into one study. But it ought to be noted that Vogel never claims to apply both diachronic and synchronic

---

[195] This multiform use of reading is discussed with great clarity in Fokkelman, *Genesis*, 4.

[196] Vogels, 'Diachronic and Synchronic', 94–8. Cf. Fleming, *Genesis 2–3*, 27.

rhetoric to the text. That is reserved for Richard Longenecker in his Galatians commentary. Rather than investigating diachronic questions such as authorship and setting (as Kessler sets out above), Longenecker labels the attempt to analyse Galatians as a piece of handbook rhetoric 'diachronic', and then applies universal categories to Galatians for his 'synchronic' approach. He turns to the latter because, it would seem, he despairs of finding sufficient enlightenment by comparing Galatians with Graeco-Roman speech while acknowledging that the epistle clearly reveals persuasive strategy.

Of importance for us is the fact that Longenecker has been criticized for designating as 'synchronic investigation' his attempt to show the conformity of Galatians to Aristotelian categories. Having concluded that the handbooks describe universally valid persuasive techniques, he distils from them a rhetoric which he also considers universally valid and then tries to show how that mode of discourse helps explain Galatians. Hence Longenecker writes under the heading 'Synchronic Rhetorical Analysis' that: 'Other ancient logical categories of persuasion can be discerned in Paul's Galatian letter as well'.[197] But referring to ancient logical categories is not symptomatic of a synchronic approach. In fact, if ancient categories of logic and rhetoric are introduced, the interpretation may focus on the text's meaning at a single point in time (i.e. its first-century setting), but this can only be synchronic if ancient logic and rhetoric are universal – but we have already seen rhetoric's exclusivity. Consistently to introduce Aristotelian categories rather than allowing the text to work on its own terms thus steps outside the received understanding of 'synchronic', the *communis sensus* of which is something like 'the way a text is read by my reading community', or at 'my point in time' – whatever that community and time may be. It does not entertain historical questions – but centres on the text itself.[198]

> The first consequence [of replacing diachronic concerns
> with synchronic] was to move the focus of interpretation
> from the author to the text. Synchronic exegesis evinces 'a
> primary exegetical respect for the final literary work itself

---

[197] Longenecker, *Galatians*, cxviii.
[198] Cf. Fokkelman, *Genesis*, 1–8. Note also that Longenecker draws his understanding of synchronic and diachronic rhetoric from Kessler (*Galatians*, cix).

and a productive concentration upon interpreting that work on its own terms' (R. M. Frye).[199]

Perhaps the shift of focus in Longenecker's work is inevitable because his tools to analyse all discourse only really describe culturally and temporally specific forms of communication.

Readings of Galatians

With the historical/literary continuum in mind we turn to Galatians itself, attempting to identify whether an approach leans toward the extrinsic or the intrinsic – or, if possible, where a text sits on the scale. We have seen that Betz considers Galatians a forensic speech, crafted in such a way that it conforms to the handbooks. His goal is clear: to prove that the epistle belongs to a particular literary world. By showing Galatians' structural and thematic conformity to a speech, he argues that Paul set out to create such a work. While Betz depends on this assessment to explicate the text, and this naturally reinforces his preliminary assessment, he has opened the door for others who wish to consider the fuller implications of Paul's employing such a rhetorical form.[200] Clearly the emphasis remains on extrinsic matters.

George Kennedy does not call Galatians a speech[201] but simply a text from a cultural milieu that overlaps with level 4 rhetoric.[202] It, like all texts, is subject to classical rhetorical analysis. Thus his work must be considered diachronic as much because it reads Galatians historically as because it argues that Galatians belongs to a certain ancient class of text. Kennedy is suggesting that since Aristotle described how all texts are persuasive (a claim which we have questioned) we should read any text with which we are concerned as Aristotle would. This is in fact only one step removed

---

[199] J. I. H. McDonald, 'Synchronic Exegesis', 657–8.

[200] Betz does draw a few conclusions: 'The fact that Paul wrote his well-composed and, both rhetorically and theologically, sophisticated "apology" forces us to assume that he founded the Galatians churches not among the poor and the uneducated but among the Hellenized and Romanized city population' (*Galatians*, 24: see introduction). Jewett similarly in his analysis claims: 'The rhetorical evidence concerning both letters may thus provide a basis for reconstructing the historical situation evoking [them] . . . as well as the precise relation between the letters themselves': cf. *Thessalonian Correspondence*, 87. Also Black, 'Rhetorical Questions', 69.

[201] *Pace* Porter, 'Theoretical Justification', 101–2.

[202] It should also be observed that Mitchell never seems to consider 1 Corinthians a speech. She simply maintains that it is a text which conforms to the suggestions of the handbooks and to texts that arise from that milieu.

from the third, mediating position described above. But if Aristotle
or Cicero provide a window into how to understand all rhetorical
discourse, then they have achieved the goal at which Perelman
aims. It remains for us only to choose which sort of rhetoric to use
for analysis: will it be 'classical Rhetoric' which reads a text as the
ancients advise, or the 'New Rhetoric' which follows Perelman?
The latter has to its advantage any psychological, sociological and
philosophical advances that have been achieved in the past two
millennia, while the first seems to fall into one of the main pitfalls
to which the historical-critical method is vulnerable – answers
relate to literary history, not meaning, and many must be regarded
as 'hypothetical'.

While it may be of interest to someone of classical curiosity to
learn how Aristotle would read Paul, this can say nothing about
meaning located in the text, nor can it answer the sociological
questions referred to above. If Kennedy were to respond that since
Paul wrote according to such canons they can help in analysing his
output, we would grant a logical consistency. He does not,
however, maintain such a line, but argues on the one hand that
Paul's cultural world was one of classical rhetoric (level 4), and on
the other, that rhetoric suggests universal modes of discourse and
so the handbooks can be applied to everything (level 2).[203] The
scheme Kennedy uses to categorize these two levels is 'primary
rhetoric' and 'secondary rhetoric', the former being the actual
instances of speeches produced for the court and the assembly, the
latter being the *influence* of rhetorical education which has trickled
down to various other forms of literature, and which may in fact
manifest itself in all kinds of Graeco-Roman communication (and
perhaps, Kennedy might add, even in our own discourse as it bears
the imprint of the ancients). He goes so far as to say that for the
above reasons, 'approaching the New Testament through Classical
rhetoric is thus historically justified' as well as 'philosophically
justifiable'.[204] But just there the blending of levels comes to the
forefront. Kennedy implies throughout that level 4 rhetoric is
universal and can be applied to anything, an implication which we
question.

Stanley Porter takes Kennedy to task at this point, rather baldly

---

[203] Kennedy, *New Testament Interpretation*, 10–11.
[204] Ibid., 10.

remarking: 'This is the extent of Kennedy's "argument": the simple assertion that the categories of classical oratory are applicable to all discourse, with no reference to any ancient sources or precedents for their analytical use'.[205] Porter then suggests that handbook rhetoric, as a subset of universal rhetoric, inevitably looks in places like universal rhetoric (at least, we would add, when the latter makes use of words).[206] But such a similarity can be misleading, and it can hold no predictive value for Galatians unless one first proves that the epistle embodies handbook, and not merely universal, rhetoric.[207] Thus we will examine Galatians from several vantage points to determine if it manifests level 4 rhetoric. When, however, we move to what Kennedy terms secondary rhetoric, we should note that we are outside the bounds of classical oratory.

Alongside Porter's critique of Kennedy we may place his positive reconstruction. He emphasizes style as a device used in texts to help maintain unity and order,[208] a virtue of his approach being that it recognizes the use of universal rhetorics within the particular rhetoric of the Graeco-Roman orators. Thus finding 'stylistic features (especially figures of speech)' is valid because they are, to a greater or lesser degree, 'common to many forms of literature, and were readily drawn upon in analysis'.[209] At the same time, Porter objects to the ferreting out and designating of species and categories of arrangement (defined as the application of 'formal terms describing categories specifically originating with oratory'),[210] because it implies that such activities (1) have precedent in the ancient world; (2) would have been intelligible to the ancients; and (3) somehow conform to the aims of classical rhetoricians.[211] Of

---

[205] Porter, 'Theoretical Justification', 106.

[206] Ibid., 108.

[207] Ibid., 106, 108.

[208] Porter, 'Argument of Romans 5'; Similarly Duke (*Irony*) sees the structure of John maintained by the device of irony. His work is less directly classical, depending on the rhetoric of, for instance, Cleanth Brooks ('Irony as a Principle of Structure', 7). Irony in Paul is found by, for example, Spencer, 'Wise Fool', 349–60.

[209] Porter, 'Theoretical Justification', 108–9. Porter at this point can cite Bultmann, *Stil*. Cf. also Gill, 'Jesus, Irony and New Quest'.

[210] Porter, 'Theoretical Justification', 109.

[211] Ibid., 109–10. Cf. also Carson ('Understanding Misunderstanding', 59–60), who objects to the notion of 'literary device' whether classically based or not, because such a labelling process tends to undermine the theological and historical aspects of the text. The studies discussed below aim to redress the imbalance while emphasizing stylistic devices.

particular value is Porter's distinction between 'universal'[212] and 'formal' rhetoric;[213] the latter must be seen as a subset of the former rather than as an embodiment or replacement of it.[214]

Porter thus latches on to stylistic studies, namely the isolation and evaluation of figures that actually appear in the text – whether or not the text is the product of a rhetor (or a rhetorical school).[215] That is, Paul's universal rhetoric overlaps with the Graeco-Roman handbooks enough for them sometimes to help discuss a Pauline device (as in Porter's own discussion of rhetorical questions in Romans 5).[216] He does not treat style as a matter of ornamentation but instead as a type of supra-sentence grammatical analysis.[217] It functions sometimes within the phrase, sometimes without,[218] not necessarily regarding the boundaries established by the sentence (i.e. some figures, for example chiasm and allegory, may go beyond the single sentence to include paragraphs or even whole works).[219] Bernard Lategan labels this the 'syntactico-rhetorical' level,[220] wherein he explores, among other things, the pronoun as a device used to 'demarcate textual space and to enable the author to manoeuvre within the space thus created'.[221]

Lategan is part of a South African scholarly community which has invested heavily in literary readings of the NT and is led by, among others, J. Eugene Botha. Botha remarks on the shortage of stylistic studies in his 1991 article, 'Style in the New Testament: The Need for Serious Reconsideration',[222] but can cite as excep-

---

[212] Though Porter exhibits a certain reluctance to speak of 'universals'.

[213] What we have been calling level 4 rhetoric.

[214] Porter, 'Theoretical Justification', 109; also 115–16.

[215] 'Stylistic', again, is not here used in a technical sense. I mean only the study of devices which contribute to the author's style and perform some task. This ranges from a rhetorical question to the use of irony.

[216] Porter, 'Argument of Romans 5'. Cf. Campbell, *Rhetoric of Righteousness*.

[217] Porter, 'Theoretical Justification', 119–22. Cf. also De Man ('Semiology and Rhetoric', 28): 'The existence of grammatical structures, within and beyond the unit of the sentence, in literary texts is undeniable, and their description and classification are indispensable. The question remains if and how figures of rhetoric can be included in such a taxonomy'. Burke, *Rhetoric of Motives*, 57.

[218] Porter, 'Theoretical Justification', 119–22 (discussing Campbell's *Rhetoric of Righteousness*); cf. Botha, 'Style in the New Testament', 81–2.

[219] Botha, 'Style in the New Testament', 81–82. Lund, *Chiasmus in the New Testament*.

[220] Lategan, 'Levels of Reader Instruction', 173–5.

[221] Ibid., 173.

[222] Botha, 'Style in the New Testament', 71. He apparently rejects works like Watson, *Invention, Arrangement and Style*.

tions the works of J. V. W. Cronjé,[223] A. H. Snyman[224] and himself.[225]

Style-centred works, often implicitly but with Porter explicitly, avoid the criticisms levelled against 'classical' analysis of the NT, for they avoid those aspects of Graeco-Roman rhetoric not applicable to our texts. Thus these exegetes do not discuss the *taxis* or species of NT texts (aspects of 'formal rhetoric') but do discuss style (less localized and thus more easily transferred to a 'universal' rhetoric). A prime example may be found in the work of Campbell, who offers a 'rhetorical study dominated by style'[226] – even where he finds dependence not on classical rhetoric but on Hebrew poetry.[227] He thus enjoys the advantage of requiring no detailed educational or sociological discussion, for he defines style primarily as the utilization of devices such as antithesis and paronomasia,[228] epanophora, parenthesis[229] and isocolic reduplication.[230]

Perhaps of even greater import is the success of these studies in shattering the bounds of 'merely' classical taxonomies and designations[231] and in adding modern stylistic techniques to analysis of Galatians.[232] J. V. W. Cronjé especially, in 'Defamiliarization in

[223] Cronjé, 'Defamiliarization'.

[224] Snyman, 'Style and Meaning in Romans 8:31–39'; 'On Studying the Figures'; 'Style and Romans'; Snyman and Cronjé, 'Toward a New Classification of the Figures'.

[225] Botha, 'Jesus and the Samaritan Woman'. In fact, stylistic studies not only cluster geographically but also around specific figures or problematic passages. For the former, see Porter, 'Argument of Romans 5'; Watson, '1 Corinthians 10:23–11:1'; Lategan, 'Levels of Reader Instruction'; Wuellner, 'Paul as Pastor'. For the latter see Porter, 'Argument of Romans 5'; P. M. McDonald, 'Romans 5.1–11 as a Rhetorical Bridge'; Crosby, 'Paul's Persuasive Language'; Jewett, 'Rhetorical Function'; cf. also Campbell, *Rhetoric of Righteousness*, especially chapter 2 (70–101).

[226] Campbell, *Rhetoric of Righteousness*, 77.

[227] Ibid., 85; speaking of antithesis.

[228] Ibid., 83–6.

[229] Ibid., 86–95.

[230] Ibid., 95–101.

[231] Botha, in his request for this deeper stylistic study ('Style in the New Testament', 76), writes: 'A mere listing or enumeration of different features contributes very little to understanding a particular document or passage, so it is not clear why it is even done in the first place'. This question could be asked of Miriam Joseph (*Shakespeare's Use of the Art of Language*) who isolates over three hundred figures. See Kessler, 'Methodological Setting', 23. For a survey of the earlier type of stylistic studies of Paul see Betz, 'Problem', 16–21.

[232] The disparaging tone is at least in part aimed at the followers of Peter Ramus, who split rhetoric into dialectic and stylistics, the term rhetoric then being used of the latter. Rhetoric thus often became a sterile sort of stylistics that did not engage the effect of the text. Cf. Wuellner, 'Where is Rhetorical Criticism Taking Us?', 462.

the Letter to the Galatians', has profitably adapted the observations of V. Shklovsky[233] and J. Mukarosky,[234] whose works discuss
the foregrounding of certain aspects of artistic works. One might
argue that the handbooks mean this all along when they speak of
retaining the hearers' attention.[235] Cronjé's suggestion that Paul
foregrounds various aspects of the epistle through *stylistic* choices
ought to challenge the student of Galatians.

The goal of these stylistic studies is to engage the pragmatics of
the text, as expressed in Cronjé's conclusion:

> In the letter of Paul to the Galatians a great number of
> devices has been applied which can all be described as
> devices of estrangement . . . These devices[236] all effectuate
> a retardation in the reading process and consequently an
> intensified perception . . . The retardation and consequent
> intensified perception occur on occasions when the writer
> really wants his readers to pay attention to what he has to
> say. A careful balance between estrangement and auto-
> matization[237] has been maintained. In addition to all this,
> most of these devices were regarded as forceful by Hellen-
> istic rhetoricians and are thus most suitable for com-
> municating the subject-matter of this emotional letter.[238]

---

[233] Shklovsky, 'Art as Device', 5–24.

[234] Mukarosky, 'Standard Language', 17–30.

[235] Historically, many have associated rhetoric with devices intended to stave off
boredom. Grassi, *Rhetoric as Philosophy*, 15–16.

[236] Estrangement has the force of foregrounding a particular element by making
that which is familiar unfamiliar. The audience is thus forced to reflect more than
would otherwise be the case. See Cronjé, 'Defamiliarization', 214–15 (depending on
Shklovsky, 'Art as Device', 11–12). Cf. also Levinson, *Pragmatics*, especially chapter
4. Longinus discussed figures, most of which 'have to do with abnormalities of
syntax and other peculiarities of structure' (cf. Wimsatt and Brooks, *Literary
Criticism*, 103). Cf. the statement: 'relative prominence in discourse often' results
from 'deviance from a linguistic norm' (from *A Dictionary of Linguistics and
Phonetics*, ed. David Crystal, 139–40). Paul Ricoeur writes: 'A metaphor . . . is in
effect, a calculated error, which brings together things that do not go together and by
means of this apparent misunderstanding it causes a new hitherto unnoticed relation
of meaning to spring up between the terms that previous systems of classification
had ignored or not allowed . . .': cf. *Interpretation Theory*, 52.

[237] Automatization relates to familiarity. 'Perception becomes habitual, it
becomes automatic'. When an element creates instant recognition it all too easily
remains in the background. Cronjé, 'Defamiliarization', 214 (citing Shklovsky, 'Art
as Device', 11–12).

[238] Cronjé, 'Defamiliarization', 226.

These works have brought style and composition to the forefront
of discussion concerning the argument of a text and therefore have
the strongest claim to both links with classical rhetoric and a close
relationship to the OT efforts begun by Muilenburg. They do not
align Paul, via the style of Galatians, with classical speeches but
with that facet of Graeco-Roman oratory which transfers most
easily to the written page.[239] Thus the handbooks are not a final
authority but one of many relevant sources, which the practitioners
knowingly supplement with modern categories when entering into
analysis.[240]

Methods of analysis

Betz: an implicit method

In keeping with the fact that he is writing a commentary, Betz does
not provide an explicit method of rhetorical criticism. His purpose
is to show that Galatians is a particular type of text: an apologetic
speech. To this end he discusses in detail Paul's adversaries and the
problem in the Galatian Christian community, and then offers a
reading which shows both Galatians' correspondence with the
handbooks and appropriateness to the rhetorical situation.[241]
Details suggesting that the epistle would be appropriate in a court
of law Betz highlights along the way. Thus his efforts can equally
be called form-critical or historical.

Kennedy: an explicit method

Kennedy suggests that using his methodology will help us grasp the
purpose of Galatians and, in contrast to Betz, transport the reader
from the realm of the merely historical to that of a continually valid
exhortation. Kennedy offers a three-step approach which Mc-

---

[239] Cf. Quintilian, *Institutio* 1.8.16; 1.9.2.

[240] Cf. Lambrecht, 'Rhetorical Criticism and the New Testament', 244. Also,
outside Galatians, the best effort may be that of Siegert (*Argumentation bei Paulus*,
especially 85–8). We will say little more about this group since they are not involved
in a 'classical rhetorical analysis'.

[241] This is understood, following the standard analysis of Bitzer ('Rhetorical
Situation'), as the particular exigence that must be treated. We mean by this that
there is an issue to be treated, and it is perceived as treatable by the speaker. The
situation thus incorporates all the participants, including their relationships and
motives, as well as the various discourses which are aimed at the issue.

Donald[242] then expands to five, as do others, by (legitimately) moving subheadings to main headings.[243]

The five steps are as follows: (1) define the rhetorical unit; (2) identify the rhetorical situation;[244] (3) identify the rhetorical disposition or arrangement; (4) identify the rhetorical techniques or style; (5) review the process to see if it adequately addresses the exigence.[245]

This last step has been summarized by Wuellner as: 'Identification of Rhetorical Criticism as a synchronic whole'.[246] Wuellner does not, however, explain how the four diachronic movements turn into a synchronic whole,[247] and it seems unlikely that Kennedy intended the change, for he does not make this shift in his reading of Galatians. Instead he attempts to measure how closely the text relates to the historical situation which produced it, a successful study being one which, upon review, shows how the exigence is resolved.

Curiously, Kennedy reveals that 'Whenever the purely classical standards are employed in appraising the New Testament its style is found wanting', and further, he acknowledges that this is the accepted opinion of both modern classicists and the church fathers.[248] His solution to the failure of the NT to live up to classical standards is, as we have already seen, to define classical Greek rhetorical analysis as the application of Greek terms to any type of discourse (level 2 rhetoric): 'if rhetorical criticism is to be valid, it must be practised with some awareness of the traditions of Jewish speech . . . and if it is to be useful it must embrace more than style'. Furthermore, 'we can significantly enhance our appreciation' of a text's 'meaning without violence to the author's intent' if we employ 'fundamental and universal features of rhetoric' to describe 'the logical and structural features of the text before us,

---

[242] McDonald, 'Rhetorical Criticism', 599–600.

[243] See also Black, 'Rhetorical Criticism and Biblical Interpretation' 254–5; 'Rhetorical Questions', 62–3 (a six-step approach). Wuellner, 'Where is Rhetorical Criticism Taking Us'?, 455–8.

[244] Kennedy (*New Testament Interpretation*, 36) emphasizes the problem as determinative of the rhetorical situation.

[245] Ibid., 33–8.

[246] Wuellner, 'Where is Rhetorical Criticism Taking Us?', 458.

[247] Ibid. He does recognize that the first four steps are diachronic.

[248] Kennedy, *New Testament Interpretation*, 11. Chapters 6 and 7 will suggest that Kennedy's observation concerning style cannot be easily dismissed. The ancients recognized that for a text to be accepted as a piece of classical rhetoric it needed to conform to certain stylistic criteria.

rather than simply quarrying a text for examples of classical figures'.[249]

But this suggests that two types of rhetoric are appropriately applied to the text: the first is a universally valid description of the persuasive power behind any kind of text; and the second is the rhetoric which actually produced the text. If the traditions of Jewish speech are manifest in the text, then why use Graeco-Roman civic oratory textbooks to describe what is happening in the NT? The validity of such an exercise is threatened by the realization that Graeco-Roman texts are irrelevant to the creation of Galatians, and that they do not attempt to describe *all* types of rhetoric. Thus we emphasize again that Kennedy does not offer an alternative to Betz, for the latter argues that Galatians *is* part of the Graeco-Roman tradition embodied in the handbooks, while the former simply argues that according to some universally derived standard, Galatians is deliberative – he is not arguing that it is a deliberative speech destined for the forum.

Longenecker: merging of methods

Longenecker employs a variety of 'rhetorics' to understand Galatians, depending, as we have seen, on what he labels synchronic and diachronic rhetoric alongside epistolary analysis. If rhetoric is the vehicle by which an author accomplishes his purpose, then all three of these can be called rhetorics; and each can be understood to address different affective levels.[250] Longenecker seeks to uncover a text's formal characteristics, which he may then explain with the aid of his trio of rhetorics. For example, when he comes upon an epistolary convention, namely the 'I am astonished that . . .' of Galatians 1.6, he interacts with the notion that this is mere formula and ought not be given too much weight.[251] Likewise, when he discusses Galatians 2.15–21 he does so in light of the fact that it is the *propositio* of a speech, and thus contains in condensed form the arguments that are to be unpacked in what follows.[252] This eclectic approach allows for a sophisticated movement through the epistle; but, as we will see, it is overly atomistic and hinders our identification of the form and genre of Galatians.

---

[249] Kennedy, *New Testament Interpretation*, 12.
[250] On this last point see Thurén, *Strategy of 1 Peter*, 60–4.
[251] Longenecker, *Galatians*, 14.
[252] Ibid., 81.

Even if every objection alluded to above were granted, Galatians might still be a piece of Graeco-Roman oratory. We therefore turn to a comparison of Galatians with the handbooks and handbook oratory, always keeping a watchful eye on scholarship's handling of the material. Successive chapters will discuss (1) *taxis*, that is, the structure of Galatians as measured by the classical handbooks (chapter 4); (2) the species of Galatians as defined by Betz, Kennedy, Longenecker and others (chapter 5); and (3) the implications of Paul's language (a) for the suggestion that rhetorical analysis was long used to assess Paul, and (b) for the question of whether the epistle could be identified as a speech (chapters 6 and 7).

4

RHETORICAL STRUCTURE AND GALATIANS

It has become practically axiomatic since the appearance of Hans Dieter Betz's Hermeneia commentary that study of the argument and structure of Galatians begins with classical rhetoric.[1] Betz's assertions that 'The body of [Galatians] is constructed as a defense speech using argumentative, judicial rhetoric',[2] and that, as a result, 'Paul's letter to the Galatians can be analyzed according to Graeco-Roman rhetoric and epistolography',[3] have exerted great force even upon those who do not share his convictions concerning the overall purpose of Galatians.

C. K. Barrett is typical when he suggests that while 'Paul conformed a little less closely than Dr Betz suggests to the contemporary models of courtroom and similar speeches . . . on the whole the parallels are convincing'.[4] He adds that Betz's 'analysis, and the parallels that he draws, are illuminating', evincing the 'methods and skills of the professional orator'.[5]

Although Barrett questions details of Betz's reconstruction, main premises (including some we will question) are accepted.[6] At issue are nothing less than the purpose and function of Galatians. This chapter compares the shape of Galatians with structural guideposts provided by the handbooks – primarily those cited in Betz's commentary, interacting chiefly with Betz because he has articulated a defence of a thorough and original rhetorical analysis of the

[1] Betz presents his conception of the arrangement of Galatians in 'Literary Composition and Function', and *Galatians*, especially 16–24.

[2] Betz, 'Problem', 24.

[3] Betz, *Galatians*, 14. He adds that this was apparently not previously acknowledged (ibid., 14, n. 97).

[4] Barrett, *Freedom and Obligation*, 50; on p. vii he describes Betz's work as 'masterly'.

[5] Barrett, ibid., 31–2.

[6] See especially Barrett, 'Apologetic Letter', 414–17. See below (pp. 91–2) for outlines which show various degrees of agreement with Betz.

epistle's structure; those disagreeing on the species of Galatians (see chapter 5) have not grappled with the details to the extent that Betz has. His outline and those with minor variations may be presented as follows:

H. D. Betz (1975)[7]	B. H. Brinsmead (1982)[8]	G. A. Kennedy (1984)[9]
1.1–5: epistolary prescript	1.1–5: epistolary prescript	1.1–5: salutation
1.6–11: *exordium*	1.6–10: *prooemium*	1.6–10: *proem*
1.12–2.14: *narratio*	1.12–2.14: *propositio*	1.11–5.1: proofs
2.15–21: *propositio*	2.15–21: *propositio*	1.11–2.21: first heading
3.1–4.31: *probatio*	3.1–4.31: *probatio*	1.11–12: topic
5.1–6.10: *exhortatio*	5.1–6.10: *refutatio*	1.13–2.14: narrative
6.11–18: epistolary postscript (*peroratio*)	6.11–18: epistolary postscript	2.15–21: *epicheireme*
		3.1–5.1: second heading
		5.1–6.10: injunctions
		6.11–18: epilogue/postscript

B. Standaert (1985)[10]	R. G. Hall (1987)[11]	J. Smit (1989)[12]
1.1–5: introduction épistolaire	1.1–5: salutation/*exordium*	1.1–5: epistolary prescript
1.6–12: annonce du thème	1.6–9: proposition	1.6–12: *exordium*
1.13–2.14: *narratio*	1.10–6.10: proof	1.13–2.21: *narratio*
2.15–21: *peroratio*	1.10–2.21: narration	3.1–14.11: *confirmatio*
3.1–4.31: *refutatio*	3.1–6.10: further headings	4.12–5.12: *conclusio*
5.1–6.10: *probatio-exhortatio*	6.11–18: epilogue	5.13–6.10: interpolation
6.11–18: épilogue		6.11–18: *amplificatio*

[7] Betz, *Galatians*, 16–24. So also Barrett, 'Apologetic Letter', 415–16; Baasland, 'Persecution', 135–50 (though he calls 5.1–12 a transitional passage: 142 and 149, n. 29); Harnisch, 'Einübung des neuen Seins', 279–96; Beker, *Der Sieg Gottes*, 9. Hans Hübner ('Galaterbrief') seems to accept Betz's outline with reservations; Jürgen Becker (*Paul*, 273–8) extends the *narratio* to 2.21, finding in 2.14b–21 an inlaid speech with its own *exordium* (2.14b); *narratio* (2.15–16); *propositio* (2.17); *probatio* (2.18–20); and *peroratio* (2.21).
[8] Brinsmead, *Dialogical Response*, 46–54.
[9] Kennedy, *New Testament Interpretation*, 147–51. This is the first work to develop Aune's suggestion that Galatians seems to contain a good deal of deliberative rhetorical forms ('Review of Betz's *Galatians*', 325).
[10] Standaert, 'La rhétorique antique', 33–40; 'La rhétorique ancienne dans Saint Paul', 78–92.
[11] Hall, 'The Rhetorical Outline of Galatians', 277–87. Hall also considers Galatians deliberative rather than forensic.
[12] Smit, 'Deliberative Speech', 1–26.

R. Longenecker (1990)[13]	J. Hester (1991)[14]	W. Russell (1993)[15]
1.1–5: salutation	1.1–5: epistolary prescript	1.1–5: prescript/salutation
1.6–10: *exordium*	1.6–10: *exordium*	1.6–10: prologue/proem/
1.11–2.14: *narratio*	1.11–12: *stasis*	*exordium*
1.11–12: thesis statement	1.13–2.21: *narratio*	1.11–6.10: proof/*probatio*/
1.13–2.14: autobiographical	2.11–14: chreia	*confirmatio*
material	2.15–21: elaboration of	1.11–2.21: historical
2.15–21: *propositio*	chreia	argument
3.1–4.11: *probatio*	3.1–4.31: *probatio*	3.1–4.31: experiential
4.12–6.10: *exhortatio*	5.1–6.10: *exhortatio*	argument
6.11–18: subscription	6.11–18: epistolary	5.1–6.10: causal argument
	postscript (*peroratio*)	6.11–18: postscript/epilogue/
		conclusio

Galatians 1–2

Many rhetorical critics now agree that parts of Galatians do not follow the advice of the handbooks – leading to alternative readings. A popular strategy has been to divide Galatians, arguing that although later chapters declare their independence, chapters 1 to 2 do conform to the handbooks' descriptions. Here then is the real battlefield, and those who maintain that Galatians conforms to level 4 rhetoric appear to have the upper hand. Therefore we must sift the data, namely the text of Galatians as compared with the handbooks, most carefully.

A word on sources before commencing: we will again conduct our discussion primarily through interaction with the handbooks since it is from them that Betz, who has largely set the agenda, derives his arguments. Speeches must neither be completely ignored nor allowed to inform the discussion to the same extent, for the greatest value of such sources to the argument that Galatians embodies classical rhetoric lies in their ability to represent stereotypical forms. Because Betz and others argue from a common stock of rhetoric familiar to, if not the masses, at least the educated, it is possible to depend too much on speeches – for there will always be oratorical activity which deviates from the norm. Relying on proof-texts is a real danger.

[13] Much of Longenecker's discussion derives from Hansen, *Abraham in Galatians*, chapter 2.
[14] This outline attempts to integrate two distinct discussions of Galatians. Some details of the first Hester now rejects. Compare James Hester's 'Rhetorical Structure', 223–33 with his later 'Placing the Blame', 281–307.
[15] W. B. Russell, 'Rhetorical Analysis of Galatians, 2', 436–37.

The *exordium*

In Betz's scheme an epistolary prescript (1.1–6) is followed by an *exordium*:[16] that part of the speech which introduces the issue[17] and aims at winning attention and favour.[18]

Betz depends on Pseudo-Cicero's *Rhetorica ad Herennium* to discuss the beginning of the *exordium*, quoting: 'the direct opening straightway prepares the hearer to attend to our speech. Its purpose is to enable us to have hearers who are attentive, receptive, and well-disposed'.[19] He then lists three occasions on which the orator might opt for a less direct approach, called the *insinuatio*: (1) when the subject itself alienates the hearer; (2) 'when the hearer has apparently been won over by the previous speakers of the opposition'; (3) 'when the hearer has become wearied by listening to previous speakers'.[20]

But rather than opting for either the usual direct approach or the *insinuatio*, Betz suggests that Galatians employs both:

> Speaking in the terms of the *Rhetorica ad Herennium*, Paul's statement of the *causa* is a mixture of two types of *exordia*, the *principium* ('direct opening') and the *insinuatio* ('subtle approach'). The former, the *principium*, is appropriate in addressing an audience where attention, receptivity, and a favorable disposition can be obtained directly and without difficulty, while the *insinuatio* should be used in cases where, for example, the audience has been won over by the previous speech of the opponent.[21]

He explains: 'Paul's case stands in the middle: he can be certain of having the attention and receptivity of the Galatians at once, but they have almost been won over, though not quite'.[22] He concedes that 'this mixture of the *principium* and the *insinuatio* may be

---

[16] Betz, *Galatians*, 44.

[17] Aristotle, *Rhetoric* 3.14.6: 'So then the most essential and special function of the *exordium* is to make clear what is the end or purpose of the speech; wherefore it should not be employed, if the subject is quite clear or unimportant'.

[18] Cicero, *De Inventione* 1.15.20. On the *exordium* generally see especially Aristotle, *Rhetoric* 3.14.1–12; Cicero, *De Inventione* 1.15.20–18.26; Quintilian, *Institutio* 4.1.1–79; Lausberg, *Handbuch*, §263–88; Martin, *Rhetorik*, 60–75.

[19] Betz, *Galatians*, 45, n. 17: *Rhetorica ad Herennium* 1.4.6.

[20] Betz, *Galatians*, 45, n. 18: *Rhetorica ad Herennium* 1.6.1.

[21] Betz, *Galatians*, 45.

[22] Ibid., 45, n. 19 further observes the present tense of Galatians 1.6–7; 4.9, 21, and others.

peculiar', but insists that 'it conforms precisely to the situation with which Paul sees himself confronted'.[23]

This explanation poses problems quite apart from the question of whether Betz accurately describes Paul's relationship with the Galatians.[24] The rhetorical handbooks present the work of con-summate categorizers, yet not once do they recommend a 'directly subtle', or a 'subtly direct' entry by the speaker. It is a rare courtroom which does not contain some listeners who are sympa-thetic to the defendant, others predisposed to side with the accuser, and a few who are undecided. Thus the situation in Galatia is probably quite close to a normal trial if only in this matter of the speaker being faced with hostility and sympathy alongside a degree of indecision.

The creation of a new category, however, is crucial to Betz's argument: he can now import Cicero to explain the θυαμάζω statement of verse 6, where Paul writes 'I am amazed that you have so quickly deserted him who called you'. Betz writes regarding this statement that 'Cicero . . . recommends the expression of astonish-ment and perplexity *as one of the means to regain the goodwill of an audience which has been won over by the opposition*'.[25] Although Paul does not really use a subtle opening,[26] Betz's argument demands that it be introduced to provide for 'an audience which has been won over by the opposition', which in turn allows for Cicero's description of the θυαμάζω statement. But once again we run into difficulties, for Cicero's full statement is,

> Or you express doubt as to what to say first, or which passage to answer before all others, at the same time showing perplexity and astonishment (*cum admiratione*). For when the audience see that he whom they think is shaken by the opponent's speech is ready to speak in reply and with confidence and assurance . . . [27]

Clearly this recommends not astonishment at the audience's dis-agreeable behaviour but admiration for the skills of one's oppo-nent. Paul neither feigns astonishment at the skill of his opponents

[23] Ibid., 45.

[24] Hall ('Rhetorical Outline', 284) considers 1.6–9, because of its attack on Paul's opponents, an example of the direct approach in an *exordium*.

[25] Betz, *Galatians*, 45, citing (in n. 21) Cicero, *De Inventione* 1.17.25.

[26] Aune writes that he cannot 'imagine what elements of the *exordium* could feasibly be regarded as "subtle"' ('Review of Betz's *Galatians*', 326).

[27] Cicero, *De Inventione* 1.17.25.

nor praises their manner of speech. Instead, addressing the Galatians, he declares himself perplexed by their entertainment of unacceptable choices.

One example Betz cites is from Plato's *Defense of Socrates at his Trial*. It reads:

> How you, men of Athens, have been affected by my accusors, I do not know; but I, for my part, almost forgot my own identity, so persuasively did they talk; and yet there is hardly a word of truth in what they have said. But I was most amazed (μάλιστα . . . ἐθαύμασα . . .) by one of the many lies that they told – when they said that you must be on your guard not to be deceived by me, because I was a clever speaker.[28]

This quotation contains an aside to the audience concerning the activity of the prosecutor, therefore not qualifying as a parallel to Paul's direct rebuke of his readers for their improper activity. The orator speaks self-consciously, the handbooks discussing the manipulation of an audience's self-awareness and its view of the speaker. Paul directs his thought in 1.6 – unlike Plato, whose concern is the speech-event itself – to the underlying crisis begging resolution. Plato and the handbooks focus on the event: Paul is too busy fighting to notice the battle.

Indeed, far from conforming to a Ciceronian rhetorical device, Paul's expression of amazement has been recognized by J. L. White, in his work on the body of the letter (and the transitions to the body), as an *epistolary* convention,[29] its function being to reproach, and its place being the outset of the body.[30] The papyri reveal that one either thanks a deity for some benevolence, or expresses amazement at an action undertaken by the addressee (often for allowing so much time to elapse since their last communication). Numerous examples demonstrate that the amazement is ironic and that the writer scolds the reader for some failure:

> I am surprised that, when so many have come up country,

---

[28] Plato, *Apologia* 17a. None of Betz's other examples in any way relates to the *exordium*; they are random expressions of surprise or amazement which happen to occur in rhetorical contexts.

[29] That is, it represents a level 4 rhetoric distinct from classical oratory.

[30] White, *Body of the Greek Letter*, 33–6; 'Introductory Formulae', 91–7; Mullins, 'Formulas', 385.

> and that with beasts unladen, you have not sent Sara-
> pammon, for you know there is need of him.[31]

> I am amazed, brother – this is a second letter which I send
> to you since my return home, and you send me nothing in
> reply.[32]

> I wonder that you did not see your way to let me have
> what I asked you to send by Corbolon, especially when I
> wanted it for a festival.[33]

Longenecker suggests that this form does not always imply irony
and reproach, providing one example:

> I find it surprising if it needs three pairs of oxen to water
> the vineyard at Chalothis, which hasn't come to much.[34]

It may be, however, that Longenecker's example should also be
treated as a reproach; in fact, the context would suggest it. The
letter reads:

> A thousand times I have written to you to cut down the
> vines at Phai . . . But today again I get a letter from you
> asking what I want done. To which I reply: cut them down,
> cut them down, cut them down, cut them down, cut them
> down: there you are, I say it again and again. They are to
> be sown with what has to go there . . . I find it surprising if
> it needs three pairs of oxen to water the vineyard at
> Chalothis, which hasn't come to much. It isn't so much a
> matter of the cost of the extra pair, as of their feed and
> other expenses.[35]

This letter betrays annoyance at the delay in cutting the vines and
the waste involved in caring for oxen used to water an unproductive
vineyard. It is only because of the next line ('But if you do think it's
needed, send on my letter to . . .'[36]) that one might claim a gentle
tone, though it need mean no more than: 'Although I think it
absurd that you are wasting money on such things, if you deem it

[31] PMert. 80.
[32] PMich. 209.
[33] POxy. 113.20. Other examples are PMich. 209.6ff., 479.4f.; BGU 1079.2; POxy.
133, 1233; PCornell 52. See White, 'Introductory Formulae', 94.
[34] POxy. 3063.11–13.
[35] Ibid., 3063.3–15.
[36] Ibid., 3063.15–17.

necessary, inquire of . . .' It is possible to find here a continuing rebuke.

A second response to Longenecker also applies to Betz. The latter acknowledges that Galatians 1.6 is 'related to [an] epistolary complaint'. He then notes that θυαμάζω occurs often in Demosthenes, Antiphon and Lysias.[37] The issue, however, is not the presence of general statements of amazement, but the place and function within Galatians of this particular statement. The papyri reveal a clear epistolary form which employs the term θυαμάζω, and Galatians conforms to it: at the point of transition from the letter opening to the body one usually finds a statement of thanksgiving or amazement in both Paul and the papyri. Although Longenecker produces an example which differs from the usual function of this epistolary form, his θυαμάζω statement does not occupy the transitional position; and Betz's examples relate neither to Galatians nor to epistolary conventions: they are expressions of surprise found within the bodies of letters and essays, not at transitional points, and as such do not conform to the form discussed by White.

It therefore seems best to recognize Paul's statement of amazement as a rebuke form and grant it full force as an epistolary device. Since this form commonly opens the body of the letter, the role of 1.6 shifts away from commencing an *exordium* to marking its end and introducing the reader to direct interaction with the actual concerns of the letter.[38] Epistolary convention lends as firm a hand to the unpacking of Galatians 1.6 as does rhetorical.[39]

Betz further states: 'The conclusion [of the *exordium*] is apparently reached in v 9, while the next major section, the *narratio*, begins in v 12',[40] proposing that the intervening verses form a

[37] Betz, *Galatians*, 47, n. 39; 'Literary Composition and Function', 359, n.2. He provides two examples from epistles, both from Demosthenes: 2.19.410: 'I marvel that so many who maintain great forces hire mercenary armies and expend so much money on them'; 9.8.435: 'I marvel also at those men who have ability in action or in speech that it has never occurred to them seriously to take to heart the conditions which affect all Greeks alike'. These are not used in the same way as in Galatians – 2.19.410 in fact comes near the end (it is the penultimate page of the epistle in the LCL).

[38] White ('Introductory Formulae', 91–2) opposes Schubert's *Pauline Thanksgiving*, which identified the thanksgiving more closely with the letter opening than with the body: Schubert's failure to determine precisely where the thanksgiving concludes argues against his analysis.

[39] White, 'Introductory Formulae', 96; Mullins, 'Formulas', 385.

[40] Betz, *Galatians*, 46.

transitio. His evidence for such a device following the *exordium* comes from Quintilian, who writes: 'However on all occasions when we have employed the *exordium*, whether we intend to pass to the *statement of facts* or direct to the *proof*, our intention should be mentioned at the conclusion of the introduction, with the result that the transition to what follows will be smooth and easy'.[41] Quintilian borrows his sample transition from Cicero: 'The introduction to my exposition of this point will be rather longer than usual, but I beg you, gentlemen, not to take it ill. For if you get a firm grasp of the beginning, you will find it much easier to follow what comes last'.[42] Cicero's version does not really resemble: 'For I would have you know, brothers, that the gospel preached by me is not human in nature'. The former draws attention exclusively to the speaker's act of 'transitioning', while the latter focuses just as narrowly on the 'non-humanity' of the gospel: the topic, not the technique. Betz appears to have confused the classical and modern transition, the latter intending to weave together the various parts of an address so that the seams are hidden, the former being an intentionally bulky seam forcing the hearer to notice the stitching in of new material.[43]

Citing Quintilian, Betz writes: 'In addition, the transition may contain an announcement of the major topic of the *narratio*'.[44] The passage in Quintilian contains eight lines, none referring to the *content* of the transition but instead to the orator's announcement of making a transition. Rather than introduce its topic, Quintilian intends his transition merely to demarcate *the act of entering* the *narratio*.[45]

An additional strand of evidence concerning the *exordium* takes us back to an earlier 'rhetorical analysis' of Galatians. Betz considers 1.6–11 the *exordium*, and calls 1.1–5 an epistolary prescript which, along with the postscript, forms an 'epistolary framework' separating 'so easily that it appears almost as a kind of

---

[41] Quintilian, *Institutio* 4.1.76.

[42] Ibid., 4.1.79, citing Cicero, *Pro Cluent* 4.11.

[43] Quintilian (Ibid., 4.1.78) writes: 'the first part of our *statement of facts* will be wasted, if the judge does not realise that we have reached that stage'.

[44] Betz, *Galatians*, 46, citing Quintilian, *Institutio* 4.1.79.

[45] Ibid., 4.1.79. Perhaps the confusion stems from the last sentence of the chapter, which reads in the LCL: 'This is practically all that I can find to say on the subject of the *exordium*'. One should understand: 'all that I can find to say concerning the subject at hand, namely the *exordium*'.

external bracket for the body of the letter'.[46] This contradicts the
assessment of John Chrysostom, one of the leading rhetors of his
age, who maintains that Galatians 1.1–3 is the *exordium*. In
chapter 6 we will argue that Chrysostom does not consider Galatians a piece of classical rhetoric, for now noting only that his
assessment of the *exordium* differs from Betz's. In reality, Galatians
1.1–3 looks no more like an actual *exordium* than does 1.6–11, but
the former verses come closer to fulfilling this function when understood as the initial overture to the audience and the allusion to the
speech's central issue.[47] Quintilian clarifies: 'In any case, there can
be no doubt that by *proem* we mean the portion of a speech
addressed to the judge *before he has begun to consider the actual
case*'.[48] Galatians 1.1–3 contains Paul's comments before he actually plunges into the matter at hand, though they are not wasted
words but, like all his prefaces, perform a task. For convenience
and by analogy, Chrysostom refers to this prologue as an *exordium*:
the function is thereby well depicted.

Finally, Aune opposes calling these verses an *exordium*, explaining that when one considers the purposes of *exordia* as
expounded in the handbooks, 'it is difficult to find anything
characteristic of a normal forensic *exordium* in Gal. 1:6–11; a
survey of Quintilian's lengthy discussion of forensic *exordia*
(4.1.5–79) reveals nothing similar to Gal. 1:6–11'.[49]

Sources which address the function and shape of the *exordium* thus oppose so identifying Galatians 1.6 11; once we
assess the data these verses appear to exhibit a different shape
altogether.

The *narratio*

Three elements of Betz's discussion of *narratio* call for investigation: type, beginning and function. Regarding the type of *narratio*,
Betz argues that the verses immediately following the *exordium*
comprise the *narratio*: that part of a speech which rehearses the
events bringing the combatants to court.[50] At the outset of his

[46] Betz, *Galatians*, 15.
[47] Quintilian, *Institutio* 4.1.1.
[48] Ibid., 4.1.3, emphasis added.
[49] Aune, 'Review of Betz's *Galatians*', 326.
[50] On the *narratio* see Aristotle, *Rhetoric* 3.16.1–11; Cicero, *De Inventione*
1.19.27–21.30; Quintilian, *Institutio* 4.2.1–132; Lausberg, *Handbuch*, §289–347;
Martin, *Rhetorik*, 75–89.

discussion of the *narratio* he writes: '[Cicero] then distinguishes between three types (*genera*) of narrative, the first of which applies to Galatians: "that form of narrative which contains an exposition of a case of law"'.[51]

We must again interact with Cicero's statement in full:

> The *narrative* is an exposition of events that have occurred or are supposed to have occurred. There are three kinds: one which contains just the case and the whole reason for the dispute; a second in which a digression is made beyond the strict limits of the case for the purpose of attacking somebody, or of making a comparison, or of amusing the audience in a way not incongruous with the business in hand, or for amplification. The third kind is wholly unconnected with public issues, which is recited or written solely for amusement but at the same time provides valuable training.[52]

Having dispensed with the third type of *narratio*, Cicero returns to the first and writes those words which Betz applies to Galatians: 'Now it seems necessary to speak of that form of narrative which contains an exposition of a case at law'.[53] This is followed by a description of the qualities that ought to characterize it: brevity, clarity and plausibility.[54] Having explained how to accomplish these goals, Cicero turns to the *partitio* with no more to say concerning the *narratio*.

Thus it appears that Cicero's statements regarding types of *narratio* are far too restrictive to apply to Galatians 1–2. The first type, which Betz unduly restricts by considering only Cicero's subsequent discussion while overlooking important aspects of his definition, cannot help since Galatians 1.12–2.14 does not really contain 'just the case and the whole reason for the dispute'. Paul neglects on the one hand any historical data concerning the churches in Galatia and on the other his present battle with 'Judaizing' opponents,[55] instead arguing against what is most likely an accusation of Paul's opponents: that he is subordinate to the

---

[51] Betz, *Galatians*, 58–59, citing Cicero, *De Inventione* 1.20.28.
[52] Ibid., 1.19.27.
[53] Ibid., 1.20.28.
[54] Ibid., 1.20.28–21.30.
[55] Unless one simply equates Paul's opponents in Galatia with the same groups he had battled earlier. The dangers of mirror-reading frequently confront the modern reader of Galatians.

apostles since he propagates a derived gospel.[56] This 'insubordination' dominates chapters 1 to 2 but is clearly subservient to the larger issues of the epistle, never reappearing in the remainder. It is not the impetus behind the altercation but a charge Paul must refute before tackling the larger questions concerning the law.

Cicero's second class of *narratio*, which Betz rightly dismisses, is equally unhelpful because, while Paul may indeed attack, compare and digress (though not amuse), his tight structure facilitates a unified argument rather than first a mention of the case, then a digression.[57] Most compelling is Hall's suggestion that 1.13–2.10 proves Paul's gospel to be from God, and 2.11–21 his lack of concern to 'please men'. Thus he accounts for the internal cohesion of 1.13–2.21 and relates it directly back to 1.10–12.[58] The third type, written for amusement and exercise, requires no comment.

A further discrepancy concerns 'the beginning of the *narratio*', which, Betz contends,

> intends 'not merely to instruct, but rather to persuade the judge'. Quintilian recommends beginning the *narratio* with a statement, the *propositio*, which will influence the judge in some way, even though he may be well-informed about the case. He mentions examples like these: 'I know that you are aware . . .'; 'You remember . . .'; 'You are not ignorant of the fact . . .'; etc. Which one of these one chooses depends entirely upon how one can best influence the judge.
>
> Paul announces his *narratio* with the words (v 11): γνωρίζω γὰρ ὑμῖν, ἀδελφοί ('I want you to know, brothers'), thus conforming to Quintilian's advice. We must conclude, therefore, that the term γνωρίζω ('know') does not simply announce information, but by pretending to tell the Galatians something new in fact reminds them of something they no doubt knew, but would at this time rather forget.[59]

[56] Becker, *Paul*, 276.
[57] Hester ('Rhetorical Structure', 223–33) argued that 2.11–14 constitutes a digression but later renounced that position. Cf. his subsequent 'Placing the Blame', 281–307. The first article's suggestion of a digression is criticized in Hall, 'Rhetorical Outline', 285.
[58] Hall, Ibid., 285–6.
[59] Betz, *Galatians*, 59–60.

Two observations concerning the beginning of a *narratio* are in order. First, when barrister Paul addresses judge and jury, can he be confident that they already know his life story? Paul pretends to tell *the Galatians* something new, but this strays from Betz's working definition of 'jury', which includes 'the combined forums of Judaism and paganism'. We cannot even know if this information is shared by Paul's Judaizing opponents, who also fit within Betz's reconstruction of the jury.[60]

Second, a closer reading of the sources may yield a different picture. Betz supports his description with three citations: Quintilian 3.9.5; 4.2.7; and 4.2.30.[61] These call for careful consideration, for Quintilian does not in fact recommend *beginning* the *narratio* with a *propositio*. In 3.9.5 he cites two concepts from Aristotle: the first relates to refutation and Quintilian disagrees with it; the second shifts the *propositio* to the slot directly after the *exordium* rather than the *narratio*, and Quintilian calls it a novelty, never allowing it to inform his exposition. Furthermore, since this reference to *propositio* appears in Quintilian's list of the parts of a forensic oration, there is no reason to distance it from his description of *propositio* found in book 4 – where he treats the dispositional components of a speech in detail. When Betz arrives at his discussion of the *propositio* of Galatians, he claims it is 2.15–21. Thus the *propositio* of Galatians is elusive: is it 1.11–12 as he now claims, or is it 2.15–21 as he argues subsequently?[62]

Quintilian claims in 4.2.7 that merely one sentence will at times suffice *instead of* a *narratio*,[63] adding in 4.2.30 that even scholastic declaimers (who are notorious for their excess)[64] occasionally substitute a single-sentence statement for a full *narratio*.[65] He then provides an example: 'I say that Horatius killed his sister'.[66] One easily sees how this sentence fulfils Cicero's notion of an 'exposition

---

[60] Sampley ('Paul's Self-Defence', 478) defines the jury more narrowly as 'those people in Galatia that will still hear Paul's pleading'.

[61] Betz, *Galatians*, 59 n. 33.

[62] Ibid., 113–15.

[63] Quintilian, *Institutio* 4.2.7.

[64] This stems from the classroom, which dictates that budding advocates include a *narratio* 'as though they were speaking first, and a refutation of the arguments of the defence, as if they were replying' (Quintilian, *Institutio* 4.2.29). It becomes tedious when the student appears in court and fails to realize that he performs the task only of the first or the second, not both.

[65] Quintilian, *Institutio* 4.2.30: *pro narratione sit propositio*.

[66] Ibid., 4.2.7.

of a case at law': it is more difficult to equate it with Galations 1.13–2.14.

This brings us back to the role of γνωρίζω. Perhaps as problematic as any of the above observations is that verse 11 has been forced to function within Betz's scheme as part of the *exordium*, the transition, and now as part of the *narratio*. Longenecker, in his investigation of epistolary convention, finds this term used as a disclosure formula.[67] It appears to function as such in Galatians to disclose the central thesis of Galatians 1–2: that Paul's gospel is not of human origin.[68]

A statement from *Rhetorica ad Alexandrum* introduces a third objection to Betz's assignment of roles: 'After [the *narratio*] comes confirmation, the method by which we shall confirm the facts already stated as being of such a nature as we undertook to show them to be, by means of proofs and considerations of justice and expediency'.[69] Thus the proof (*probatio*) defends what was introduced in the *narratio*. Betz himself quotes sources that imply the same function when he writes:

> Among the specific devices Quintilian recommends, we notice that it is 'useful to scatter some hints of our proofs here and there, but in such a way that it is never forgotten that we are making a *statement of facts* and not a *proof*'.[70] Simple and brief arguments may be thrown in, but these should be taken as only preparatory for the arguments to be developed in the *probatio*.[71] Such remarks should remain part of the *narratio*, since they are most effective when they are not recognizable as arguments.[72]

But 1.12–2.14 does not introduce what is proven in the *probatio*. Even if the chief point of Galatians 3–4 is open to debate, to my knowledge nobody has suggested that it argues that Paul's gospel is not from men. Chapters 1 to 2 clearly comprise a self-contained argumentative section dealing with concerns distinct from, though

[67] Longenecker, *Galatians*, 20, 22.

[68] Sanders goes so far as to say that when attention is fixed on exegetical rather than historical (i.e. attempting to correlate Galatians and Acts) matters, 'the normal explanation' is that Gal. 1.12 contains the point to be proven: cf. 'Paul's "Autobiographical" Statements', 335, n.4.

[69] *Rhetorica ad Alexandrum* 1438b.30.

[70] Quintilian, *Institutio* 4.2.54.

[71] Betz (*Galatians*, 61, n. 59), referring to Lausberg, *Handbuch*, §324.

[72] Betz, ibid., 61.

definitely preliminary to, those of the *probatio*. Hence Hall, in his rhetorical outline, views the narrative in 1.10–2.21 as a self-contained argumentative unit with its own *propositio*, 1.10–12, allowing the entire portion to unfold in a chiastic pattern.[73]

Betz has written: '[Paul's] case requires a long statement of facts, since he has to cover his entire history from birth on'.[74] If he attempts to prove his gospel is not from men by introducing data reaching back to his birth, Paul violates the instruction of the *Rhetorica ad Herennium* that 'We shall be able to make the Statement of Facts brief if we begin it at the place at which we need to begin; if we do not try to recount from the remotest beginning . . .'[75] Betz adds: 'He begins with his birth because it is relevant to the case'; unfortunately we never learn how it establishes that Paul's gospel was not conferred by the apostles. Nor does the account of his pre-conversion persecution activities advance this case. When, however, the narrowness of a legal context is peeled away, these 'superfluous' elements take on argumentative significance.

Becker, who follows Betz's construction almost entirely, acknowledges that this narrative steps outside the bounds of a *narratio* in that it develops matters foreign to the case, while at the same time neglecting pertinent material. He writes:

> Yet, if we view the historical presentation in its rhetorical aspect, Gal. 1:11–2:21 is only in a limited way a historical exposition of the case at hand. For Paul devotes himself to his own life only as it relates to the problem and seeks in it only elements that belong here. He does not examine at all the history of the Galatian churches and the Judaizers. His procedure is not quite that orthodox.[76]

Becker correctly observes that Paul stresses his own experience beyond what is appropriate to a trial even as he neglects those who have brought the case to court. How unorthodox can Paul's oratory be before we decide that it is something else?

Finally, it seems that nobody has asked the most basic question: Is narrative equal to *narratio*? Chrysostom brings this question to

---

[73] Hall, 'Rhetorical Outline', 282–3.
[74] Betz, *Galatians*, 61.
[75] *Rhetorica ad Herennium* 9.14.
[76] Becker, *Paul*, 276; Kennedy (*New Testament Interpretation*, 145) also maintains that 'the narrative . . . is not an account of the facts at issue'.

the fore when he writes that Paul is 'about to narrate (διηγεῖσθαι) his former life, and sudden conversion, and to demonstrate clearly that it was sincere'.[77] We have already highlighted difficulties with identifying 'the *narratio*', and add here that the Greek term behind *narratio* was often used nearly coterminously with the English 'narrative'. Thus Luke compiles an 'account' (διήγησιν: Lk. 1.1) which we instinctively recognize as narrative, but not as a rhetorical *narratio*.[78] When *The Republic* suggests that everything said by a poet or μυθολόγων is διήγησις, the reader does not imagine that poetry is forensic discourse;[79] likewise Plutarch envisages no court-room when he reports: 'You are aware . . . that of the dialogues of Plato, some are narratives (διηγηματικοί) and others dramatic'.[80] Cosgrove calls this portion of Galatians 'a story', while Lightfoot's outline labels chapters 1 to 2 'Personal, chiefly in the form of a narrative'.[81] These modifiers approach both Chrysostom's estimation and the nature of Paul's text.[82]

It is significant that, though Betz and Kennedy end the *narratio* at 2.14,[83] Chrysostom and Lightfoot let Paul's narrative run to 2.21 – presumably because 2.15–21 are indeed part of the story.[84]

The *propositio*

Galatians 2.15–21 has proven to be central to deciphering the message of Galatians. Many consider Betz's reconstruction of the rhetorical activity undertaken in these verses to be the most convincing element in his commentary. Richard Longenecker writes: 'In our view, Hans Dieter Betz has gone a long way toward resolving this dilemma in proposing that 2:15–21 is in reality the *propositio* of Galatians, which "sums up the *narratio's* material content" and "sets up the arguments to be discussed later in the *probatio*"'.[85] Again mentioning Betz, he adds that the argument of 2.15–21 becomes clear when read in the light of instruction offered

---

[77] Chrysostom, *Galatians*, on 1.10 (NPNF 1st 13: 9).
[78] Though surely BAGD errs in including no reference to a forensic use of the verb or noun; see *in loc.*
[79] Plato, *Republic* 3.6.392d.
[80] Plutarch, *Moralia*, 'Table Talk 7' 8.711c (in LCL Plutarch, *Moralia*, vol. IX).
[81] Lightfoot, *Galatians*, 65.
[82] Cosgrove, *Cross and Spirit*, 121.
[83] Betz, *Galatians*, 58–112; Kennedy, *New Testament Interpretation*, 148.
[84] Hall ('Rhetorical Outline', 286–87) also extends the 'narration' to 2.21.
[85] Longenecker, *Galatians*, 80, citing Betz, *Galatians*, 114. On the *propositio* see Quintilian, *Institutio* 4.4.1–5.28; Cicero, *De Inventione* 1.22.31–23.33; *Rhetorica ad*

by Aristotle and others concerning the 'nature and function of a *propositio*', prompting the conclusion that although Galatians may at points differ from the apologetic letter, the first two chapters and part of the third conform to the genre. 'In particular, 2:15–21 should be seen as Paul's *propositio*'.[86]

Betz describes the *propositio* as that which follows on the heels of the completed *narratio* and 'sums up the *narratio's* material content'. It is, however, distinct from the *narratio*, and exists to prepare the audience for the arguments of the *probatio*.

> The points of presumed agreement are set forth first (2:15–16). This passage is a summary of the doctrine of justification by faith . . . The summary is made to appear as the logical conclusion one would draw from the *narratio* as a whole. Verses 17–18 contain the point of disagreement. Here especially language from the opposition is borrowed. Verses 19–20 contain the exposition in the form of four theological theses, to be elaborated upon later. Verse 21 concludes with a *refutatio*, a sharp denial of a charge. Paul does not use *partitio* or *enumeratio* because there is only one point against which the whole defense has to be made (2:17). The *propositio* is extremely concise and consists of largely dogmatic abbreviations, i.e. very short formulaic summaries of doctrines.[87]

But this description blurs categories until it no longer conforms to the handbooks. First, if the summary is the logical conclusion drawn from the *narratio*, then according to Betz's reading of previous portions of Galatians, 2.15–21 ought to 'set up' the argument that Paul's gospel is not from men. This notion, however, has no prominence in these verses.

Second, Betz denies that Paul uses '*partitio* or *enumeratio* because there is only one point against which the whole defense has to be made'. This seems to oppose the actual text of *Rhetorica ad Herennium*: 'The Distribution has two points: The Enumeration and the Exposition. We shall be using the Enumeration when we tell by number how many points we are going to discuss. The number ought not to exceed three . . . The Exposition consists in

---

Herennium 1.10.17; Volkmann, *Rhetorik*, §15; Lausberg, *Handbuch*, §346; Martin, *Rhetorik*, 91–5. Aristotle and *Rhetorica ad Alexandrum* do not discuss it.

[86] Longenecker, *Galatians*, 81–2.

[87] Betz, *Galatians*, 114.

setting forth, briefly and completely, the points we intend to discuss'.[88] At least in this source, exposition clings to enumeration. Thus, if one says 'in what follows I shall argue three points', the exposition is a list of those points. Betz admits that there is no enumeration – and there obviously is not – so he is forced to conclude that only one point is argued: 2.17. But, if 2.17 is that point then verses 19–20 cannot be an exposition of four points to be unfolded in the remainder of Galatians. That would put verses 19–20 in competition with verse 17.[89]

Third, Cicero in *De Inventione* calls the *propositio* the *partitio* and describes its task as setting out points of agreement and disagreement.[90] Quintilian, in his much longer discussion, speaks of *partitio* as a subset of the *propositio*, describing it thus: '*Partition* may be defined as the enumeration in order of our own *propositions*, those of the adversary or both'.[91] Betz, who observes in his commentary that Cicero has adopted a different name for the same portion, claims that though Paul omits the *partitio*, he does provide points of agreement (2.15–16) and disagreement (2.17–18).[92] He cites Cicero's description of a *partitio* which consecutively sets forth points of discussion, but then follows Quintilian to argue that 'Paul doesn't use *partitio* or *enumeratio* because there is only one point against which the whole defense has to be made (2:17)'.[93] This requires that chapters 3 to 6, or at least 3 to 4, argue a single point. But while the notion that Christ is not a minister of sin would appear to be that point, it is not the one introduced in the *exordium* and *narratio*, nor is it defended in what follows.[94]

Consequently Betz needs to handle 2.17 with great care: he writes, 'The disagreement does not pertain to the doctrine of the justification by faith for the Jewish Christians, but to the implications of that doctrine for Gentile Christians. This means, of course, that the entire doctrine of justification by faith in Jesus Christ is at stake. In Paul's view, the implications of this doctrine show what

---

[88] *Rhetorica ad Herennium* 1.10.17.

[89] Dunn (*Galatians*, 132) agrees that 2.15–21 plays the role of *propositio* as summary and transition – though he rejects the notion of four theses to be expanded.

[90] Cicero, *De Inventione* 1.22.31.

[91] Quintilian, *Institutio* 4.5.1.

[92] Betz, *Galatians*, 114, n. 10.

[93] Ibid., 114. Cf. Quintilian, *Institutio* 4.5.8.

[94] Hall, following similar logic, insists that these verses do not support the main thesis: that 'Paul founded the Galatian church rightly', thus 1.6–9, which do introduce this theme, are the *propositio*: cf. 'Rhetorical Outline', 283–6.

the doctrine itself means'.[95] In this way Betz transcends any restrictions imposed by the content of Paul's words as the one point which summarizes the argument of the epistle. But can 2.17 constitute the single point argued throughout the remainder of Galatians, or even embody the entire gospel of justification by faith? 'But if seeking to be justified in Christ we ourselves have also been found to be sinners, does Christ then serve sin? μὴ γένοιτο!' Neither suggestion has previously marked discussion of this verse, yet the purpose of the *propositio* is to define the case to be proven. Absolute transparency is vital when defining the issue of a court-room speech; the handbooks recommend raising all possible sign-posts: even entry into various parts of the speech is explicitly stated. Cicero's description begins:

> In an argument a partition correctly made renders the whole speech clear and perspicuous. It takes two forms, both of which greatly contribute to clarifying the case and determining the nature of the controversy. One form shows in what we agree with our opponents and what is left in dispute; as a result of this some definite problem is set for the auditor on which he ought to have his attention fixed. In the second form the matters which we intend to discuss are briefly set forth in a methodical way. This leads the auditor to hold definite points in his mind, and to under-stand that when these have been discussed the oration will be over.[96]

So then, the *propositio* exists only to state clearly, concisely and in order, that is, unmistakably, what is being argued. Quintilian provides this example: 'I understand, gentlemen, that the accusa-tion falls into three parts, the first aspersing my client's character, the second dealing with his candidature for the magistracy, and the third with the charges of bribery'.[97] The requisite transparency is evident, but Paul provides nothing like this. Either Paul is an ineffective rhetor or 2.17 functions otherwise.[98]

---

[95] Betz, *Galatians*, 119.

[96] Cicero, *De Inventione* 1.22.31.

[97] Quintilian, *Institutio* 4.5.12, citing Cicero's *Pro Murena* 5.11.

[98] It would appear that at least some of the confusion is caused by a blending of terms. Betz (*Galatians*, 114 and n. 10) writes that *propositio* is Quintilian's term, while Cicero calls the same element the *partitio*, and *ad Herennium* the *divisio*. This gives the correct impression that Cicero means by *partitio* what Quintilian and Betz call the *propositio*. But then Betz says that Paul does not use *partitio*. The explanation

To conclude our discussion of chapters 1 to 2, we note that there is little evidence that Paul reflects the advice of the handbooks. He does argue by way of narrative, but his words neither conform to the *narratio* of the handbook, nor introduce the arguments which occupy the remainder of Galatians. They, like the whole of the two chapters, present arguments which are intended to instruct and persuade – not to serve as the preliminaries of a case. Furthermore, he never provides the sort of structural guideposts recommended by the handbooks in their discussion of the *exordium* and the *propositio*. In this, Galatians resembles Paul's epistolary style as a whole, of which Dahl writes: 'In order to follow the flow of thought in the Pauline letters, one should pay more attention to thematic statements, gradual transitions and "ring compositions" than to the division into chapter and verse or to headings and systematized outlines.'[99] The divisions are often hard to identify precisely because Paul does not flag them in the manner of the orators.

Galatians 3–4

Betz introduces chapters 3 and 4 by confessing that rhetorical description is elusive since 'Quintilian instructs to diversify by a thousand devices'.[100] He labels these chapters the *probatio* – the proof. It is not readily apparent, however, how 3 to 4 connect with the arguments presented earlier, for they fail to prove the proposal pushed to the fore in chapters 1 to 2. Our discussion of the *propositio* revealed that Betz defines the issue to be proved in a rather peculiar way; furthermore, chapters 3 and 4 do not argue the point he claims is set forth in 2.15–21 as the single issue of the trial.

The rhetorical devices which he finds in chapters 3 and 4 are: (1) interrogation in 3.1–5;[101] (2) Abraham as an example in 3.6–14;[102] and (3) analogy by comparison to a contract in 3.15–18.[103] By the

---

is that these terms are not entirely synonymous, for to Cicero the latter is one of the main portions of the speech, while Quintilian views it as a function of a subset of the *propositio*.

[99] Dahl, 'Missionary Theology', 79. J. Barclay takes Dahl to mean that Paul himself does not supply the headings and subdivisions: cf. *Obeying the Truth*, 149 and n. 1.

[100] Betz, *Galatians*, 129, depending on Quintilian, *Institutio* 5.14.27–35. Longenecker (*Galatians*, cxi) calls this 'a somewhat thin and rather desperate justification for keeping Galatians 3 within the bounds of classical rhetoric'.

[101] Betz, *Galatians*, 130.

[102] Ibid., 137.

[103] Ibid., 154.

time he has reached 3.26 his attention has shifted away from
classical rhetoric to Christian, focusing now on structure and
composition and finding a Christian baptismal liturgy in 3.26–9.[104]
Although in Betz's scheme 4.1–7 discusses 3.26–9,[105] none of the
footnotes relates to rhetoric except one which observes a pronom-
inal change, and says it 'may be a rhetorical device of the diatribe
style'.[106]

Furthermore, as has been observed by Paul Meyer, imposing
rhetorical categories on these arguments robs the unit of its
cohesiveness. 'When "thus" [καθὼς] in 3:6 is transformed into "as
[it is written]" (137), the link with the preceding [verse] is broken. In
Galatians 3, Betz makes vs. 11a follow from 10, whereas Paul's
syntax makes it follow from 11b (146)'.[107] And surely 4.1–7 is not
the explanation of 3.26–9, but resumes the line briefly left at the
end of 3.24.[108] In fact, so closely is 4.1–7 linked to 3.23–6 that a
reading which excludes 3.27–9 loses little of the immediate argument (though its omission leaves arguments introduced in 3.6–9
and 16 incomplete).

Section 4.12–20 is labelled the fifth argument.[109] Although
discussion of this part again refers seldom to rhetorical convention,[110] Betz does note:

> What Paul offers in the section is a string of topoi
> belonging to the theme of 'friendship' (περὶ φιλίας). This
> theme was famous in antiquity, as the large number of
> works on 'friendship', many of which are extant, demon-
> strate. By the time of Paul, the subject was treated also in
> the diatribe literature and in epistles. In the epistolary
> literature it was even a standard topic.[111]

This reference to diatribe introduces an issue which is closely
related to discussion of classical rhetoric. Although space constraints forbid a full discussion of the relationship of rhetoric to
diatribe, a few words are in order.

First, Betz fairly consistently bases his understanding of rhetoric

[104] Ibid., 181–5.
[105] Ibid., 202.
[106] Ibid., 211, n. 96.
[107] Meyer, 'Review', 319.
[108] Ibid.
[109] Betz, *Galatians*, 220.
[110] Ibid., 221–37.
[111] Ibid., 221.

on handbook descriptions, yet the classical handbooks he depends on offer no detailed discussion of diatribe.[112] This is because they represent two different sorts of rhetoric. If we define level 4 rhetoric as a codification of communicative techniques aimed at a specific venue (so that Aristotle primarily discusses speeches in court or the assembly) then it is clear why diatribe is omitted from their discussion: it is not the oratory of the court, the forum or the public gathering. Although more work remains to be done, Stowers has presented the most compelling explanation, linking diatribe to the classroom.[113]

Second, Aune further explains that 'the diatribe style must, it appears, be regarded as a popular style (a characteristic vehicle of popular Hellenistic moral philosophy) which was in some sense antithetical to the concerns and practices of the major rhetorical schools and traditions.[114] The fact that Paul does utilize the diatribe style flies in the face of Betz's designation of him as a "skilled rhetorician"'.[115] If the rhetorical handbooks do not provide us with a source for diatribe, we must look elsewhere; often it is called 'Cynic–Stoic diatribe', but neither Cynics nor Stoics epitomize handbook rhetoric in the ancient world.[116] Marrou describes philosophy as a 'minority culture' within a larger culture which was 'literary, rhetorical and aesthetic', and suggests that each culture was intolerant of the other.[117]

Thus we conclude with Aune that the presence of diatribe does not support Betz's form of 'rhetorical' reading of Galatians, and add that NT studies need to exercise greater caution when defining rhetoric. A host of level 4 rhetorics was available in Paul's day, even as today, only one of which was Aristotelian oratory.

The so-called sixth argument, in 4.21–31, is also expounded apart from classical insights, rhetoric's only task being to explain

---

[112] I have been unable to find any discussion of diatribe in the handbooks; so also Watson, 'Diatribe', 213.

[113] Stowers, *Diatribe and Romans*, 48–78; Watson, 'Diatribe', 213.

[114] Cf. Gottschalk, 'Diatribe Again', 91. He adds (p. 92) that diatribes are 'lectures on ethics, in an informal style using simple, even homely, language; the audience is frequently addressed directly and there are some passages of "dialogue" with an imaginary partner (not always opponent)'. So also Capelle and Marrou, 'Diatribe', 998. Cf. Jocelyn, 'Diatribe', 89–91who recognizes this cluster of attributes but denies that they form a distinct genre.

[115] Aune, 'Review of Betz's *Galatians*', 325.

[116] Watson, 'Diatribe', 213.

[117] Marrou, *History of Education*, 206, 210. He detects traces of this antagonism down to the twelfth century.

why this argument comes last.[118] It seems that though Quintilian says not to end with a weak argument (and allegory can be weak because of its ambiguity), Pseudo-Demetrius is more informative in allowing that 'any darkly-hinting expression is more terror-striking', for 'things clear and plain are apt to be disdained'.[119] This competition among handbooks well illustrates the danger of eclecticism: Paul's words are either weak or terror-striking, but not both. When scholarship can choose between conflicting advice without a clear rationale for that choice, it raises the question of whether the options have any value at all until after the discourse in question is shown to conform to a given handbook's instructions. The ability of either of these sources to explain the order of this last argument is doubtful. Indeed, the more important question must be whether the arguments Paul uses are effective: that is, would we gain greater insight into Paul's rhetoric, or even early Christian rhetoric generally, if we avoided this preoccupation with handbook rhetoric and restricted our focus to Galatians?

We have seen that for the proof, chapters 3 and 4, the only substantive contributions of rhetoric are to reveal that 3.1–5 contains an interrogation, that Abraham is an example, and that a contract analogy exists in 3.15–18.[120] None of this had gone unnoticed apart from rhetoric. In fact, dealing with 3.1–5 and its interrogation of the witnesses seemed more natural before rhetorical criticism suggested that the jury was being interrogated. Weaknesses such as this prompt Hansen to suggest that 'Forensic rhetoric must therefore be judged to be too narrow a category to encompass adequately Paul's eclectic use of a wide variety of rhetorical features'.[121] This expansion into level 4 rhetorics beyond Aristotelian forensic speech is vital to understanding Galatians.

Galatians 5–6

Galatians, in typical Pauline fashion, provides paraenesis after doctrine. Scholarship has differed, however, on where that paraenesis begins and even its role in the epistle, so any method claiming

---

[118] Betz, *Galatians*, 238–52.

[119] Ibid., 239–40.

[120] Longenecker (*Galatians*, cxi) also acknowledges that rhetoric cannot contribute much.

[121] Hansen, *Abraham in Galatians*, 70.

to solve this structural conundrum deserves a full hearing.[122] Barrett holds that at this very point rhetorical analysis shows its real worth, for it takes us beyond the impasse which compelled Ropes to propose that Paul was waging a war on two fronts.[123] Others have been less sympathetic to finding in these chapters an element of classical rhetoric.

Betz begins his discussion of this portion with a concession: 'it is rather puzzling to see that paraenesis plays only a marginal role in the ancient rhetorical handbooks, if not in rhetoric itself'.[124] Naturally this has not gone unnoticed. Betz's critics, however, might rightly go further and say that rhetorical handbooks are *not at all* concerned with paraenesis. Joop Smit for this reason proposes that since Galatians is a speech, 5.13–6.10 must be a later addition.[125] Furthermore, for a third of a courtroom speech to exhort the jury to good works is simply inconceivable.

Our discussion of the species of Galatians will demonstrate that classical rhetoric's failure to explain the presence of paraenesis in judicial oratory is a prime impetus behind Kennedy's proposal that Galatians is deliberative oratory. But these other proposals prove at least as problematic.[126] The shortcomings of rhetorical categories are manifest not only in criticism of Betz's reconstruction, but also in the ongoing search for the purpose and shape of this section. Disagreement concerning the commencement of paraenesis is widespread. Highly influential is Otto Merk's article arguing that it

---

[122] The essential article is by Merk, who provides bibliographies for the various views concerning the beginning of the exhortation ('Paränese im Galaterbrief', 84). The proposals range from 4.12 to 5.13. Discussions after Merk's break down as follows. Longenecker defends 4.12 because it contains the first imperative of the letter (*Galatians*, 186).

For 5.13 see Oepke, *Galater*, 165–7; Mussner, *Galaterbrief*, 364–6; Hübner, 'Galaterbrief', 5; Barclay, *Obeying the Truth*, chapter 1; Fung, *Galatians*, v–viii; Lührmann (*Galatians*, 100–2), who denies that this section conforms to Paul's normal ethical exhortation; Matera, *Galatians*, 193–4; Dunn, *Galatians*, 261.

For 5.1 see Bonnard, *Galates*, 101; Hull, 'Teaching Outline of Galatians', 429–30; Montgomery, 'Galatians', 432; Brinsmead, *Dialogical Response*, 53–4; Osiek, *Galatians*, 1; Getty, *Galatians and Romans*, 37; Pilch, 'Galatians', 6; Ebeling, *Truth of the Gospel*, 239–40; Barrett, *Freedom and Obligation*, 3; Rohde, *Galater*, vii–viii; Longenecker, *Galatians*, 221–2; Thompson, 'Teaching/Paraenesis', 922.

For 5.2 see Bruce, *Galatians*, 228; Cousar, *Galatians*, 111.

For 4.31 see Cosgrove, *Cross and Spirit*, 147–8.

[123] Barrett, 'Apologetic Letter', 416.

[124] Betz, *Galatians*, 254.

[125] Smit, 'Deliberative Speech', 8–9, 25–6.

[126] See chapter 5, especially on Kennedy.

actually begins not with Galatians 5.1 but 5.13.[127] Bligh binds all of
4.31–5.13 to the incident at Antioch, suggesting that it originally
appeared in Paul's debate with Peter though as an earlier recension.
This leans on similarities between 2.14–3.4 and 4.31–5.13.[128]

Frank Matera suggests that simply labelling this portion 'paraenesis' is too restrictive since 5.1–6.17 functions as a unified
climax to Paul's argument.[129] He emphasizes the continuity of
this portion with the preceding theological arguments, highlighting the reality that circumcision is only acknowledged, not
treated, in the first four chapters.[130] Dunn, however, is probably
right to criticize Matera for overlooking the broad parallels
between 5.1–12 and 6.11–17, which 'serve more to underline the
climactic character' of 5.1–12.[131] Primary is the observation,
which Matera himself has made, that circumcision is discussed
mainly in two places: 5.1–12 and 6.11–17. Clearly more work
needs to be done.[132]

Only at 6.11–18 does Betz return to categories described in the
handbooks. Concerning these verses he writes:

> As a rhetorical feature, the postscript of Galatians serves
> as the *peroratio* or *conclusio*, that is, the end and conclusion
> of the apologetic speech forming the body of the letter. The
> general purpose of the *peroratio* is twofold: it serves as a
> last chance to remind the judge or the audience of the case
> and it tries to make a strong emotional impression upon
> them. The three conventional parts of the *peroratio* carry
> out this task: the *enumeratio* or *recapitulatio*
> (ἀνακεφαλαίωσις) sharpens and sums up the main points
> of the case, the *indignatio* arouses anger and hostility
> among the opponents, and the *conquestio* stimulates pity.
> In an actual case, the *peroratio* can, of course, take many
> different forms, but it must conform to the case at issue,
> and it must be concise. It also must be clearly related to the
> individual parts of the speech, especially to the *exor-
> dium*.[133]

127 Merk, 'Paränese im Galaterbrief', 83–104.
128 Bligh, *Galatians*, 414–16.
129 Matera, 'Culmination', 79–91.
130 Ibid., 79.
131 Dunn, *Galatians*, 261.
132 Ibid.
133 Betz, *Galatians*, 313.

Although these verses do sum up and recapitulate, this proves little concerning Galatians' relationship to classical rhetoric. Does not all good didactic material conclude with a brief recapitulation?[134] The sort of generalization found in this discussion of *peroratio* cannot clarify 6.11–18 more than the thematic treatments found, for example, in Lightfoot. Indeed, Galatians again corresponds to epistolary material to at least the same degree as rhetorical – though Paul's mention of handwriting (Gal. 6.11) tips the scales in favour of identifying Galatians as a letter.

Furthermore, Betz quotes his source in full to support the notion that the *enumeratio* functions this way. It reads:

> There are two kinds of peroration, for it may deal either with facts or with the emotional aspect of the case. The repetition and grouping of the facts, which the Greeks call ἀνακεφαλαίωσις and some of our writers call the enumeration, serves both to refresh the memory of the judge and to place the whole of the case before his eyes, and even though the facts may have little impression on him in detail, their cumulative effect is considerable. The final recapitulation must be as brief as possible and, as the Greek indicates, we must summarize the facts under the appropriate heads.[135]

This differs from Betz's expression of the *peroratio*'s purpose; he ascribes 'three conventional parts' to the *peroratio* which are actually subsumed by Quintilian under two headings: (1) 'the *enumeratio* or *recapitulatio* sharpens and sums up the main points of the case'; and (2) arousal of anger and moving to pity relate to 'the emotional aspects of the case'. Thus Quintilian describes a part of speech which may 'deal *either* with facts or with the emotional aspect of the case'.[136] Alternative functions of two distinct types of *peroratio* have been merged in Betz's description.

This is legitimate for certain speeches, for Quintilian goes on to state that 'private cases also admit of both kinds of peroration, namely, that which consists in the recapitulation of the proofs and that which takes the form of an appeal to pity, the latter being employed when the position or reputation of the litigant seems to

---

[134] White (*Body of the Greek Letter*, 47) includes recapitulation among the roles of an epistolary 'superscription'.
[135] Betz, *Galatians*, 313, quoting Quintilian, *Institutio* 6.1.1–2.
[136] Ibid. 6.1.1.

be in danger'.[137] At first glance it appears that this conforms quite nicely to the situation in Galatia; it does not, however, hold up to scrutiny. Betz maintains that these verses are polemical until 6.17, which he says 'although reduced to a minimum . . . does have the appearance of a *conquestio* [that part which provokes pity]'.[138] Quintilian adduces an example from Cicero which appeals to a defendant's 'worth, his manly pursuits, the scars from wounds received in battle', though Quintilian's full statement is: 'If we turn to the defendant, we must note that his worth, his manly pursuits, the scars from wounds received in battle, his rank and the services rendered by his ancestors will all commend him to the good-will of the judges'.[139] But it is not immediately clear that Cicero's pointing to the long list of accomplishments, including battle-wounds, carries the same tone or sparks the same emotions as Paul's injunction not to trouble him since he bears scars. The latter command, immediately after a pronouncement of blessing on those who accept his message, may even sound more like a threat from a position of strength than a plea (cf. Gal. 4.16, 20 which also imply a position of strength). At least as far back as 5.7 ('you were running well; who hindered you from obeying the truth?'), Paul's more personal words partake of the vigour of his didactic portion; they do not aim to provoke pity but instead betray apostolic confidence.[140] Paul is at last fully on the offensive and exercises his authority to lay down rules even while offering encouragement to the faint. In 6.6 he even hands out instruction concerning the payment of teachers. Whether he includes himself in that camp or not, it would be an audacious piece of instruction from one who in just a moment must become submissive and pitiable.[141] Betz is thus right to observe that these verses only appear to fulfil this function 'if we are anticipating the *conquestio*'.[142] But were the Galatians expecting one? Has anyone before Betz?

[137] Ibid. 6.1.36.
[138] Betz, *Galatians*, 323.
[139] Quintilian, *Institutio* 6.1.21.
[140] Stirewalt (in an unpublished paper delivered to the SBL Paul Seminar [1974]) goes as far back as 5.2, which, he maintains, is the authoritative decision (of an official letter) handed down by Paul to the Galatians via a delegation they sent to ask about circumcision: cf. 'Official Letter Writing and the Letter of Paul to the Churches of Galatia', 34–5.
[141] Schütz (*Apostolic Authority*, 114–15) demonstrates that even the narrative of Galatians is not defensive but offensive. So also Lyons, *Pauline Autobiography*, 83–95, 136–76; Gaventa, 'Autobiography as Paradigm', 304–26.
[142] Betz, *Galatians*, 323.

Even if Paul's audience had in the process of digesting the letter begun to project themselves into the role of a jury listening to a judicial speech (or any speech for that matter) the illusion is smashed in this portion. For Paul has in 6.11 foregrounded the fact that he is not delivering a speech but is *writing* a letter. Had he said something like 'notice my tone', as alluded to in 4.20, the possibility of oratorical illusion could have been maintained, but instead he refers to the ink-covered page – 'see with what large letters'. This is, of course, a common feature of Paul's letters, and as Betz indicates, serves to authenticate the epistle.[143]

Betz further writes, 'Seen as a rhetorical feature, the *peroratio* becomes most important for the interpretation of Galatians. It contains the interpretive clues to the understanding of Paul's major concerns in the letter as a whole and should be employed as the hermeneutical key to the intentions of the Apostle'.[144] But why is this so? Should not the *propositio*'s clear statement of intent provide these clues? Difficulties arise if the last words of Galatians provide the 'interpretive clues' and 'hermeneutical key' to all of the epistle, for if Paul is presenting essentially oral material, it is important that determinative elements such as these stand at the beginning, not the end. Speeches unfold in a linear fashion and must accordingly create a sense of direction at the outset.[145] While on occasion this procedure can be distorted to great effect by reorienting the whole speech at the conclusion, this effect can only be achieved if it is unusual and therefore unexpected. The clues and keys to a speech are normally at or near the beginning: the *exordium* and *propositio* should establish them.

This again raises that same dilemma: What is the point to be argued throughout Galatians? Section 1.11–12 suggests a different theme for the epistle from 2.15–21; and chapters 3 to 4 argue something different again. Which of these is summarized and therefore seen as the intent of the speech as a whole? Kennedy argues that 'what Paul thinks he has demonstrated to the Galatians is not that they should alter their judgment of him, but that "neither circumcision counts for anything nor uncircumcision, but a new creation"'.[146] While this motif underpins

---

[143] Ibid., 314. Cf. 1 Cor. 16.21; 2 Cor. 13.10; Col. 4.18; 2 Th. 3.17.

[144] Betz, ibid., 313.

[145] Kennedy, *New Testament Interpretation*, 146. See my discussion of species in chapter 5 (esp. concerning Kennedy).

[146] Kennedy, *New Testament Interpretation*, 151.

Galatians, it is not the explicitly stated and expounded theme of the letter. Thus the persuasive techniques detailed in the rhetorical handbooks are found in neither Gal. 6.11–18, nor in Gal. 5–6 as a whole. A great deal remains to be discovered concerning these two chapters, but it is doubtful that the handbooks can contribute much.

Conclusion

Describing the structure of Galatians as 'rhetorical' again appears suspect. Not only does rhetorical analysis fail to produce agreement concerning the outline, but even more, the epistle does not conform to the descriptions culled from the handbooks. Considering two outlines of Galatians which antedate Betz's commentary may prove helpful.

J. B. Lightfoot (1896)

 I. Personal, chiefly in the form of a narrative. 1.1–2.21
   1. salutation and ascription of praise so worded as to introduce the main subject of the letter 1.1–5
   2. rebuke 1.6–10
   3. 'This Gospel came directly from God' 1.11–21
 II. Doctrinal, mostly argumentative. 3.1–4.31
III. Hortatory. Practical Applications injunctions 5.1–6.10
    conclusion 6.11–18.[147]

E. D. W. Burton (1921)

 I. Introduction. 1.1–10
   1. salutation and assertion of authority. 1.1–5
   2. expression of indignant surprise. 1.6–10
 II. Personal portion of the letter
'The general theme established by proving the apostle's independence of all human authority and direct relation to Christ'. 1.11–2.21
   1. proposition: 1.11–12
   2. evidence substantiating the preceding assertion . . . 1.13–2.21
III. Refutatory Portion of the Letter. 3–4
 IV. Hortatory Portion of the Letter. 5.1–6.10
   1. Exhortations directly connected with the doctrine of the letter. 5.1–6.5
   2. Exhortations having less direct relation to the principal subject of the epistle. 6.6–10
  V. Conclusion of the letter. 6.11–18.[148]

---

[147] Lightfoot, *Galatians*, 65–7.
[148] Burton, *Galatians*, lxxii–lxxiv.

These outlines not only resemble one another, they also share much with rhetorical outlines. With the notable exception of the paraenesis, Galatians yields a rather straightforward structure – but to the resolution of this one difficulty the handbooks contribute nothing. It seems that the most the handbooks can offer when adapted for description rather than prescription is a proposal of function for each of the various parts of a speech; but before they can describe these functions the analyst must first identify the sections – which is done by comparing the handbook descriptions to the shape of the parts of Galatians. Unfortunately, these shapes do not correspond to the handbooks' descriptions, thus begging the question of what the handbooks can contribute when analysis turns from shape to function; logic seems to suggest that they can, in fact, add little. We now turn from attempts to classify the individual parts of Galatians to a consideration of the letter as a whole.

5

RHETORICAL SPECIES AND GALATIANS

The third chapter of Aristotle's *Rhetoric* introduces three 'kinds of rhetoric . . . corresponding to the three kinds of hearers'(1.3.1),[1] a scheme which springs from the notion that the speaker, the issue and the hearer all exert a force upon the speech. Each of the three species[2] (this division was accepted by subsequent handbooks) can be understood according to its effect on the hearer (its purpose) and its temporal distinctives.[3] The first type, judicial (or forensic [δικανικόν, *iudiciale*]), represents the rhetoric of the law-courts addressed to a judge or jury (ὅ δικαστής; 1.3.2),[4] the purpose of the 'litigant' (1.3.3) being to defend or accuse concerning a past action (1.3.4). Its stated end (τέλος) is the just or the unjust (*Rhetoric* 1.3.5).[5]

Deliberative (συμβουλευτικόν, *deliberativum*)[6] or parliamentary

[1] It is widely held that Isocrates first spoke in terms of the three species. See Solmsen, 'Aristotelian Tradition', 35–50, 169–90; Perelman and Olbrechts-Tyteca, *The New Rhetoric*, 21; Atkins (*Literary Criticism in Antiquity*, 132) suggests that Lysias was in fact first. Anaximenes (see Quintilian, *Institutio*, 3.4.9) referred to only two types – deliberative and forensic. Clearly he did not intend these two to include all discourse.

[2] Most ancient writers followed the definitions offered by Aristotle. See Kennedy, *New Testament Interpretation*, 19.

[3] Cf. also *Rhetorica ad Herennium* 1.2.2; Cicero, *De Inventione* 1.5.7; *Topica* 23.91; *De Partitione Oratoria* 3.10; Quintilian, *Institutio Oratoria* 2.21.23, 3.3–4. For the secondary literature, see especially Martin, *Antike Rhetorik*, 177–210; Kennedy, *Persuasion in Greece*, 152–203; *Rhetoric in the Roman World*, 17–23; Lausberg, *Handbuch*, 1:51–61.§53–65. Hinks, 'Tria Genera Causarum', 170–6; Perelman and Olbrechts-Tyteca, *The New Rhetoric*, 21. Cf. also Hughes, *Early Christian Rhetoric*, 30–3.

[4] The Roman system often included preliminary proceedings held before a magistrate. Cf. Caplan, ed. *Rhetorica ad Herennium* 1.12.22, n. a (LCL). See also Cicero, *De Partitione Oratoria* 4.11.

[5] Cf. Pseudo-Cicero, *Rhetorica ad Herennium* 1.2.1: 'The judicial is based on legal controversy, and comprises criminal prosecution or civil suit, and defence'.

[6] In *Rhetorica ad Alexandrum* deliberative is called δημηγορικόν, which Rackham translates 'parliamentary' for the Loeb volume (see 1421b). Cf. Cicero, *De Partitione Oratoria*, 4.11.

oratory aims to exhort or dissuade the assembly concerning some *future* action,[7] persuading the audience to embark on an expedient course or to avoid a harmful one (the τέλος of deliberative: *Rhetoric* 1.3.5). This is later specified as 'the discussion of policy'.[8]

Epideictic (demonstrative, ἐπιδεικτόν,[9] *demonstrativum*, panegyric), the oratory of praise or blame (*Rhetoric* 1.3.3), focuses on the present ('for it is the existing condition of things that all those who praise or blame have in view' 1.3.4), though Aristotle adds 'It is not uncommon . . . for the epideictic speakers to avail themselves of other times, of the past by way of recalling it, or the future by way of anticipating it' (1.3.4). The handbooks report that epideictic treats the honourable and disgraceful (1.3.5), its purpose reduced to winning acclaim for the speaker from an audience of spectators (θεωροί) who delight in the artistry of the speech. Aristotle writes that unlike the two other species, epideictic gives no thought to persuading an arbiter since controversy is lacking;[10] but this does not deny that praise and blame perform a practical function.[11] In fact, this species does not step outside the political/legal realm of the first two: 'For there is no class of oratory', writes Cicero of panegyric, 'capable of producing more copious rhetoric or of doing more service to the state'.[12]

Although NT specialists often recognize that pinpointing species necessarily relies on conclusions derived from a combination of function, temporal distinctives and ends, they sometimes fail to observe that species cannot be addressed from an Aristotelian perspective without discussing the particular audience posited for each type of speech (and the arguments perceived to be most effective in light of that audience).[13] All three elements – function, time and audience – are sculptors manipulating the clay which

[7] Cicero, *De Partitione Oratoria* 3.10. But compare Aristotle, *Rhetoric* 1.8.7: 'We have now stated what things, whether future or present (ἐσομένων ἢ ὄντων), should be the aim of those who recommend a certain course'; and 1.6.1: 'It is evident then, what things, likely to happen or alreading existing (ἐσομένων ἢ ὑπαρχόντων), the orator should aim at, when exhorting, and what when dissuading'.

[8] *Rhetorica ad Herennium* 1.2.1. Much can be learned about deliberative speech generally and its application to 1 Corinthians from Mitchell, *Rhetoric of Reconciliation*, 20–64.

[9] ἐπιδεικτικόν in *Rhetorica ad Alexandrum*.

[10] Aristotle, *Rhetoric* 2.18.1 – the spectator is cast in the role of judge. Cf. also *Rhetorica ad Alexandrum* 1440b, 13; Cicero, *De Partitione Oratoria* 21.71. See Johanson (*To All the Brethren*, 40) for discussion.

[11] Quintilian, *Institutio* 3.7.1.

[12] Cicero, *De Partitione Oratoria* 20.69.

[13] Johanson, *To All the Brethren*, 40.

becomes the speech, for their totality constitutes the context.[14] The first type then, the judicial, *defends or accuses* concerning some *past* action before a *judge* (or jury), the three elements teaming together to shape the event. The issues appropriate to forensic speech are conjectural (i.e. not hinging on technical legal matters but on how an event happened), legal and judicial – all with clear links to the courts.[15] Thus to declare a discourse forensic because it defends or accuses concerning a past event – apart from a judge or jury – falls short of classical definitions. And to prove that a given text accuses or defends may link it to a sort of forensic rhetoric, but not necessarily the sort discussed in the handbooks. Likewise a deliberative speech has three elements – the third being the senate or forum which must choose whether to accept or reject the proposed course.[16]

In fact, one could argue that audience deserves pride of place since instances of forensic oratory focused on a *future* event exist, including so-called 'right to die' cases and legal disputes over the termination of a pregnancy. No valid conception of rhetoric would deny that law-court speeches related to such matters are forensic because they do not fix on a past event. Thus it is the fact of the judge and jury, the legal matter, and the appearance in a court that labels such speeches forensic, not merely their temporal focus.

So all three elements establish a frame[17] within which 'classical rhetoric' must be understood, for Johanson correctly insists that 'Aristotle's classification was an attempt to cover the existing fields of oratory of his day and consequently it can only be defended from those circumstances'.[18] This induces him to state what exactly is missing from much recent discussion of species: 'regarding the forensic and deliberative genres, these must be seen as rooted in the political and judicial types of rhetorical contexts of his time. As such, they will only be useful in categorising speeches that reflect

[14] Lausberg, *Elemente*, 21–3; Consigny, 'Rhetoric and its Situations', 175–86; Brinton, 'Situation in Rhetoric', 234–48; McGuire, 'Structural Study', 1–22. This last article distinguishes the particular situation from the larger historical setting.
[15] *Rhetorica ad Herennium* 1.11.18.
[16] Crucial to Aristotle's work, but less so for our present argument, are the *topoi* which are employed for the purposes of the particular species (*Rhetoric* 1.3.1–5).
[17] The term 'frame' refers to the total context within which the speech exists. Thus the frame for a forensic oration requires at least a courtroom, a judge or jury, a defendant, and prosecutor.
[18] Johanson, *To All the Brethren*, 40. Cf. Hinks, 'Tria Genera Causarum', 174; Kinneavy, *Theory of Discourse*, 227.

more or less the same types of rhetorical contexts'.[19] He further notes of epideictic that there is a 'generality of . . . audience . . . [and] varying celebrative contexts (funeral, festivals, sophistic exercises, etc.)'.[20]

The limits of the three Aristotelian species are recognized by Hugh Blair, the writer of a text on rhetoric appearing in 1783. He replaces epideictic with a new species of rhetoric which is appropriate to his age, describing the change this way: 'I have already treated the Eloquence of Popular Assemblies, and of the Eloquence of the Bar. The subject which remains for this Lecture is, the strain and spirit of that Eloquence which is suited to the Pulpit'.[21]

Blair recognized that rhetorico-social restrictions must be part of any discussion of species, a truth latent in the work of classicists and historians;[22] the rhetoricians maintained their focus – they did not merely instruct in eloquence or how to persuade, but intended to prepare men for their proper roles in a dignified legal and civic process.[23] Thus the *Rhetorica ad Herennium* asserts: 'The task of the public speaker is to discuss capably the matters which law and custom have fixed for the uses of citizenship, and to secure as far as possible the agreement of his hearers'.[24]

Education, including its exercises,[25] prepared for roles played out in legal and political arenas, and it was with the decline of opportunities provided therein that rhetoric and rhetorical education began to decline.[26] Thus, when Greek, and in turn Roman, oratory declined, many who lamented this tragedy most loudly

[19] Johanson, *To All the Brethren*, 40.

[20] Clearly epideictic roamed on a longer leash than the other species. This diversity ultimately 'led to divergence and confusion among subsequent theorists, and ultimately [epideictic] became a repository for all types of speeches and other literary forms that could not be subsumed under the other two genres'. So Johanson, *To All the Brethren*, 40.

[21] Blair, *Lectures*, 2.101, as cited in Olbricht, 'Aristotelian Rhetorical Analysis', 225, n. 53.

[22] Anton D. Leeman, president of the International Society for the History of Rhetoric, writes that Aristotle, while advancing rhetoric theoretically, 'restricted the field of activity of the orator to public meetings – the law-court, the political assembly, the ceremonial gathering' ('Variety of Classical Rhetoric', 44).

[23] On the role of rhetoric in Isocrates' thought see Hudson, 'Field of Rhetoric', 8.

[24] *Rhetorica ad Herennium* 1.2.1. Plato, *Gorgias* 454b: Oratory serves to produce 'that kind of persuasion, Socrates, which you find in the law-courts and in any public gatherings'.

[25] See especially Quintilian, *Institutio* 2.4 for discussion of exercises.

[26] M. L. Clarke, 'Quintilian on Education', 102. Though some said that rhetoric was to be learned by spending time in court, not in school. See Winterbottom, 'Quintilian and the *Vir Bonus*', 96.

were aggrieved not merely because it spelled the loss of a favoured activity, but because it reflected a decline in cherished sociopolitical arrangements, one of which was an effective democratic process.[27]

> For the outstanding fact about first-century oratory is that the only orators to achieve any prominence or influence *by means of their oratory* are the *delatores*. The rest were decorative but impotent: the *Dialogus* tells us why – education lacked touch with reality, and political conditions took away all scope.[28]

'There was room only for panegyric now [in the first years of Trajan's reign], and the driest of legal advocacy: only occasionally the spice of a trial for misdemeanours in the provinces. There was basically nothing to do in the senate.'[29] Limits on freedom of speech, centralisation of bureaucracy and the 'development of Roman law, which provided equitable solutions to many problems on the basis of formulae and precedent rather than through argument from probability, ethos, and pathos' led to restrictions on forensic rhetoric at the same time as deliberative declined.[30]

Rhetoric's links with specific contexts also contributed to a much later decline in the use of Quintilian. Muretus noted the decreasing use of the *Institutio* during his career in the sixteenth century. 'This work in the span of one generation had gone from the center to the periphery – though the reason is easily discerned: over-concern with *forensic speech* combined with excessive detail render it impractical'.[31]

---

[27] Dio Cassius, *History*, 53.19.3–4; Kennedy, *Classical Rhetoric*, 108, 111–12; Atkins, *English Literary Criticism II*, 215; Sloan and Perelman, 'Rhetoric', 10:20.

[28] Winterbottom, 'Quintilian and the *Vir Bonus*', 90–2. Talk in this passage is of oratory, of rhetors on their feet. Domitius Afer is spoken of as defender and prosecutor; the setting is the forum and the senate; participants are called 'accusers' throughout.

[29] Winterbottom, 'Quintilian and the *Vir Bonus*', 97; See also Mack, *Rhetoric and the New Testament*, 15. For a brief discussion of the effect on literature exerted by rhetoric's decline, see Kennedy, *Classical Rhetoric*, 112. He especially refers to 'Longinus', and Tacitus.

[30] Kennedy, *Classical Rhetoric*, 112. Cf. Cameron, *Christianity and Rhetoric*, 73–5.

[31] Muretus, *Variae Lectiones*, XVII.15, discussed in Clarke, 'Quintilian on Education', 114. Attention to Quintilian and his concerns is here offered as evidence of the role of the rhetor in political life. Another rhetor/rhetorician who perhaps more ably than even Quintilian illustrates the connection is Cicero. For a brief, well-paced introduction to his political life see Griffin, 'Cicero and Rome'.

Thus the decline of rhetoric argues for its restricted nature. It was so tightly bound up with politics and the courts that injury to one spelt a weakening in the other.

The limits of forensic rhetoric

Chapter 2 defended an understanding of handbook rhetoric which limits it primarily to the courts and the political assembly. We wish to supplement those observations by adding that the three species are similarly restricted, evidence for the limits of forensic rhetoric being inferred from definitions offered in the handbooks. Injustice, the stated concern of forensic, Aristotle defines as voluntarily causing injury contrary to the law (*Rhetoric* 1.10.1). Furthermore, inartificial proofs 'properly belong to forensic oratory. The proofs are five in number: laws, witnesses, contracts, tortures, oaths' (1.15.1–33). Aristotle supplies numerous illustrations, often beginning thus: 'For example, a man on trial does not always deny . . .' or '. . . a trial would be unnecessary'.[32] Illustrations of forensic speech consistently arise from court scenes.

While Aristotle probably limited his time at actual trials, Quintilian's teaching career began after years of experience in court – and did not put an end to his former profession.[33] Cicero similarly knew the cut and thrust of the forensic drama. Thus it should not surprise us that their writings have an air of reality as they locate their forensic discussion in the courts.

The limits of deliberative rhetoric

Not only forensic rhetoric works within limits; deliberative is similarly restricted. Aristotle writes:

> We have now stated what things, whether future or present, should be the aim of those who recommend a certain course; from what topics they should derive their proofs of expediency; further, the ways and means of being well equipped for dealing with the characters and institutions of each form of government, so far as was within the scope of the present occasion; for the subject has been discussed in detail in the *Politics*.[34]

[32] Aristotle, *Rhetoric* 1.3.6.
[33] Clarke, 'Quintilian on Education', 103.
[34] Aristotle, *Rhetoric* 1.8.7.

It is the 'member of the general assembly that the speaker wishes to persuade (κρίνων οἷον ἐκκλησιαστής)';[35] the subjects (topics) which deliberative treats are identified by Aristotle as ways and means, war and peace, the defence of the country, imports and exports, and legislation.[36] Even when the *Rhetorica ad Alexandrum* adds religious rituals to the list it further bonds deliberative to political matters, for it soon becomes apparent that the author is speaking of adaptations made to the civil religion.[37]

Cicero, his attention likewise fixed on the concerns of the state, writes that 'we have to discover with whom and against whom, and when and where it is in our power to employ what resources of arms and money and allies or of the things contributing to our effecting a particular result'.[38] Aristotle, with such ends in view, emphasizes types of government and the ends of each; for such knowledge is indispensable to persuading the body responsible for making decisions that determine the future of a state.[39]

The limits of epideictic rhetoric

Epideictic is paid scant attention in the handbooks, and for that reason seems to fall outside much of chapter 2's discussion concerning the narrowness of rhetoric. It also rarely works its way into studies of the NT apart from a few passages which are said to praise or blame (e.g. 1 Cor. 13)[40] – but it has appeared in studies of Galatians in revised form. It has been defined variously. Johanson asks: 'What is the basic function of epideictic? Is it the praise of beauty, the reinforcement or the gaining of adherence to traditional values, the inducement of partisanship, or the display of the luminosity of noble acts and thoughts?'[41] These purposes share

[35] Ibid., *Rhetoric* 1.3.2.

[36] Aristotle, *Rhetoric* 1.4.7. He writes not that these are the only 'subjects about which all men deliberate and deliberative orators harangue' but that they are the most important. In the same context he has already written that he will not list the subjects which are open to discussion, but that 'more than its legitimate subjects of inquiry have already been assigned to it'. He would probably include among these many biblical subjects. Cf. Pogoloff, 'Isocrates and Contemporary Hermeneutics', 347.

[37] *Rhetorica ad Alexandrum* 1423a.30–1424a.9.

[38] Cicero, *De Partitione Oratoria* 27.95.

[39] Cicero (*De Oratore* 2.82), and following him, Quintilian (*Institutio* 3.8.1), dissent, arguing that the concern is not with expediency but with what is honourable (though their frame has not changed).

[40] See Smit, 'Genre', 193–216.

[41] Johanson, *To All the Brethren*, 40, n. 210, citing respectively: Lausberg,

little with Aristotle's discussion of praise and blame for the glory of
the speaker, or the narrower definition offered in *Rhetorica ad
Herennium* that 'epideictic . . . is devoted to the praise or censure of
some particular person' (1.2.1).[42] They are abstractions derived
from speeches, not simple reiterations of the handbook prescriptions, and describe the *effect* of epideictic. Thus while Aristotle
speaks of glorifying a person or quality, Perelman sees that such
praise affirms the values making that person great – likewise the
same praise, in displaying the 'luminosity' of an act or thought,
affirms it.

By attending to the source – Perelman – in brief, the transition
from ancient epideictic to modern can be seen. He explains that in
contrast to political and forensic speeches, epideictic oratory was
unopposed speech presented to spectators. It was viewed as a sort
of game, an opportunity to display the virtuosity of the orator.
Although Aristotle had found a purpose in epideictic's concern
with beauty, such value judgements almost immediately dissolved
into interest in the beauty of the speech itself, not its subject.[43]

Perelman does not, however, leave epideictic where he finds it.
He insists first that it forms a 'central part of the art of persuasion',
and second, that 'the lack of understanding shown toward it results
from a false conception of the effects of argumentation'. Its
purpose is not to argue logically but to 'increase the intensity of
adherence to certain values, which might not be contested when
considered on their own but may nevertheless not prevail against
other values that might come into conflict with them'. The goal is
thus 'a sense of communion centered around the particular values
recognized by the audience' in pursuit of which the orator uses all
the available tools of rhetoric.[44]

Significantly, redefinition leads to wider application. From Aristotle to Cicero, epideictic was held to reflect only apparent struggles, not real ones,[45] but 'the new rhetoric' as articulated by
Perelman removes this restriction. Thus, although the tensions

---

Handbuch, 130; Perelman and Olbrechts-Tyteca, *The New Rhetoric*, 50–1; Berger,
Exegese, 53; Rosenfield, 'Celebration of Epideictic', 132–4.
    [42] Though Cicero still insists that it serves the state (*De Partitione Oratoria* 20.69).
    [43] Perelman and Olbrechts-Tyteca, *The New Rhetoric*, 47–48. I disagree, however,
with the unsupported notion that the orator often did not appear in public. Above
all, epideictic is a 'live' performance. This I only note in passing since it does not
affect our thesis.
    [44] Ibid., 49–51.
    [45] Cicero, *De Partitione Oratoria* 21.71.

surrounding Paul and his new converts – who existed as a religious minority often harassed by bands of Jews and also by those who had long mistrusted those same Jews – created a situation 'that would give a real as opposed to a merely apparent agonistic dimension to [Paul's] letters with varying degrees of urgency',[46] some label it epideictic based on this new perspective.

Furthermore, in keeping with its purposes, style plays a lead role in classical epideictic. Cicero writes that

> because virtually the whole method in [panegyric] is directed to giving the audience pleasure and entertainment, in the style employment must be made of those brilliant touches in particular words which are such an extremely agreeable feature – that means that we must use frequent repetitions of parallels and similes and contraries and doublets and rhythmic periods not designed to resemble verse but to satisfy the ear with what may be called a suitable verbal harmony.[47]

Galatians does not approach the style required of any species of oratory (Saunders claims that every extant example of Greek oratory employs the Attic dialect[48]), much less that demanded of epideictic,[49] yet this shortcoming is also side-stepped when rhetoric is defined as encompassing all discourse.

Those who consider Galatians epideictic thus mean little more than that (1) it is neither forensic nor deliberative, and (2) it seeks to praise or blame and in so doing reaffirm traditional values.[50] They disregard Aristotle's assertion that such speeches do not address real struggles; and they make no attempt to relate the epistle to the audience and event for which ancient epideictic speeches were intended. Once again we see that the primary identifier of species has been overlooked. The ancient world regarded as epideictic (the word itself means 'display speeches'[51]), those speeches delivered at funerals (which usually honoured fallen

---

[46] Johanson, *To All the Brethren*, 41.

[47] Cicero, *De Partitione Oratoria* 21.72.

[48] Saunders, *Greek Political Oratory*, 8.

[49] The next two chapters defend these assertions.

[50] In fact, the ancient world was not always convinced that rhetoric confirmed traditional values. Consider the attitude expressed in Aristophanes' *The Clouds*, and the expulsion of the heads of three major schools of rhetoric (155 BC). See Finley, *Politics*, 28.

[51] Saunders, *Greek Political Oratory*, 12.

armies)[52], contests and public spectacles. Since their purpose was primarily to display the skills of the orator, they were often little more than events to be enjoyed, the performers being the celebrities of the day.[53]

Naturally, these limits on epideictic, and therefore Galatians, are classical and only concern those wishing to understand species from that perspective. If one creates a more general category to include all levels of rhetoric and every speech which praises or blames, then the new definitions become relevant even to Galatians – but the discontinuity with classical rhetoric ought to be acknowledged. Admittedly, epideictic is an anomaly: Aristotle treats it differently from the other species in that he allows it to wander outside its accepted domain. This does not, however, justify finding what Aristotle calls epideictic everywhere someone or something is praised or blamed, for he remarks that *within an apologetic speech* it may be appropriate to praise the defendant, that prosecuting speeches must involve blame, and that sometimes praise and blame also have a role in deliberation. Thus the cumulative boundaries for the three species are not really broadened, but epideictic is allowed to wander rather freely within the frontiers established for the three.[54] Likewise, the explicit statements of *Rhetorica ad Herennium* oppose the broadening found in many studies: 'Nor should this kind of course be the less strongly recommended just because it presents itself only seldom in life. Indeed when a task may present itself, be it only occasionally, the ability to perform it as skilfully as possible must be desirable'.[55] Surely this writer did not anticipate epideictic's extension to each utterance that is neither judicial nor deliberative.

The limits of rhetoric and Galatians

These restrictions highlight problems attending those who understand species exclusively, or even primarily, according to function; for to them overlap of function can only create chaos. Such

[52] See especially the funeral speech of Pericles in Thucydides 2.35–46. Such speeches, especially in the Greek tradition, were not eulogies for the departed but were tributes to the Athenian way of life through the virtue of unnamed soldiers.

[53] In a satire, Lucian reports an occasion when the jury, bored by the dry oratory, was distracted by the marvelous hall within which a case was tried. Even the jurors expected to be entertained (ΠΕΡΙ ΤΟΥ ΟΙΚΟΥ [The Hall], especially 21–32).

[54] Aristotle, *Rhetoric* 1.3.1. So also *Rhetorica ad Herennium* 3.8.15.

[55] Ibid.

confusion manifests itself in discussions of Galatians, since most readers recognize elements of a Pauline defence, even more see deliberation standing alongside, and some describe the epistle as epideictic.[56]

For the ancients, rhetoric had its place in the preparation and delivery of orations to be delivered on specific occasions in particular places. Kennedy, in his discussion of the 'rhetorical situation' describes it as something akin to the *Sitz-im-Leben* of form criticism. But 'rhetorical situation' centers on the particular exigency which the discourse intends to affect, while *Sitz-im-Leben* lives outside the particular (describing the recurring social context for which the text exists), and transports the reader into a realm of ideas which transforms historical artists into generic ones often capable of little more than embodying the traditional functions of their texts. For example, while a psalm may be written for employment at an inauguration ceremony, *Sitz-im-Leben* describes not the particular ceremony for which it was first created, but rather that generality which we may label 'inauguration ceremonies'.[57] According to Bultmann, 'The *Sitz im Leben* is not . . . an individual historical event, but a typical situation or occupation in the life of a community'.[58] If rhetoric has any discernible *Sitz-im-Leben* it consists not in the particulars of a debate but in the larger sociological setting. Thus forensic finds its *Sitz-im-Leben* in the courtroom and deliberative in the assembly.[59] But this vital context is overlooked in Kennedy's redefined *Sitz-im-Leben*. Its extension to the analysis of biblical texts requires justification incomprehensible to those with whom we associate classical rhetoric. Thus analysis of species, though a common element of recent work, would to the rhetors have been viewed as an odd exercise; the mere statement of context ought with finality to settle the matter.[60]

---

[56] See also Aristotle, *Rhetoric* 1.9. Kessler highlights the difficulty of isolating genre, a difficulty which grows out of the interaction of motifs common to literature: cf. 'Methodological Setting', 27–8.

[57] Kessler, ibid., 30.

[58] Bultmann, *History*, 4.

[59] *Pace* Thurén's framing of the issue in *Strategy of 1 Peter*, 54, especially nn. 54, 55.

[60] That is, species of the speech. When the rhetorical unit is identified as something other than a speech, the rules lose their value. This, however, says as much about the analysis as the speech, for the rhetoricians recognize that praise and blame (the concern of epideictic) have a role to play in defence and accusation (the concern of forensic), and so on. It seems nonsensical to argue that a forensic speech ceases to be that for a few moments, then resumes after the invective (or praise) is completed.

We will now evaluate attempts to identify the species of Galatians, again allowing the analysts to set the agenda (i.e. the handbooks are the prime source of data).

Galatians as a forensic speech

In his programmatic assertion that 'Galatians can be analysed according to Greco-Roman rhetoric and epistolography',[61] Betz is consciously dependent on demonstrating that the portrait closely fits the frame.[62] He goes to great lengths to show that this speech[63] was presented to a (fictional – but nevertheless valid) judge and jury.

> The apologetic letter, such as Galatians, presupposes the real or fictitious situation of the court of law, with jury, accuser, and defendant. In the case of Galatians, the addressees are identical with the jury, with Paul being the defendant, and his opponents the accusers. This situation makes Paul's Galatian letter a self-apology, delivered not in person but in a written form.[64]

Betz attempts to prove that Galatians is an apologetic letter by explaining its form,[65] an endeavour that could proceed one of two ways. He could compare it to actual letters and contemporary

The speech remains forensic throughout – though not simply because of the function of a sub-unit. The analyst should not confuse mode and species.

[61] Betz's classification of Galatians as forensic convinces to varying degrees: Brinsmead, *Dialogical Response*, 41–55; Lüdemann, *Paul*; Johanson, *To All The Brethren*; Standaert, 'La rhétorique ancienne'; Beaudean, *Paul's Theology of Preaching*; Smiles, *Gospel and Law*; Becker, *Paul*, 273–8.

[62] Betz, *Galatians*, 14.

[63] Betz seldom overtly calls Galatians a speech – rather he labels it an apologetic letter and attempts to show that it looks like a speech with epistolary prescript and postscript appended. Perhaps his clearest claim is as follows: 'As a rhetorical feature, the postscript of the letter to the Galatians serves as the *peroratio* or *conclusio*, that is the end and conclusion of the apologetic speech forming the body of the letter': cf. 'Literary Composition', 356–57.

[64] Betz, *Galatians*, 24; so also 'Literary Composition', 377, which differs from the commentary (until the final sentence) only by inserting definite articles and putting 'apologetic letter' in quotation marks. This twice-repeated paragraph appears to be a formative part of Betz's thought.

[65] Betz (*Galatians*, 14) writes: 'Paul's letter to the Galatians is an example of the "apologetic letter" genre. The evidence for this hypothesis must, of course, be derived from an analysis of the composition of the letter'. Classen observes the interaction between form and function: 'The correct observation that Paul describes his earlier actions in a fairly long section and partly also justifies them, leads Betz to the unjustified conclusion that the whole letter is apologetic, especially in the light of

descriptions of similar material;[66] but he instead opts for a new method which seeks to demonstrate that Galatians conforms to the handbooks; that is, the various components of the epistle look, when closely scrutinized, like parts of speeches discussed by Aristotle, Quintilian, Cicero, etc. Though unable to present a cache of letters parallel to Galatians in defence of his designation, he overcomes this lack with a precise demonstration of the epistle's conformity to handbook advice.[67] Surely with the minutiae tallied up, we cannot resist his conclusions.

Having observed this similarity, Betz seems to suggest, we may confidently identify troublesome passages based on their functional and structural roles within the species as described by the handbooks. The ancients provide data which, when properly distilled and reconstituted, comprise an overlay to place upon the text of Galatians, revealing both points of conformity and points at which the text departs from the established pattern. Thus, if he can demonstrate that, for example, 1.8–9 looks and functions like part of an *exordium* as described in the handbooks, he is well on his way to establishing certain expectations which cohere with the function of the *exordium* within the species to which these verses belong. The promise that such species-created expectation will give way to exegetical reward seems amply fulfilled when, for instance, Betz writes: 'Viewing Galatians from a rhetorical perspective suggests at once that chapters iii and iv must contain the *probatio* section'.[68] He displays similar confidence when evaluating Merk's identification of the beginning of *paraenesis* in Galatians: 'since the conclusions are not based upon a composition analysis they are not convincing'.[69]

Betz recognizes that before he can speak thus, he must solidify his position, a task performed by identifying specific, effective,

---

individual formulae which could be used in a defence speech': cf. 'Antike Rhetorik', 29, my translation.

[66] Meeks ('Review of *Galatians*', 306) criticises Betz for failing to produce actual letters.

[67] Longenecker (*Galatians*, cix) labels this approach 'diachronic analysis', for Betz's approach emphasizes 'the rhetorical forms in their historical context and seeks to trace out lines of genetic relations with other writings of the time'. Diachronic analysis is concerned with persuasion within the specific historical and cultural context which produces the discourse. Thus Betz says little concerning persuasion in the abstract and much concerning how the rhetoricians describe persuasion in Greek and Roman courts.

[68] Betz, 'Literary Composition', 369.

[69] Ibid., 375, n. 2.

devices which heighten the link between Galatians and its forensic provenance. For example, he writes of Galatians 1.6 that Paul employs a device from legal and political rhetoric.[70] But more exciting potentialities lie in his next words: 'It is important for understanding what Paul means that the rhetorical background of his language be taken into consideration'.[71] Betz seems to invite the reader to be engulfed by the full 'rhetorical' force of the forensic setting, for Paul's meaning is taken to be intertwined with the 'packaging', that is, with the sights and sounds of the courtroom. Thus we are conscripted into imagining, alongside an implied reader, an implied context which arises from the text itself. In such a world, judicial rhetoric would create expectations appropriate to its particular setting: it would unveil an atmosphere capable of exerting an emotive and cognitive effect upon those whose imaginations are sufficiently engaged.[72] In Galatians the packaging exerts a powerful metaphorical force which, even apart from Paul's utterance, transports the hearer in directions Paul considers favourable.

But with these observations Betz's thesis runs into difficulty. For when asked what benefits the 'rhetorical background of his language' bestows upon the enlightened reader, we must answer that in actuality it adds little, for who ever thought that μετατίθημι does other than 'to cast a negative judgement on the Galatians, to question their stability and loyalty, and to characterise their plans as typical "party politics"'?[73] Paul's language at 1.6 has not been a great stumbling-block to interpreters operating apart from recognition of Galatians' judicial setting; and furthermore, it docs not compel the reader to envisage a court scene. Most significantly, this very verse has pushed some away from rhetoric to an epistolary analysis, for θαυμάζω is the antithesis of Paul's usual εὐχαριστῶ statement which, as seen in our previous chapter, is a recognized epistolary convention.

What then clues the reader in to the forensic nature of Galatians? Is there anything which will immediately flag the judicial setting? The situational context (i.e. the fictional courtroom) cannot be used to define species unless it is readily discernible (i.e. one would surely know if he or she is responding to a summons or sitting on a

[70] Betz, *Galatians*, 47.
[71] Ibid.
[72] See Sperber and Wilson ('Rhetoric and Relevance', 145) for amplification of this concept of discourse's 'cognitive effect'.
[73] See Josephus, *Antiquities* 20.38; *Life* 195. Cf. Longenecker, *Galatians*, 14.

jury).[74] This setting is nowhere explicit, nor does it necessarily follow from Paul's lexical selections (if such were the case, perhaps the judicial nature would have been noticed before Betz discovered it). He himself has written: 'The effectiveness of rhetoric depends primarily upon the naiveté of the hearer, rather than upon the soundness of the case. Rhetoric works only as long as one does not know *how* it works'. But does this compete with his statements concerning the original readers' education?[75] Further, how naive can one suppose Paul's audience to be if sophisticated enough to identify a judicial speech disguised as a letter? Nothing requires that Paul use the fictional device of the judicial speech in his letter – it is testimony to his creativity if he did – but is it not the case that inviting his readers into such a connotation-filled fictional world requires that they recognize their entry? How can the full effect of the strategy be realized if the readers are not aware of the manoeuvre?[76]

Further, if one grants, for the sake of joining Betz in his experimental reading of Galatians, that Galatians conveys judicial rhetoric, the confusion is not thereby dispelled; the adoption of this receptive stance makes it no easier to isolate the various participants in the court scene. For example, in addressing the matter of judge and jury that lack of focus becomes evident. Betz suggests that

> Paul's letter contains a *defense of his version of the gospel addressed to his churches in Galatia*. To this degree it is an inner-Christian 'apology,' or an apology within the Pauline cluster of churches. However, since Paul's Jewish-Christian

[74] Additionally, Galatians is not sufficiently different from other epistles to demand this dramatically different set of classifications.

[75] Cf. *Galatians*, 24. We have already cited Betz's view that 'The fact that Paul wrote his well-composed and, both rhetorically and theologically, sophisticated "apology" forces us to assume that he founded the Galatians churches not among the poor and the uneducated but among the Hellenized and Romanized city population': cf. *Galatians*, 2. This seems to be a departure from most other rhetorical studies which (1) are more concerned with the education of the speaker than the audience; and (2) often conclude simply that at least a base rhetoric was 'in the air' (the language of Longenecker, *Galatians*, p. cxiii, paraphrasing Kennedy, *New Testament Interpretation*, 10). Of course, to speak of a 'Hellenized and Romanized city population' does not restrict Betz's lateral movement. Cf. also Hansen, *Abraham in Galatians*, 55; Thurén, *Strategy of 1 Peter*, 49. Downing ('A Bas Les Aristos', 224) claims this as support for his suggestion that the early church possessed some literary sophistication.

[76] The question of recognition will reappear in the next two chapters.

opponents have almost succeeded in winning the Galatians over to their side, which is also the side of Judaism, *the apostle's defense amounts to a defense of his theology before the forum of Judaism*. On the other hand, since the Galatians were pagans before becoming Christians, *Paul's defense is at the same time a defense before the forum of paganism*.[77]

How likely is it that these three parties simultaneously serve similar functions? Can Paul address with the same words the particular rhetorical situations and exigencies of three disparate, even warring factions?[78]

A similar breadth of scope manifests itself when considering the defendant's identity. Betz claims that

> *Paul defends primarily his 'gospel without law,'* that is the inclusion of the Gentiles into God's salvation on the basis of their 'faith in Jesus Christ' but without committing them to the Torah covenant. Such a defense must, of course, include *Paul's defense*, because he is the one who claims to have been appointed by Christ himself to preach this gospel and to convert these Gentiles.[79]

Paul's responsibilities as attorney for the defence are not yet exhausted, for 'the founding of the Galatian churches was initiated by an ecstatic experience of the Spirit. Therefore, *if anything needs a defense it is this experience of the Spirit*'.[80] So Paul must defend his gospel, himself, and the Spirit. Longenecker does not clarify things when he insists that 'at times in [chapters 1–2] Paul is the accuser

[77] Betz, 'Defense of the Spirit', 102–3. This jury is later restricted to 'the addressees', but, on the same page: 'Because of the fundamental issues under discussion, the readers do not simply include the Galatian churches but all churches. What the apostle had to say, he has to say to the whole of Christianity: Jewish and Gentile Christians, Paulinists and anti-Paulinists' (*Galatians* 214). The emphasis is Betz's.

[78] Mack, *Rhetoric and the New Testament*, 67.

[79] Betz, 'Defense of the Spirit', 107.

[80] Ibid. Betz (108) adds: 'Once we have identified the central issue of the letter, we may raise some puzzling questions. Is it not absurd to try to defend the Spirit of God? . . . Paul does not consider it impossible or inappropriate to present a defense of the Spirit of God . . . *How* can the Spirit be defended?'; and again ('Literary Composition and Function', 378): 'Having to use this rather suspect form of logical argumentation becomes even more questionable when one realizes that *no* kind of rational argument can possibly defend the position Paul must defend. In effect, his defense amounts to a defence of the πνεῦμα which was given to the gentile Galatians outside of the Torah'.

and the prosecutor as well as the defendant, and his converts are in the dock as deserters as well as being the jury'.[81]

This breadth of scope betrays an inbuilt imprecision, calling into question the designation 'legal brief'. Working with the premise that a chief concern of the rhetoricians is clarity, one must conclude that if Paul used the handbooks, he did a very poor job; but if he did such a poor job, what compels us to assume, indeed how could we know, that he used them?[82]

We thus conclude that though Betz's diachronic approach reveals a profound understanding of the need to establish the frame within which Galatians can exist as a speech, his efforts to tie Galatians to that frame in the end fall short. We simply lack compelling evidence that Paul's words manufacture the judicial setting.

Galatians as deliberative rhetoric

Not surprisingly, Betz has been challenged on the question of species. The most significant response to his reconstruction comes from the eminent classicist George Kennedy, who insists that the rejection of atomistic approaches reveals Galatians' membership in the deliberative species.[83] Kennedy, who deserves credit for many advances in the field of classical rhetoric, is well qualified to employ the tools needed for this paradigmatic shift.[84] In fact, his guidebook is responsible for the shape of much rhetorical analysis of the NT, for, as we observed in chapter 1, a major part of Kennedy's step-by-step method is the determination of species.

Kennedy justifies this step by insisting that 'as the discussion of Galatians . . . reveals, [identifying species] can be crucial in under-

---

[81] Longenecker, *Galatians*, cxi; also Hansen, *Abraham in Galatians*, 59. Neither of these scholars appear troubled by the imprecision.

[82] Longenecker (*Galatians*, cxiii) criticizes Betz for 'understanding the impact of classical rhetoric on Paul in too scholastic and rigid a fashion'. This assertion raises the same question: what grounds do we have for inaugurating an enterprise that assumes Galatians is an example of classical rhetoric if Galatians does not closely conform to the handbooks?

[83] More now agree that Galatians is deliberative than forensic. See, besides Kennedy, Church, 'Rhetorical Structure', 17–33; Aune, 'Review of Betz's *Galatians*', 323–8; Lyons, *Pauline Autobiography*, 173–4; Hall, 'Rhetorical Outline', 277–9; Cosgrove, *Cross and Spirit*, 124; Vouga, 'Rhetorischen Gattung', 291–2; Smit, 'Deliberative Speech', 1–26.

[84] See especially his historical surveys: *Persuasion in Greece*; *Rhetoric in the Roman World*; *Classical Rhetoric*.

standing the unit'.[85] Thus, Galatians is Kennedy's test case to determine the value of this element of his methodology[86] – and he intends to capitalize on the differences between those readings which treat the epistle as judicial and those which stamp it deliberative.[87] But his reading does not, despite appearances, run parallel to Betz's, for there is nothing in *New Testament Interpretation* to indicate that Galatians is a different species of *speech*, only that it is a different species of *text*.[88] Kennedy argues not that Paul constructed Galatians along lines suggested by the handbooks, but that Galatians, like all texts, can be analysed according to insights provided by Aristotle, Quintilian, Cicero, etc. Not only will we attempt to demonstrate that he undermines his own position when he offers a reconstruction, and therefore cannot take us beyond the work of Betz, but also that his analysis does not even engage 'classical rhetoric' the way Betz does.[89]

Kennedy states that Betz 'was apparently led to [the view that Galatians is an example of judicial rhetoric], at least in part, by the existence of a narrative section in Galatians 2, a feeling that narration is characteristic of judicial rhetoric, and a resulting effort to see in the letter the traditional parts of a juridicial oration as described by Quintilian and to see the letter in a traditional genre'.[90] In his response to Betz, after stating that each species employs narrative but for different ends, he asserts that the narrative portion of Galatians does not recount the facts of the case. Instead it supports the assertion of 1.11 (already mooted in 1.1–2) that his gospel was from God rather than men.[91] 'That there is no other gospel' is repeatedly asserted by Kennedy to represent 'a general statement of the proposition of the letter, which will be taken up and given specific meaning in the headings which follow [the *proem*]'.[92]

---

[85] Kennedy, *New Testament Interpretation*, 36.

[86] J. I. H. McDonald, 'Rhetorical Criticism', 600.

[87] Or perhaps, to be more precise, one should say that the readings begin with the presupposition that Galatians is deliberative or judicial.

[88] Unlike Smit, who treats Galatians as a speech. He provides no evidence accept a supposed dispositional conformity to the handbooks. So our arguments in chapter 4 apply again; as do chapters 6 to 7 which demonstrate that Paul's language is most 'unrhetorical'.

[89] See our discussion (in chapter 1) of Kennedy's method and the discussion of Hansen and Longenecker which follows.

[90] Kennedy, *New Testament Interpretation*, 144.

[91] Ibid., 145.

[92] Ibid., 148. Cf. 148–50.

He possesses further ammunition: highlighting the difficulty Betz faces when confronted with the fact of paraenesis, he remarks that the 'exhortation of 5:1–6:10 is strong evidence that the epistle is in fact deliberative in intent.[93] This exhortation is a problem for Betz's theory, since exhortation, as all recognise, is not regarded as a part of judicial rhetoric by any of the ancient authorities'.[94]

So we see that Kennedy employs a two-pronged strategy, basing his offensive on the observations that (1) Betz's strength, the presence of narrative, does not demand Betz's explanation; and (2) the presence of paraenesis undermines that explanation while driving us to another – that Galatians is deliberative. But Kennedy's reconstruction is vulnerable to precisely the same attacks as he launches against Betz. First, Kennedy links the paraenesis, indeed the entire epistle, to the notion, found early in Galatians, that Paul's gospel is not from men. But a careful reading reveals that Galatians does not base its exhortation on the notion that 'there is no other gospel' but on something else, something less precise: the eschatological standing of the believer.[95] Moreover, these differences are not matters of degree but represent wide-ranging alternatives. The question of new behaviour thus resolves itself not with a deepening recognition that there is only one gospel, or even with proper resolution of the matter of law, but instead these concerns coalesce into a seminar on the believers' eschatological relationship with the Spirit.

Kennedy himself sometimes supports this reading, for in discussing the epilogue – the postscript of 6.11–18 – he writes: 'It is important to notice that what Paul thinks he has demonstrated to the Galatians is not that they should alter their judgement of him, but that "neither circumcision counts for anything nor uncircumcision, but a new creation" (6:15)'.[96] Kennedy thus correctly emphasizes the importance of 'what Paul thinks he has demonstrated', but errs in thinking that the statement from Paul contributes more to his own position than Betz's, for it supports not arguments for the

[93] So also Hall, 'Rhetorical Outline', 277–87; Black, 'Rhetorical Questions', 66.

[94] Betz elsewhere suggests that 2 Cor. 8.16–23 are 'commendation' and 'exhortation', for which he has also been criticized since 'none of these partitions is paralleled in ancient rhetorical theory'. So Black, 'The Rhetorical Form', 63.

[95] 'Eschatology' characterizes Galatians from start to finish. Cf. Gal. 1.4; 2.19–20; 6.15. See Cosgrove, *Cross and Spirit* 140–1; Martyn, 'Apocalyptic Antinomies'; Cook, 'Prescript as Programme', 513–15, 518.

[96] Kennedy, *New Testament Interpretation*, 151; cf. Mack, *Rhetoric and the New Testament*, 72.

validity of the one (Pauline) gospel, but eschatology's dominant role in the epistle. Thus, at least the paraenesis and the epilogue are severed from Kennedy's particular brand of argument concerning deliberative speech.

A far more important observation remains to be made, for the presence of paraenesis dominates Kennedy's assault on Betz. Consider again Kennedy's assertion that 'exhortation is a problem for Betz's theory, since exhortation, as he acknowledges, is not regarded as a part of judicial rhetoric by any of the ancient authorities'.[97] He adds that it 'is one of the two forms of deliberative rhetoric, the other being dissuasion'.

But note first that Betz's trouble does not grow out of the lack of handbook discussion concerning exhortation in *forensic speech*; it is born of his observation that the handbooks do not discuss exhortation (paraenesis) *anywhere*. Betz, as we have seen, writes: 'It is rather puzzling to see that paraenesis plays only a marginal role in the ancient rhetorical handbooks, if not in rhetoric itself'.[98] Thus Kennedy's position suffers from the mere presence of paraenesis in Galatians to precisely the same degree as that of Betz.[99] Furthermore, when this gives way to the notion that exhortation comprises one of the two forms of deliberative we must again hesitate, for Kennedy uses the term 'exhortation' differently from the handbooks, a difference which seems to shrink with the addition that 'Paul exhorts the Galatians to quite specific acts, in particular to a rejection of the practice of circumcision'. The more specific the focus of Paul's exhortation, the more it favours Kennedy's position.[100] But in actuality, Galatians alternates between general and

---

[97] Kennedy, *New Testament Interpretation*, 145.

[98] Betz, *Galatians*, 254.

[99] The same misreading mars the results of Jewett's *Thessalonian Correspondence*. He labels 2 Thessalonians 3.6–15 '*exhortatio*' without recognizing that this category does not exist as part of ancient rhetoric. Smit ('Deliberative Speech', 8) properly recognises and builds upon this lack by eliminating parts of chapters 5 and 6 from Paul's 'speech'.

[100] See also Hansen, *Abraham in Galatians*, 60: 'Paul points to the harmful effects of the actions which he seeks to dissuade the Galatian believers from following . . . Deliberative rhetoric seeks to exhort or dissuade an audience regarding future actions by demonstrating that those actions are expedient or harmful'. Then follows a footnote (*Abraham in Galatians*, 230, n. 39) which cites Aristotle (*Rhetoric* 1.3.5): 'The end of the deliberative speaker is the expedient or harmful; for he who exhorts . . . recommends a course of action as better, and he who dissuades . . . advises against it as worse'. Note the switch from 'action' in Aristotle's text to 'actions' in Hansen's. The singular in the former is significant – but does not fit Galatians. Mack (*Rhetoric and the New Testament*, 73) sidesteps this difficulty by asserting that

specific instruction in a way quite unlike anything found in the speech-related material.

Aristotle speaks of exhortation and dissuasion (1.3.2), but the former term in Pauline studies is often linked to *Haustafeln* or other diverse series of instructions (as in Gal. 5–6) while in classical speeches the goal, as shown above, was to persuade the nation-state concerning one of five matters: ways and means; war and peace; defence; imports and exports; legislation (1.4.7). Only in epideictic speeches does there seem to be the sort of broad-based exhortation found in Paul. Funeral orations exhorted children to virtue (Plato, *Menexenus* 246B–249E) and gave reasons for grieving and not grieving (Pseudo-Lysias, *Funeral Oration* 71–8).[101] Such exhortation, however, shares little with the persuasion of deliberative speeches, and we will address the possibility of Galatians being epideictic with our comments on that species which follow.

The accumulation of material as diverse as 'bear one another's burdens' (6.2) and 'through love serve one another' (5.13) on the one hand, and on the other 'all who are circumcised are obligated to perform the entire law' (5.3) does not strike the reader as particularly out of character for the Paul of the New Testament, though it would be out of place in a speech delivered before the senate. With these observations I conclude that Kennedy's statements concerning the final third of Galatians, though damaging to Betz's hypothesis, are not compelling evidence in favour of the deliberative species.

Furthermore, with regard to Kennedy's method, we find that his real interest lies apart from measuring Paul's conformity to classical handbooks or basing conclusions and exegetical decisions on the fact that Paul has constructed a speech according to the instructions found on their pages when he writes:

> Betz is puzzled by [the handbooks'] silence and notes that exhortation, or *paraenesis*, is a regular feature of philosophical letters. It is, but philosophical letters like those of Seneca are not judicial: they either inculcate belief without calling for action, in which case they are epideictic, or they exhort the recipient to a particular course of action, in which case they are deliberative.[102]

'[Paul's] argument about the gospel was worked out to support his deliberative appeal to "stand fast" in freedom (from the law)'.

[101] See Hughes, 'Rhetoric of 1 Thessalonians', 106.

[102] Kennedy, *New Testament Interpretation*, 145–6.

So then Kennedy, in contrast to Betz, does not define species according to the frame of the speech, nor, from his perspective, do species manifest themselves upon careful examination of the handbooks, but are revealed by the overall *function* of the 'rhetorical unit' – even if that unit is not a speech.[103] Since Kennedy has in large part set the agenda, we find others who follow his lead.

Hall writes in his discussion of the structure of Galatians:

> The major purpose of Galatians is not to defend some past action (judicial) or to praise some and to blame others (epideictic) but to persuade the Galatians to cleave to Paul and his gospel and to reject his opponents and their gospel . . . Since the debate requires the Galatians to decide between two antithetical modes of life and behavior and since the participants in the debate are not primarily concerned about Paul's past action but about what future action the Galatians will take, Galatians is most naturally classified as a deliberative work.[104]

Walter B. Russell III similarly writes: 'Galatians is deliberative because Paul was seeking to persuade his audience to make a definitive decision about their identity and behavior in the immediate future'.[105] Christopher Stanley argues that Galatians is deliberative because 'Only a strong dose of clear thinking, coupled with a vigorous appeal to the Galatians' own best interest, offered hope for reversing the trend'.[106] Aristotle is then cited to show that expediency points to deliberative.[107]

This strategy of depending on function to reveal species has come to dominate studies of Galatians and so must be evaluated.[108] We therefore turn aside briefly to consider the work of Duane Watson, for he presents what is for our purposes perhaps the most useful expression of a functionally motivated decision regarding species

---

[103] Nils Dahl, in 'Paul's Letter to the Galatians: Epistolary Genre, Content, and Structure' (unpublished paper presented to the 1973 SBL Paul seminar), also finds a change in function.

[104] Hall, 'Rhetorical Outline', 279.

[105] Russell, 'Rhetorical Analysis 2', 417. Not all functional readings conclude that Galatians is deliberative: Hester ('Rhetorical Structure', 227) once argued for the judicial species because Galatians defends Paul's independence from Jerusalem, though he now holds that it is epideictic, primarily because it praises and blames. See below, pp. 162f.

[106] Stanley, ' "Under a Curse" ', 490.

[107] Ibid., citing Aristotle, *Rhetoric* 1.3.21–5.

[108] Cf. Schüssler-Fiorenza, 'Rhetorical Situation in 1 Corinthians', 391–3.

due to his clarity and completeness of argument, and the fact that
he finds the deliberative species in the passage he investigates. In his
analysis of 1 Corinthians 10.23–11.1 he maintains that these verses
are deliberative for four reasons:

> First, this subsection is intended to advise and dissuade the
> Corinthians regarding a particular course of action.
> Second, the time referent is future, regarding policy for
> occasions that will arise after the writing. Third, Paul
> concerns himself with what is beneficial and harmful,
> expedient and inexpedient for the Corinthians individually
> and corporately, that is, with the desired ends of delibera-
> tive rhetoric . . . Finally, example and comparison of
> example supply the major portion of the deliberation
> through the section.[109]

But the assertion that this portion deserves the label deliberative
'for it exhibits the major characteristics of this species' raises new
questions. Although we may grant that these verses intend 'to
advise and dissuade' could we not argue that nearly all religious
material functions this way at one level or another?[110] Second, how
helpful is it to observe that literature which advises or dissuades
concerns a future time referent (or, following Quintilian, either a
present or future referent)? The rhetoricians discuss what they
observe happening in speeches; and they rightly link deliberative
with a future referent, for what profit lies in exhorting an audience
to undertake an action in the past? Thus the time referent enjoys no
life of its own, merely pointing backwards to function. Third, to
exhort someone to undertake an action contrary to their desires
will nearly always require that the speaker demonstrate that the act
is 'beneficial or edifying'. However, with regard to religious rhetoric
the value of this observation is mitigated by the elusiveness of the
'beneficial'. If Paul wishes the reader to perform some act not
immediately deemed beneficial, he need only reorient the instruction in such a way as to bring eschatological blessing into view.[111]

[109] Watson, '1 Corinthians 10:23–11:1', 302. Watson depends on a similar
method to assess 2 John ('Analysis of 2 John', 109).
[110] I.e. religious discourse functions this way in 'advising' one to embrace or
maintain the doctrines of the faith, or by 'dissuading' one from participation in
improper activity, even as Johanson (*To all the Brethren*, 41) argues that 'the *ultimate*
persuasive goal will almost invariably be to strengthen adherence to the Christian
gospel, whatever specific exigence(s) may occasion a particular letter'.
[111] In some Christian churches in America the members regularly drink poison

Thus 'beneficial' is too broad to classify religious material. Finally, Watson's fourth observation, that examples provide the major portion of deliberation, seems more specific, thus more helpful, than the first three until we examine the text under discussion. The examples he identifies are 10.25: 'eat everything which is offered for sale in the meat market, nothing being questioned because of conscience'; and 10.27: 'If an unbeliever invites you and you will go, eat everything put before you, questioning nothing because of conscience'.[112] Watson thus calls two situations 'examples'. But at what points do 'examples' and 'situations' coincide? Do these verses contain what the handbooks designate examples? The handbooks speak of what we might term models: characters or historical events which demonstrate how, if one undertakes a certain act, particular results will follow.[113] Chapters 9–10 contain instructions which depend on this type of example; but 10.23–11.1 seems to be free of such devices until 11.1, where Paul presents himself as a model of how the Corinthians ought to live (even as he imitates Christ; cf. Gal. 6.17). Indeed, the two situations Paul discussed may be neither examples nor hypothetical situations, but real dilemmas which regularly confronted the Corinthians. They may have been so real that church members submitted questions which Paul answered in the verses. Only with difficulty, however, can one conclude that examples drive this deliberation.[114] For these reasons I conclude not that the substance of these verses eliminates the possibility of deliberation, but that Watson's four bits of evidence do not compel us to find in them 'deliberative rhetoric'.

Self-described classical rhetorical studies which base identification of species on function are limited, for they divorce function from sociological setting, from audience appropriate to the propounded species, and often, from the structure of the text. Function in the end seems not far removed from what might be termed a generalized authorial intent (or, if one prefers, intent of the text). Thus if the intent is to persuade, the text is labelled deliberative: if it

and handle snakes; in others, they sign away social security checks, all because they regard it as 'beneficial'.
[112] Watson, '1 Corinthians 10:23–11:17', 306; following Watson's translation.
[113] Quintilian, *Institutio* 5.11.3–6.
[114] It seems that overlap in content has ensnared the exegete. Examples, for instance, are common to a great deal of communication and thus by their presence can prove very little. Although the handbooks may recommend employing particular devices more in one species than another, to read backward from their presence is not a promising enterprise.

intends to defend it is labelled forensic. This intent, though, arises not from recognition of the species, for to Kennedy, it must be identified prior to, and is the controlling factor in, recognition of species; it can only be determined by evaluating the subject-matter as developed in the text. This, however, reverses a major component of the analytical cycle: recognition of the species should arise from the frame, which informs the reader as to the text's purpose (courtroom speeches will accuse or defend). An analysis that begins with the function of the text circumnavigates the same circle, though anti-clockwise, the difficulty being that this reversal limits confidence to the degree that one trusts one's own ability to discern a content-based intent. Furthermore, it seems that though the inevitable result of such analysis would be recognition of the frame of the speech, in reality biblical exegetes seldom get their day in court, usually settling for identification of the species without linking the text to its sociological setting.[115]

Can we benefit by listening to those who discuss genre-theory? The insights of their debate may assist us, for, at least in the matter at hand, the attempt to identify species closely parallels the attempt to identify genre. We thus note the contribution of W. G. Doty, who maintains that generic definition should 'focus upon formal, structural composition of the literary work rather than on thematology'.[116] Surely structure has much to say concerning genre, but rhetorical studies of Paul rely on it very little (and on those few occasions when more is asked, the difficulties often increase). This situation exists because the three species are not thought to differ much in overall structure.[117] Granted, narrative plays a greater role in forensic, while examples drive deliberative, and a vast number of other features appear more often in one species than another, but a cursory investigation of recent research reveals the facility with which biblical exegetes can side-step such obstacles.[118] In the end we admit that the three species overlap too much for structure to identify species, and that the tools at our disposal can only help to

---

[115] Discussion at this point often turns to universal aspects of communication rather than classical.

[116] Doty, 'Genre', 439; cf. Hansen, *Abraham in Galatians*, 21; 219, n. 1.

[117] Cf. Lyons, *Pauline Autobiography*, 112–19: 'All three speech types used more or less the same divisions'.

[118] As seen in the use both Betz and Kennedy make of the narrative in Galatians. Cf. Hughes ('The Rhetoric of 1 Thessalonians', 100), who finds narrative in a supposedly epideictic text.

ascertain the distance between different types of texts, not between 'related genres and sub-genres'.[119]

With structure offering minimal help, where do we turn? An appropriate strategy may be to ask about the overall function of the largest rhetorical unit before us (i.e. Galatians as a whole). We find that Paul clearly does more than defend his apostleship – thus Betz expands his reading to include defence of apostleship, gospel and the Holy Spirit. Only chapters 1 to 2 really seem apologetic, however, so we must ask about the effect of the whole, which does seem to invite the reader to choose a particular way of life – a code of conduct (which, ironically, has no code). In the process, Galatians defends, exhorts, and praises and blames, all of which are appropriate to any of the three species of classical rhetoric. But function, when so understood, does not help a great deal.

Once exegetes give up the claim to classical rhetorical analysis they could even ask how *all three* species direct the reader; thus with any given portion one could ask who is being accused; who is being defended; what quality (or person) is being praised; what quality blamed (denigrated); and what sort of action the audience is invited to deliberate over. The first two questions have been part of synoptic scholarship for some time, helping define the *Sitz-im-Leben* of the pericope. One might also profitably ask how far from the surface the answers lie; that is, does the text explicitly ask the reader to consider an altered way of life, as in Galatians 5 to 6? Or does it praise some quality which then ought to effect a change in the reader's life (as e.g. 1 Cor. 13)? This of course is unrelated to classical rhetoric.

In fact, all such function-related questions distance the discussion from classical rhetoric, for they address an aspect of discourse related to level 2 rhetoric. Thus, if all discourse arguing for a particular course of action is deliberative, then this species includes everything from a parliamentary speech to a parent telling a child that 'A penny saved is a penny earned'. If our understanding of rhetoric classifies discourse according to function, we might describe both examples as deliberative, but the second is clearly not an example of handbook oratory. Attempts to narrow the list of texts to exclude the second need a sound methodological base – but

---

[119] Johanson, *To All the Brethren*, 42. In fact, the structure of speeches does vary according to species – but since the exegete need only claim that Galatians is an exception, we simply grant the point for argument's sake and seek other avenues of investigation.

this is missing from analyses of Galatians; furthermore, if the ground for exclusion is nonconformity with the prescriptions of the handbooks, then Galatians must also be rejected, for it differs substantially from both handbook advice and any classical speech.

Additionally, functional analyses of rhetoric were not part of the critical arsenal of the ancients, nor, as has been suggested above, are they an enterprise which could have been appreciated.[120] Kennedy does not bring the handbooks into play in anything more than a general way (as opposed to the exacting work of Betz). In fact, Kennedy's reading of Galatians (and Watson's work on 1 Cor. 10.23–11.1) has broken its ties with classical rhetoric and infringes on the 'new rhetoric'. Although not a bad thing, this adaptation leaves us questioning the relevance of the detailed explanations of Aristotelian and other ancient rhetoric which are prolegomena to their investigations. Without wishing to speculate on the reasons, we admit that such a preamble from the pen of one so expert in classics as Kennedy contains immeasurable rhetorical force, but does not link the result to the handbooks.[121]

This invites us to explore Kennedy's fidelity to Graeco-Roman oratory, for he alternates between embracing and rejecting, rendering the determination of his exact relationship to level 4 rhetoric nearly impossible. He writes, for example, 'There are three *species* of rhetoric . . . Although these categories specifically refer to the circumstances of classical oratory, they in fact apply to all kinds of discourse'.[122] But Kennedy's choice of verb, 'apply', is ambiguous. He has in fact 'applied' rhetorical categories to non-classical texts, but he does not thereby prove that such texts are classical speeches or even that they closely resemble them. To apply such categories to a pre-Homeric biblical text is just as possible, but is it desirable?

---

[120] So Porter, 'Theoretical Justification', especially 107–10. Hughes states otherwise: 'Thus rhetorical criticism has the virtue of being a form of analysis whose presuppositions ancient writers are likely to have understood; hence it is a kind of analysis that has intrinsic historical plausibility: cf. 'Rhetoric of 1 Thessalonians', 95'. (Note 9 then adds: 'In order to make an analysis as historically plausible as possible, the rhetorical critic should above all strive not to become a slave of a single ancient handbook or a synthetic compendium of handbooks'.) His methodology consists of applying classical labels to various parts of 1 Thessalonians.

[121] See comments by Porter, 'Theoretical justification', 109.

[122] Kennedy, *New Testament Interpretation*, 19. Thurén (*Strategy of 1 Peter*, 51) writes: 'Furthermore it should be borne in mind that the three principal rhetorical genres mentioned in the handbooks . . . were not restricted to classical civic oratory, but could be applied to any kind of situation, and thus should not be seen as fixed'. Also adopting Kennedy's notion of applicability is Wanamaker, *Thessalonians*, 46.

Thomas Olbricht has challenged the universal applicability of Aristotle's discussion of species: 'In this regard Kennedy and I apparently understand Aristotle differently. Kennedy may be right that to some extent (in some cases very limited), the three genres are "in fact applicable to all discourse" (*New Testament Interpretation*, 19). But Aristotle clearly identified types of discourse where even rhetoric itself is not applicable, much less the three genres (*Rhetoric* 1.2.20–22). Examples are discourses on philosophy, physics, and medicine. Aristotle makes it clear that the province of rhetoric is ethics, hence politics (1.2.7)'.[123] Olbricht correctly sees the limits of Aristotle's discussion.[124] Furthermore, when he concedes that the three may apply to some extent, Olbricht means that having ripped species from its appropriate domain by reducing it to a base function, the label can be applied so that even a poem which defends someone may be called judicial, though Aristotle never envisaged such a use.

A distinction exists between what some NT exegetes mean by the universality of rhetoric and what the ancients meant.[125] The latter felt that any subject could be worked into a level 4 speech if standardized means were mastered, so that, for instance, one need not be a doctor to discuss a poisoning in forensic rhetoric. This differs from what those scholars mean by 'universal', who suggest that any type of literature can be analysed using rhetoric. If by this one anticipates the application of certain tests to a text to see how the *tester* (i.e. the reader) is manipulated, then such an understanding possesses a certain validity – but this practice transcends the concerns of the ancients. Again we insist that the modern approach is not being denigrated, but it remains a distinct enterprise with limited contact with the classical world. In this light we agree with Johanson's stance: 'It is questioned here whether the rhetorical genres as defined by Aristotle are of a sufficiently general and inclusive character to be so universally applicable as Kennedy and many others appear to allow'.[126]

Admittedly, Aristotle does make statements that on first reading seem to imply an interest in level 1 rhetoric. He allows that 'all, up to a certain point, endeavour to criticise or uphold an argument, to

[123] Olbricht, 'Aristotelian Analysis', 225, n. 51.
[124] See E. Black, *Rhetorical Criticism*, 118.
[125] See above, pages 12–34, for a discussion of the restricted nature of level 4 rhetoric.
[126] Johanson, *To All the Brethren*, 39.

defend themselves or accuse'.[127] All argue – but Aristotle soon
manifests his narrow concerns, for the same chapter reveals that
they are tethered to specific formal settings. He speaks of trial,
state, court, dicasts, business of the litigants, laws, cases, judges and
judgements.[128]

Aristotle inserts into his description of deliberative the notion
that 'the most important and effective of all the means of persuasion and good counsel is to know all the forms of government and
to distinguish the manners and customs, institutions, and interests
of each; for all men are guided by considerations of expediency,
and *that which preserves the State is expedient*'.[129] This is part of
five paragraphs on types of government and the ends of each – all
of which, at least to Aristotle's thinking, are related to deliberation.
Even when discussing aspects of rhetoric which have undeniably
universal relevance, he confines his advice to specific settings and
purposes. For example, when discussing style, he reduces it to an
element of 'political contests', thus pushing it outside the ring of
general discourse.[130]

Aristotle further observes that 'when compared, the speeches of
writers appear meagre in public debates, while those of the rhetoricians, however well delivered, are amateurish when read. The
reason is that they are only suitable to public debates; hence
speeches suited for delivery, when delivery is absent, do not fulfil
their proper function and appear silly'.[131] Paul would be opposing
this advice if he merely appended epistolary material to a speech.
Kennedy, however, ignores this notion and simply merges his
particular definition of universal applicability with the supposition
that rhetoric was an analytical tool:

> Though classical rhetorical theory was developed as a
> system to teach students how to speak in public, and found
> its fullest development in formal oratory, it was also
> utilized to teach and to analyze literary composition. To
> what extent is an awareness of the conventions of different

[127] Aristotle, *Rhetoric* 1.1.1.
[128] We again quote in full an Aristotelian passage which limits the applicability:
'Now we may say that the most important subjects about which all men deliberate
and deliberative orators harangue, are five in number, to wit: ways and means (περί
τε πόρων which is restricted to the financial affairs of the state), war and peace, the
defense of the country, imports and exports, legislation' (*Rhetoric* 1.4.7).
[129] Aristotle, ibid., 1.8.1, emphasis added.
[130] Ibid., 3.1.4.
[131] Ibid., 3.12.2.

literary forms essential for valid rhetorical criticism? The answer seems to be that it can be helpful, but that it is not fundamental. Any discourse may be classified as judicial, deliberative, or epideictic and will have the rhetorical characteristics of its species.[132]

Those 'rhetorical characteristics' are then briefly defined as ethos, logos and pathos. But Kennedy, having whetted our appetites, does not instruct us in the analysis of literary composition based on the rhetoric of the handbooks, nor even present good evidence that the ancients undertook such an activity. Instead, he changes his focus to matters of style, introducing the handbooks into the equation with the remark that Quintilian recommends reading classical authors; but this misleads, for the recommendation does not link Quintilian to literary analysis, much less rhetoric to literary analysis; what he recommends is reading widely in order to develop an abundance of words and ideas.[133] Finally, when Kennedy abandons discussion of style he asserts that the New Testament writers *do not* conform to classical generic models, concluding: 'In general, identification of genre is not a crucial factor in understanding how rhetoric actually works in units of the New Testament'.[134]

To understand Kennedy properly one must recognize his goal of linking the creation of speeches with the creation, and with one more step the analysis, of literary material. He does not offer evidence for this connection beyond his questionable assertion that all discourse belongs to one of the three species of rhetoric, and that Quintilian has something to say about reading literature. This repeated proposition that the ancients used rhetorical categories for analysis vivifies Kennedy's efforts, but it fails when Quintilian's statements are read critically. All that can be garnered from the material Kennedy presents is that speakers, like writers, should maximize the power of words.[135]

[132] Kennedy, *New Testament Interpretation*, 30–1. He thus uses level 4 rhetoric to analyse other levels of discourse. See our discussion of Kennedy in chapter 3, especially 61–4.

[133] Quintilian, *Institutio* 10.1.

[134] Kennedy, *New Testament Interpretation*, 33. At this point Kennedy speaks of literary genre, not of rhetorical species.

[135] Hughes (*Early Christian Rhetoric*, 26) quotes Cicero to show that 'when official messages, presumably in the form of letters, must be sent to or from the Senate and must be written in an elaborate style, no other *genus* of rhetoric is needed, "since the ability acquired by a ready speaker, from the treatment of his

Clearly Kennedy's analytical approach has departed from the concerns of the rhetoricians. But Kennedy moves even further, for in *New Testament Interpretation* he writes that while in the ancient world rhetoric was for 'civil life' (and thus the handbooks are restricted to 'legal and political rhetoric'), modern critics look to another category: the 'rhetoric of religion'. This nearly universal rhetoric depends not on logical argumentation but on 'authoritative proclamation' which gains credibility from the personal qualities of the speaker or from the intuitive agreement of the hearer. 'Absolute demands, deliberate rejection of worldly reason, sometimes paradoxes or even obscurity, become a persuasive factor in the enunciation of a new religious message. This phenomenon is known as "sacred language" '.[136]

These words seem to contradict Kennedy's statement that all discourse rests under the umbrella of one of the three species. Perhaps he would contend that even this 'sacred language' conforms to one of the three species of rhetoric, but if so, the material thus labelled differs from classical material in persuasive technique, frame and function. Why then classify it with work influenced by the rhetoricians when in fact he cites some examples which branch off at level 3, and even those which remain branch off by level 4?

Kennedy enjoys no monopoly on introducing additional sorts of rhetoric. Mack similarly suggests that the social setting of early Christianity required a new rhetoric because it did not 'correspond to the traditional occasions for each type of speech'. Thus a new means of communication was crafted 'in which every form of rhetorical issue and strategy was frequently brought to bear simultaneously in an essentially extravagant persuasion'.[137]

Olbricht defends those who expand the roster of species (following his own admission that 1 Thessalonians does not match the frame of any speech suggested in the handbooks). He correctly argues that the poor fit requires not stuffing the epistle into a too-tight Aristotelian garment, but rather, 'in the spirit of Aristotle'

---

other subjects and topics, will not fail him in situations of that description" (*On the Orator*, 2.12.49)'. This instruction cannot support the transfer of rhetoric to epistolary matters, however, for Cicero, in his mention of the work of the 'ready speaker', discusses how one should conduct himself in regard to 'this type of speaking'. That is, the discussion concerns the writing of speeches (which constitute the official messages), not the crafting of the presumed letters. Cf. Porter, 'Theoretical Justification', 115–16, n. 40.

[136] Kennedy, *New Testament Interpretation*, 6.
[137] Mack, *Rhetoric and the New Testament*, 35.

crafting a new one.[138] He moreover asserts that the only reason for omitting the church from Aristotle's level 4 categories is that it did not yet exist. 'Had Aristotle lived in the fourth century A.D., his modus operandi would have driven him to this fourth genre'.[139] As we have seen, this creation did indeed appear in subsequent literature: Hugh Blair (in the eighteenth century) still offered three species, but replaced epideictic with 'that eloquence which is suited to the pulpit'.[140]

Johanson reasons that,

> with Paul in the role of a religious authority addressing religious audiences with regard to shared interests (whether conflicting or not) in pertinent beliefs and practices, the *ultimate* persuasive goal will almost inevitably be to strengthen adherence to the Christian gospel, whatever specific exigence(s) may occasion a particular letter. In other words, one has to do with a basically different audience-role than those of the legal judge, the political deliberator, or the spectator . . . The concern for continual adherence discloses a future focus in common with the deliberative genre, but the topics are not the mundane concern with the politically expedient or harmful but rather with salvation as revealed in the gospel.[141]

These developments should not surprise us, for we need only return to Amos Wilder to find that they are foreshadowed in what is perhaps the earliest modern rhetorical investigation of the NT. He observes that 'The whole compendium of Israel's literature is built upon peculiar rhetorics that find no place in the textbooks of Aristotle or Quintilian'.[142] Wilder, whose primary interest lies in the rhetoric of the gospels, finds allies in Johanson and Koester, who develop this 'peculiar rhetoric' as they find it in 1 Thessalo-

---

[138] Olbricht, 'Aristotelian Analysis', 225. His work is thus the epitome of a 'Neo-Aristotelian analysis'.

[139] Olbricht, 'Aristotelian Analysis', 225.

[140] Blair, *Lectures on Rhetoric*, 2:101. See Olbricht, 'Aristotelian Analysis', 225, n. 53. Further growth in the list comes at the hands of E. Black who describes: a 'genre . . . in which the evocation of an emotional experience in the audience induces belief in the situation to which the emotion is appropriate instead of following as a consequence of belief in the situation': cf. *Rhetorical Criticism*, 118. Classen ('Antike Rhetorik', 20) adds γένος διδακτικόν based on his study of Melanchthon (see chapter 6).

[141] Johanson, *To All the Brethren*, 41.

[142] Wilder, *Early Christian Rhetoric*, 15.

nians, and show little patience with those who, like Kennedy and Boers, fail to distinguish classical from Christian rhetoric.[143]

Only after the difference between Paul's exhortation and the classical variety has been understood can we turn from Kennedy to François Vouga's proposal.[144] In his brief article he suggests that limits imposed by the handbooks are overcome by attending to actual speeches[145] and then attempts to move via *dispositio* to species (a move we elsewhere conclude to be unhelpful).[146] This effort leads to the conclusion that Galatians is deliberative. Vouga argues that the epistle's structural similarity to an acknowledged deliberative speech which contains exhortation – Demosthenes' *On the Peace* – removes the obstacles to labelling Galatians 'deliberative', including the paraenesis which so troubled Betz.

Our response to Vouga is threefold. First, he states that with regard to Kennedy's proposal, 'The difficulty of this thesis resides in the broad development of the *narratio* (Gal. 1.12–2.14), which surely does not belong to the deliberative *Gattung*'.[147] He then eliminates this difficulty by presenting *On the Peace* as an example of a deliberative speech containing just such a *narratio*. Apart from the question of whether *On the Peace* 4–12 closely resembles Galatians 1.12–2.14, it is important to note what such an argument really proves: that having removed ourselves a step from the handbooks, we find actual speeches which contain dispositional elements foreign to their particular species. But once this is granted we find that Vouga has removed the main plank of Kennedy's platform – the inescapable presence of *exhortatio* in Galatians – for if *narratio* can float so freely, why not *exhortatio*? But if the parts are in a state of flux, we have no basis to distinguish between species.

Second, the 'narrative' of *On the Peace* is slightly different from Paul's story in Galatians. In fact, it is no story at all but a list of three occasions when Demosthenes stood up in the assembly to resist the majority. In the first case, he opposed joining Plutarchus in a campaign in Euboea;[148] second, he addressed the Athenians concerning Neoptolemus, a man who eventually sided with

[143] Johanson, *To All the Brethren*, 39–40; Koester, 'I Thessalonians Experiment', 34–6. Olbricht also refers to Hinks, 'Tria Genera Causarum', 170–6.
[144] Vouga, 'Rhetorischen Gattung', 291–2.
[145] Ibid., 291.
[146] See above, pp. 144–45 and notes.
[147] Vouga, 'Rhetorischen Gattung', 291; my translation.
[148] Demosthenes, *On the Peace* 4–5.

Philip;[149] and third, he opposed abandoning the Phocians to Philip.[150] In each instance he was justified. These examples, against Vouga, do not really constitute a typical *narratio*, but present an argument which will help carry Demosthenes' speech. They establish that he has three times shown both courage and good judgement while opposing public sentiment, and even more, that he has spoken each time with the good of the state as his sole motivation.

Thus we find two similarities between Paul and Demosthenes: (1) they show that their interests lie with the audience and have already been vindicated with regard to the present issue; (2) they create a forceful argument out of a series of events from their past. This second observation is not enough, however, to prove that we are dealing with *narratios*. The portions in question do not present the actual cases to be argued but instead present a pair of preliminary arguments which prop up what follows. Perhaps neither should be called a *narratio*.

Third, we need to consider what it is that characterizes deliberative rhetoric. Not only is general exhortation as a rule foreign to all types of rhetoric, not just forensic, but Demosthenes' exhortation (which in the end equals his purpose) in *On the Peace* is unlike Paul's. At one level all deliberative speeches can be thought to be exhortative, since the speech as a whole, as well as its constituent parts, urges its audience to adopt a particular course of action: yet when one turns to Galatians 5.2–6.10 the nature of the pleas is radically different. *On the Peace* urges the Athenian *polis* to adopt a particular course in dealing with Philip of Macedon – recommending caution against his military and political ambitions – but the final chapters of Galatians cannot be reduced to a simple thesis statement other than something like a call to Christian love. But such a reduction fails to represent the epistle in its entirety, while a classical speech, whether forensic or deliberative, would fail miserably if the auditors were unable to reduce it to a called-for act such as acquit, convict, levy a tax, attack, etc. In the end Galatians differs substantially from Demosthenes' speech.[151]

A third major attempt to classify Galatians as deliberative rhetoric has been submitted by Joop Smit, who writes: 'Paul's

---

[149] Ibid., 6–7.
[150] Ibid., 10.
[151] The greatest difference is perhaps in the nature of the language used. One is appropriate to rhetoric: one is most certainly not. In the next two chapters I defend this assertion.

speech . . . corresponds entirely to the norms the handbooks of rhetoric set for the deliberative genre'. He thus interacts with Betz's assessment of Galatians instead of Kennedy's, for only Betz emphasizes the fact that the handbooks discuss speeches. Smit argues that Betz got the genre right – Galatians is classical oratory – but misconstrued the species. But many of our problems with both Betz and Kennedy apply to Smit, and we also add the following objections.

First, Smit insists: 'The question whether rites of religion should be changed or not, is explicitly listed by the *Rhetorica ad Alexandrum* among the subjects proper for the deliberative genre, and in that context, amply discussed'. Smit offers a truly classical reading of Galatians in that he tries to measure the text's conformity to the handbooks, but at this point he has over-stretched the fabric. We have seen that deliberative rhetoric submits proposals to governing assemblies, and that religious questions enter into one handbook's range of deliberative interest: but this inclusion arises from one author's desire to cover all conceivable spheres of state interest, one of which, naturally, is the state religion.[152] This again highlights the dangers of an eclectic use of the handbooks: Aristotle, for example, does not include such questions in his *Rhetoric*.

Second, Smit allows portions of the handbooks which clearly relate to forensic discourse to inform his discussion. Since Betz and Kennedy have prompted us to focus on the first chapters of Galatians, with Smit we will interact with subsequent ones. An example of his merging of forensic with deliberative speech appears in his discussion of the *indignatio*, where he lists seven items which incite indignation.

> The gravity of the crime, as it appears from the attention that authorities like the gods, ancestors, the state and the law have given to the matter under discussion.
> The victims of the crime.
> The rejection of tolerance and indifference because in this case that amounts to a dangerous precedent.
> The danger that the crime will spread if not checked now.
> The irrevocability of the impending decision. It cannot be

---

[152] See *Rhetorica ad Alexandrum* 2.1423a.30–1424a.9 and our discussion of the limits of deliberative (given above). Only in the fourth century does deliberative rhetoric take on a prominent role in Christianity as councils and synods are now conducted by the secular/religious authority.

revised later on and the harm done cannot be remedied.
The intention of the guilty person or persons. The crime
was committed on purpose and with premeditation.
The cruel and sacrilegious character of the crime.[153]

Smit then insists that 'in Galatians 5. 7–12 Paul seemingly
touches on each of these typical points of the *indignatio*, lightly and
in the indicated order'.[154] Not only should we note that, remarkably, Paul uses seven items from Cicero in the same order as the
handbook presents them,[155] but that all relate not to deliberative
but to *forensic*. The mention of crimes, cases and, in the most
ambiguous instance, the fifth, punishment (for the actual statement
is: 'once the decision has been made it cannot be changed by any
judicial body'[156]) does not incline one toward the notion that the
epistle is deliberative.

Furthermore, the actual texts do not always seem to match
Smit's description of their function. For example, does 'You were
running well: who hindered you from obeying the truth?' (5.7)
really depend on the gravity of the crime and point to its victims to
incite indignation? It is clear that pointing to a victim in court plays
on the emotions, especially if the victim is feeble or has been
disabled by an assault, but Paul does nothing like this. Also, Smit
must first demonstrate that the Galatians consider themselves
victims, but it seems unlikely that they do: if they have submitted to
Paul's opponents it is through an exercise of the will.[157]

Another element which does not quite conform to the description
is the seventh. Cicero says: 'The seventh topic is used when we
express our indignation, saying that a foul, cruel, nefarious, and
tyrannical deed has been done by force and violence or by the
influence of riches, and that such an act is utterly at variance with
law and equity'.[158] 'Sacrilege' has thus been introduced to the

[153] Smit, 'Deliberative Speech', 19–20. He is following Cicero, *De Inventione* 1.53.100–54.105.
[154] Smit, 'Deliberative Speech', 20.
[155] In actuality the order is different. Smit ('Deliberative Speech', 20) writes in the very next sentence: 'First Paul presents the Galatians as victims of deceivers who are leading them away from the true gospel'. Then he continues: 'Subsequently he stresses the gravity of the crime.' Thus we see that already with the first two items the order is reversed.
[156] Cicero, *De Inventione* 1.53.102.
[157] Smit cannot argue that the purpose of Galatians is to prosecute the opponents for a crime against the churches, since that would mean that the epistle is a judicial, not deliberative, speech.
[158] Cicero, *De Inventione* 1.53.102.

discussion not by Cicero but by Smit, who then writes of Gal. 5.12:
'With a sacrilegious sneer Paul stresses their scandalous behaviour
and therewith rounds off this part'.[159] But the handbooks are
addressing the criminal deeds of the accused, not the expression on
the face of the prosecutor. Thus at least the first and the last of
Smit's seven items do not seem to fit Galatians.

Finally, a main strength of Betz's analysis lies in his taking the
frame of the speech seriously. He argues that Galatians is judicial
because there is a defence, a judge and jury, a defendant and the
like. Smit, who repeatedly stresses that Galatians is a speech, does
not substitute a deliberative scene for Betz's law-court. The letter
does not look or sound like the sort of speech Cicero or the author
of *Rhetorica ad Alexandrum* would recognize. In fact, in keeping
with Smit's claim that, 'Force of habit was the only reason for Paul
to conform to the familiar model',[160] we may be forgiven for
thinking that Galatians is indeed like the discourses Paul habitually
writes (at least those which we possess) with respect to form,
content and level of language. This conformity is not, however,
with the requirements of oratory but with the epistolary form
which Paul himself has in part established.

Galatians' links with deliberative rhetoric as argued by Kennedy
have not been proven – unless, that is, the definitions are broadened
extensively. Before such a broadening nears completion, though,
the analysis will betray a distance from ancient rhetorical material
which severs any connection with classical rhetoric.

Smit and Vouga present arguments which are troubled by broadening of a different sort, for they depend primarily on level 4
rhetoric to explain Galatians. Unfortunately Galatians does not
resemble classical oratory enough to establish their cases.

Subsequent solutions to the question of species

Betz applies classical rhetoric to Galatians because he thinks Paul
wrote in conformity with the rules of the handbooks (i.e. Galatians
looks like a forensic speech); Kennedy argues that *all discourse* can
be analysed with the aid of *classical* rhetoric (i.e. Galatians acts like
a deliberative speech); and further along this same trajectory,
Walter Hansen and Richard Longenecker introduce the notion that

[159] Smit, 'Deliberative Speech', 20. Galatians 5.12 reads: 'those who are harrassing
you ought to cut themselves off'.
[160] Smit, Ibid., 23. By 'familiar model' Smit means the rhetorical speech.

Galatians, like all discourse, is subject to both diachronic and synchronic rhetorical analysis.

Galatians as mixed rhetoric

Both Longenecker and Hansen argue that the diachronic model begs for supplementation by 'synchronic' analysis, described as 'strictly a compositional method' which 'examines the argument on its own, classifying its stages of development in terms of general, more universal modes of persuasion'.[161] Longenecker goes on to isolate several persuasive devices utilized in Galatians: enthymeme; example; argument by definition; argument by dissociation of ideas; argument by the severance of a group and its members; means-end argument; argument by repetition and amplification.[162] The agenda thus widens through the introduction of synchronic analysis – for such an undertaking attempts to uncover the persuasive force of a text regardless of its cultural and historical orientation; or, as Hansen insists, it uses 'the parallels which are applicable from the Rhetorical handbooks simply as descriptive tools'.[163]

In most cases, synchronic investigations lie outside the bounds of our interest, for such efforts depend on the assumption that classical rhetorical handbooks should no longer monopolize our understanding of persuasion. The best modern handbooks, in order to succeed, must take up the insights of their predecessors and hopefully (if we have learned anything about how humans convince one another in the last 2,500 years) supersede them. But for two reasons Hansen/Longenecker's discussion of synchronic rhetoric remains firmly within the rubric of classical rhetoric. First, Longenecker explicitly states the necessity of both diachronic and synchronic analysis.[164] Second, when he enters into his discussion of synchronic rhetoric, Longenecker consistently demonstrates that the techniques Paul appropriates find their description in the classical handbooks, and he understands their persuasive function solely on the information contained therein. Longenecker has been described as 'a bit confused over what constitutes synchronic

---

[161] Longenecker, *Galatians*, cix. Cf. Hansen, *Abraham in Galatians*, 56, and 229, n. 15.
[162] Ibid., cxvi–cxix.
[163] Hansen, *Abraham in Galatians*, 56
[164] Longenecker, *Galatians*, cxiv.

rhetorical analysis when he actually performs it, relying upon the classical categories of invention'.[165] He defines synchronic as the universal or ahistorical analysis of persuasion, but he obtains his data from Graeco-Roman handbooks.[166] Thus a specific cultural/ rhetorical tradition informs the reading – which at least looks like a diachronic reading; and since that informant is Graeco-Roman rhetoric, it falls within our investigation.

With regard to methods of investigation (as chapter 3 implied), the distance between Kennedy and Hansen/Longenecker is not great in practice, as all three depend on the notion that rhetoric is

> a universal phenomenon which is conditioned by basic workings of the human mind and heart and by the nature of all human society. Aristotle's objective in writing his *Rhetoric* was not to describe Greek rhetoric, but to describe this universal facet of human communication; the categories he identifies are intended to exhaust the possibilities, though the examples of them which he gives are drawn from the specific practice of the Greek city state. It is perfectly possible to utilize the categories of Aristotelian rhetoric to study speech in China, India, Africa, and elsewhere in the world, cultures much more different from Greek than was Palestine in the time of the Roman empire.[167]

Although it is possible to study speeches from these other cultures – each possessing their own particular rhetoric – with the aid of the handbooks, all such a study can reveal are points of agreement and disagreement with classical oratory – but surely a worthwhile reading offers more than this. It is because Aristotle's categories describe Athenian political oratory rather than universals that such efforts fall short. One might further ask if universal description is ever possible – even if it is the author's goal. In the end, Longenecker's reading is not synchronic because he mistakes an anti-

[165] Porter, 'Theoretical Justification', 106, n. 16.
[166] Longenecker's bibliography lists none of the standard handbooks (e.g. Perelman and Olbrechts-Tyteca) for the synchronic mode of analysis. Instead he consistently refers to Graeco-Roman sources. He even begins a new paragraph with the words: 'Other ancient logical categories of persuasion can be described in Paul's Galatian letter as well' (Longenecker, *Galatians*, cxviii). If the method depends on application of ancient categories, the work is diachronic.
[167] Kennedy, *New Testament Interpretation*, 10–11; quoted in Hansen, *Abraham in Galatians*, 57.

quated and culturally specific (level 4) rhetoric for a universal (level 1) rhetoric.

Perhaps a line can be traced back from Longenecker via Hansen to Kessler. We saw in chapter 3 that Kessler separates aspects of his investigation into columns containing historical and ahistorical classifications, the latter group comprising a synchronic approach;[168] Hansen, however, apparently believes that recognizing a text's conformity to a classical handbook without asking whether the author intended that conformity implies synchronic investigation.[169] But Kessler states that synchronic methods 'deal with the meaning of the text in its present form without reference to the provenance of it'.[170] Thus Kessler opens the door to discussion of textual features apart from any particular cultural explanation. All insights, whether first-century or twentieth, ought to be employed if relevant; for the purpose lies neither in identifying a device as Aristotelian, nor in explaining why Aristotle finds a device persuasive, but rather explaining how a device affects the reader. Should Aristotle offer the best explanation, it must not be overlooked – but the goal is not finding adherence to the handbooks. In fact, finding such adherence characterizes diachronic analysis unless the handbooks describe a universal rhetoric. Hansen's so-called 'synchronic analysis' uses only Graeco-Roman informants to explicate the text, and thus falls short of being synchronic.

Turning from questions of method to the analysis produced by Hansen and Longenecker, one quickly finds that results differ from those offered by Betz and Kennedy. The new explanation calls Galatians a mixed letter containing aspects of both deliberative and

---

[168] See above, pp. 76–9.

[169] Hansen (*Abraham in Galatians*, 56) writes: 'Betz often appears to be engaged in . . . a source-critical analysis. He quotes at length from the ancient rhetorical handbooks and demonstrates that Galatians is structured in accordance with the requirements of classical rhetorical theory, and is constantly concerned to show the influence of Greco-Roman rhetorical theory on Paul's argumentative discourse. According to Betz, the structure of Paul's argument is best understood by observing how Paul "conforms" to the requirements of the handbooks of Aristotle, Cicero, Quintilian, and others. Betz's frequent use of such terms as "conforms", "follows", and "obeys" to depict Paul's relationship to classical rhetoric conveys the impression that it is his purpose to demonstrate Paul's direct, even conscious, dependence upon classical rhetoric in the development of his argument'. Such evidence does indeed point to a diachronic analysis (and at the same time make Betz's work of greater interest for the purposes of this thesis), but finding that Paul uses the same devices without suggesting that he depended on the handbooks or a rhetorical education does not constitute synchronic analysis.

[170] See Kessler, 'Methodological Setting', 24.

judicial rhetoric as well as many epistolary conventions.[171] Of
4.12–6.10 Longenecker writes:

> Rhetorically, a major shift in Paul's argument occurs at
> 4:12.[172] There are, of course, still elements of forensic
> rhetoric to be found in what follows, particularly in Paul's
> accusation against the errorists . . . and his statements of
> self-defense. But the dominant tone from 4:12 onwards is
> that of deliberative rhetoric, not forensic rhetoric . . . In
> 4:12ff. Paul is no longer so much concerned to accuse or
> defend as to persuade his Galatian converts to adopt a
> certain course of action.[173]

Longenecker further states that 'Greco-Roman deliberative
rhetoric [is] prominent in 4:12–6:10'.[174] He then informs us that
'rhetorical conventions were simply part of ancient Greco-Roman
society, which everyone, whether formally educated or simply
exposed to the marketplace of ideas, was influenced by and used to
his own advantage'.[175] From such statements we gather that he
considers much of Galatians forensic, the final third being deliberative,[176] and that though he will not commit himself to explaining
where Paul obtained the conventions (in school or in society), the
rhetoric employed by Paul remains that of the handbooks.

Longenecker does not find a great wealth of rhetorical devices in
4.12–6.10 – but he administers the stamp of a rhetorical species
because he deems part of Kennedy's argument persuasive, namely,
that part which emphasizes Betz's inability to deal with the

---

[171] Evidently function drives much of Hansen's rhetorical analysis of species while
content controls the epistolary analysis: cf. *Abraham in Galatians*, 59.

[172] Galatians 4.12–20 motivate Hansen and, following him, Longenecker, to
describe the epistle as mixed in style and function. Hansen (*Abraham in Galatians*,
224–5, n. 80) offers a discussion of these verses and demonstrates that they contain a
rich deposit of epistolary formulae. This wealth betrays, in Hansen's estimation, a
turning point in the epistle.

[173] Longenecker, *Galatians*, 184; the wording is nearly identical to Hansen,
Abraham in Galatians, 59.

[174] Longenecker, *Galatians*, 185; Hansen, *Abraham in Galatians*, 58. They commit
the same errors for the same reasons as Kennedy. See above on Kennedy for
discussion.

[175] Longenecker, *Galatians*, 185–6, citing Malherbe, *Social Aspects*, 33–5, 41–5.

[176] More precisely, Longenecker finds forensic rhetoric in 1.6–3.7, and 4.8–11;
Jewish rhetoric in 3.6–4.7; and deliberative in 4.12–6.10. The 'rhetoric' which
determines the designation of the first and last sections Longenecker describes as the
'dominating' and the 'prominent' rhetoric of the respective section, again highlighting failure to consider the frame: cf. *Galatians* 185; also cxi–cxii.

exhortation in Galatians.[177] He then offers extensive quotations from Kennedy which argue that, due to the 'linear and cumulative' nature of a speech, Galatians can only be one species – and Galatians ends with exhortation, so the epistle must be deliberative.[178] Longenecker finds fault with such an assertion, though perhaps not with its most problematic facet: rather than question whether Galatians encapsulates a speech at all, he challenges the notion that a speech must be 'only one rhetorical genre per composition'.[179]

The difficulty with Longenecker's methodological step resides in its failure to concede that speeches are public oral discourses (a mistake which Kennedy makes elsewhere, but not on this point). Two observations follow: (1) Kennedy has a great deal in his favour as he argues that a speech partakes of one species, for his argument is simply that this is how a speech is heard. Furthermore, Longenecker can offer no examples of his type of mixed speech (note that he does not argue that a forensic speech may for example praise or blame, but that one speech consists of more than one species); (2) speeches, as we have attempted to demonstrate repeatedly, are shaped by their frame: and species ought to be identified by that frame rather than by the precarious means currently employed.

The work of Hansen and Longenecker offers this benefit: it forces the student of Galatians to recognize that a single species cannot describe the whole of the epistle. But it raises the problem of how any speech can be more than one species (recalling that species relates to audience and frame at least as much as to function). We thus ask two questions: (1) does Paul write informed by a model other than classical speech? Hansen himself (followed by Longenecker) seems to imply as much; (2) should Galatians be read as a complete text irrespective of its provenance? That is, would a synchronic reading – one that seeks to discover Galatians' persuasive underpinnings through employment of a more universal canon of persuasion – offer more to the reader? I would answer yes to both.

---

[177] Ibid., 185; Hansen, *Abraham in Galatians*, 58.
[178] See also Elliott, *Rhetoric of Romans*, 69.
[179] Longenecker, *Galatians*, 185; cf. Hansen, *Abraham in Galatians*, 59. Both depend on Aune, 'Review of Betz's *Galatians*', 325; Church, 'Rhetorical Structure', 19.

Galatians as epideictic rhetoric

Two recent discussions of Galatians suggest that it is epideictic. John L. White writes:

> To comprehend Paul's primary intent we must look to the social reality which Paul conceives as a possibility in Christ. In this sense epideictic rhetoric best describes Paul's intent, because it sought to fix or alter the disposition of people toward certain values. To be sure, Paul concerns himself with the future conduct of the Galatians, as Hall suggests. However, the central issue is the past and how it impinges upon the future as a basis of commitment.[180]

We thus learn that though Paul's concern is with the past, present and future, his overarching desire is to alter values – making Galatians epideictic. But before stating this conclusion White too refers to Aristotle's classification of the three species and interacts with Betz's proposal.[181] In short, White implies that his work runs parallel to Betz but reaches a different conclusion. This is not the case, for Betz maintains, as we have seen, that Galatians is a piece of forensic classical oratory, while White, allowing function to inform his reading, speaks of fixing or altering values. These are not parallel readings because this notion of manipulating values is not an aspect of handbook rhetoric at all, but arises instead from modern reflections on the *result* of certain types of speech which have been placed under the umbrella of epideictic. These would not necessarily have been so classified by the ancients, nor were such results the stated goal of epideictic; they have been discovered in the second half of this century to be the result of epideictic.[182]

Thus, when one urges the army to fight or praises the deceased or some virtue, there is an inevitable affirmation of certain values – usually traditional ones – so that epideictic has a conservative tendency. The crucial point is that this tendency to affirm traditional values does not necessarily signal the presence of epideictic – it characterizes its function. Judicial and deliberative rhetoric fulfil

[180] White, 'Apostolic Mission', 159–60.

[181] Ibid., 157–58.

[182] Cf. Calvin Porter: 'within the traditional system . . . Rom 1.18–32 is epideictic speech'. He then demonstrates that it is not epideictic according to Aristotle's categories, but according to modern conceptions. This provokes the question, why begin with 'within the traditional system . . .' rather than with 'in opposition to the traditional system'? Cf. 'Romans 1.18–32', 216.

this same function when, in condemning failure to conform to societies' notions of right and wrong, the courts validate and reinforce those same notions; and we need only recall the parliamentary and congressional discussions of economic policy of the 1980s to appreciate the relationship between economics and social values.[183]

Epideictic oratory, as described in the handbooks and understood as discourse without an agonistic dimension, clearly does not describe Galatians. But if we abandon all connections with classical rhetorical categories, Perelman can add even more to our understanding of epideictic when he links it with education.

> [It] is not his own cause or viewpoint that he is defending, but that of his entire audience. He is, so to speak, the educator of his audience, and if it is necessary that he should enjoy a certain prestige before he speaks, it is to enable him, through his own authority, to promote the values that he is upholding.[184]

Modern understandings of epideictic thus envisage a connection with educational discourse; and so, if White is right to introduce this category to explain Galatians, we can argue that the similarity depends on the fact that Paul intends to educate his hearers. Of course, this pushes the epistle completely outside the bounds of any category of classical oratory, but it does provide a way forward in the analysis of Galatians.[185]

The same qualifications apply to James Hester's attempt to classify Galatians, for he also depends on modern redefinitions of epideictic.[186] Before drawing any conclusions, however, Hester provides a preliminary argument: looking to epistolary theory and finding letter types such as blaming, reproachful, rebuking, admonishing, vituperative, praising, commending and congratulatory,[187]

[183] Economics is a chief concern of deliberative oratory.
[184] Perelman and Olbrechts-Tyteca, *The New Rhetoric*, 52.
[185] Though even designating Galatians 'educational' following Perelman and Olbrechts-Tyteca's scheme falters on the agonistic dimension of the letter: 'It is because epidictic discourse is intended to promote values on which there is agreement that one has an impression of misuse when in a speech of this kind someone takes up a position on a controversial question, turns the argument toward disputed values and introduces a discordant note on an occasion that is liable to promote communion, a funeral ceremony for instance. The same abuse exists when an educator turns propagandist' (*The New Rhetoric*, 53).
[186] Hester, 'Placing the Blame', 294–5.
[187] Ibid., 288; following Stowers, *Letter Writing*, 27–8.

he writes: 'I believe Galatians can be characterised as a letter of blame'.[188] Then, since 'epideictic is the rhetoric of praise and/or blame', Galatians must be epideictic rhetoric.[189] Thus Hester offers a purely functional reading. He describes Galatians' letter type, equates that with a species of rhetoric, and then imports definitions supplied by the 'new rhetoric' to solidify his conclusion. Classical writers only contribute epistolary classifications and structural guidelines.

The logic of this approach is flawed, however, because it mixes competing level 4 rhetorics to identify the text, and then imports level 2 rhetoric to describe it. Epistolary theorists discuss letters which praise and blame even as rhetoricians discuss speeches which aim for that same goal; but there is no warrant for automatically merging the two so that the rhetorician's discussion of a blaming speech is used to describe a letter of reproach – unless the rhetoricians are again assumed to discuss universal categories.[190] The same applies to the importation of modern definitions: there may be grounds for understanding Galatians as an epideictic discourse according to recent broadened explanations of that species,[191] but a great deal of confusion is introduced each time ancient and modern definitions of epideictic are conflated. They often refer to two quite distinct types of discourse.[192]

Conclusion

Having considered various attempts to describe the species of Galatians, I conclude that the participants have lost sight of the boundaries established by classical rhetoric. In the majority of studies we witness the (perhaps inevitable) transformation of

---

[188] Hester, 'Placing the Blame', 288.

[189] Ibid.

[190] See Porter ('Theoretical Justification', 100–22) for a discussion of the applicability of epistolary theory to rhetoric; he includes a survey of all the extant epistolary handbooks of the Graeco-Roman world and concludes that their only significant point of contact with the rhetorical theorists is in the matter of style. Cf. also Malherbe, 'Ancient Epistolary Theorists', 3.

[191] If outsiders have used 'epideictic' speech to mislead Paul's 'students', then he would need a heavy dose of polemical instruction to win them back. So we conclude that Galatians cannot be considered epideictic as defined by Aristotelian rhetoric, but modern expansions may help more by positing a classroom setting for Galatians than classical readings which suggest a court or political assembly.

[192] Though the classical form represents a small, somewhat marginalized, subset of the modern class called epideictic.

rhetorical situations into undefined (because barely relevant) textual backgrounds, or, at best, into historically conditioned exigencies that are treated outside the appropriate sociological spheres as enunciated in the handbooks. Betz inaugurates the new methodology in promising fashion by attempting to define the frame of that oration which he thinks Galatians pretends to be. Smit then alters the conclusion but maintains much of the agenda by arguing that Galatians is a deliberative speech. Subsequent writers, however, betray no awareness of Betz's preliminary step nor its vital role in the ascertainment of species. For this reason I conclude that only Betz and Smit offer a true classical rhetorical analysis, though Galatians does not bear the stamp of either species.

Other attempts to read Galatians depart from classical rhetoric to the extent that their designation of the epistle as one of the species must be understood as only true by analogy: that is, Galatians may function in a way similar to one of the species of rhetoric though it is in fact something else, namely an epistle.

Kennedy says that the handbooks 'apply' to all literature – not that Galatians is a speech. Thus when he says that the epistle is an example of deliberative rhetoric, he works with an alternative non-classical understanding of both 'deliberative' and 'rhetoric' even as he uses the handbooks to describe them. Longenecker and the rest move further away from the limits of classical oratory, for they speak of a letter displaying different types of rhetoric – judicial, deliberative, Jewish, epistolary – all operating at different levels, meaning that Paul reflects his various environmental, educational and religious experiences.

Analysts rarely base their conclusions on the oral nature of speeches, which may in some instances reflect a lack of awareness of this aspect of rhetoric, though it more probably results from adherence to Kennedy's insistence that species labels apply to all discourse. One cause for encouragement is that studies, as evidenced by White's discussion, are moving ever further from linking Paul to classical oratory. When this link is completely broken (or only maintained where its validity is demonstrable) the ground will be clear for scholarship to replace attempts to uncover classical rhetoric with efforts to describe early Christian rhetoric, first-century Jewish rhetoric and, ultimately, Paul's rhetoric. Efforts in this direction are under way, but often the analysis is hindered by the intrusion of classical standards.

So, then, I conclude that (1) Galatians does not manifest the structural elements which have been claimed for it, and (2) it does not fit any of the three species of rhetoric as described by the handbooks. In the next two chapters I will consider Paul's language and what it says about his relationship to rhetoric. The first stage will consider the views of early Christians who in some cases were the leading rhetoricians of their day.

6

THE LANGUAGE OF PAUL'S LETTERS: 1. AS EVALUATED BY EARLY CHRISTIAN WRITERS

At least since Celsus put down his pen there have been only two possibilities: either Paul wrote badly in the classical style, or he chose another mode of expression altogether. If he chose another, many would still think that his words lack any literary quality – for there was, at least for Celsus, no other standard. And by classical we mean the polished pieces that have come down to us from the great Greek writers of literature. Those who compared Paul to these authors found his style wanting. But is this the proper standard?

In order to assess Paul's style in such a way as to shed light on the relationship between Galatians and classical rhetoric, it is necessary to evaluate the level of the language he used. We will attempt to satisfy this need by travelling two distinct pathways. In this chapter, we will consider the attitude of those closer than we are to Paul in time and in manner of education. They have much to say concerning Pauline style, sophistication and eloquence (or lack of each), all of them informed by their education and mastery of Graeco-Roman rhetoric. In the next chapter we will consider what, if anything, can be gathered from the various data which constitute our picture of Paul's background. To provide the details for this portrait and to get beyond the limits of previous rhetorical inquiries into this question, we will then attempt, on a much larger scale, to interact with those who have evaluated the level of Paul's writing by comparing it to other extant documents of the ancient world. Conclusions there will serve as confirmation of important facets of this chapter, for if we find that the rhetorically trained early readers of Paul instinctively reach the same conclusions as those later scholars who undertake a comparative investigation of his level, we have strong grounds for confidence. Similarly, if we find widespread agreement among those competent to determine that Paul did not employ the mode of speech appropriate to Graeco-Roman oratory, we will have another substantial piece of evidence that Paul did not write Galatians as classical rhetoric.

What follows is intended to serve two purposes. First, our survey will bring together what evidence we have concerning Paul's literary level and writing skill; and second, it will provide evidence for arguments which lie outside the ability of the non-specialist. By looking to the earliest Christians and their assessment of Paul's style, we can move things along a great deal, for these early writers are in effect deciding for us whether Paul adopted the language of an educated writer. While literature and oratory did not necessarily look the same in matters of *taxis* and in regard to species, they did (inevitably) overlap in their application of a particular type of language. We will see that Paul was not thought to write in this type of language. We thus challenge Mack's assertion that history, stretching from the church fathers to Bultmann[1] and Betz, witnessed a rhetorical reading of the text.[2]

We therefore turn now to a survey of early Christian writers who were experts in classical rhetoric, our assumption being that their views concerning biblical material, and more especially of Paul, ought to have some influence on our understanding of Galatians. This is so because they meet two criteria: they possess (1) thorough education in the classical system of rhetoric; and (2) intimate acquaintance with the biblical text – especially the writings of Paul. Several of the 'fathers' pass such a test, for 'Of the great Latin Fathers, five – Tertullian, Cyprian, Arnobius, Lactantius and Augustine – had taught rhetoric at some time, while others – Minucius Felix,[3] Ambrose, Hilary and Jerome – were at least thoroughly acquainted with classical literature'.[4] Such an investiga-

---

[1] Mention of Bultmann illustrates the imprecision that accompanies discussion of rhetoric. Kennedy gives the impression that he is discussing the rhetoric of the handbooks. Bultmann deals, however, not with handbook rhetoric but, as his title indicates, with *Der Stil der paulinischen Predigt und die kynischstoische Diatribe*. Diatribe is not one of the standard rhetorical forms or species but a competing level 4 mode of discourse often employed by those openly hostile to handbook rhetoric.

[2] Mack, *Rhetoric and the New Testament*, 10–12. See also Betz ('Problem', 17) who refers to Clement of Alexandria, Gregory of Nyssa (especially comments on 1 Cor. 15.28), Augustine, and extends to Erasmus and Melanchthon. He further cites Luther on Galatians and claims that 'Calvin's commentary on Romans has a thoroughgoing rhetorical analysis of the letter'. I use the term church fathers, like Kennedy and Betz, to include writers as late as Augustine.

[3] Minucius Felix was a Roman lawyer unknown apart from an apology in dialogue form called *Octavius* (it vies for the title of first Christian Latin document of importance). See Von Campenhausen, *Fathers*, 5.

[4] Kennedy, 'Christianity and Criticism', 336–7.

tion will need to consider their opinion of both Paul and Paul's prose. Others, writing even earlier than these, have a place in the discussion, though in many ways the most important is the last, Augustine, whose writings will be treated at greater length than those of his predecessors. Another subset demanding consideration, both because of the nature of their education and because of Betz's statements, come along much later than the fathers.

The church fathers

During the period of roughly fifty years when NT scholars are said to have produced few rhetorical studies, significant works aimed at dissecting patristic literature did appear, perhaps because such writers had clear links to the world of paganism and rhetoric which they left behind when converted. One need only cite Thomas Amergen's *Stylistic Influence of the Second Sophistic on the Panegyrical Sermons of St. John Chrysostom: A Study in Greek Rhetoric*.[5] As the title implies, however, this book emphasizes style and treats a work which has links to Graeco-Roman rhetoric.[6] Thus we do not find patristic scholars imputing rhetorical skills to their subjects but rather finding them where they clearly await discovery. One must further note that though these earliest writers lived in a world marked by rhetoric, it ought to be demonstrated, not merely assumed, that the same could be said of the masses.

Although we know less about biblical exegesis in the second century than in subsequent periods, it seems correct to say that at that date the Bible usually 'was interpreted without regard to its literary or historical context'.[7] If rhetoric is defined in such a way as to be associated with these contexts, we then have reason to conclude that it did not have an influence on the analysis of texts. In fact, one finds a near total separation of rhetoric from all church activity revealed in the excommunication of Paul of Samosata around 270 for 'oratorical delivery'.[8] Also crucial is the observation that the subject-matter of early Christian works would have lent itself to the appropriation of classical techniques and devices, for

[5] Amergen, *Stylistic Influence*.
[6] See below (pp. 176–81) for more on Chrysostom.
[7] Dockery, *Biblical Interpretation*, 72.
[8] Kennedy, *Greek Rhetoric under Christian Emperors*, 185. Paul of Samosata's downfall was heresy and 'oratorical delivery'. Eusebius, *Ecclesiastical History* 7.29–30.

both apology and exhortation mark early Christian writing, yet the texts bear no 'thematic or structural references to the classics'.[9]

According to Kennedy, not until the third century does one find an

> increasing sign not only of the adaptation of dialectic, but of the influence of rhetoric among Christians. The earliest extant example of the utilisation of the structure and topics of classical epideictic oratory to create Christian panegyric is apparently a farewell speech of Gregory Thaumaturgus to Origen in 238.[10]

We thus do not find evidence of a rhetorical world which represents the only mode of discourse available to the early Christians. In fact, Kennedy adds that Gregory's is 'the only extant example of a Greek farewell speech' and that Origen reacted to it negatively, telling him to reject his philosophizing and to embrace Christianity.[11] Kennedy goes so far as to write: 'It is clear that some tension existed between rhetoric and religion in Gregory's society'.[12] These concessions which, as we will see, apply beyond Gregory's social boundaries, support the notion that rhetoric was deemed an inappropriate vehicle for Christianity.

Greek fathers

Lack of artistry in the NT was not regarded as a fault by early rhetorically trained Christians.[13] They were able, in fact, to find virtue in the qualities which provoked pagan adversaries to slander.[14] Consider the words of Tatian:

> retiring by myself, I sought how I might be able to discover the truth. And, while I was giving my most earnest attention to the matter, I happened to meet with certain

---

[9] Sider, *The Gospel and its Proclamation*, 60–4.

[10] Kennedy, *Classical Rhetoric*, 140.

[11] Ibid., 140–1.

[12] Ibid., 141.

[13] But cf. the Corinthian congregation, who, it would appear, were in search of rhetorical flourish. Norden, *Antike Kunstprosa*, 493; Litfin, *Theology of Proclamation*, 154–5.

[14] Such slander, significantly, is lacking in much Jewish criticism of the writings in question. Was their particular rhetoric near enough to the Christian writings that Jews hostile to Christianity find fault not with style and technique, but with content? They seem to accept the means of communication.

barbaric writings, too old to be compared with the opinions of the Greeks, and too divine to be compared with
their errors; and I was led to put faith in these by the
unpretending cast of the language, the inartificial character
of the writers.[15]

Theophilus, in a parody of the classical *exordium*, takes a different
line: 'Fluent speech and euphonious diction produce delight and
praise – resulting in empty glory, among wretched men who have a
depraved mind. The man who loves truth, however, pays no
attention to defiled language, but examines the fact behind the
word to see what it is and what it means'.[16]

A more significant figure is Origen, whose *Contra Celsum* embodies a detailed response to an attack on Christianity.[17] His quotations from Celsus and the responses reflect an awareness that the
biblical texts, including Paul's writings, are not literary.[18] T. R.
Glover writes that though we possess only fragments of Celsus, we
have 'enough to show how Christianity at once provoked the
laughter, incensed the patriotism, and offended the religious tastes
of educated people'.[19] Nevertheless, Origen mounts a defence free
from artificial claims of biblical literary sophistication – even going
so far as to find virtue in biblical 'boorishness'.

Celsus swings the axe at the very root of the tree when he brings
the charge that Jesus' teaching is 'successful only among the
uneducated because of its vulgarity and utter illiteracy';[20] Jesus was
poor, 'had no general education and had learnt no arguments and
doctrines by which he could have become a persuasive speaker to
crowds'.[21] His apostles were mere fishermen.[22] Origen, far from

[15] Tatian, *Address of Tatian to the Greeks*, 29 (c. 170).
[16] Theophilus of Antioch, *Ad Autolycum*, 1.1.
[17] *C.* 185–254. Most of our knowledge of Origen's life comes from Eusebius'
Ecclesiastical History, book 6.
[18] E.g. Origen, *Contra Celsum*, 7.62: 'We ought also to notice that the idea about
being long-suffering is not *corrupted* by the poor literary style'. Origen concedes that
the style is poor, though we will see that his overall argument makes a virtue of the
stylistic poverty, for Paul's lesser style offers universal benefit, while the sophistication of a Plato renders him accessible to the few. Other pagan criticisms of biblical
style are found in Lactantius, *Divine Institutes* 5.1.15–16; 30; Augustine, *Confessions*
3.5.9. Jerome, *Letter 22*.
[19] Glover, *Conflict of Religions*, 239. Cf. A. H. N. Jones, 'Social Background', 20.
[20] *Contra Celsum* 1.27. Ibid., 6.12 adds that Christians are 'uneducated and
stupid', and 6.23 that their teachings are 'matters only fit for fools and slaves to
listen to'.
[21] Ibid., 1.29.
[22] Ibid., 1.62.

denying these criticisms, concedes that Jesus' apostles were 'unlettered and ignorant men'.[23] Celsus characterizes proselytizing Christians as religious 'scoundrels' who 'frequently take advantage of the lack of education of gullible people'.[24] Not only is the Christian appeal restricted to 'stupid and uneducated yokels' (or, as even Origen himself puts it, 'the stupid' and the 'barbarian'),[25] but, according to Celsus, they go so far as to 'drive away every intelligent man from arguing about this faith, and invite only the stupid and low-class folk'.[26]

Thus Jesus, the apostles and early Christians were accused of being vulgar, and even worse, to Celsus' mind, illiterate. Unavoidably, then, these same 'shortcomings' are manifest in biblical texts: 'But Celsus thinks the books of the Jews and Christians are utterly crude and illiterate'.[27]

While always conceding a great deal, Origen answers the accusation with a consistent argument: the apostles depended on God's power rather than verbal art or 'ordered narrative by the standards of Greek dialectical or rhetorical arts'. This lack of 'persuasive words of the wisdom that consists in literary style and composition' prevented Christianity's confusion with philosophical schools. Thus Origen identifies the 'fisherfolk and tax-collectors who have not even a primary education' with Paul, who says: 'And my word and my preaching were not in persuasive words of man's wisdom, but in demonstration of the spirit and of power, that our faith may not be in the wisdom of men but in the power of God [1 Cor. 2.4–5]'.[28]

Origen's reply suggests that the designations 'fisherfolk and tax-collectors' mean more than the typical disparagement of certain occupations: his interest is in the level of their literary output. This persuasion which functions independently of accepted persuasive literary modes works in all the apostles; even as all share in the same shortcomings, so their writings must all partake of the same spiritual *dunamis*. Accordingly, he argues for simplicity in order to defend the integrity of the Bible, reminding his reader that

> men who had not learnt the technique taught by the
> pernicious sophistry of the Greeks, which has great plausi-

23 Ibid., 8.47.
24 Ibid., 1.9.
25 Ibid., 6.1.
26 Ibid., 3.18.
27 Ibid., 4.87.
28 Ibid., 1.62.

bility and cleverness, and who knew nothing of the rhetoric prevalent in the law-courts, could not have invented stories in such a way that their writings were capable in themselves of bringing a man to believe and to live a life in conformity with his faith. I think it was for this reason that Jesus chose to employ such men to teach his doctrine, that there might be no possible suspicion of plausible sophisms, but that to those able to understand, the innocence of the writer's purpose, which if I may say so was very naïve, might be obviously manifest; and that they might see that the writers were considered worthy to be endowed with divine power, which accomplished far more than seems to be achieved by involved verbosity and stylish constructions, and by a logical argument divided into distinct sections and worked out with Greek technical skill.[29]

Could Origen have displayed such an attitude toward rhetoric in his description of the evangelists while believing that Paul was a rhetor?

The composition of the Bible's audience and its authorship demand that it be written in a common style – even word choice exhibits this artlessness, for NT vocabulary, which falls far short of 'the brilliance of a literary composition', was purposely chosen to convey truth and to win the masses rather than impress the sophisticated.[30]

In a specifically Pauline context he likewise suggests that 'If [Celsus] devotes himself to attentive reading, I know well that . . . he will admire the mind of the man who uses ordinary vocabulary to contemplate great truths'.[31] Again he insists, it is 'not in recondite writings which are read only by a few scholars, but in popular literature that "the invisible things of God are clearly seen from the creation of the world, being understood by the things that are made"' [Rom. 1.20].[32] Paul, in Origen's estimation, does not depend on the heights of *paideia* but instead writes popular literature with an ordinary vocabulary.

This does not mean that Origen necessarily considers Paul incapable of a higher level: he only discusses what Paul has actually

[29] Ibid., 3.39.
[30] Ibid., 6.1–2.
[31] Ibid., 3.20.
[32] Ibid., 7.37.

done in his epistles. Moreover, as seen already, he provides a rationale for simple acts of communication: writers with a 'meaner style' offer benefit to a wider sphere than one in possession of, say, Plato's sophistication. He does not mean to disparage Plato but to explain by this contrast Paul's claim that his preaching was 'not in persuasive words of wisdom, but in demonstration of the spirit and of power'.[33]

So with respect to persuasive technique and vocabulary, Origen and Celsus agree that the Bible, and particularly Paul himself, derive no part of their force from similarity to classical persuasive material. Indeed, Origen, depending on Paul, claims that the source of the gospel's power lies apart from its spokespersons' sophistication, and that foolish things confound the wise. Paul uses 'the word "wise" in a loose sense to mean those who seem to have made progress in learning, although they have fallen away to atheistic polytheism'.[34] Origen specifies that he means 'foolishness in so far as that applies to preaching';[35] and insists that the 'gospel is not for the wise of this age'.[36] Wisdom for him is education in the best doctrines, the value of a doctrine being commensurate with its truthfulness.[37] Its failure to partake of this zeal for truth compels him to eschew rhetoric altogether. In keeping with such a position, says Origen, the mere appearance of intelligence matters little alongside true intelligence.[38] Thus the accusation of this age that the gospel is foolishness poses no threat.

The rhetor himself plays only a small part in Origen's response.[39] Celsus has asserted that it is nonsensical to argue that God has made evil and that he is 'incapable of persuading and admonishing men'.[40] Addressing the notion that God cannot persuade, Origen insists that persuasion, like getting a haircut, is a reciprocal relationship: it requires an effective argument of one party and submission of the other. So the fault lies not with God but with those who refuse to 'accept God's persuasive words'.[41] He then

[33] Ibid., 6.2.
[34] Ibid., 3.73, citing 1 Cor. 1.27.
[35] Ibid., 1.13: citing 1 Cor. 1.21 and 23–4.
[36] Ibid., 3.47, citing 1 Cor. 1.18ff. 1 Cor. 1–2 appear for this purpose at 1.62; 3.47, 48, 73 and elsewhere.
[37] Ibid., 3.49.
[38] Ibid., 3.49.
[39] Ibid., 6.57.
[40] Ibid., 6.54.
[41] Ibid., 6.57.

narrows his focus by comparing God's persuasion with that of the rhetorician, insisting that

> If anyone applies this also to men, who are called 'creators of persuasion', he would not be wrong. For it is possible even for a man who has grasped in the highest degree the principles of rhetoric, and who uses them in the right way, to do all in his power to persuade men, and yet, because he fails to gain the will of the man who ought to be persuaded, he seems to be unconvincing. And that, even if the persuasive words are given by God, yet the act of assent to them is not caused by God, is clearly taught by Paul when he says: 'The persuasion is not from him who calls you'.[42]

He does not equate divine persuasion with rhetoric, but depends on the latter to empower an analogy. The similarity lies in the observation that the rhetor, like God, awaits the response of the listener. But the argument is structured as a *reductio* which applies his observation to another sphere; he never suggests that the Bible contains classical rhetoric, only that they intersect at the point where both depend on a persuasion requiring the submission of the hearer/reader.

Origen clearly holds that the Bible, including the Pauline corpus, does not depend on persuasive ability stemming from a rhetorical education, but rather embodies a non-artistic statement of the truth which is fortified by the power of the Spirit. He does not champion a rhetorical interpretation of Paul: he opposes it. He also does not seem to think that all writers who have their origin in the Graeco-Roman world 'breathe the air of rhetoric' in such a way that it necessarily determines the shape and strategy of their discourse.

Basil (*c.* 330–79), another well-trained speaker, regrets time lost to a wisdom made foolish by God.[43] 'An address about the saints cannot be made to conform to the laws of encomium. The best encomium of the martyrs is to exhort the congregation to virtue'.[44]

---

[42] Ibid., citing Gal. 5.8.

[43] Basil, *Letters*, 223.2. NPNF 2nd 8:263. Jacks, *St Basil and Greek Literature*; Campbell, *Influence*; Kustas, 'Basil and Rhetorical Tradition', 221–79. Quasten, *Patrology*, 3.204–36.

[44] Kennedy, *Greek Rhetoric under Christian Emperors*, 240, citing Basil, Sermon 19, para 2. Further cf. Basil's *To the Young on How They Should Benefit From Greek Writings*. He argues for the usefulness of 'writers like Hesiod, Homer, and Plato, but does not discuss orators, style, or sophistry'. Cf. N. G. Wilson, *Basil on Greek Literature*.

He adds: 'Our writers do not waste time in polishing periods, we prefer clarity of expression to mere euphony'[45] and 'the school of God does not recognize the laws of the encomium', 'nor does it deal in "sophistic vanities"'.[46] In a letter to Leontius the Sophist, he confesses that constant exposure to 'commonplace speech' has robbed him of the confidence to 'address Sophists like you, who are certain to be annoyed and unmerciful'.[47] This estimation Basil also applies to the Bible,[48] but elsewhere insists that the gospel is true though written in an unlearned style and 'a barbarian tongue'.[49]

Chrysostom studied[50] and then taught rhetoric.[51] Not surprisingly, then, his writings reveal an attitude toward rhetoric which provides grounds for discussion. First, regarding his practice, one finds that Chrysostom's sermons

> make abundant, even excessive, use of the stylistic devices of the sophists, especially tropes and figures involving pleonasm, such as anaphora, or sound, such as paranomasia, or vivacity, such as rhetorical question or question and answer. Progymnasmatic forms appear, such as the ecphrasis of deserted Antioch (2.5–6) or of the works of creation (9.6; 10.5–6) or the human body (11.5).[52]

Of his encomia, Kennedy writes: 'Although he uses the stylistic artifices of the sophists . . . he does not seek to imitate their structural forms and topics'.[53] We thus see the coincidence of use and disuse by Chrysostom, in that he appropriates stylistic elements even while his structure does not correspond to that proposed for a classical oration (of any species). This pattern recurs time and again, though its value need not go unchallenged, for it opens the question of how much pleonasm, figures of sound and vivacity

---

45   Murphy, 'Augustine', 403, following Campbell, *Influence*.
46   Murphy, ibid., 403.
47   Basil, *Letters*, 20.
48   Murphy, 'Augustine', 403.
49   Basil, *Letters*, 309. Cf. Fox, *Basil*, 89.
50   Chrysostom (*c.* 354–407), along with Theodore of Mopsuestia, studied under Libanius, the leading rhetorician of their day. Dockery, *Biblical Interpretation*, 109.
51   Zeno states that just when Chrysostom's career was about to begin he abandoned it for a life of solitude. Quasten, *Patrology*, 3.424–82; Bauer, *Chrysostom*; Carter, 'Chronology', 357–64. See Jones, 'Chrysostom's Parentage', 171–3.
52   Kennedy, *Greek Rhetoric under Christian Emperors*, 248. References are to Chrysostom's homilies *Concerning the Statutes*, for which see Schaff, NPNF 1st 9: 331–489.
53   Kennedy, *Greek Rhetoric under Christian Emperors*, 249.

actually tell us about a writer's relation to classical rhetoric. Perhaps they comprise a few of the hallmarks evidenced to varying degrees in nearly all examples of good writing – or at least writings of a certain level. Of things specifically rhetorical, for example *dispositio*, Kennedy finds little in Chrysostom.

This nexus of Chrysostom, Paul and language allows for another observation: Chrysostom and Paul spoke sharply contrasting levels of Greek. Chrysostom's manner of speaking does not share the apostle's simplicity – for he spoke the Greek appropriate to his level of *paideia*. We thus read of an elderly woman who, in the midst of one of his sermons, voiced her inability to comprehend even half of what he was saying, 'so remote was his language from that of the people'. Chrysostom therefore departed from his usual level of written and spoken Greek to complete his sermon.[54] On his lips the peculiar words and expressions of the NT and LXX appear as 'technical terms or quotations from a foreign tongue, i.e. at a purely lexical level', though he rejects 'the morphological and syntactical features of the Greek Bible'.[55] Thus, while Paul wrote to be understood by all with the result that he was unappreciated by some, Chrysostom adopts an elevated form misunderstood by some though surely appreciated by others. They represent well the linguistic distance between the common and the elevated tongue.

How does Chrysostom himself evaluate the language of the NT? More specifically, what does he say concerning Paul? We read in his homily on 1 Corinthians 1.10–17 of a debate that he has observed: a Christian argues with a Greek that Paul's eloquence outshines Plato's, while the Greek argues for Paul's ignorance. Chrysostom suggests that each argues what ought to be the other's case, for if the Greek is right and Paul is ignorant, then the ignorant has overcome the great philosopher; and if the Christian is right, if Paul surpasses Plato, then Christianity is vulnerable to the criticism that its power resides in words. Chrysostom then instructs that to avoid ridicule (even to earn praise) Christians should not protest the charge that the apostles were untrained and 'rude', but should even add that they were also 'untaught, and unlettered, and poor, and vile, and stupid, and obscure'. The irony is that 'the fisherman, the tentmaker, the publican, the ignorant, the unlettered, coming from the far distant country of Palestine, and having beaten off their

[54] This story, given without reference, is found in Browning, *Medieval and Modern Greek*, 55.
[55] Ibid.

own ground the philosophers, the masters of oratory, the skilful debaters, alone prevailed against them in a short space of time'.[56]

Admittedly, these words describe the apostles as a group, but they appear in Chrysostom's commentary on *Paul*'s words in 1 Corinthians in reaction to a debate concerning *Paul*'s eloquence, and as such apply to him as much as any apostle. Speaking elsewhere of Corinthian disparagement of Paul, Chrysostom writes that admitting Paul's inabilities means little, for his mere presence refuted the demons, revealing that he possessed 'a greater power by far than power of speech'.[57]

An imaginary debate with Basil reveals more concerning Chrysostom's estimation of Paul's literary ability.[58] Chrysostom is asked to respond to the charge that Paul is 'rude of speech'. He therefore distinguishes 'the tricks of profane oratory' from understanding how to contend for the truth, then continues that Paul only claimed rudeness of speech, not knowledge. Further,

> were I to insist upon the polish of Isocrates, the weight of Demosthenes, the dignity of Thucydides, and the sublimity of Plato, in any one bishop, St. Paul would be a strong evidence against me. But I pass by all such matters and the elaborate ornaments of profane oratory; and I take no account of style and delivery; yea let a man's diction be poor and his composition simple and unadorned, but let him not be unskilled in the knowledge and accurate statement of doctrine.[59]

Chrysostom recognizes the source of Paul's power. It lies not in the tricks of the orator but in harmony with divine truth.

We again find little interest in *dispositio* and Chrysostom never offers a complete 'rhetorical' outline of Galatians. On occasion he employs the terminology of the handbooks, but not to produce Kennedy's kind of analysis save one exception: in discussing Galatians, as we have seen, he identifies an 'exordium'. He disagrees, however, with modern critics concerning which verses constitute that *exordium*, specifying 1.1–3[60] and in so doing

---

[56] Chrysostom, *First Corinthians*, Homily 3, 8.
[57] Chrysostom, *On the Priesthood* 4.6.
[58] For the identity of 'Basil' see Staats, 'Chrysostomus', 226.
[59] Chrysostom, *On The Priesthood* 4.6.
[60] Chrysostom, *Galatians* 1. See also Migne, *Patrologiae Graeca* LXI, cols. 610–82, with Latin trans. But see also on Gal. 1.5. Cf. Betz (*Galatians*, 44–56) who

creating the impression that rather than treat the *exordium* as part of a speech he simply draws an analogy between an epistolary device and its rhetorical counterpart. This succeeds because such a comparison efficiently describes that element which introduces the participants and the issue at hand, much the same as an *exordium* does for a speech. Lest too much be made of this term, one should be aware that the term used (τὸ προοίμιον)[61] is not originally from the oratorical sphere at all but, as Quintilian explains, was borrowed from music, and was given quite wide application even by the first century.[62] Thus Chrysostom may be communicating the general purpose of introduction by using a wide-ranging metaphor. If this analysis is right, '*exordium*' here means no more than what Betz and others mean by 'epistolary prescript'.

We have already discussed a second apparent use of a technical term which appears in Chrysostom's comments on Galatians 1.10.[63] We repeat only that Chrysostom calls 1.10–2.21 a narrative – which does not demand that he envisages a *narratio* of a speech. This in turn requires that Chrysostom oppose recent rhetorical descriptions of the function of 2.15–21: he calls it 'hortatory', but says it is 'couched in the form of reproof' – with no suggestion of a *propositio*.[64] His structure for Galatians thus shares little with recent rhetorical analyses other than to acknowledge that 1.10–2.21 is a narrative – a notion with which all would agree.

Galatians 5.13, according to Chrysostom, begins a digression into 'moral discourse'.[65] He neither considers the entire epistle hortatory, nor even 5.1 and beyond – instead specifying 5.13–6.10[66] – but finds elements of exhortation and instruction woven into the entire fabric of the epistle.

Chrysostom teaches us still more concerning the intersection of rhetoric and Galatians: 'Observe throughout the transparent humility of this holy soul; his earnestness in his own vindication is as

---

designates as *exordium* Gal. 1.6–11; Mack (*Rhetoric and the New Testament*, 69) Gal. 2.6–10; Longenecker (*Galatians*, 12–19) Gal. 1.6–10.

[61] Migne, XI, *in situ.* (col. 612).

[62] Quintilian, *Institutio* 4.1.2 reads: 'It may be because οἰμή means a time, and players on the lyre have given the name of *proem* to the prelude which they perform to win the favor of the audience before entering upon the regular contest for the prize, that orators before beginning to plead make a few introductory remarks to win the indulgence of the judges'.

[63] See the discussion of *narratio* in our chapter 4.

[64] Chrysostom, *Galatians* 13: 20.

[65] Ibid., 13: 39.

[66] Cf. Kennedy, *New Testament Interpretation*, 145.

great as if he had to render an account of his deeds, and was pleading for his life in a court of justice'.[67] He also comments on 1.22, 23, 24, all of which mention modesty or humility. Humility could easily have been discussed as a commonplace – yet he avoids 'rhetorical categories'. Surely he would have often heard discourses treating these commonplaces during his career, yet we find no attempt to develop them in Galatians. Even more pointedly, he talks about an earnestness that reminds him of the courts, yet that recognition never compels him to find and isolate a judicial setting or any other conventional elements of forensic discourse beyond this 'earnestness'. He notes only that Paul's intensity matches that of a defendant and then moves on, never comparing his actual mode of speech to that of the courts. Of 3.1 we read: 'Here he passes to another subject' but find no trace of the rhetorical label for such a transition.[68]

The distance between Paul and oratory can be seen in Chrysostom's comments on Galatians 1.10 which stress that 'he who wishes to persuade men, is led to act tortuously and insincerely, and to employ deceit and falsehood, in order to engage the assent of his hearers'.[69] He further remarks that Paul has sought neither honour nor a personal following, instead seeking to please God alone: these words relate directly to the sophist and his conduct, excluding Paul from that sphere.

Finally, in response to a specific Graeco-Roman rhetorical term which does appear in Galatians, both Chrysostom and his companion Theodore of Mopsuestia suggest that Paul gets it wrong. Chrysostom writes of Galatians 4.24: 'Contrary to usage, he calls a type an allegory'.[70] Theodore similarly comments: 'Paul knew the Hellenistic term but not the Hellenistic application which would treat the texts like dreams in the night'.[71]

This wealth of reasons for distancing Galatians from oratory within Chrysostom's thought is all too easily overlooked because of a handful of allusions to courtroom drama. We have already noted one, and add that at 1.10 we find another. Chrysostom, inevitably

---

[67] Chrysostom, *Galatians*, on 1.20.

[68] Ibid., *in loc.*

[69] Ibid.

[70] Ibid. Bouwman, 'Die Hagar-und Sara-Perikope', 3143–4; Kepple, 'Antiochene Exegesis', 239–49. Cf. Hanson, *Paul's Technique*, 94–103, 126–7, 160–1.

[71] Theodore, 'Galatians 4.22–31', 95–103. Cf. also Dockery, *Biblical Interpretation*, 112; Theodore, *Epistolas b. Pauli commentari* 1.73–74. Quasten, *Patrology*, 3.402.

one might say, relates persuasion to oratory, but – and this is the crucial point for Chrysostom – only to *deny* that Paul depended on rhetorical means. While some today may question Paul's integrity on this point, or attribute his renunciation of sophistry to irony, we have no basis for holding that Chrysostom shared such an assessment of the text. To him, 1.10 reflects Paul's rejection of a summons, not the beginning of a defence.[72] Thus, if forensic imagery appears in his commentary on Galatians it is as a device imposed upon the text to help communicate its message, even as Paul depends on forensic language in Romans.

Chrysostom does not argue that Galatians is modelled on a Graeco-Roman oration or that it can be analysed with the help of rhetoric; indeed he casts doubt on Paul's awareness of, and conformity to, such a manner of discourse.

Another Greek speaker, Gregory of Nyssa,[73] was heavily influenced by philosophy and employed a more artificial style than previous Christian writers; indeed, he is said to have come closest to the structure of classical orations.[74] When he focuses on matters near to our concern he tells us that 'Peter, Andrew and John caught fish, Paul made tents, Matthew collected taxes, and the others all made their own living; none were rulers, commanders or captains, nor were they admirers of rhetors and philosophers but were poor and unlearned and eagerly pursued their humble occupations'.[75]

For Gregory, as we will see for others, biblical non-conformity to Graeco-Roman oratory never led to despair; it meant only the application of different standards. For our purposes, though, he clearly did not consider Paul an accomplished or sophisticated orator but a member of a different social class.

Latin fathers

Perhaps because of his oft-cited question: 'What indeed has Athens to do with Jerusalem? What concord is there between the Academy and the church? What between heretics and Christians?',[76] Ter-

---

[72] Chrysostom, *Galatians*, *in loc.* Chrysostom refers to 1 Cor. 4.3 to assert again that Paul will not be tried by his converts.

[73] *C.* 330–89; Dockery, *Biblical Interpretation*, 101.

[74] Stein, *Encomium*. See also Owen, 'St Gregory', 64–71. On his use of rhetorical forms see Mann, 'Gregor', 126–47.

[75] Gregory of Nyssa, Epistle 17; cited in Hagendahl, 'Piscatorie', 189.

[76] Tertullian, *Prescription*, 7. See the notably similar words of Jerome below.

tullian[77] has been thought to have rejected all classical influences.[78] This is reinforced when in the same place he describes dialectics as the source of heresy.[79] Kennedy, however, attacks such a reading: recently students of Tertullian have come to realize that his writings merge with Christian thought material as diverse as elements of Stoicism and Platonism, history, law, rhetoric and even 'the satiric techniques of Juvenal and Tacitus'.

> Classical literature was there to use for Christian purposes and was a rich source of examples. A knowledge of letters is necessary, he says (*De corona* 8.2), for the business of life. Some study of literature cannot be avoided by a Christian, but he must not teach it (*De idolatria* 10). Demosthenes and Cicero were eloquent men (*Apology* 11.15–16); Plato has dignity, Aristotle equanimity (*De anima* 3.2); but Aristotelian dialectic is the mother of heresy (*De praescriptione haereticorum* 7). With character-istic irony, Tertullian recommends the reading of the scriptures for those who would seek entertainment.[80]

So we must grant Tertullian greater complexity than is sometimes admitted – forcing us to evaluate carefully what remain rather meagre data. We learn that he has a respect for eloquence, but never suggests that Paul was a model of oratorical skill; and we neither hear him suggesting that Paul makes use of oratorical techniques nor find him doing so himself within a church setting. Yet he recognizes that practical needs can sometimes only be met by falling back on aspects of classical culture, such as its education (*On Idolatry* 10). Thus, Marrou tells us, Christians 'never throughout the whole of antiquity, except for a few particular cases' moved into segregated schools. Instead they supplemented their shared pagan education with specifically Christian learning undertaken at church and at home.[81] The real danger is not every

---

[77] *C.* 155–255, born Quintus Septimus Florens Tertullianus, to a subaltern in the army. See Dockery, *Biblical Interpretation*, 67, von Campenhausen, *Fathers*, 5–9 for biographical data. On Tertullian and rhetoric see further: Sider, *Ancient Rhetoric*; 'Approaches to Tertullian', 228–60; Barnes, *Tertullian*.

[78] So Ellspermann, *Christian Writers*, 23–42. According to von Campenhausen (*Fathers*, 5) he studied both rhetoric and law and may have practised law for a time.

[79] Tertullian, *Prescription*, 7.

[80] Kennedy, 'Christianity and Criticism', 337. Cf. also his *Classical Rhetoric*, 13.

[81] Marrou, *History of Education*, 317–18; cf. Murphy, 'Augustine', 402. On pagan education in early Christianity generally see Marrou, ibid., 315ff., especially 315–19.

exposure to things classical but combustible combinations of Christianity and paganism. For Tertullian, classical techniques, though powerful, do not determine the shape or content of the biblical text.

As for the style of his own discourse, Tertullian did not imitate classical models.

> He wanted to strike and unmask the reality of his time; he wanted above all to grip, enchain, and captivate his hearers . . . [His Latin] was without precedent in the literary field . . . the living language of the Christians of that time . . . It observes and adopts at the same time even in grammatical details the language actually spoken by the society of Carthage, and by the people whom Tertullian knew, observed and sought out.[82]

All this adds up to discourse which 'often violently exceeds the bounds of good taste'. Even the ancients complain about its obscurity,[83] but when he applies this style the results are dramatic. Tertullian, surveying previous defences of Christianity, discovers that they are formless, haphazard shots fired in all directions, rather than arguments narrowly focused on crucial concerns – and they lack the sophistication needed to win a hearing.[84] He responds with his *Apologeticum*, a discourse aimed at political leaders and patterned after orations delivered before a tribunal.[85] He thus employs rhetoric only in its proper sphere, and gives no indication that the church and rhetoric have ever been formally introduced, adopting the practice of Paul himself.[86]

Cyprian also deserves attention, for he, by birth a member of the ruling class, inaugurated significant changes in the role of the priesthood.[87] He was the first bishop to fulfil his clerical functions 'in the magisterial style of the consuls and pro-consuls' – an approach without precedent in the Greek church.[88]

---

[82] Von Campenhausen, *Fathers*, 8. Glover has nothing but praise for his 'brilliant' Latin – see *Ancient World*, 325.

[83] Von Campenhausen, *Fathers*, 9.

[84] Ibid., 11.

[85] Ibid., 12.

[86] See chapter 7 on Acts 24.

[87] Caecilius Cyprianus, bishop of Carthage. See Von Campenhausen, *Fathers*, 36ff.

[88] Ibid., 37.

Gregory of Nazianus[89] classified the speeches of Cyprian into three groups based on their objective, yielding the categories of (1) moral exhortation; (2) teaching; and (3) lives of Christians. We learn that in the appropriate setting (i.e. at funerals), he preached epideictic sermons.[90] But his other speeches make concessions to sophistry only with respect to style, eschewing 'classical structural elements and classical allusions'.[91] We again observe the tendency manifest in Tertullian; in fact, of Cyprian it is said not only that he writes 'a more Ciceronian Latin than Tertullian'[92] but also that in rejecting 'paganism he put off all interest in literature and never quotes a Classical writer'[93] whether pagan poet, rhetorician or orator.[94] His language reveals his *paideia* even as his rejection of pagan literature hides it.

This does not, however, mean that he necessarily rejected all non-stylistic links with his pagan past. He too asserts that in the appropriate sphere rhetoric has its place – as long as it is not dragged into the church. 'In courts of justice, in the public meetings, in political discussions, a full eloquence may be the pride of vocal ambition, but in speaking of the Lord God, a pure simplicity of expression which is convincing, depends upon the substance of the argument rather than upon the forcefulness of eloquence'.[95] Cyprian reserves rhetoric for the spheres intended by the handbooks, while recognizing its inappropriateness in the church; surely he provides no precedent for finding classical rhetoric in Paul's epistles.

Arnobius had taught rhetoric, and gained renown as a critic of Christianity,[96] at Sicca Veneria in Africa Proconsularis before his conversion at the age of 60.[97] He thereafter attains to the height of rhetoric even while decrying it in his public works:

---

[89] Gregory of Nazianus, *Oration* 24.

[90] Kennedy, *Greek Rhetoric under Christian Emperors*, 238.

[91] Ibid.

[92] Though Von Campenhausen credits him with 'a new Latin religious style'. Augustine would later adopt his teaching on rhetorical restraint: *Fathers*, 50. See *De doctrina Christiana* 4.14.31. Cf. Von Campenhausen, ibid., 221.

[93] Kennedy, 'Christianity and Criticism', 338.

[94] Bardy, 'L'église', 1–28. Von Campenhausen (*Fathers*, 37) questions the position, first expressed by Jerome, that Cyprian had taught rhetoric.

[95] Ellspermann, *Christian Writers*, 51, citing *Adversus Donatus* 2.

[96] Frend, *Rise of Christianity*, 450–51.

[97] Nominated for post of teacher of rhetoric at Nicomedia in 292, Arnobius was converted about 300 (at approximately 40 years of age). See Ellspermann, *Christian Writers*, 67.

> Because you are skilled in declining verbs and nouns by cases and tenses, and in avoiding barbarous words and expressions; because you have learned either to express yourselves in harmonious, and orderly, and fitly disposed language, or to know when it is rude and unpolished; because you know what the issues to be proposed in lawsuits are, how many kinds of cases there are, how many ways of pleading, what the genus is, what the species, by what methods an opposite is distinguished from a contrary – do you therefore think that you know what is the nature of the lowest and the highest?[98]

In his rejection of rhetoric in the church, like so many others, he depends on 1 Corinthians: 'Have the well known words never rung in your ears, that the wisdom of man is foolishness with God?'[99] He goes so far as to declare the rules of grammar unnecessary,[100] wondering, with Christian authors in view, how smooth pronunciation or grammatical precision could possibly facilitate comprehension.

> Let that pomposity of style and strictly regulated diction be reserved for public assemblies, for lawsuits, for the forum and the courts of justice, and by all means be handed over to those who, striving after the smooth influences of pleasant sensations, bestow all their care upon splendour of language.[101]

When confronted with the charge that biblical texts 'were written by unlearned and ignorant men', he too argues that this renders them all the more believable: they come from the hands of the simple and innocent who know nothing of artifice or treachery. The 'language is mean and vulgar' precisely because truth requires no polish.

> Syllogisms, enthymemes, definitions, and all those ornaments by which men seek to establish their statements, aid those groping for the truth, but do not clearly mark its great features. But he who really knows the subject under discussion, neither defines, nor deduces, nor seeks the

[98] Arnobius, *Heathen* 2.6.
[99] Ibid., citing 1 Cor. 3.19.
[100] Ibid., 1.59.
[101] Ibid.

other tricks of the words by which an audience is wont to
be taken in, and to be beguiled into a forced assent to a
proposition.[102]

While this may seem faint praise, it is intended to be taken
seriously: he responds to the charge that Christian texts are
'overrun with barbarisms and solecisms, and disfigured by mon-
strous blunders' with the retort that such criticism reveals a
'childish and petty spirit; for if we allow that it is reasonable, let us
cease to use certain kinds of fruit because they grow with prickles
on them'.[103] He does not deny that the NT exhibits linguistic
crudeness, for it is apparent to all; instead Arnobius, like others
before him, defends its lowliness.

He provides a reason for using a lower form of expression – even
when the writer is capable of better. By now we are familiar with its
form:

> When we are discussing matters far removed from mere
> display, we should consider what is said . . . especially
> since we know that some even who devoted themselves to
> philosophy, not only disregarded refinement of style, but
> also purposely adopted a vulgar meanness when they
> might have spoken with greater elegance and richness, lest
> forsooth they might impair the stern gravity of speech and
> revel rather in the pretentious show of the Sophists.[104]

He, again resembling his predecessors, grants rhetoric a place,
albeit grudgingly, in the venues envisaged in the handbooks,[105] but
considers the Scriptures to speak with a sweet simplicity; thus they
alone provide an appropriate model for the church's discourse.[106]
Arnobius may not be counted as a predecessor to the work of Betz
or Kennedy, for he does not allow rhetoric in the church, nor
champion its expansion into neighbouring spheres.

Lactantius, who studied rhetoric under Arnobius before either
were converted,[107] responds to false teachers who assail Paul and

---

102 Ibid., 1.58.
103 Ibid., 1.59.
104 Ibid.
105 Ibid.
106 Crutwell, *Literary History*, 632.
107 Lactantius Firmianus Africanus. He knew law but never appeared as a lawyer.
The thrust of his efforts had been neither toward the practice of law nor oratory but
to be a rhetorician. Cf. Von Campenhausen, *Fathers*, 62; Crutwell, *Literary History*,

Peter with the traditional charge of apostolic artlessness and ignorance:[108] 'because the prophets spoke in common and simple language, as though they spoke to the people', the learned reject their message. Indeed they

> are despised by those who are willing to hear nothing except that which is polished and eloquent; nor is anything able to remain fixed in their minds, except that which charms their ears by a more soothing sound . . . So entirely do they regard nothing as true, except that which is pleasant to the ear; nothing as credible, except that which can excite pleasure: no one estimates a subject by its truth, but by its embellishment. Therefore they do not believe the sacred writings, because they are without pretence. [109]

Those who expound Christian truths he describes as 'either altogether ignorant, or at any rate possessed of little learning'.[110] But the benefits of pursuing broader education cannot outweigh the liabilities, for pagan literature equals 'sweets which conceal poison'.[111]

He does maintain that elegance and copiousness help to communicate the truth to the educated non-Christian;[112] he does not, however, find rhetoric in the NT, only defending the use of classical

---

642–7; Frend, *Rise of Christianity*, 451. That he had taught rhetoric is plain from his *Divine Institutes* 5.2.

[108] Lactantius, *Divine Institutes* 5.2; cited in Hagendahl, 'Piscatorie', 186. In this important article Hagendahl cites Celsus ('Origen, *Contra Celsum*. I 62 S. 113, 8' ['Piscatorie', 185]); Lactantius (*Divine Institutes* 5.2 [186]); Julianus (Epistle 55, LCL [186]); Eusebius ('De Theophonia' 5 [PG 24, 624f.] [186]); Hieronymus (Jerome) [187]; Leo the Great (188); Augustine (188–89); Gregory of Nyssa (189); and Sulpicius Severus (192) to show that Peter was consistently viewed by early churchmen, all trained in rhetoric, as reaching no greater rhetorical heights than one should expect of a *fisherman* (clearly intended as pejorative). Such evidence, while not always immediately impacting our work on Galatians, does obviate such claims as that of Pogoloff, who writes that the 'New Testament writer' and the 'recipients' 'lived in a socio-linguistic world shaped by the *conscious rhetoric of Hellenism*' (italics added). This, Pogoloff explains, means 'that the preachers' desires to provoke πιστις were incarnated in Hellenistic rhetoric': cf. 'Isocrates and Contemporary Hermeneutics', 350–1. He seems to imply that all the NT writers cloak their rhetoric in Graeco-Roman forms, but this is denied by those early readers of the texts to whom Hagendahl refers. (Could Pogoloff mean that the gospel of Mark was shaped by, and reveals, Graeco-Roman rhetoric?)

[109] Lactantius, *Divine Institutes* 5.1.

[110] Ibid. Cf. Sider, *Gospel and its Proclamation*, 123; Ellspermann, *Christian Writers*, 90.

[111] *Divine Institutes* 5.1.

[112] Ibid., 5.2. Cf. also 1.1.

forms of eloquence in apologetics and evangelistic material (such as his own *Institutes*).[113] Thus rhetoric for Lactantius, as for those before him, fulfils its true potential when communicating with outsiders, presumably again because they cannot be expected to absorb the unadorned truth. He finds no sophistication anywhere in the Scriptures which would indicate its presence – or validate its use with insiders.

Turning to Jerome, one finds perhaps the clearest statement of rejection of rhetoric. In 372, he moved to Antioch and increased his learning, especially with respect to Greek. He discovered, however, an inner turmoil as his love of pagan wisdom threatened to overwhelm his faith. 'In a dream, the Lord asked Jerome who and what he was. Jerome replied, "I am a Christian". But the response came: "You lie, you are a follower of Cicero and not of Christ, for where your treasure is, there will your heart be also"'.[114] He does not defend himself with the argument that he simply follows his model Paul and his appreciation for rhetoric as revealed in Galatians (or elsewhere). Instead he accepts the accusation that being a 'follower of Cicero' means being out of step with Christ.[115]

Jerome's writings reflect a sensitivity to style and a striving for polish, so it comes as no surprise that he assesses Paul's manner of writing.[116] He locates in Paul 'fault of sentence structure', but never denigrates him for that. Instead he too turns to 1 Corinthians to suggest that Paul could never have drawn 'the whole world to Christ if he had preached the Gospel *"in sapientia verbi"*'.[117] Jerome even refers to Paul in response to an attack on his own writing, insisting that the words 'though I be rude in speech, yet not in knowledge' well described one who had studied under the great Gamaliel, and who

> thought Greek eloquence of no account, or at all events, in his humility, he would not parade his knowledge of it . . .

[113] Ellspermann, *Christian Writers*, 95. *The Institutes* is teeming with allusions to Greek and Latin figures of the past and the gods of their literature.

[114] Dockery, *Biblical Interpretation*, 130. The story is found in Jerome, *Letters* 22.30. Cicero surely represented more than philosophy or rhetoric; he was to Jerome a symbol of classical learning. Later, in his Bethlehem monastery, Jerome taught rhetoric. So Von Campenhausen, *Fathers*, 158.

[115] Though his writings betray a continued interest in 'pagan' matters including rhetoric.

[116] Ellsperman, *Christian Writers*, 128; Lund, *Chiasmus*, 5.

[117] Ellsperman, ibid., 135–6, citing *Commentarius in epistulam Pauli ad Ephesios* 2.587–88.

Still it was not to an illiterate man who stumbled in every sentence that Festus cried, as he stood before his judgement seat: 'Paul thou art beside thyself; much learning doth make thee mad'.[118]

Elsewhere Jerome the allegorical interpreter, speaking of the prodigal who threw husks to swine, writes: 'We can interpret the husks another way. The food of demons is the songs of the poets, secular wisdom, the pomp of rhetorical words. These . . . when they have been studied with their greatest zeal and labor . . . contribute nothing else to their readers, but empty sound, a noisy speech'.[119]

Finally, he asks: 'What communion hath light with darkness? And what concord hath Christ with Belial? How can Horace go with the Psalter, Virgil with the Gospels, Cicero with the Apostle [Paul]? . . . we ought not to drink the cup of Christ, and, at the same time, the cup of devils'.[120] If there is an appropriate place for rhetoric it is not in the writing of Scripture. Such a disjunction is further supported when Jerome instructs:

> read the book of Tully *To Herennius*; read his *Rhetoricians*; or, since he tells us that these books fell from his hands in a merely inchoate and unfinished condition, look through his three books *On the Orator*, in which he introduces a discussion between Crassus and Antony, the most eloquent orators of that day; and a fourth book called *The Orator* which he wrote to Brutus when already an old man; and you will realize that History, Oratory, Dialogue, Epistolary writing, and Commentaries, have, each of them, their special style.[121]

Jerome does not allow for the use of undifferentiated styles across the spectrum of literary genres: each to its own. So the notion that Paul's epistles reproduce the style of oratory would violate his sense of decorum. While Jerome is too complex and has produced too much material for us to analyse fully here, his occasional disapproval of Cicero, rhetoric and even Paul's sentence structure allows some confidence in concluding that he could not equate Paul's style with that of classical rhetoric.

---

[118] Jerome, *Apology* 1.17.
[119] Jerome, *Letters* 21.13.
[120] Ibid., 22.29. See also Jerome's *Perpetual Virginity*.
[121] Jerome, *Apology* 1.16.

Augustine,[122] like Jerome, enjoyed a place among the best educated of his day, yet Douglas Campbell (naming the former), suggests that early Christians possessed of classical backgrounds exhibited a surprising lack of interest in rhetorical approaches to the NT.[123] This, however, only holds for rhetoric as a tool for analysis; Augustine says much concerning rhetorical theory. Indeed some believe that he renewed rhetoric after sophistry rendered it impotent.[124] Kenneth Burke assesses his position this way:

> Regarding his turn from teacher of pagan rhetoric to Christian theologian and bishop, Augustine twice refers to the role of word merchant (*venditor verborum*). In a way, the fourth part of his *De Doctrina Christiana* marks the same crossing, or conversion, as the *Confessions*. It, too, concerns the development from the selling of words to the preaching of the Word. But in the work on Christian rhetoric, he is partly asking how to adapt for ecclesiastical purposes the verbal skill of the pagans, and partly attempting to show that Christianity already had an eloquent body of letters, whereas the autobiography places the emphasis upon the break rather than the bridge between the two realms.[125]

Thus one of Augustine's concerns is with achieving eloquence, but this raises the question of what sort of eloquence he would pursue. The early Christians often view Graeco-Roman rhetoric as something to be rejected, and Augustine stands within this tradition (as well as revealing what he considers to be the sociological sphere of rhetoric) with his reminiscence: 'No longer should I sell weapons to arm the frenzy of young men, who were not so much interested in Your law or Your peace as in the madness of lies and the battles of the law courts'.[126] This opinion poses no obstacle to his assess-

---

[122] 13 November 354 to 28 August 430, born at Thagaste and a contemporary of Athanasius, Basil, Gregorys of Nyssa and Nazianus, Theodore of Mopsuestia, Chrysostom, Theodoret, Cyril of Alexandria, John Cassian, Jerome, Ambrose and Marius Victorinus (cf. Marrou, *St Augustine*, 5–10). *De doctrina Christiana*'s (hereafter *DDC* though some of our quotations render it as *On Christian Doctrine*) present obscurity does not correspond to its former prominence. It was the first work of Augustine to be printed in the Renaissance (Hagendahl, *Augustine*, 568).

[123] Campbell, *Rhetoric of Righteousness*, 71.

[124] Baldwin, *Medieval Rhetoric*, 51.

[125] Burke, *Rhetoric of Religion*, 29.

[126] Augustine, *Confessions* Book 1:9.2.2. For another statement of the sphere of rhetoric, namely for the statesman and in court, see 4.12.27. That Augustine

ment of Paul since Augustine never saw him as a pleader in court in the first place – in fact, he scoffs at the notion that Paul employed rhetoric. Having quoted Romans 5.3–5, he asks

> Now were any man unlearnedly learned (if I may use the expression) to contend that the apostle had here followed the rules of rhetoric, would not every Christian, learned or unlearned laugh at him? And yet here we find the figure which is called in Greek κλιμάχ (climax) and by some in Latin *gradatio* . . . Another ornament too is found here.[127]

So he rejects Paul's conformity to the rules of rhetoric in this passage even as he admits that Paul employs certain devices which are discussed in the handbooks. This pattern, complete with the recognition of stylistic devices alongside the non-use of rhetoric, is widespread: exegetes laboured 'to identify the metres, tropes and figures of "pagan" literature in the biblical writings', even while speaking of a 'special divine eloquence' which freed NT writers from the need for formalized rhetoric. 'Thus Augustine the rhetorician documented the figures of classical rhetoric in biblical texts. On the other hand, when the Augustine nurtured on the Hellenistic classics found the style of Scripture in comparison rude and vulgar, Augustine the allegorical interpreter found in this same roughness the evidence of its spiritual eloquence'.[128]

Indeed, far from attributing to Paul an oratorical eloquence revealed by the use of figures, Augustine strengthens the case that Paul did not conform to the rules of rhetoric. This is in keeping with the younger, searching rhetorician's view of the Bible as a

elsewhere treats rhetoric more favourably is not to be doubted. If techniques are learned in one's youth and quickly absorbed, Augustine suggests that knowledge of them may be useful – but he has resigned his post as teacher of rhetoric and he will not teach the technique in his writings. See Hagendahl, *Augustine*, 2: 567 for discussion. Further, while no longer an armsdealer, Augustine did, on behalf of church members, 'plead with the powers that be and the magistrates for the guilty or the oppressed'. So Marrou, *St Augustine*, 45, n. 61. See *Letters*, 152–4; Murphy, 'Augustine', 409.

[127] Augustine, *DDC* 4.7.11; see also 4.7.12. Cf. Campbell, *Rhetoric of Righteousness*, 76; and Hughes (*Early Christian Rhetoric*, 19–20), who cites the same reference to *climax* to show that Augustine does treat Scripture as rhetoric. Our disagreement is surely because the use of figures relates to style – and as such is an inevitable part of discourse (i.e. marks the presence of level 2 rhetoric) – but does not signify the presence of level 4 rhetoric.

[128] Poland, 'Rhetorical Sublime', 37. Contrast Smit ('Deliberative Speech', 24) and Barrett ('Apologetic Letter', 31–2) and their reference to Paul's 'professional' skill as a rhetorician.

whole. Presumably free of polemical constraints, he writes that he had turned to the Bible but was dismayed by its stylistic short-comings: 'Its words seemed impalatable, "unworthy to be compared with the dignity of Tully (Cicero)"'.[129] Indeed, Augustine was, post conversion, forced by biblical stylistic shortcomings to redefine eloquence altogether.[130] Since classical rhetoric cannot be defended as a tool used by Paul or any other biblical writer, he is free to reject such standards and to offer his honest assessment of the text, writing: 'how wisely and eloquently he speaks! But wisdom is his guide, eloquence his attendant; he follows the first, the second follows him, and yet he does not spurn it when it comes after him'.[131] Furthermore, while claiming no expertise in Greek, he offers the opinion that Paul's wording does not 'run very harmoniously even in the original tongue'.[132]

Of Galatians he writes:

> although the whole epistle is written in the subdued style, except at the end, where it rises into a temperate eloquence, yet he interposes one passage of so much feeling that, not withstanding the absence of any ornaments such as appear in the passages just quoted [2 Cor. 6.2–10; Rom. 8.28–9], it cannot be called anything but powerful [quotes Gal. 4.10–20] . . . Is there anything here of contrasted words arranged antithetically, or of words rising gradually to a climax, or of sonorous clauses, and sections, and periods? Yet, notwithstanding, there is a glow of strong emotion that makes us feel the fervour of eloquence.[133]

To circumvent Scripture's 'difficulty and obscurity' he insists that, because God's truth is too big for the rules of grammar, the writers of the Bible step outside of common usage.[134] While this view satisfied Augustine, he is neither the first nor the last to depend on it to overcome the obvious limits of the text.[135] He appears to be the first, however, to propose a new type of rhetoric

---

[129] Von Campenhausen, *Fathers*, 190 (citing *Confessions* 3.5.9).
[130] Augustine, *DDC* 4.6.9. See 4.7.11–13 for Paul.
[131] Ibid., 4.7.12. Chapters 10–11 continue in this vein, arguing that clarity is all important, but that there is no reason to be 'inelegant'.
[132] Ibid., 4.20.
[133] Ibid., 4.20.44.
[134] Evans, *Language*, 5, citing *Enarrationes in Psalmos* 105.18; and 104.18.
[135] Evans, ibid., 5–6.

that is distinctly Christian: Book 4 of *De Doctrina Christiana*.[136] In it Augustine gives instruction concerning the public presentation of the gospel. Wisdom surpasses eloquence; yet one cannot instruct a disengaged audience, and so Augustine insists that effective communication requires effort, though without leaving truth behind.[137] But this outgrowth of the work of Cicero[138] does not consist in a reissuing of the earlier non-Christian rhetoric, as Augustine declares at the outset:

> In the first place, then, I wish by this preamble to put a stop to the expectations of readers who may think that I am about to lay down rules of rhetoric such as I have learnt, and taught too, in the secular schools, and to warn them that they need not look for any such from me . . . and if any good man should happen to have leisure for learning them, he is not to ask me to teach them either in this work or in any other.[139]

He furthermore does not employ rhetoric as an exegetical tool. For an aid to reading one must turn back to the first three books of *DDC*, where he details those arts which help to understand texts – but rhetoric is not among them. He offers to exegesis an interest in (1) history; (2) natural science; (3) the mechanical arts (for understanding biblical figures[140]); and (4) reasoning and numbers (considered the highest learning).[141] While these pursuits can help the reader to understand the Bible, apart from these (and with the exception of history their function is primarily limited to comprehension of allusions in the text) there is no self-conscious attempt to develop a method for explication.[142]

> Book IV of *On Christian Doctrine* is usually considered the first rhetorical theory specifically designed for the minister[143] . . . The first three books of *On Christian Doctrine*,

[136] Hagendahl, *Augustine*, 2: 558. Cf. Fortin, 'Augustine', 85.
[137] Murphy ('Augustine', 400) speaks of Augustine's 'espousal of a union between meaning and expression' as that which marks his rejection of sophistry.
[138] He considers Cicero the pure source while fourth-century sophistry was perverted beyond redemption. *DDC* 4.5.7, 4.28.61. Cf. *Confessions* 9.2.4.
[139] *DDC* 4.1.2.
[140] Ibid., 2.30.47. Cf. Ellspermann, *Christian Writers*, 190.
[141] Ellspermann, ibid., 176–9.
[142] Though it has been described as 'a Christian theory of literature' by Huppé in *Doctrine and Poetry*, v.
[143] Murphy, 'Augustine', 408; Hagendahl, *Augustine*, 2: 558. The latter points out

which describe procedures for a proper interpretation of the Bible, actually set forth the invention part of Augustine's rhetoric. There is no basis here for replacing either logic or theology with rhetoric as the capstone of professional training. The work does represent, however, one of the first theoretical efforts to bring together interpretation – that is, interpreting a text, as opposed to interpreting the facts of a case – and rhetoric.[144]

More precisely we learn that Books 1 to 3 aid in the understanding of Scripture as a preliminary to sermon preparation. The books treat, in order, 'signs of realities'; 'words as conventional signs'; and ambiguity. The concern throughout the three books is with 'the use of words'; and they teach that 'the preacher needs a knowledge of language to equip himself with the tools of understanding'. Hence Augustine addresses 'both ambiguities growing out of words used literally, and ambiguity deriving from words used figuratively'.[145]

So the analytical parts of *DDC*, the first three books, do not introduce rhetoric as employed in NT studies. Furthermore, those who would bring Augustine into the discussion seem to neglect his assertion that rhetorical art 'is not to be used so much for ascertaining the meaning as for setting forth the meaning when it is ascertained. But the art previously spoken of, which deals with inferences, and definitions, and divisions, is of the greatest assistance in the discovery of meaning'.[146]

We would misunderstand *DDC* were we to overlook the distinction between the 'means of discovery' and the 'means of expression', and the fact that Augustine explains the first while merely arguing for the second.[147] That is, he does not offer a guide to homiletics as a sequel to the three books explaining how to extract meaning from the text. Book 4 is less prescriptive than argumentative, defending eloquence.[148] Moreover, the first three books do not form part of the 'first Christian rhetoric' – and they certainly never

that while the spheres and subject-matter change the need for effective verbal communication binds them together (cf. 563).

[144] Sloan, 'Rhetoric', 806.

[145] Murphy, 'Augustine', 407. It is also necessary to bear in mind that roughly thirty years elapsed between the completion of Books 1–3, and Book 4.

[146] Augustine, *DDC* 2.37.55.

[147] Murphy, 'Augustine', 409.

[148] *DDC* 4.1.2.

suggest or even envisage an analysis based on the rhetorical hand-books. So the analytical portions in no way relate to classical rhetoric,[149] and the portion that deals with eloquence (Book 4) exists to argue for its necessity. Perhaps one can surmise from Book 4's production thirty years after the completion of the first three books[150] that an anti-intellectualism regarding pagan techniques had robbed preachers of eloquence and that Augustine sought to raise the standard.

Furthermore, Hagendahl argues that *DDC* is not intended to be a general manual of Christian education but rather exists to equip a particular group, the clergy,[151] for preaching.[152] This is in reaction to Marrou's claim that it represented 'a thesis on Christian educa-tion'; but even Marrou in the same place adds that its aim is 'biblical knowledge and priestly eloquence'.[153] Von Campenhausen discusses the motivation behind its composition, agreeing that it is a handbook for preparing potential preachers in the catholic church.[154]

When the question of pagan examples in literary education arises (imitation of Homer and Virgil being a dominant aspect of educa-tion), Augustine suggests that one would do well to take examples instead from the Bible.[155] He thus proposes an altogether 'new type of eloquence'[156] and illustrates it with numerous examples from Paul.[157] He does not, it must be noted, equate this eloquence with Graeco-Roman forms; instead he identifies divine power as elo-quence which 'uses events in the same way a human rhetorician uses words'.[158] Eloquence need not spring from Graeco-Roman rhetoric, and for that matter, 'rhetoric' need not be associated with that tradition either, but may be a 'Christian rhetoric'. Accordingly, as Classen discovers, 'Augustine never analyses the structure of an entire *Schrift*, whether a gospel or an epistle, with help from the categories of ancient rhetoric, and furthermore, in his commen-

---

[149] Classen, 'Antike Rhetorik', 16.
[150] Murphy, 'Augustine', 407; Hagendahl (*Augustine*, 554) dates *DDC* to the year 426.
[151] Clarke, *Rhetoric at Rome*, 197, n. 18. Cf. also the comments of Oroz in *La retórica augustiniana*, 484–95 (especially 489).
[152] Hagendahl, *Augustine*, 566.
[153] Marrou, *St Augustine*, 55.
[154] Von Campenhausen, *Fathers*, 270.
[155] Murphy, 'Augustine', 408.
[156] Ibid.
[157] *DDC* 4.6.9; 4.18.36.
[158] Bernard, 'The Rhetoric of God', 96.

taries, we find no such attempt so far as I can see'.[159] One searches in vain for evidence of a rhetorical analysis in studies such as Augustine wrote on Romans: he employed no such technique.

Before leaving our survey of the fathers and their attitude toward rhetoric, we need to highlight the force which pulls together patristic discussion of the level of biblical language: 1 Corinthians 1–2 solidifies the response to criticisms of the Bible – though it does not refute those charges. We have observed the variety of situations in which early writers depended on Paul's words concerning the wisdom of this world and the foolishness of Christian preaching. This was the repeated defence of the Scriptures: they are free from manmade persuasive technique, instead relying on simple truth as conveyed and empowered by the Holy Spirit. These verses circulated widely because there was no other response; the Bible simply falls short of the level demanded by the educated person of that day. Paul, by defending 'truth' rather than the means of persuasion, provided a way of escape to those challenged by the 'inferiority' of their sacred texts – texts which the fathers also knew, since they enjoyed the benefit of a high level of education, to be less than 'literature'.

Other early Christians

Others add to this picture. Asterius of Cappadocia stopped teaching rhetoric upon his conversion.[160] 'But the Cross', preaches John of Antioch, 'wrought persuasion by means of unlearned men; yea, it persuaded even the whole world'.[161] Tatian claims that 'You have contrived the art of rhetoric to serve injustice and slander'.[162] Leo the Great adds:

> For when Christ was about to summon all nations to the illumination of the Faith, he chose those who were to devote themselves to preaching of the Gospel not from among philosophers or orators, but took humble fishermen as the instruments by which He would reveal himself, lest the heavenly teaching, which was of itself full of mighty

[159] Classen, 'Antike Rhetorik', 16, my translation.
[160] Socrates, *Ecclesiastical History* 1.36. Cf. Quasten, *Patrology*, 3.194–7.
[161] Murphy, 'Augustine', 401, citing John of Antioch, *On the Heroes of the Faith*.
[162] Tatian, *Address to the Greeks* 1.

power, should seem to need the aid of words. And hence the Apostle protests and says, [complete text of 1 Cor. 1.17–20].[163]

He then issues a direct attack on 'rhetorical arguments and clever debates of man's devices', for 'Christ's Gospel needs not this art'.[164]

Thus the Scriptures were considered crude by those most equipped to judge (even most favourably disposed to giving the text high marks), 'notwithstanding their occasional recognition of a trope or figure'.[165]

Nils Lund correctly observes that 'whenever the purely classical standards are employed in appraising the New Testament, its style is found wanting. Modern classicists agree in this respect with the conclusion of the early Fathers of the Church'.[166] This remains the case even though, according to Kennedy 'The Fourth Century brought a radical change in the relationships of Christians to rhetoric . . . the disputes of the church became important national issues and openly utilized devices of classical rhetoric and dialectic'.[167] This of course refers to what the handbooks perceive as oratory (i.e. national political issues, and is accordingly moving into the proper deliberative sphere). While rhetoric could thrive in this atmosphere, by the end of the era 'the fourth Council of Carthage (398) forbade bishops to read *libros gentilium* unless necessary'.[168] One must wait nearly a half-century, for Theodoret of Cyrrhus (393–466), to find a prominent churchman who actively encourages a rhetorical education for children of the well-off.[169] There remains no wholesale absorption of rhetoric into the activities of the church even if churchmen concede by this time that such rhetoric has value in the sociological settings for which it was originally intended.

---

[163] Leo the Great, *Letter* 164.2.

[164] Ibid.

[165] Campbell, *Rhetoric of Righteousness*, 76.

[166] Lund, *Chiasmus*, 8.

[167] Kennedy, *Greek Rhetoric under Christian Emperors*, 185–6. Furthermore, 'Among extant works of the Fourth-Century Fathers, the best representative of opposition to dialectic is probably Epiphanius of Salamis (*c.* 315–403), especially in his treatise on heresies known as *Panario* or *Breadbasket*. Epiphanius vigorously opposed virtually any departure from the customs of the early church, all heresies, all compromise with classical culture, all the work of Origen, and all use of statues and paintings of Christ or the saints . . .' (202).

[168] Murphy, 'Augustine', 402. It is uncertain that this is a plenary council. See Munier, 'Carthage', 147.

[169] Dockery, *Biblical Interpretation*, 147. See Strauss, *Schriftgebrauch*, 104–13.

Our conclusion coincides with that of Judge, who writes that Paul represents 'what the new cultivation [at the end of the second century] had not been prepared to tolerate, surviving only thanks to the operation of non-literary interests'.[170] Once we reach *the fourth century*, however, a form of preaching arises called the panegyrical sermon.[171] Kennedy informs us that it had no Jewish antecedents, usually showed significant differences from sophistic orations, and when it reached its highest form, came from the lips of Christians highly critical of rhetoric.[172] Thus even when uniquely Christian forms do appear they are late, maintain only tenuous links to classical rhetoric, and add nothing to the argument that the early church engaged in oratorical delivery or analysis.

Post-patristic 'rhetoricians'

Chapter 2 considered the expansion of handbook rhetoric beyond the confines of its intended three branches. History reveals, however, that only with the onset of the thirteenth century does a convincing transfer of preaching into the realm of rhetoric take place. Thomas of Chobham, in his *Summa de Arte Praedicatoria* adds the sermon to the three species.[173] The fact that this development was the cause of Thomas' fame invigorates the claim that this inevitable migration did not occur earlier. We have no ground for widening classical rhetoric to accommodate preaching and then claiming such a designation for Galatians. At least until this quite late date, the evidence suggests that Paul would not be considered a rhetor. Thus Olbricht's words, cited in chapter 5, that Aristotle omitted the church and its rhetoric from his handbook only because the church did not yet exist, and that 'had Aristotle lived in the fourth century A.D., his modus operandi would have driven him to this fourth genre'[174] must be read critically. While we cannot say with certainty where the fourth century would have pushed Aristotle, we can say it did not force the rhetoricians of that day to annex preaching into their cluster of species. And even when, with Thomas, the addition did occur, it was used of a form of oral discourse, not a method of textual analysis.

---

[170] Judge, 'St Paul and Classical Society', 21.
[171] Kennedy, *Classical Rhetoric*, 141.
[172] Ibid., 142–43.
[173] Evans, *Language*, 9. See Murphy, *Rhetoric in the Middle Ages*, 317–27.
[174] Olbricht, 'Aristotelian Analysis', 225.

He further writes: 'The sacred page has its own special topics beside those of the dialecticians and rhetoricians, for the praise of God and the destruction of vices'.[175] With others to whom we have already referred, Thomas believes rhetoric (like dialectic) to possess its own subject-matter – as we have earlier tried to demonstrate with the help of the handbooks – and moreover, those topics appropriate to rhetoric are not the ones considered in the Bible. It seems sage to say that he would reject the classification of Galatians as a piece of classical rhetoric for the reasons given in chapter 2, and now, even more, because Paul's concern is not appropriate to Aristotelian rhetoric.

Two centuries after Thomas, rhetoric becomes a tool for analysis of the Bible. Wilhelm Wuellner remarks that since the Reformation began, 'the question persists why and for what purpose was reference to rhetoric necessary when studying the word of God or religious truth'.[176] The major figures of the period reveal great sophistication when using rhetoric as a tool for study.

Seldom cited of the great characters from the Reformation era is Philipp Melanchthon,[177] another writer trained in rhetoric who, like many humanists of his day, had been influenced by a new interest in method for its own sake.[178] This new emphasis was derived from Aristotle, known primarily through Cicero and Averroes. The Reformation scholar T. H. L. Parker explains how a work of Rudolf Agricola, significantly titled *De Inventione Dialectica* (1479), worked its way into the reformers' thought-world.

> Agricola, dissatisfied with the 'scholastic' method of discussion, wishes to replace it by a dialectic that is closely allied to rhetoric. He therefore makes use of a conceptual tool that he takes over from Cicero, and which Cicero had

---

[175] Evans, *Language*, 9–10 and 170, n. 48, citing Cambridge: Corpus Christi College, MS 455 fol. 77rb. Evans adds in the same place, 'cf. fo. 76ra on the legal topic'.

[176] Wuellner, 'Paul as Pastor', 75. See Hausamann, 'Die Rhetorik', 305–14.

[177] Melanchthon does not appear in Betz's admittedly selective bibliography to *Galatians* though he does warrant mention in the text (14, n. 97). He goes unmentioned in Kennedy's *New Testament Interpretation*, as well as in the bibliographies of Mack's *Rhetoric and the New Testament*, Longenecker's *Galatians* and Mitchell's *Rhetoric of Reconciliation*. Perhaps this is due to the inaccessibility of Melanchthon's German and the scarcity of English translations. On this see Classen, 'St Paul's Epistles', 271, n. 17.

[178] 1497–1560. On Melanchthon see especially Scheible, 'Melanchthon'; for an extensive bibliography of both Melanchthon's works and scholarly studies of them, see 395–410.

borrowed from Aristotle. This is expressed in the title: *inventio*, the searching out in a document of its leading concepts, those which together comprehend the meaning of the whole. Aristotle had called these concepts by the word τόποι, which had passed into Cicero as *loci* and which became current in the age of the Renaissance in such titles as *Loci communes* and *Loci theologici*.[179]

Agricola's work reached Melanchthon via Oecolampadius.[180] Melanchthon then journeyed back from Agricola to Aristotle himself and developed a deep-seated attraction to the philosopher. All this led to a strategy of applying dialectic to a text by which the reader embarked on a mission of 'search and discovery, his purpose [being] to find and co-ordinate the major concepts, his office to reduce confusion to order . . . His journey is *inventio*, his specimens *loci*'.[181] This means that when one reads Melanchthon's commentary on Romans, it would be wrong to expect a running exposition of the text as found in, say, Chrysostom. Instead what one finds is an uncovering of the themes in the text.[182] When actually commenting on Romans, Melanchthon does not introduce grammatical or verse divisions; instead he lists and elucidates concepts. Parker offers by way of illustration the *exordium*, the first verses of the epistle. They break down as follows:

> Paul, a servant of Jesus Christ, called to be an apostle, etc./ Called./ Separated to the Gospel of God./ By the prophets in the Holy Scripture, etc./ Concerning his Son./ Through whom we have received, etc./ Grace to you and peace.[183]

These are then treated not as portions ready for an exegetical examination, but rather as doctrinal kernels requiring expansion and exposition.[184] This approach yields a rather strange commentary – one not particularly helpful for readers of Paul – which causes Parker to ask if the singling out of *loci* is a good, 'or even a valid, way of understanding and expounding the New Testament?'[185]

---

[179] Parker, *Calvin's New Testament Commentaries*, 31.
[180] Ibid.
[181] Ibid., 33.
[182] Ibid.
[183] Ibid., 34–5, citing Melanchthon, *Corpus Reformatorum*, 15.545–53.
[184] Parker, *Calvin's New Testament Commentaries*, 35.
[185] Ibid.

Melanchthon's analysis of Romans uses categories of rhetoric in such a way as to treat the epistle as a defence given in court. He further lists a series of *propositiones*, followed by *argumenta*.[186] But this rhetorical terminology clearly adds up to a device that Melanchthon places over the text of Romans, not one which he derives from the text itself. It is successful because Romans does undoubtedly contain a series of both theological propositions and arguments. Parker, however, tells us that to treat Paul's text thus merely assisted in its exposition; it said nothing concerning the subject-matter of Romans.[187] Joachim Classen insists that Melanchthon knew, despite calling Romans an *oratio*, that it is no such thing by classical definitions, for he spoke of an *inscriptio*. Classen adds that the commentary finds a *narratio*, though it is not a narrative portion but 'a list of arguments Saint Paul intends to prove later'.[188] To both Quintilian and to modern rhetorical studies, this last device is more aptly referred to as the *propositio* – but here it merely reinforces the impression that Melanchthon was not concerned to draw too close a connection between his use of terms and the handbook definitions.

Further evidence for the discontinuity between Melanchthon's rhetoric and classical rhetoric arises when we turn to Galatians. He begins, like Betz, with the identification of its species (*genus*), but he does not conclude that it is one of the three species which we have come to recognize; instead he calls it an example of the *genus didacticum*.[189] As Classen correctly observes, Melanchthon 'feels free to modify [the rhetorical tradition] and to introduce a new element where he considers the old standards incomplete or inadequate'.[190] This manipulation of the tradition is further revealed in his labelling verses 1 and 2 the *epigraph*,[191] verse 3 the *salutatio* (a term taken not from rhetoric but epistolography) and verses 1.6–2.21 the *exordium*; moreover he finds the *propositio* not at 2.15–21, but rather 3.1: 'O foolish Galatians, who has bewitched you'.[192]

[186] Parker, *Romans*, 3–4.
[187] Ibid., 5–6.
[188] Classen, 'St Paul's Epistles', 272–3.
[189] Ibid.
[190] Ibid.
[191] See Melanchthon, *Colossians*, 111, n. 1 on ch. 1: Parker, the editor, states that *epigraph* was 'Melanchthon's usual description of the opening lines of an epistle'.
[192] Classen, 'St Paul's Epistles', 273. Colossians (in Melanchthon, *Colossians*, 21) is also outlined in a way that deviates widely from the standard definitions:

According to this evidence, Melanchthon uses rhetoric as a template to place over the text of Galatians in order to assist in its analysis. He does not, however, pretend that the text conforms to expectations created by that template, nor does he encounter difficulty when the schema falls short. He expands the categories as much as necessary, but, most importantly '[the] construction of the whole he does not explicate with the help of an established schema of the theory'.[193]

So then, Melanchthon uses rhetoric in a more sophisticated way than anything we have yet encountered, but this says more about him than about Paul. He neither considers letters orations nor suggests that Paul is responsible for the notion that parts of an oration exist within the text (for Melanchthon invents them himself); and he creates a new genre, *genus didacticum*,[194] to describe both Galatians and Romans[195] precisely because the epistles do not fit the classical mould of any of the three species. Moreover, he calls Romans a *doctrinae christianae compendium*.[196] Apart from the question of what this label means, if he calls Romans a compendium it is unlikely that he considers it argumentative public discourse, much less a speech modelled on the form appropriate to the courts or the senate. While Melanchthon's work surely is a 'rhetorical analysis', it only serves to reveal that Galatians is *not* the level 4 rhetoric discussed in the handbooks. In the end, Melanchthon does not support the thesis that Paul wrote speeches, though his analyses do employ a significant number of rhetorical terms.

A final humanist of note and contemporary of Melanchthon,

1.3–11 *exordium*
1.12–2.15 *narratio*
2.16–19 *epilogus*, or *conclusio*
2.20–23 addition to the *conclusio*
3.1–4.18 moral precepts.

Melanchthon writes at 3.1: 'In the following chapters [Paul] deals with moral precepts' (Parker, 87). Melanchthon attaches no rhetorical handle, nor does he search for a functional label similar to those applied to the first two chapters; instead he simply summarizes the contents of chapters 3 and 4. This inability to label paraenesis with help from the handbooks has never been resolved.

[193] Classen, 'Antike Rhetorik', 19.
[194] Cf. the use made of this category by Berger, 'Hellenistische Gattungen', 1295–9.
[195] Classen, 'Antike Rhetorik', 20.
[196] Scheible, 'Melanchthon', 389; Aune, 'Romans as *Logos Protreptikos*', 112.

Erasmus,[197] offered his opinion of proper Christian expression: 'Ciceronian Latin is an inappropriate vehicle for the writing of a Christian world, and apart from anything else its employment on topics for which it is not suited breaks the fundamental ancient law of *decorum*'.[198] Like many before him, Erasmus thought the evil lies not in rhetoric's use but its misuse. He would have thought it abuse had Paul employed it.

Conclusion

A survey of supposed progenitors reveals that claims for a rhetorical approach to Paul contained in certain recent works may require rethinking. As classical and patristic scholars have observed, the earliest Christians found in Paul no rhetorician or highborn orator but a humble author of weighty letters. We are inclined, in light of the evidence presented above, to agree with Malherbe's observation that 'The Church Fathers, measuring Paul by the criteria of Classicism, were embarrassed by his rudeness of style'.[199] But this is not the whole story, for these readers rarely judged Paul by such standards. Especially for the early church, the text was powerful enough so as not to need 'the subtle and complicated outward expressions of verbal debate'.[200] Quacquarelli goes so far as to argue that recognizing Paul's eloquence apart from rhetoric freed the fathers to develop alternative modes of discourse, and already by Augustine this resulted in profound alterations to the classical educational system.[201] It is not until the Reformation era that we find Pauline texts treated with the help of rhetoric in any significant way, and even then it is with the awareness that external categories are being forced on to the text. We find no suggestion that the epistles were actually orations. This survey would then oppose the notions that Paul's style and language were informed by Graeco-Roman rhetoric and that previous ages commonly used classical rhetoric to understand the NT.

[197] According to Wilamowitz-Moellendorff (*Classical Scholarship*, 40–1) he lived from 1466 to 1536. The date is thrown into doubt by Erasmus' need to push his birth back to a time before his father took orders. See Dorey, *Erasmus*, ix.

[198] From Knott's introduction to *Dialogus Ciceronianus*.

[199] Malherbe, *Social Aspects*, 34.

[200] Florescu, *La Retorica*, 7; cited in Quacquarelli, 'Rhetoric', 735.

[201] Ibid., 736.

7

THE LANGUAGE OF PAUL'S LETTERS: 2. THE CONTRIBUTION OF MODERN STUDIES

Acts 24: a courtroom analogy

William Kurz in discussing Paul's defence before Felix in Acts 24 declares that 'Luke's ability to give the appearance of a full speech is striking to a modern reader, and comparable to that of the classical and Hellenistic historians'.[1] Fred Veltman adds that the speech exhibits 'all the earmarks of a typical apology'.[2] Kurz concludes that to identify a Lukan awareness of the rules of Greek rhetoric is simply to 'argue from observable effects to their required cause'.[3]

It is commonly agreed that Acts 24 contains a court-scene and that Luke provides touches which give the account an air of authenticity. But what is it that stimulates such a response in the reader? And more to the point: do those same factors which evoke the forensic atmosphere fill the Galatian air? We will develop this analogy by isolating the elements which transport the reader into a forensic setting. If kept brief enough to avoid becoming a distraction, isolating such elements can contribute to our understanding of the task which confronts the writer intent upon creating a fictitious piece of forensic discourse: Paul's supposed purpose in Galatians.[4]

The creation of context is assisted by the narrative introduction – those elements which at the outset determine the atmosphere of the scene. In accordance with the standard practice as revealed in ancient court records, we are told in Acts that the accusors arrive

[1] Kurz, 'Christological Proofs', 195.

[2] Veltman, 'Defense Speeches', 254. Veltman's concern is the relationship of a speech to the genre of the literature within which it rests. He concludes that form, arrangement and shared general elements are constant from historiography to romance to Paul's speeches; see especially 256.

[3] Kurz, 'Christological Proofs', 195.

[4] And in fact the analogy will apply to the attempt to create any classical oration.

acompanied by a 'rhetor'.⁵ Luke, following custom, employs the genitive absolute to introduce the dispute.⁶ Thus in Acts it is at the bench's beckoning (κληθέντος δὲ αὐτοῦ) that Tertullus begins.⁷ We hear of the plaintiffs' activities in the expected legal terminology: they prosecuted their case (οἵτινες ἐνεφάνισαν τῷ ἡγεμόνι),⁸ and Tertullus began to 'accuse' (κατηγορέω).⁹ Luke uses the terminology needed to create the impression of an official court proceeding, which is supplemented by the presence of a hired advocate.¹⁰

Kennedy correctly notes that Tertullus comes across as a professional, for he too displays a familiarity with Roman courtroom procedure.¹¹ His attempts to win the good will of Felix are overdone to be sure; they nevertheless accord with what one would expect, employing the language customary to such introductions: the reference to peace, brevity and the desire not to be tiresome.¹² And he displays just enough flourish: πάντῃ . . . πανταχοῦ. . . πάσης (Acts 24.3).

Having seen Luke and Tertullus express themselves in a forensic atmosphere, we must examine Paul's conduct in the dock. His rebuttal opens with a brief *captatio benevolentiae*, takes seriously and responds to the charges,¹³ and displays the requisite *brevitas*. He follows form by inserting πολύς at the beginning (24.10, cf. 24.2),¹⁴ and he too knows how to use courtroom terminology: both κρίνειν and διαγινώσκειν mark forensic discourse.¹⁵ Even re-

⁵ Acts 24.1. This term (we are told that the elders came with ῥήτορος Τερτύλλού τινός) appears only here in the NT.
⁶ P. Oxy. 1204.13: κληθέντος Πλουτάρχου (the name of the accused). Winter, 'The *Captatio Benevolentiae*', 508. Winter also cites P. Fouad 26.2.31–5 and P. Oxy. 2131 as examples of the speech itself commencing with the genitive (as in Acts 24.2).
⁷ Paul is called, not Tertullus. See P. Oxy. 1204 cited directly above for an exact parallel: there it refers to the defendant.
⁸ Acts 24.1.
⁹ Acts 24.2.
¹⁰ For discussion of trials in the provinces, and especially of the freedom of governors to dictate the events, see Crook, *Law and Life of Rome*. Jolowicz and Nicholas (*Study of Roman Law*, 5–6) speak of instability in Roman proceedings before the second century.
¹¹ Kennedy, *New Testament Interpretation*, 135. So also Gempf, *Mission Speeches*, 175.
¹² Tajra, *Trial*, 120. Cf. also Lösch, 'Dankesrede', 306–14.
¹³ Veltman, 'Defense Speeches', 254.
¹⁴ Cf. also Acts 1.3, Heb. 1.1 – these are typical of the widespread use of the term in documents (or portions thereof) possessing a degree of sophistication.
¹⁵ Trites, 'Legal Scenes', 282. This article thoroughly documents the legal terminology in Acts.

garding grammatical forms Paul makes the right decisions: his use of the rare optative within a conditional clause (24.19) reveals 'the use of slightly antique language in the presence of Felix'[16] which must be regarded as nothing other than the appropriate level of formality. According to Bruce, 24.21 uses ἧς by Attic attraction for ἥν,[17] and παραστῆσαι is used in much the same way by Paul as by Attic orators and philosophers.[18]

Additional observations contribute to the picture: Paul's manner of speech differs from his more usual patterns;[19] and though he does not depend on a flamboyant Atticised Greek throughout, he does commence defending with what Kennedy terms a 'good classical Greek periodic sentence'.[20] The actual speech, furthermore, breaks down rather tidily into its constituent parts: Paul offers the requisite *exordium* (24.10), followed by a single verse statement of facts (24.11).[21] Kennedy labels 24.12 the proposition, and 12–21 the proof.[22] Significantly, commentators as diverse as Kennedy and Winter arrive at agreement concerning (1) the presence of classical oratory; (2) the species of the speech; and (3) the general rhetorical *dispositio*.[23] Such concord is lacking where Galatians is concerned.

The concluding elements of a standard legal dispute are of course the verdict and adjournment. Although Felix offers no verdict, even in this omission the Lukan vocabulary effectively maintains the forensic imagery. The term διαγινώσκω is used only twice in the NT, both occurring at the end of speeches in Acts. It can mean, as in Acts 23.15, 'to make inquiry'; on the other hand it can mean 'to

[16] Turner, *Grammar, III*, 126.

[17] Bruce, *Acts*, 479.

[18] Ibid.

[19] Kennedy, *New Testament Interpretation*, 139. Obviously this can be attributed to Luke rather than Paul, but such an observation does not affect our point – which is that someone has taken the appropriate means to portray a forensic setting for this event and has therefore adapted Paul's utterance to match the occasion.

[20] Kennedy, *New Testament Interpretation*, 136. Marshall (*Acts*, 376) considers ἐκ πολλῶν ἐτῶν an exaggeration born of rhetorical effect.

[21] Kennedy, *New Testament Interpretation*, 136; cf. Neyrey, 'Trial Speeches', 214–15.

[22] Kennedy, *New Testament Interpretation*, 136.

[23] Winter calls 10b the *exordium*, 11 the *narratio*, 12–13 the *confirmatio*, 14–18 the *refutatio*, and adds that 18–21 are the *peroratio*: cf. 'The *Captatio Benevolentiae*', 522. When one compares the discussions of Kennedy and Winter, it becomes apparent that apart from this final designation, the disagreements are largely semantic – and Winter's comments on the *peroratio* merely reflect further refinement of Kennedy's one-paragraph analysis.

render a decision'.[24] It is not necessary to argue for a particular reading of Acts 24.22 to further our observation that Luke throughout depends on technical legal terms to confront the reader with a forensic setting: either way we find Luke attaining closure without a verdict. Finally, as Haenchen recognizes,[25] ἀναβάλλω is the legal term for adjournment.

The result of the details provided by Luke is that we have a clear portrait of a forensic battle. Tertullus' speech has been described as a 'masterpiece', that is, it conveys 'exquisite rhetorical artistry'.[26] Paul's speech in turn requires less of Luke's attention since the setting has been created long before Paul gets the nod from Felix. Thus, with a forceful opening Paul is on his way. Nevertheless, Luke does maintain the technical vocabulary of the courts. There is no mistaking the scene that he has created, and in fact, it has been recognized throughout its interpretative history as a forensic contest: it could be nothing else.

This cursory reading of Acts 24 allows two observations concerning the illusion of courtroom drama. First, there is a host of devices by which the writer can construct a courtroom around the reader. Whether that courtroom be historical or fictional, the literary means are clearly the same. The announced presence of participants including plaintiffs, defendants, judges, juries and rhetors all accomplish this, as do activities such as approaching the bench and adjourning the trial.[27]

Second, the forensic 'register' announces that the readers (and the narrated characters) have entered the province of the judge. That is, an accepted vocabulary coheres to a 'particular topic, subject or activity'.[28] Courtrooms delimit the topic of discourse, the subject and perhaps above all the activity undertaken within their walls. This is the judge's dominion, as countless clues reveal. We thus introduce a related sociolinguistic concept: 'a domain is a combination of factors which are believed to influence choice of code (language, dialect or style) by speakers. Such factors might

[24] MM 147. Cf. P Petr III.43; P Amh II.29.18.
[25] Haenchen, *Acts*, 656. BAGD and LSJ support this reading though with few citations.
[26] Lösch, 'Dankesrede', 317, my translation.
[27] Lakoff (*Talking Power*, 87–9) adds from the American court scene: mirandize, arraign, indictment, preliminary hearing, peremptory challenge, direct examination, cross examination, redirect, recross, closing arguments, summation. Any small cluster of these terms, and many of them used alone, conjure up the forensic setting.
[28] Trudgill, *Introducing Language*, 62.

include participants, topic and location'.[29] Clearly the court, based on these three factors, exerts an influence on one's utterance. Legal language is formalized, sometimes calcified; the participant, including the illiterate hauled before the justice, is aware of the distinction between the halls of justice and the stalls of the market – even if unable to attain to the requirements of the former.[30]

How do these factors impinge on our thesis concerning Galatians? The mere fact of Paul bringing his readers into a courtroom would accomplish a great deal. It would, for example, convey certain assumptions concerning both Paul's and his readership's authority, help clarify the role expected of the reader and, if the readers are allowed by Paul to sit in judgement on him and his apostolate, communicate to them a great deal of respect, possibly even flattery. Finally, it would exert immeasurable psychological force. In short, such a device has power and its employment would reflect a certain genius skilled in the harnessing of that power. But three observations follow from our glance at Acts 24.

First, Paul has a vast array of devices available to transport the reader into the fictional courtroom, so that the desire to create such a frame is easily satisfied. In fact, one may go so far as to say that if Galatians were a forensic speech, the use of such formulae would be inevitable. Second, there is a particular register, a vocabulary and level of discourse, appropriate to the courts that goes beyond stereotypical phrasing. Formalized, even polished, language would be evident were Paul to disguise his epistle as a trial document. Third, and derivative of the first two, the level of Paul's language relates to the assertion that rhetorical readings of the NT were commonplace throughout history. We saw in chapter 6 that patristic experts in oratory, not finding in Paul the language of rhetoric, sought alternative explanations for his means of expression. What follows will show that twentieth-century scholarship struggles similarly with Paul's language, for it too searches for alternatives rather than attribute to Paul the skills of an orator.

Leaving Acts 24, and having observed that Paul is there portrayed as an orator familiar with the language and structure of judicial arguments, we now have a basis for comparing Galatians with forensic speeches. This picture, whether it reveals more of

[29] Ibid., 29.
[30] Thus in America a defendant may have no understanding of legal vocabulary, but almost certainly knows that the judge is addressed as 'your honour'. In many legal systems the attire of the judge is also determinative.

Luke or of Paul, well illustrates the sort of oratory described in the handbooks, and as a consequence has engendered agreement among analysts concerning species and structure. We now know what Paul would sound like in court: does Galatians share that tone?

Our introduction has indexed the conclusions concerning Paul's education drawn by recent scholarship from Paul's rhetorical abilities, but the studies examined never attempt to solidify their conclusions by measuring Paul against the form of discourse appropriate to oratory. We will argue that Paul's epistles fail to betray an advanced education, a significant datum in that while we have already seen cause to reject the position that Galatians is an oration, the observation that Paul did not use the language of the orator is even more sure. In other words, when we move to a firmer foundation, a more objective set of criteria, none who claim oratorical prowess for Paul follow.

The subsequent inquiry into Paul's language level will argue primarily that Galatians fails to attain to the literary level demanded of oratory, and secondarily, that mitigating circumstances preclude the drawing of hard and fast conclusions from the letters themselves concerning Paul's education and background.[31] As the history of this discussion was progressing in a rather straightforward fashion, the more recent 'rhetorical criticism' swept in, cutting against the grain to yield a totally new set of results. But the incursion of this new approach has not produced satisfying answers to the question of where Paul learned rhetorical strategies, or of how they are executed in practice. Few acknowledge that the orator necessarily depended upon a particular register reflecting the 'oratorical domain' and revealing the speaker's level of *paideia*.

The question is vital, for, as we saw in chapter 1, some have attempted to work back from a supposed rhetorical discourse discovered in a NT text to estimations of the source of Paul's ability.[32] The reconstruction of Paul's background – social, educational, financial – informs too many conclusions to be determined by excessively hypothetical propositions. Manifold explanations for Paul's oratorical prowess are proffered, ranging from prolonged

---

[31] As, for instance, Deissmann (*Light*, 246–51) argues for Paul's low class.

[32] This thesis does not question the logic of this move, but merely wishes again to emphasize the weakness of an edifice without a foundation. If it is unlikely that he wrote classical orations, it is equally unlikely that Paul provides evidence of the *paideia* which leads to their production.

higher education in the manner of his day to a rejection of the question altogether as irrelevant to the matter of classical rhetoric. Thus the position of the rhetorical critic appears to be that Paul probably had a rhetorical education, but if not it makes little difference since he would inevitably have learned the techniques of persuasion in the course of daily life. This composite picture downplays the subtlety of today's exegetes; nevertheless, rhetoric is often understood as the common rhetorical conventions of Paul's day, and is sufficiently broad that a skilful listener would instinctively know when to use the various parts of an oration or how to score a point by dropping a device – a clever phrase or a rich word – into the discourse. But such an approach, if we aim to be precise, leaves us unable properly to categorize the texts in view. If the presence of an introduction or a conclusion, of a listing of argumentative points, of metaphor, metonymy, pun, parataxis and periphrasis signals the presence of rhetoric, then we cannot mean level 4 oratory. As soon as we refine our test, that is, if we demand of a piece of judicial rhetoric those things ascribed to it by Aristotle, texts fall by the wayside – and when we begin to identify specific aspects of oratory, Paul is trimmed away with the same stroke as all the other biblical texts. This occurs because rhetoric is not simply dependence on a set of formal considerations (such as species and structure) and stylistic devices, which alternatively envelop or exist within any piece of discourse, but, as understood by the ancients, was a piece of discourse reflecting a convention not easily imitated: as a product of sophisticated Greek *paideia*, it reflected a level of language appropriate to that *paideia*.[33] We shall see that the NT writers generally, and Paul in particular, are held not just by the church fathers but also by more recent scholars to have failed to attain to that level.

Orientation to Paul's background

In light of the array of conclusions drawn from a supposed employment of rhetoric, we shall briefly consider Paul's personal background to see if it can help us isolate the source of his rhetoric.[34] It

[33] Consider, for instance, Hatch (*Greek Ideas*, 48): 'There was a complex system of education, the main elements of which were the knowledge of literature, the cultivation of literary expression, and a general acquaintance with the rules of argument'.

[34] Downing suggests that nothing can be made of an *audience*'s status from the

does not, in fact, take much before we stretch Paul's biographical data to the breaking point. We have (1) a few textual references to his citizenship, upbringing and early activities; (2) our general picture of education in the first century of this era; and (3) the stylistic data teased out of his texts. All this can be stirred into the same mix, but once it has been considered we are forced to admit that too much remains unknown, and too much uncertainty attends the implications of what we do know concerning Paul's background.

We begin with the claim that Paul was from Tarsus (Acts 22.3). The capital of Cilicia, and a vital link between east and west, the city enjoyed fame both as a main station on the information and trade networks of the ancient world and as an academic centre, offering an education to the aspiring rhetor, philosopher or professional person.[35] Strabo, in his *Geography*, tells us that philosophy and other disciplines were studied to the point that Tarsus surpassed even Athens and Alexandria.[36] A distinctive feature is that the natives populate the schools while 'foreigners are not inclined to sojourn there; neither do these natives stay there, but they complete their education abroad; and when they have completed it they are pleased to live abroad, and few go back home'.[37] We also learn that Tarsus 'has all kinds of schools of rhetoric'.[38] We must grant Strabo some licence when he suggests that Tarsians 'could instantly speak offhand and unceasingly on any given subject'[39] but to illustrate their worldly success he offers that Rome was full of 'learned men' from Tarsus.[40]

Dio Chrysostom, writing closer to Paul's era, addressed the assembly of Tarsus in his *Discourses* 33–4, revealing in discourse 34 that the city had a council, an assembly and what appears to be an autonomous group of elders.[41] He implies that there was civil unrest because one of the guilds, the linen-workers, had been barred from the franchise,[42] even though other trades had

address delivered to them ('A Bas Les Aristos', 220–2). Dio depends on the same 'kinds of argument and illustration – and language' in discourses for the court as for the crowd (see especially Dio, *Discourses*, 57.10–12).
[35] Strabo, *Geography* 14.5,13,673. See Kim, *Origin*, 32.
[36] Strabo, ibid., 14.5.13.
[37] Ibid., 14.5.13. Cf. Nock, *St Paul*, 22.
[38] Strabo, ibid., 14.5.13.
[39] Ibid., 14.5.14.
[40] Ibid., 14.5.15.
[41] Dio, *Discourses*, 34.16.
[42] Ibid., 34. 21, 23.

not.[43] Importantly, Dio gives the impression that though these
linen-workers were looked down upon by a substantial portion of
the citizenry, their presence was none the less accepted at popular
assemblies.[44] Finally we learn that five hundred drachmas secured
Tarsian citizenship.

A somewhat different picture arises from Philostratus, who
writes in *The Life of Apollonius of Tyana* that his hero was
unpopular there after reproaching its citizenry with the charge that
'through their languid indifference and sensual indolence they
could not put up with the vigour of his remarks'.[45] Adding to this
picture he writes: 'Nowhere are men more addicted than here to
luxury; jesters and full of insolence are they all; and they attend
more to their fine linen than the Athenians did to wisdom'.[46] He
alludes to the gifts by which Augustus further increases the stature
of the city,[47] leaving one to wonder whether the sloth was born of
too much wealth and leisure,[48] or was simply a fanciful picture
invented to assist the story. Its veracity is supported by the notion
that there is danger in wrongly portraying a famous subject.

William Ramsay thinks that Paul might have descended from
one of the Jewish families repatriated in Tarsus by Antiochus
Epiphanes in 171–170 BCE. They were given some political
authority and, one might suppose, a certain accompanying pres-
tige.[49] Others have suggested that an ancestor was enslaved by
Pompey's forces (when in 63 BCE Palestine was taken), but subsequently freed by a member of the Roman *gens* Paulus. This
reconstruction would account for Paul's citizenship and his Latin
name.[50] Jerome, being at once more and less specific, writes that
Paul's family originated in Gischala (northern Galilee) but that
either they emigrated or were deported following a Roman inva-
sion.[51]

---

[43]   Ibid., 34. 23. He tells that a dyer, a cobbler and a carpenter would have escaped
reproach. Cf. Broughton, 'Roman Asia', 791.

[44]   Dio, *Discourses* 34.21: ταῖς ἐκκλησίαις.

[45]   Philostratus, *Life of Apollonius* 6.34.

[46]   Ibid., 1.7.

[47]   Dio, *Discourses*, 34.7ff.

[48]   Another explanation lies in Tarsus' supposed history of Epicureanism. Sarda-
napalus, the seventh-century BCE founder of the city, had inscribed on his grave,
esthie, pine, paize. Malherbe, 'Beasts at Ephesus', 71–80.

[49]   Ramsay, *St Paul the Traveller*, 169–86.

[50]   Dahl, *Missionary Theology*, 3.

[51]   Ibid., 3, n. 2. Lietzmann, *Beginnings of Christian Church*, 104. Cf. Jerome, *On
Illustrious Men*, 5; *Commentary on Philemon*, v. 23.

Even a piece of evidence so widely accepted as Paul's Tarsian origin, however, no longer receives universal assent. Helmut Koester first questioned it, and Hans-Martin Schenke more recently argued against it on the grounds that (1) its mention is restricted to Acts; (2) the source for the claim, provided in Acts 9.11, allows equally that 'of Tarsus' is a patronym analogous to Simon of Cyrene (Mark 15.21) thus commenting only on his familial origin; and (3) evidence suggests that Paul was resident in Damascus for some time, making the use of a modifier like 'of Tarsus' more appropriate.[52] Since items 2 and 3 can only solidify an already established hypothesis, conclusions on this matter are bound up with one's estimation of the veracity of Acts.

The same sort of difficulties adhere to Paul's Roman citizenship. Koester, Wolfgang Stegemann and others dispute this Lukan claim because (1) Paul would have depended on citizenship to escape the lash more often; (2) appealing to Caesar was not a right restricted only to citizens of Rome; and (3) Roman citizenship was less widespread in the early days of the empire than later.[53] This is opposed by Lüdemann who suggests that item (1) is overruled by the facts that the prohibition on flogging citizens was often over-looked; Paul may for good reason have elected not to appeal to his citizenship; and there may have been difficulty in instantly proving Roman citizenship when confronted with punishment.[54] Items (2) and (3) only question the probability of an individual's citizenship; they do not outweigh the evidence in favour of Paul's. Thus Lüdemann concludes that Paul was probably a citizen of Rome.[55]

Regarding Paul's education in Jerusalem we meet with further uncertainty. Bornkamm notes that we have no evidence for a Pharisaism outside of Palestine, and that Jerusalem is surely the headquarters of the movement.[56] But he denies that Paul studied under Gamaliel because it is tendentious: Luke habitually rates Pharisaism highly, and continues to treat the post-Damascus Paul as a practising Jew.[57]

---

[52] Schenke, 'Four Problems', 319–21; Koester, *Introduction*, 2: 97–9.

[53] Koester, ibid., 2:98–9; Stegemann, 'Römischer Bürger?', 200–29.

[54] Lüdemann, *Early Christianity*, 240–1. He accepts Paul's Roman citizenship primarily because of (1) his name; (2) the ease with which he moved through colonized territory; and (3) the circumstances of his ultimate transport to Rome.

[55] Ibid., 241. For a stimulating and wide-ranging discussion see Kehnscherper, 'Paulus als römischer Bürger'.

[56] Bornkamm, *Paulus*, 168.

[57] Ibid., 35, 168. On this cf. Kim, *Origin*, 34; Weiss, *Earliest Christianity*, 1: 181.

This entire discussion has failed to move us forward since, negatively, even if we grant such a Lukan practice it would not demand that he is pressing his understanding of Paul back into his account of preconversion days – for this *tendenz*-theory best exercises its authority over Lukan descriptions of Paul after Damascus;[58] and positively, at least some of the difficulties are offset by the observation that Paul too makes certain claims for himself. For example, he goes out of his way to claim an orthodox upbringing: his claim to being a Pharisee and a 'Hebrew of the Hebrews' zealous for the law is well known (Phil. 3.5–6) and must be allowed to inform the discussion.[59]

An additional objection to a Jerusalem education springs from Paul's claim in Galatians 1.22 that he was unrecognized by the Christian churches in Judaea. One may cite Bultmann, followed by Haenchen, on this score.[60] It has been observed, however, that Jerusalem's population expanded between the time of the Hasmonaeans and 66 CE from *c.* 32,000 to *c.* 80,000.[61] A city of such size contains too many 'neighbourhoods' for us to assume that the entire populace knew one another. Even more, discussion must not treat Paul's statement as though he refers to Jerusalem, for the reading is ταῖς ἐκκλησίαις τῆς Ἰουδαίας. The argument based on Jerusalem's population grows in proportion to the increase of the area under consideration. In the end we can only agree with Kim that 'there is no inherent reason why Gamaliel the elder could not have been Paul's teacher',[62] nor for denying the concomitant that Paul was then educated in Jerusalem.[63]

---

[58] The very fact of, for example, Luke's claim that Paul is a citizen of Tarsus illustrates that he does not excise all data opposing his tendency, for it remains despite its inability to further his portrayal of Paul as a Pharisee and an orthodox Jew. One might even suggest that Luke is at his most accurate when he discusses the early phases of Paul's life, but that he misunderstands the later Paul. This would make sense of the supposed discrepancies between the Paul of Acts and the Paul of the epistles.

[59] Phil. 3.5f.; Rom. 11.1,2; 2 Cor. 11.22. Though see Lentz (*Luke's Portrait*, 54) on the difficulty of Pharisees 'born overseas'.

[60] Haenchen, *Acts*, 554, citing Bultmann, 'Paulus', 1020–2.

[61] Hengel, *Pre-Christian Paul*, 24. Wilkinson argues for a population of *c.* 55,000 in the city before the reign of Agrippa. His approach is more refined than estimates based solely on population densities: cf. 'Ancient Jerusalem', 50. Broshi offers 32,000 to 82,500 for the period in question: cf. 'La Population', 13.

[62] Kim, *Origin*, 34.

[63] Cf. Dibelius, *Paul*, 33: 'There is no doubt connected with the fact that it was in the Jewish motherland, in Jerusalem itself, that Paul was schooled in the doctrines of the law'.

A final consideration with links to Paul's education is his financial security. Our data include Paul's payment for four Nazirite vows (Acts 21.23),[64] Felix waiting for a bribe (Acts 24.26), and Paul's ability to pay two years' worth of rent on a residence in Rome. All of this implies a certain wealth.

But rather than accumulate evidence to support a few tentative and controversial conclusions, we instead admit that for our purposes they can be only preliminary and of limited value.[65] Judge correctly observes that a childhood spent in Tarsus could not guarantee for Paul either a rhetorical or a philosophical education – for they were available only to the wealthy. Furthermore, being raised in Jerusalem does not ensure a complete insulation from Greek thought and culture. 'Half of Gamaliel's pupils are said to have been trained in the wisdom of the Greeks'.[66] Hence knowing the place of Paul's education helps us less than would knowing its level, but we have little data from which to solve that mystery. We have seen that, at least in the opinion of close contemporaries, it attained to no great heights. This question will rise again in what follows. For now we will attempt to learn what we can concerning the various types of language in the ancient world and Paul's place within that language family.

The level of Paul's language

Our attempt to investigate the various literary strata of the NT and to discern Paul's place will be assisted by two preliminary investigations. First, we will demonstrate that Paul has been believed to be of a lower stratum not only by the Fathers discussed above, but also by a significant group of turn-of-the-century philologists. Significantly, some assessed Paul only from the perspective of the known classical literature,[67] which at that time was consistently of a high level. Second, we must examine the charge of being 'uneducated' as it was thrown around in the ancient world. Taken literally and without attending to its social implications, this charge

---

[64] Gray details the cost of each in *Sacrifice in the Old Testament*, 38–9.

[65] Lentz expresses the difficulty of gaining a clear picture of even the Paul of Acts, let alone merging that picture with other sources: cf. *Luke's Portrait*, 1–6.

[66] Judge, 'Classical Society', 29.

[67] The significance of this date, as will be shown below, is that it marked the introduction of the papyri into the discussion.

produces skewed results. We thus find it necessary to embark on these ground-clearing inquiries.

Philologists found Paul to be a lesser writer

Eduard Norden compared Paul's technique to *antike Kunstprosa* – the prose style of the ancient literary world – and declared Paul difficult to understand, strange and unhellenic.[68] Carl F. G. Heinrici (1900) in his commentary on 2 Corinthians defended Paul's style but noted that he imitates no established form. Paul wrote according to his own rhetoric: 'No classicist, no Hellenist has written thus, and also no church father'.[69] At the end of the nineteenth century Johannes Weiss found oratorical figures in Paul, identifying one of the most prominent not as Graeco-Roman but as Hebrew parallelism,[70] and later writing (in agreement with Deissmann) that Paul's epistles were not literary.[71] At the end of his self-described preliminary investigation he appealed to specialists in Graeco-Roman rhetoric to examine Paul.[72] Franz Overbeck argues that the NT contains *Kleinliteratur*, while the classical and patristic texts to which it has, inappropriately, been compared represent *Hochliteratur*: the NT texts are free of the forms of real literature, and cannot provide the shape for even subsequent Christian writings.[73]

Paul Wendland is particularly direct: he finds it 'highly improbable and not demonstrable' that Paul formed his discourse according to the regulations of a rhetorical theory; and that 'the artistic forms of Greek oratory certainly already existing in Tarsus reached his ears on occasion; they will not have made a deep impression on him'.[74] Finally, he glosses over, as if well-established, the notion that Paul had no direct contact with 'höheren Literatur'.[75]

There is little that is distinctly classical in Paul. The Pauline

---

[68] Norden, *Antike Kunstprosa*, 2: 499.
[69] Heinrici, *Zweite Korinther*, 453; as translated in Hughes, *Early Christian Rhetoric*, 22. Heinrici *Literarische Charakter*, 69 describes Paul as τέχνη ἄτεχνος.
[70] Weiss, 'Beiträge', 168.
[71] Weiss, *Neutestamentlichen Wissenschaft* , 10–11.
[72] Weiss, 'Beitrage', 247.
[73] Overbeck, *Patristischen Literatur*; *Über die Christlichkeit*, 86.
[74] P. Wendland, *Die Urchristlichen Literaturformen*, 354, my translation.
[75] Ibid., 356.

corpus contains two citations of Greek authors: Menander's *Thais* in 1 Corinthians 15.33[76] and Epimenides' *De oraculis*, περί χρησμῶν in Titus 1.12[77] – but these statements have become proverbial by Paul's day.[78] To say 'All the world's a stage' proves little about the education of the speaker, and Paul may not have read the authors from whom these words originate.[79] Minn quotes with approval Thomas Wilson's conclusion that 'St Paul was never a university student, but just a well-educated artisan, and something of an expert in rabbinical learning',[80] and Hengel adds that the 'language of Homer and the Greek tragedians is as alien to Paul as the imitation of the Attic orators or the purity of the classical language'.[81] The attempt to prove Attic purity's foreignness to Paul should not distract us from another implication of Hengel's words: Homer, both as a source of language and as the literary basis of all Greek education, shines through so much of the ancient world's literature and oratory[82] that his absence suggests Paul's lack of interest in having Galatians considered literature.[83] For this reason we conclude that even the few supposed classical quotations are not necessarily useful for our portrayal of Paul.

The charge of being uneducated

Was Paul, as Celsus and even some Christian writers maintain, among the illiterate of society? What should we conclude from the insistence of such a diverse group of Paul's readers, many well-versed in classical rhetoric, that Paul was uneducated?[84] These

[76] Minn ('Classical Reminiscence', 93) demonstrates that the form of the 'citation' corresponds to the proverb but not the play. Conzelmann (*1 Corinthians*, 278, n. 139) asserts that this can say nothing about Paul's background.

[77] Authorship of Titus has no bearing on the question before us.

[78] Renehan, 'Classical Greek Quotations', 33; Hengel, *Pre-Christian Paul*, 3 and 94–5, n. 28 (see especially n. 28 for technical studies related to this question); Malherbe, *Social Aspects*, 43. Recent attempts to find classical parallels in Paul must proceed with caution. Failure to recognize that these may be widespread, traditional statements is the undoing of, for example, Howell, 'St Paul', 328–32.

[79] Minn, 'Classical Reminiscence', 96.

[80] Ibid., 97, citing T. Wilson, *St Paul and Paganism*, 6.

[81] Hengel, *Pre-Christian Paul*, 3.

[82] Scott, *Homer and his Influence*; Marrou, *History of Education*, 160–75.

[83] Harmon defends a particular attitude in Lucian toward Homer simply because the former was an Atticist ('The Poet κατ' Εξοχην', 41). Use of Homeric themes, terms and quotations was a mark of Atticism.

[84] Literacy *per se* is discussed in Harris, *Ancient Literacy*; Kenney, 'Small Writing and Less Reading', 168–9. For NT concerns see Botha, 'Greco-Roman Literacy as

accusations carried different implications then than now; and they illustrate social stratification's numerous causes and varied results. Loveday Alexander provides an example of this from Galen:

> I had a father who was rigorously correct in the language of the Greeks, and my teacher and paedagogus were Greeks too. I was reared on these words. I do not recognize yours (i.e. the words used by Archigenes). Don't quote me the usage of merchants or tradesmen or tax-collectors – I haven't mixed with such people. I was brought up on the books of the men of antiquity.[85]

This assault implies neither Archigenes' inability to communicate, nor the illiteracy of every tradesman and tax-collector; surely not all conversation heard in the house of a Galen displays the orators' verbal stature. What we see is one class's unwillingness to accept the lesser refinement of a class which may be in reality not very far below, the determinative issue in this case being Archigenes' failure to employ Attic words – which highlights his lack of *paideia*. Thus criticisms of the sort uttered by Celsus or Galen serve not to close the question of literary level but rather to open it: they point to a continuum on which we must place Paul's epistles, although by telling us that Paul did not use the Atticized Greek preferred by those at the top, they contribute more to excluding Paul from the upper limits than to defining his precise place.

Another example of social stratification as revealed by language is found in Philostratus' *Life of Apollonius*. We meet a youth who, according to his accuser, has no education: Apollonius reproaches him for speaking 'the vilest Greek dialects'. But this man does not live in poverty, for the text subsequently reveals that he is well bred and of sufficient means to support a retinue of 'parasites'. The necessary course of action for him is clear: 'there is in all cities a class of men, whose acquaintances you have never made, but who are called schoolmasters . . . they will teach you the rhetoric of the Forum'. The young man acts upon the advice, goes to school, and is eventually commended for 'the improvement both of his judgement and of his tongue'.[86] The condescension Apollonius displays

---

Setting for NT Writings'. All three conclude that the rate of literacy in antiquity is far too easily overestimated.

[85] Galen, in Kühn, *Galeni Opera Omnia*, 8: 587. This quotation is found, as she translates it, in Alexander, *Preface to Luke's Gospel*, 182.

[86] Philostratus, *Life of Apollonius* 6.36.

towards this young man results from his speech, but even at this age the youth does, with the aid of the rhetorician, overcome his lack. From this we learn two things. First, the charge of being uneducated contains meaning only within its sociological setting; it is unlikely that this young man is literally and completely uneducated – he is too well-off for that, and is, moreover, able to move directly into a course of higher education.[87] Hence Apollonius adopts this tone with one who is somewhat refined in appearance, well-off, and possesses at least a basic education. Social stratification allows one above a certain line to declare the masses below to be totally devoid of *paideia* – indeed (ironically) to be unacquainted with teachers altogether – based solely on patterns of speech.

Second, rhetorical education 'strengthens' this man's speech patterns.[88] It obliterates those qualities which betray his lack of education and impose social limits (if subjection to ridicule should be so understood). Rhetorical training so alters the man's patterns of speech that he no longer exhibits those qualities which earlier subjected him to abuse. In short, patterns of speech were assumed to indicate social standing.

Interestingly, Apollonius, though not from Athens, escaped this embarrassment prior to his own schooling. In fact, his 'biographer' shares that it was his good fortune to speak pure Attic from the time he began to learn letters: already in his youth his speech was uncontaminated by the common Greek spoken by the rest of his community.[89] Even without knowing if this blessing derives from his personal genius or from the favour of some deity, one can appreciate the social benefit derived from such ability.

Quintilian's apposite comments on ignorance even within the judicial system must not be neglected here. He writes: 'As we most often express our views before an ignorant audience, and more especially before popular assemblies, of which the majority is usually uneducated, we must distinguish between what is honourable and what is expedient and conform our utterances to suit

---

[87] Even in the face of an argument that rhetoric was not restricted exclusively to a tertiary education, we cannot go so far as to grant that it was primary. Apuleius (*Florida*, 20) says the student goes first to the *literator* to learn to read, then the *grammaticus* and finally the *rhetor*. But cf. Marrou (*History of Education*, 233f.) for the suggestion that the *grammaticus* had co-opted some of the responsibilities of the rhetorician.

[88] Philostratus, *Life of Apollonius* 6.36 reads: ὑφ' ὧν καὶ γνώμη αὐτῷ καὶ ἡ γλῶττα ἴσχυσεν.

[89] Philostratus, ibid., 1.7.

ordinary understandings'.[90] 'We . . . have to compose our speeches
for others to judge, and have frequently to speak before an
audience of men who, if not thoroughly ill-educated, are certainly
ignorant of such arts as dialectic'.[91] This corresponds to Cicero's
statement that in court 'ignorant people commonly judge an
orator's power by the test of a triumphant result'.[92] Quintilian's
lament, inconveniently for solicitors, applies to more than just the
audience: if questions are not phrased in everyday speech, 'the
witness, who is often an uneducated man', may fail to understand.[93]

Sufficient trouble stems from uneducated audiences and witnesses, but according to Quintilian, the ignorance spreads even
further: 'The judge often comes to his panel from the countryside
and is expected to give a decision on what he can understand . . .'[94]
Our judges are the people, or drawn from the people, and those
who are appointed to give sentence are frequently ill-educated and
sometimes mere rustics'.[95] He elsewhere writes that 'a learned judge
must not be addressed in the same tone that we should employ
before a soldier or a rustic', where the final two should be understood as 'unlearned judges'.[96]

But can we accept the charge that cases were tried by simpletons?
We should probably conclude that their education, while sometimes
considerable, could not measure up to Quintilian's vision of
paideia.

Alexander concludes that to members of 'society', outsiders were
exposed by their lack of education. On the other hand, the Jewish
understanding of 'Hellenism' was much broader, embracing not
only the Greek educational elite but also members of society whom
the elite would have regarded with disdain.[97] Even the best
philosophers support the stereotype of the ignorant labourer.[98] One

---

[90] Quintilian, *Institutio* 3.8.2.
[91] Ibid., 5.14.29.
[92] Cicero, *De Oratore* 2.12.72.
[93] Quintilian, *Institutio* 5.7.31.
[94] Ibid., 4.2.45.
[95] Ibid., 12.10.53.
[96] Ibid., 11.1.45.
[97] Loveday Alexander, *Contemporary Setting*, 134. Pleket ('Urban Elites', 133–4)
thus insists that 'fundamental *social* differences' exist even between 'one who hires
another to manage his business and one who conducts business himself. The
difference must not be understood in economic terms'. He adds (p. 136): 'Investing
in trade was normal for an aristocrat; to be a trader, humiliating'.
[98] Cf. Plato, *Republic* 6.495d–e, 522b, 590c, *Laws* 919c–920d (some of this is hard

sees not only the limited perspective of the elite, but also the standard: *paideia* is the overriding factor, the issue rendering intelligible the reproach found in Philodemus and Quintilian, and also those criticisms levelled at Paul even by his admirers.[99]

This assessment of the *literati* is consistent,[100] and, as we have seen, even the most articulate members of the church did not defend their sacred texts from assault but followed Paul in redefining eloquence altogether (1 Cor. 2.1–5). This is not, however, the assessment that a member of the middle or lower classes might give the early church or its texts. Hengel reminds us that we have been hearing 'the voice of the intellectual of antiquity, who despised manual labour'.[101] Like Paul, many in the early church practised a trade, even as Paul urged the Thessalonian congregation to do;[102] and a number may have enjoyed the wealth of those Jews who, according to Hegesippus, were dragged before Domitian but were immediately dismissed because their calluses proclaimed them to be 'common people'.[103] Martial calls the parents of a cobbler 'ignorant' (*stulti*), though they possessed enough education to teach their son to read, revealing both 'the ambiguity of the term "educated"', and the possibility of learning to read without attending an established school.[104] Lars Rydbeck, making use of Galen, demonstrates that even medical writings were sometimes subjected to the same criticisms as contemporary Christian texts.[105] So we see again that while the term 'uneducated' may place a ceiling on the extent of one's education, it tells

to read today as anything other than ironical). From Aristotle we learn that Thebes admitted nobody to public office who had engaged in trade during the ten years prior to the appointment (*Politics* 3.1278a, especially lines 25ff.). See further Plutarch, *Life of Pericles* 2; *Life of Marcellus* 14f.; Valerius Maximus 8.14.6. These are cited in Alexander, 'The Living Voice', 228, n. 1.

[99] Alexander, *Contemporary Setting*, 139. This accords with Pleket's observation that 'scholars were generally members of the landowning upper-class': cf. 'Urban Elites', 137.

[100] Perhaps this also explains John 7.15 and its charge that Jesus was illiterate and unlearned.

[101] Hengel, *Property and Riches*, 62.

[102] Ibid., 62. On Paul as a tent-maker and its implications for determining his social strata, see Hock, 'Paul's Tentmaking', 555–64. Hock suggests that Paul's self-conscious way of speaking about his occupation reveals a member of the higher classes who is well aware of the loss of status his labour costs him. This publicly displayed 'loss of status' can scarcely be reconciled with the notion that Paul's personal presentation corresponded to that of an orator.

[103] Hengel, *Property and Riches*, 63–4. See Eusebius, *Ecclesiastical History* 4.20.

[104] For this see Alexander, *Preface to Luke*, 181, and Martial, *Epigrams*, 9.73.7.

[105] Rydbeck, *Fachprosa*, appendix *c*.

222 Rhetoric and Galatians

us nothing specific until we apprehend the level of the judge. Even then, though, it seems to mean little more than 'less educated than I am'.

Josephus, a man of letters and active diplomatic service who exceeds the literary standards of the NT,[106] was scoffed at by critics of his work for its poverty of style.[107] This is in contrast to the assessment of Henry St John Thackeray, who finds allusions to Sophocles and Thucydides in *Antiquities* which were introduced by secretaries employed to improve his writing.[108] Feldman adds that 'Josephus is a major example of the atticising reaction against the *koinē* that occurred at the end of the first century and continued into the second century'.[109] Josephus was a self-conscious intellectual who attempted to adopt a literary sophistication, yet he was ridiculed. Surely he was not uneducated by any modern standard, and had advantages that would have been the envy of the NT writers.[110]

This analysis raises the question of dating the Attic revival. Since it did not originate with Josephus we must date it at least a little earlier, for he lived from *c.* 37 to 94 CE, completed the *War* no later than 80, and *Antiquities* no later than 94. Thus if the style was in vogue in the 70s and 80s it could well have been the standard by which writings and even more, speakers, were measured in the 50s, 60s and 70s. Indeed the earliest extant example of writing influenced by Atticism seems to be from Dionysius Halicarnassus, in the first century BCE.[111] Kilpatrick observes not only that Dionysius was the first, but that Plutarch was the next 'Atticist in his own right', and that he 'shows the stamp of Attic Greek in syntax, in vocabulary and forms'. This form of Greek influenced novelists, orators and sophists, becoming for them the norm after Plutarch,[112] but did not

---

[106] Wilder, *Early Christian Rhetoric*, 36.

[107] Josephus, *Against Apion* 1.23–7.

[108] Thackeray, *Josephus*, 107–118. He finds Sophocles in *Antiquities*, Books 15–16, and Thucydides in Books 17–19. Feldman opposes Thackeray, asserting that by the time of his writing *Antiquities* Josephus had been in Rome for twenty years – ample time to develop his style – and that the same authors have a certain influence on other writings of Josephus as well, most notably *The Jewish War*: cf. 'Josephus Revisited', 860.

[109] Feldman, ibid., 859.

[110] See further the example of the same attitude as found in Lucian, *The Ship or the Wishes* 2, referred to by Hengel, *Pre-Christian Paul*, 3–4, and 96, n. 34.

[111] Kilpatrick, 'Atticism', 126–7. He speaks of Dionysius as the first to commend the Attic virtues.

[112] Plutarch was born before 50 CE. Cf. *OCD*², 848–9.

affect technical writers to the same degree.[113] Such a dating of the rise of Atticism is conservative if Leonard Palmer is right. He writes that Greek rhetoricians at Rome urged an Attic style – and the copying of 'ancient Attic models of speech and eloquence' – already in the Ciceronian age.[114] Cicero links Atticism in Rome with Calvus at the middle of the first century CE,[115] and it must have existed even earlier in Greek schools.[116] *Orator* 6.23 speaks of Attic oratory as an established phenomenon.[117] Pelletier argues effectively both for an early date for the Attic revival, and for Atticizing in Josephus.[118]

Merely to reduce the differences in style to Atticisms – and Paul's failure to use them – may have value for other ventures, but is too restrictive for our purposes. The question of *levels* must be understood in terms of *paideia*, only one element of which may be considered the use of Atticisms. The narrowness of language acceptable to oratory is our chief concern. Evidence for this narrowness[119] is found in Cicero, who through Antonius, in *De Oratore*, speaks of Diogenes and dialectic. He concludes that Diogenes 'introduces a kind of diction that is not lucid, copious and flowing, but meagre, spiritless, cramped and paltry; and if any man commends this style, it will be only with the qualification that it is unsuitable to an orator'.[120] Only a very precisely defined language is suitable to rhetoric, and all other, including the speech of men as successful as Diogenes, must be rejected. The fathers acknowledged the dilemma confronting them because Paul did not use the expected language.

The preceding chapter has argued that Paul's language was not what the fathers expected of rhetoric, from which they inferred that he lacked the *paideia* of an orator. They did not subject Paul's

---

[113] Kilpatrick, 'Atticism', 126–7; Rydbeck, *Fachprosa*.

[114] Palmer, *The Greek Language*, 172–3.

[115] Cicero, *Brutus* 82.284 (Calvus: 82–47 BCE; he is also complimented in Quintilian, *Institutio* 10.2.25).

[116] Hendrickson, in Cicero, *Brutus* 82.284.

[117] Hommel, 'Rhetorik', 1403; Schmid, *Atticismus*; Norden, *Die Antike Kunstprosa*, 357–67.

[118] Pelletier, *Flavius Josèphe*. For the dates of Josephus see Grabbe, 'Josephus', 365. Cf. also on the matter generally, Judge, 'Classical Education in the New Testament', 9. Kilpatrick ('Atticism', 127) has not neglected Josephus, but follows Thackeray in attributing much of his Atticism to secretaries.

[119] The teacher of rhetoric was, significantly, called the *sophistés*. See Stambaugh and Balch, *Social World*, 122.

[120] Cicero, *De Oratore* 2.38.159.

writings to a classical rhetorical examination because they knew them to represent a discourse distinct from the Graeco-Roman rhetoric they had been taught. And it is clear that at times they were troubled by the differences. Thus rhetorical criticism was not a mode of analysis practised for two millennia, only to be discarded for a time in our century. Attempts to equate Paul's epistles with the literature of the ancient world could have only led to embarrassment, and hence were not pursued by those expert in both rhetoric and Paul.

Paul does not share the literary heights of the sophisticated writers of his day, but, as has been well-argued since the days of Deissmann,[121] this is simply the wrong standard. A middle ground existed which suited many who were interested in communication but who succumbed to no literary pretensions, as we have seen for Diogenes via Cicero. Indeed, even Cicero argues only that certain language is not suitable to oratory, not that Diogenes fails to communicate. Paul should be put on a plane closer to Diogenes than to Cicero, though not because Paul resembles Diogenes but because his epistles also fall short of the language of rhetoric. Neither, however, is ignorant of Greek.

In fact, one easily finds evidence that Paul falls short of rhetorical Greek, beginning with the presence of a host of words which appear in colloquial forms or are foreign to Attic Greek. Many more are old words used in new ways. Examples include 'the highly colloquial types γέγοναν . . . καυχᾶσαι, ζηλοῦτε and φυσιοῦσθε as subj., νοῖ, ἐφ' ἐλπίδι,[122] σπείρης, νοός νοῖ, ἡμίσους, ἀπεκατεστάθη, ἐλελύκεισαν, γέγοναν δοῖ, ὀδυνᾶσαι, φάγεσαι, λυέτωσαν, οἶδας οἴδαμεν, ἤμην, ἐλήμφθην and δόξα, all of which distinguish Hellenistic from Attic Greek'.[123] Significant for the argument of Galatians is the non-classical use of ἀνάθεμα, a term signifying consecration or devotion (and usually spelt ἀνάθημα) in non-biblical literature. This term has come to mean, via the LXX, 'given over to destruction'. The LXX renders ḥērem (ban, devoted to the ban) with ἀνάθεμα. One finds the 'Greek' meaning at Luke 21.5, while Paul consistently adopts the 'LXX meaning' (Rom. 9.3; 1 Cor. 12.3, 16.22; cf. Lev. 27.28–29; Deut. 7.26, 13.17; Josh. 6.17–18, 7.11–13, 15).[124]

---

[121] See below (pp. 233f.) for a discussion of Deissmann, as well as alternative discourse models developed to explain Paul's non-Attic Greek.

[122] Moulton and Howard, *Grammar, II*: 9.

[123] Moulton and Howard, *Grammar, II*: 10.

[124] See Longenecker, *Galatians*, 17.

Perhaps most important for our concerns is διαθήκη, meaning 'will' or 'testament' in classical writers[125] and in Josephus (illustrating Josephus' tendency towards classical word use).[126] Only one non-biblical instance of the term meaning simply 'treaty' or 'agreement' is known: Aristophanes, *The Birds* 439f., where Peisthetaerus demands a pledge of protection, complete with guarantor.[127] More typical are: Isaeus' *On the Estate of Cleonymus* 1.24: 'If, gentlemen, Cleonymus, as my opponents allege, bequeathed the estate to them by the will in its present form', and Lysias, *On the Property of Aristophanes* 19.39: 'For Conon's death and the dispositions made under his will in Cyprus have clearly shown that his fortune was but a small fraction of what you were expecting'.[128] B. F. Westcott notes that readings of Hebrews after Chrysostom revert to this classical use of the term meaning 'will' rather than 'covenant'.[129]

In the LXX, however (clearly depending on *berît*), and in the NT, we find that συνθήκη, the normal Greek word for covenant, has yielded to διαθήκη. Paul follows the colloquial form and speaks primarily of a covenant, not of a will and testament (though at times the concepts seem to merge in Galatians).[130] Other terms that represent LXX influence or simply move away from their older meaning are πρόσωπον λαμβάνω for *nephesh panim* (Gal. 2.6); ἐν χείρι, from the Aramaic *b'yad* via the LXX (Gal. 3.19);[131] and κτίσις which now takes over the role of κτίσμα.[132] 'πίστις is changed from 'proof' or 'evidence' to 'a state

[125] It is a legal term, i.e. last will and testament, in Aristotle, *Wasps* 584, 589; Plato, *Laws*, 11.923e; Epictetus, *Dissertations* 2.13.7; BGU 19.2.5; P.Lond. 177; IG, 7.3426.14. It more rarely means (though the extension of the legal term is clear enough) the last words of a philosopher: Philostratus, *Life of Apollonius* 7.35; Lucian, *On the Passing of Peregrinus* 41. These references are from Westcott, *Hebrews*, 300–4.

[126] See, for instance, *Antiquities* 17.3.2;9.7; *Jewish War* 2.3.

[127] Aristophanes, *The Birds* 439–41.

[128] Lysias, *On the Property of Aristophanes* 19.39. So also Isaeus, *On the Estate of Menecles* 2.14; *On the Estate of Nicostratus* 4.12.47, 14.48; *On the Estate of Aristarchus*, 10.10.80; Demosthenes, *Against Aphobus* I.7.13.817, *Against Stephanus* 2.46.25.1136. Each of these clearly refers to the will of the deceased. For many of these references I am indebted to Burton, *Galatians*, 496.

[129] Westcott, *Hebrews*, 304.

[130] The importance of this term was noted already by Deissmann, *Light From the Ancient East*, 337–8. On the problems in Galatians see Bammel, 'Gottes ΔΙΑΘΗΚΗ', 313–19; Selb, 'Διαθήκη im Neuen Testament', 190–2; Llewelyn, 'Revocation of Wills', 41–7.

[131] From Leviticus 26.46: ἐν χειρὶ Μωυσῆ.

[132] I.e. it comes to speak of the thing created rather than the act of creating. Hatch, *Biblical Greek*, 5.

of mind';[133] at Gal. 4.13 τὸ πρότερον should be πρῶτον in classical Greek;[134] and finally, nominatives + the article with simple substantives in classical Greek address only inferiors, who are in effect referred to in the third person, while Paul even writes ὁ θεος, ὁ πατήρ, etc., rendering the articular Semitic vocative with the Greek articular nominative.[135]

Further indicators of Paul's level are his failure to employ the dual, the final optative,[136] εὖ instead of the encroaching καλῶς,[137] his use of παιδεύω to mean punishment rather than teaching, and his participating in the reorientation of παρακαλέω. The more proper conditional εἰ + optative, followed by optative + ἄν, does not occur in the NT; ἐν + dative becomes εἰς + accusative, revealing the confusion of 'motion into' with 'resting in' which appears in 'late vulgar texts . . . more and more';[138] and οὐ is used to negate all indicatives while μή negates all other moods.[139]

Galatians 2.3–5 may threaten the notion that Galatians could have passed for a piece of oratory as much as any passage. Consider the words of 2.3: 'Yet not even Titus, who was with me, Ἕλλην ὤν, was compelled to be circumcised'. If circumcision stands at the heart of the crisis in Galatia, then the ambiguity contained in Paul's first reference to it ought to disturb us. Why did he not, if he meant 'although he was a Greek',[140] use a form of καίπερ or καίτοι? He has left open the possibility of being understood to

---

[133] Ibid., 83–8; p. 85 lists citations from Philo where our term appears to be used with the same meaning as in the Bible: *On The Creation* 14.45; *Allegorical Interpretation* 3.81.228; *On the Migration of Abraham* 9.43.442 (references have been brought into conformity with LCL).

[134] N. Turner, *Grammatical Insights*, 91: 'It is precarious to suppose that St. Paul refers to the first of only *two* visits (i.e. comparative). Nor need the word be non-elative, i.e. "the first of at least three times"'.

[135] BDF, §147(3).

[136] Cf. Browning, *Medieval and Modern Greek*, 37: 'The optative disappears as a separate category, except in a few fossilised usages which are becoming lexical rather than grammatical'. The obvious example of this fossilization is Paul's use of μὴ γένοιτο, which represents every use of the optative in Paul (on this see Turner, *Grammar, III*: 121). Moulton and Howard consider the presence of the potential optative a 'primary test' and concludes that all but Luke are free of this 'artificialism' (*Grammar, II*: 7).

[137] BDF §102(3). Cf. Lee, 'Speech of Jesus in Mark's Gospel', 12.

[138] Browning, *Medieval and Modern Greek*, 41–2.

[139] Ibid., 49.

[140] This is the more usual understanding: see, for example, Burton, *Galatians*, 76; Lagrange, *Aux Galates*, 28; Mußner, *Galaterbrief*, 106; Betz, *Galatians*, 57 (his discussion at 88 and 89 of Gal. 2.3 is less clear than his translation on 57); Longenecker, *Galatians*, 50.

mean 'because he was a Greek he was not compelled to be circumcised', though this would be better expressed with διὰ τὸ εἶναι . . .[141] Lightfoot hesitantly embraces this reading,[142] Turner lending weight by remarking both that the present text is ambiguous and that the concessive use appears infrequently in the NT.[143] There is no better reason to reject it than that Paul certainly would have emphasized the notion that the Jerusalem church accepted an uncircumcised Titus precisely *because* he was not a Jew: if that clinched the argument, the Galatians too would be exempt. While one might assert that the clause contains an ingenious ambiguity which allows Paul, in the interests of his case, to say what he does not mean (like the television lawyer who knows his utterance will be stricken from the record only after it affects the jury), it must be borne in mind that this imprecision merely introduces the greater problems found in the verses which follow. The confusion would be considered intolerable by sophisticated hearers.

Verse 3 marks only the beginning of the difficulties in 2.3–5. Even worse for Paul's sake, his words have sparked an argument over whether or not Titus was actually circumcised – his report eliminating only the possibility that Titus' circumcision was coerced. F. C. Burkitt queries: 'who can doubt that it was the knife which really did circumcise Titus that has cut the syntax of Gal. 2:3–5 to pieces?'[144] Duncan similarly writes: 'The very incoherence of his language . . . suggests that Paul is dealing with a matter of extreme delicacy. If the issue had been a clear-cut one, if e.g. Paul had positively refused to have Titus circumcized, and the other party had accepted this position, Paul . . . would have expressed himself in emphatic and unambiguous language . . .'[145] The evidence though, favours the conclusion that Titus remained uncircumcised, 2.5–6 catapulting us in that direction: we also note favourably Manson's assessment: 'If he was circumcised, the fact

---

[141] Cf. 2.11: ὅτι + genitive + ἦν; or James 4.2: διὰ τὸ μὴ αἰτεῖσθαι ὑμᾶς.

[142] Lightfoot, *Galatians*, 105. He has few followers in this.

[143] Turner, *Grammar, III*: 157.

[144] Burkitt, *Christian Beginnings*, 118. Others who maintain that Titus was circumcised are Farrar, *Life and Work of Paul*, 233–6; Nock, *St Paul*, 109; he introduces the notion that Titus slipped away while Paul was occupied and diffused a difficult situation by submitting to circumcision. This introduces more problems than it solves according to Manson, 'The Problem of Galatians', 176, n. 1.

[145] Duncan, *Galatians*, 43.

would be well advertised in Galatia by Paul's opponents and the involved and stumbling verbiage of these verses would be worse than useless as a camouflage for that nasty fact'.[146] No matter the conclusion drawn, the language is troublesome: 'Paul wrote a bad piece of Greek';[147] 'The counsels of the Apostles of the Circumcision are the hidden rock on which the grammar of the sentence is wrecked';[148] 'The style of this sentence is remarkably problematic'.[149] The language rarely escapes criticism, for 2.4 begins with an anacoluthon, and the sentence merely trails away at verse 5, while what lies in between lacks both subject and main verb.[150]

Verses 6 to 10, according to Betz, appear at first glance to be 'one convoluted sentence, a strange phenomenon in the otherwise so well-composed letter'.[151] He then, however, manages to turn the apparent difficulties into virtues. He continues: 'detailed analysis . . . reveals that the section is by no means carelessly composed. On the contrary, it is simply more complex. The enormous care which the author has apparently devoted to this section can only be explained if the event on which he reports constitutes the center of his "statement of facts"'.[152] This smacks of special pleading. A careful reading of Lightfoot reveals that the damaging effects of the hidden rock at verse 4 continue in 6–10.[153] Bligh, resorting to desperate measures, reorders 2.1–10 until much of the confusion is dispelled.[154] Surely the passage which introduces the central issue of an oration should not require such efforts.[155]

Given the evidence drawn from Paul's vocabulary and syntax, it seems safe to conclude that Galatians lacks rhetorical polish. James Hope Moulton properly places all the NT writers in the same category, even while recognizing different levels of sophistication:

[146] Manson, 'The Problem of Galatians', 175–6.
[147] Barrett, *Freedom and Obligation*, 112, n.12.
[148] Lightfoot, *Galatians*, 106.
[149] Schlier, *Galater*, 69, my translation.
[150] For implications of the grammar see Orchard, 'Ellipse between Galatians 2,3 and 2,4', 469–81; Blommerde, 'Is There an Ellipsis?', 100–2; Walker, 'Why Paul Went to Jerusalem', 503–10.
[151] Betz, *Galatians*, 92.
[152] Ibid.
[153] Compare Lightfoot, *Galatians*, 106 with 108.
[154] Bligh, *Galatians*, 152–4.
[155] We do not engage in textual criticism since, even when reconstructed most favourably for Paul, the grammar is not thereby clarified. All the options discussed spring from similar texts. The variants can, however, contribute to our argument that the text at its best presents difficulties. For intelligent discussion of the textual options see Bruce, *Galatians*, 113–14, Barrett, *Freedom and Obligation*, 112, n. 12.

In the use of popular forms [Paul] and Luke go as far, with
rare exceptions, as the least cultured of NT writers. These
facts are the strongest possible disproof for both Paul and
Luke of any charge of using book Greek: no author who
could favour the Atticist rules would fail to purge his pages
of vernacular inflexions. If, however, the two friends keep
company in their inflexions, they part again in vocabulary
and in so typical a matter as the use of the optative, and in
both Paul leans away from the literary style.[156]

To the *literati, koinē* words are vulgar: obsolete meanings and
declensions are revived and are alone regarded as correct; employment of these words and forms becomes 'a mark of culture and of
literary acceptability', the index of acceptability being the presence
of the element in question in the literature of Golden Athens.[157]
Atticisms (and freedom from elements considered non-Attic) thus
often characterize the language of those who have completed the
course of higher education, and certainly of the orator. Inquiry into
the origins of the Atticizing movement, which reveals that the
primary impetus has come from developments which occurred
within the educational system, confirms this. Browning lists five
causes of Atticism's rise:

(1) education was based on literary texts far removed from
     spoken speech.
(2) 'It is probable that the beginnings of a new dialect differ-
     entiation were taking place within Koine though there is
     very little direct evidence of this'.
(3) The opposition of rhetoricians to ornament and verbosity
     led to a heightened academic interest in, and imitation of,
     the style of the classical orators – and classical grammatical
     forms followed closely on style. 'This occurs particularly
     easily in Greek, in which the linguistic form used is largely
     a function of the situation, i.e. in works of literature a
     function of the literary genre'.
(4) the themes of teachers of rhetoric related almost exclusively
     to the time between the Persian Wars and Alexander the
     Great.
(5) Those who could afford a literary education possessed, by

---

[156] Moulton, *Grammar, II*: 9.
[157] Browning, *Medieval and Modern Greek*, 50–1. This work tells the story of the
Greek language most accessibly.

virtue of their distinct, refined speech, a status symbol
which instantly separated them from the masses. The
'living developing' *koinē* was therefore detested by those
who craved such a symbol.[158]

Four of these causes relate to education: (1), (3), (4) and (5), and
two relate to rhetoric: (3) and (4). Atticism, rhetoric and *paideia*
thus worked closely together by Paul's day.

This conclusion seems sure: handbook rhetoric, both in its
surviving incarnations and in theory, partakes of a form of Greek
which is in several ways distinct from the *koinē*. But the NT,
including Galatians, does not employ this register and therefore
could not masquerade as oratory. In portions of the NT where Paul
is presented as delivering actual forensic speeches a rather marked
change comes over his mode of expression, but throughout his
epistles we find constant employment of a *koinē* free of artifice.[159]

Alternative explanations of Paul's language

As argued in the previous chapter, many early readers found that
Paul's letters do not conform to classical eloquence. Modern
scholarship also notices this and therefore proposes several alternative explanations for Paul's communicative strategy. One vital
aspect of these alternatives is that they never suggest a return to the
days when eloquence equalled classical modes.[160]

The beginning of this century provides a convenient starting
point for discussing the nature of NT Greek. The archaeological
discoveries of the late nineteenth century, as well as refined
methodologies, gave great impetus to the discussion which flowered
in the 1890s and thereafter. One should note, moreover, that each
model proposed by scholarship further solidifies our argument, for,
as with the fathers,[161] each begins with the assumption that the NT

[158] Browning, *Medieval and Modern Greek*, 49–51.

[159] So also Köster, 'Did Paul Model his Language?'; Hatch, *Biblical Greek*, 9,
83–8; Jannaris, *Historical Greek Grammar*, 8; Moulton, *Grammar, II*: 9–10; Colwell,
'Greek Language', 480; BDF, §3; Nock, *Early Gentile Christianity*, 94–6; Turner,
'Literary Character', 107–8.

[160] Cf. Judge, 'St Paul and Classical Society', 35: 'They still found his letters
weighty and strong, and these clearly made no concessions to Atticism'.

[161] Cf. Dibelius (*From Tradition to Gospel*, 9) who writes: 'The company of
unlettered people which expected the end of the world any day had neither the
capacity nor the inclination for the production of books, and we must not predicate
a true literary activity in the Christian church of the first two or three decades'. He

texts do not correspond to the level of classical literature.[162] In fact, the very existence of these attempts to describe biblical Greek is predicated upon these shortcomings. The NT is simply understood not to be classical; thus what follows is intended to reinforce our argument that Paul did not attain to this level – the level of Graeco-Roman oratory – by discussing the alternatives open to Paul.

One stream of evidence for non-rhetorical language is the argument that the NT was composed in a biblical or 'holy' language.[163] Kümmel traces this view back to Hermann Cremer, who in his *Biblisch-theologisches Wörterbuch der neutestamentlichen Gräcität* saw the Greek of the NT as the 'organ of the spirit of Christ' and therefore as 'the language of the Holy Spirit'.[164] Along a related line, Henry Gehman's careful look at the LXX and, simultaneously, Nigel Turner's comparison of the NT to apocryphal writings, led them to conclude that travellers to certain parts of first-century Syria would have heard a distinct Palestinian-Greek dialect.[165] Turner's evidence is that, on the one hand, Semitic influence alone cannot account for all that sets the region apart, while, on the other, the NT reveals an 'almost complete lack of classical standards in every author'.[166] Matthew Black similarly calls the Greek of the NT 'a peculiar language, the language of a peculiar people'.[167] Although we might agree within limits, it cannot be too peculiar if it is the language of the synagogue and thus was understood by god-fearers and other gentiles at whom Paul directed his proselytizing efforts.[168] More importantly, regardless of the accu-

pushes in the direction of an active oral rhetoric; thus his concern is not to identify classical aspects of rhetoric.

[162] See Neill and Wright, *Interpretation of the New Testament*, 158–9.

[163] For the pre-history of this movement see Deissmann, 'Hellenistic Greek', 39–41; Voelz, 'Language of the New Testament', 895–906. Also essential is McKnight, ' "Holy Ghost" Greek?', 87–93.

[164] Kümmel, *Investigation of Problems*, 194, citing Cremer, *Biblico-Theological Dictionary*. The battle was in fact much older: during the seventeenth and eighteenth centuries factions argued that the text was either 'Hebraic' Greek or 'Purist' Greek (i.e. untouched by Hebrew or any other influence). By the middle of the eighteenth century the Hebraist position was accepted. See on the history Winer, *Grammatik*, 4–14.

[165] Porter, *Language of the New Testament*, 28. See especially n. 3 for a bibliography of Turner's many related works.

[166] Porter, *Language of the New Testament*, 28, quoting Turner, *Grammar, III*:2; see also *Grammatical Insights*, 182.

[167] M. Black, 'Biblical Languages', 11.

[168] Paul's missionary strategy according to Acts and his own statements depends on this ability to communicate widely. See Jaeger, *Early Christianity and Greek Paideia*, 7.

racy of their conclusions concerning the nature of NT Greek, if Paul had simply used the Greek of the rhetors this alternative would never have been proposed.[169]

The discovery of the papyri,[170] and their subsequent analysis (along with other new documents) by Adolf Deissmann, had the effect, on the one hand, of freeing the NT from much of the stigma accrued to it by not living up to the standards of classical literature,[171] and, on the other, of attacking this notion that the Bible employs a unique 'holy' language. He especially attacked this second notion, and in so doing revealed the prominence which it enjoyed in his day, when he spoke of the 'dogma' of a Greek Bible which was 'linguistically sealed off and isolated'. His agenda then was to move 'towards a knowledge of its individual and heterogeneous elements, and investigate these upon their own historical bases'.[172]

The papyri revealed a completely unknown class of letters which seemingly shared more with the NT correspondence than did the work of known authors and orators.[173] This allowed for a reorientation among scholars, as indicated by Malherbe's observation that turn-of-the-century German philologists agreed with both the

[169] Also worthy of consideration is Wibbing, *Tugend- und Lasterkataloge im Neuen Testament*. Wibbing draws many linguistic and conceptual parallels between Qumran and the NT, especially the pastorals.

[170] Eight hundred papyrus rolls were found at Herculaneum in 1752. More, discovered in 1778 in Gizeh in the Fayum district, were unceremoniously burned. Thebes and Memphis gave up a great deal of material concerning the temple of Serapis in 1820, and in 1821 Book 24 of the Iliad was uncovered. Orations were found in 1847 (three, given by Hyperides). In 1877 a large number of fragments were found in Crocodilopolis, many subsequently destroyed, the bulk of the remains going to Vienna for the private collection of Archduke Rainer. The years 1889–90 saw Flinders Petrie lead an organized search of Gurob, where he found valuable materials in mummy cases. His discoveries included the lost *Constitution of Athens* by Aristotle and the *Odes* of Bacchylides. See Barclay, 'New Testament and Papyri', 57–8. A modern standard is E. G. Turner, *Greek Papyri*.

[171] Deissmann writes that it had been a long time since 'the Greek of the New Testament was looked upon as the genuinely classical'. And: 'Whoever surrenders himself frankly to the impression which is made by the language of the early Christians is fully assured that the historical connecting-points of New Testament Greek are not found in the period of the Epos and the Attic classical literature. Paul did not speak the language of the Homeric poems or of the tragedians and Demosthenes, any more than Luther that of the Nibelungen-Lied': cf. *Bible Studies*, 63.

[172] Ibid., 66 (see also 65). Cf. Kümmel, *Investigation of Problems*, 219.

[173] For the notion that popular speech is preserved in inscriptions, papyri and ostraca but not in literary works see Deissmann, *Light from the Ancient East*, 4–61.

church fathers and Paul that he was 'unskilled in speaking' (2 Cor. 11.6) and not worthy of comparison with ancient orators.

> To Deissmann, such a comparison was inappropriate, for Paul did not write artistic prose. He argues that one should keep in mind the contrast between artless, nonliterary prose, like Paul's, and artistic prose, which followed the canons of rhetorical theory. Paul was a man of the people, and his letters show none of the artificiality of the sophists.[174]

Deissmann insists that a reconstruction of the ancient world based on artful literary texts could not be undertaken, that a reconstruction 'which has been pieced together fragmentarily out of fragments, might easily prove erroneous'.[175] And he has enough ammunition to go against established scholars like Eduard Norden who, in a critique of the language and literature of early Christianity, compared Paul with the ancient world in such a way that the results were invalid: they were 'mere contrasts between artless non-literary prose and the artistic prose of literature'.[176] Deissmann then proposes that it is the '*non-literary* written memorials of . . . the period which led up to and witnessed the rise and early development of Christianity' which run most closely parallel to the NT texts: 'the innumerable texts on stone, metal, wax, papyrus, parchment, wood, or earthenware' freshly discovered during the years prior to his investigations.[177]

Deissmann perceived immediately that these documents do more than supplement the known witnesses to the language of the 'Imperial Period': they reflect language of a fundamentally different kind.[178] Previously held literary witnesses to the era came from the pens of the cultivated, of writers who wrote about their own society and its peculiar social habits. When the 'lower classes . . . do come to the front – in the comedies, for instance – they stand before us for the most part in the light thrown upon them from above'.[179] The failure of scholarship to reckon with this stratification and its effect on literature he labels a 'fatal generalisation'.[180] Because the

---

[174] Malherbe, *Social Aspects*, 54–5.
[175] Deissmann, *Light from the Ancient East*, 3.
[176] Ibid., 3–4.
[177] Ibid., 4. Deissmann's emphasis.
[178] Ibid., 7.
[179] Ibid., 7.
[180] Ibid.

common has been identified with the elite, Christians have been measured against an inappropriate standard.[181]

Having demonstrated with the aid of the papyri the existence of long-neglected lower and middle classes, he ascribes membership in them to the NT writers.[182] The greatest benefit, he maintains, from exposure to the 'non-literary written memorials of the Roman Empire' lies in their correcting the universally held portrait of Roman antiquity – a portrait distorted by viewing it 'exclusively from above. They place us in the midst of the classes in which we have to think of the apostle Paul and the early Christians gathering recruits'.[183]

From this second argument Deissmann concludes that the NT is undoubtedly a 'monument of late colloquial Greek, and in the great majority of its component parts the monument of a more or less *popular* colloquial language'.[184] When he turns to Paul, his conclusions exude similar confidence. With undisguised admiration for the Pauline style he insists that its force comes from elsewhere than classical idiom: even at its finest, or at its most argumentative, Paul's

> Greek never becomes literary. It is never disciplined, say, by the canon of the Atticists, never tuned to the Asian rhythm: it remains non-literary. Thickly studded with rugged, forceful words taken from the popular idiom, it is perhaps the most brilliant example of the artless though not inartistic colloquial prose of a travelled city-resident of the Roman Empire, its wonderful flexibility making it just the very Greek for use in a mission to all the world.[185]

When Deissmann speaks of this new standard of writing he is speaking of phonology and accidence, summed up as 'morpholo-

---

[181]   Ibid.

[182]   Ibid. On p. 7, note 1 he says that the entire book is a defence of this thesis.

[183]   Ibid., 9. He adds (9, n. 1) that within the new findings, even the Imperial documents do not conform to the higher standard which one might expect of them, but instead they are 'at least linguistically, representative not of the higher but of an average culture'.

[184]   Ibid., 69.

[185]   Ibid., 70. Compare his subsequent discussion of Hebrews: 'the contrast in which the Epistle to the Hebrews, for instance, stands linguistically to the earlier texts of Primitive Christianity, is peculiarly instructive to us. It points to the fact that the Epistle to the Hebrews, with its more definitely artistic, more literary language (corresponding to its more theological subject-matter), constituted an epoch in the history of the new religion. Christianity is beginning to lay hands on the instruments of culture; the literary and theological period has begun' (pp. 70–1).

gical details'.[186] He argues from the presence of a host of words which appear in the NT but not in classical literature,[187] as well as the distinctives of syntax when compared with classical style,[188] the last illustrated by, for example, the widely noted difference between classical and biblical uses of prepositions.[189] We should note that these are the very differences that may have brought ridicule upon Josephus,[190] and may also explain the charge of being uneducated which was thrown at the young man and the judges discussed above. Deissmann's work not only helps explain these accusations, but it makes sense of that monolithic reaction to the literary quality of the NT which was uncovered in our last chapter. He writes that Christianity's defenders embraced the simplicity of the NT in the face of a culture of learning which ridiculed the 'language of the New Testament as a boatman's idiom'.[191] One cannot escape the conclusion that the NT does not measure up to the standards of classical antiquity; realizing this, Deissmann describes as hopeless any effort to defend the literary qualities of the NT.[192] But, he insists, this need not be a problem when one reads the texts within their own milieu.

An aspect of his work which applies directly to the study of Paul is his well-known distinction between letters and epistles:[193] Paul's letters are not literary creations (i.e. not epistles written for the public).[194] He then boldly asserts that

> Almost all the mistakes that have ever been made in the
> study of St. Paul's life and work have arisen from the
> neglect of the fact that his writings are non-literary and
> letter-like in character[195] . . . St. Paul was not a writer of

---

[186] Ibid., 72.

[187] Ibid., 72–118. He directly assaults the idea of 'Biblical words' as comprising a special 'Biblical Language' in these pages. Kümmel recounts that Deissmann's *Bibelstudien* of 1895 relied on the papyri to provide the meaning of previously unknown NT words (*Investigation of Problems*, 218–19). This did and should provide strong evidence that the papyri provided a solution to larger problems.

[188] Ibid., 119–31.

[189] Ibid., 120–1.

[190] This is not to imply that Josephus sounds like the papyri fragments or even like many of the texts of the NT. His work is clearly of a higher level.

[191] Ibid., 71. See Norden, *Antike Kunstprosa*, II. 512–13.

[192] Ibid., 71; cf. 66.

[193] Ibid., 227–51. For the letter see especially 228–9, and for the epistle 229–30; though Doty, 'Classification of Epistolary Literature', 183–99, and E. Richards, *The Secretary*, 212–16, expose the shortcomings of Deissmann's classification.

[194] Deissmann, *Light from the Ancient East*, 234.

[195] Ibid.

epistles but of letters; he was not a literary man . . . [but] a non-literary man of the non-literary class in the Imperial age . . . prophet-like in personality, rising above his class and surveying the contemporary educated world with the consciousness of superior strength.[196]

Paul's lines are 'unbookish', described as 'so unassuming and yet written with such powerful originality'.[197] In this context appears Deissmann's well-known description of Galatians as, in contrast to the coolly rational Thessalonian correspondence, 'the offspring of passion, a fiery utterance of chastisement and defence, not at all a treatise. "De lege et evangelio", the reflection rather of a genius flashing like summer lightning'.[198]

The dialogue engendered by Deissmann represents something of a revitalization of our first alternative to the classical language model. Among those who accepted his conclusions were such prominent scholars as Thackeray, Radermacher and A. T. Robertson.[199] Alternatively, his critics never sought to prove classical influence on the NT, but consistently maintained that Jewish/Semitic influences were being overlooked. For this position see C. F. Burney, G. Dalman, R. H. Charles and, above all, N. Turner.[200] This dialectic has more recently yielded the awareness even among followers of Deissmann that the NT contains 'Semitisms',[201] though when the disputants attempt precise definition the evidence for a distinct Christian dialect diminishes.[202] Both positions

---

[196] Ibid., 240–41.

[197] Ibid., 246.

[198] Ibid., 237.

[199] See Thackeray, *Grammar of the Septuagint*; Radermacher, *Neutestamentliche Grammatik*, especially 1–12 on the character of the *koinē*; Robertson, *Grammar*, 76–7. He insists that the nature of NT Greek is 'now obvious to everyone' (77).

[200] Burney, *Aramaic Origin of the Fourth Gospel*; *Poetry of Our Lord* (see also Burrows, 'Johannine Prologue', 57–69); Dalman, *Words of Jesus*; Charles, *Revelation*; Turner, *Christian Words*. Significantly, most advocates of this position attended to Johannine literature or the LXX.

[201] See especially Howard's appendix in Moulton, *Grammar II*: 412–85; Moule, *Idiom Book*, 171–91; Metzger, 'Language of the New Testament', 54–55. By 'Semitisms' we mean all words introduced via the LXX or Aramaic speech of the early community. Since Dalman 'Hebraisms' has been used of the former and 'Aramaisms' of the latter.

[202] Most helpful are the works of Silva; he proposes four categories of words used distinctively in the NT: (1) words in keeping with general *koinē* development but which, as if by accident, do not appear in extant literature; (2) words used creatively; (3) NT theological vocabulary which develops in parallel to any technical literature addressing a specialized topic; (4) semantic loans. Many from category (4) also belong to (3), while others may be individual instances of *parole* and *langue* in

of course argue against Paul's having used the language of Graeco-Roman literature.

So Deissmann and others who subsequently discuss the nature of NT Greek take seriously the fact that Paul does not attain to the standards of the classical world's literary figures:[203] he was of another stratum altogether, and hence would never have been accepted as an orator.

A third view of NT Greek came from Albert Wifstrand, who in his 'Stylistic Problems in James and Peter'[204] made much of the fact that Hebrews, James and Peter reveal a higher literary level than may have been commonly supposed in the post-Deissmann environment.[205] His study arrived at the conclusion that these writings are best explained by merging the influence of the Hellenized synagogue[206] with technical writings, though not to create a 'dialect' spoken by Jews. The mix was grammatically *koinē* with some Semitic phrasing.[207] This notion was taken up by Lars Rydbeck, who explored the hypothesis that professional people employed prose similar to that of the biblical text. The result was to lend support to Wifstrand's conclusions. Rydbeck's survey looked at grammar, style and content,[208] and led him to argue, for example, that there were certain characteristics[209] of the astronomical writings of Ptolemaeus, the mathematics of Nichomachus, and the pharmacological texts of Dioscurides which are shared by the NT.[210] Thus if one writes, say, ἥτις instead of ἥ, that does not prove vulgarity (and certainly does not make the writer 'Semitic'), it simply causes one to be designated less than

tension (Silva, 'New Lexical Semitisms', 253–57). Ordering of relevant terms was offered already in Silva, 'Semantic Borrowing', 104–10. Indispensable to the larger discussion are Voelz, 'Language of the New Testament', 893–977; Horsley, 'Jewish Greek'. Cf. Betz, 'Hellenismus', 19–35.

[203] Already in his 1911 Croall Lectures, George Milligan states that 'Paul stands midway between the literary and non-literary writers of his day' (published as *New Testament Documents*; see 104–5). This refinement of Deissmann was inevitable and continues unabated.

[204] Wifstrand, 'Stylistic Problems', 170–82.

[205] This superiority, at least in comparison with Paul, had been recognized by Deissmann as well.

[206] Wifstrand, 'Stylistic Problems', 180.

[207] Ibid., 180–1.

[208] Rydbeck, 'Linguistic Levels', 195.

[209] Many of which he identified as Ionic/Attic or even more purely Ionic rather than Attic. See Rydbeck, 'Linguistic Levels', 194–5. Cf. Wifstrand, 'Det grekiska Prosaspråket', 149–54. Rydbeck (p. 195) specifically contrasts 'this type of prose . . . from the periodic and smoothed out prose of the type of Isocrates'.

[210] Rydbeck, *Fachprosa*; cf. Malherbe, *Social Aspects*, 41.

classical.[211] By marrying Wifstrand's proposed synagogue Greek
to the style of these scientific treatises, one arrives at the sort of
language used in the NT; a 'linguistic "middle zone", a
"Zwischenprosa" which is by no means vulgar, which bears the
marks of a well-used written language (it has been called a
"Schreibtischprodukt"), but which is distinct from the literary
Greek of the period'.[212]

The motivation for employing such a style, Rydbeck suggests, is
to communicate matters of practical concern rather than to satisfy
literary ambitions. Thus the writer needed a vehicle capable of
precise expression.[213] This eventually spread to a wider sphere: the
voice of science became the language of government writs and
contracts.[214] So then, he concludes, a writer free of literary pretensions who wishes to communicate in 'writing at the beginning of
the Imperial era, could thus fall back on this standard language,
this normal prose'.[215]

But classicists know that this distinction between various sorts of
prose existed in more sophisticated writers long before the first
century: Aristotle, W. Rhys Roberts tells us, maintained that
ornamentation has no place in scientific inquiry: 'nobody', he says,
'uses fine language when teaching geometry'.[216] 'The style of
written prose', observes Roberts, 'is not that of oratorical debate,
nor are those of political and forensic speaking the same. Both
written and spoken have to be known. To know the latter is to
know how to speak good Greek. To know the former means that
you are not obliged, as otherwise you are, to hold your tongue
when you wish to communicate something to the general public'.[217]

This question of propriety is crucial. Robert Browning, speaking
of Apollonius Dyscolus, finds that he 'writes a Hellenistic *koinē*, as
befitted a technical writer. Atticism was confined to belles-lettres
... Apollonius takes no thought for style'.[218] Apollonius was,

[211] Rydbeck, 'Linguistic Levels', 198. 'Less than classical', again, means not
showing evidence of Greek *paideia*.
[212] Alexander, *Preface to Luke's Gospel*, 171.
[213] Rydbeck, 'Linguistic Levels', 195.
[214] Ibid., 195–96.
[215] Ibid., 196.
[216] Roberts, *Greek Rhetoric and Literary Criticism*, 52, citing Aristotle, *Rhetoric*
1404.1.12.
[217] Roberts, *Greek Rhetoric and Literary Criticism*, 54, depending on Aristotle,
Rhetoric 3.12.1–3. Roberts elsewhere (p. 9) describes Plato's style as becoming 'less
beautiful and more austere' as he strove for 'scientific truth' and 'moral goodness'.
[218] Browning, 'Apollonius Dyscolus', 86. Cf. Alexander, *Preface to Luke's Gospel*,

however, neither ignorant of expressive nuance, nor lacking in linguistic sophistication, for the writings in which he employed this non-reflective style were discussions of grammatical subtleties. In the words of Priscian he is *'maximus auctor artis grammaticae'*,[219] yet he pays little attention to style because his goal demands that communication outweigh artistry.

Although these works help classify certain biblical texts, they neither suggest a particular education for Paul, nor demonstrate that his writings are comparable to the non-Christian corpus suggested as a touchstone by Wifstrand and Rydbeck. The former implies not an elevated style in Paul alongside that of James or Peter, but a still different style.[220] And the work of the latter, at least in Malherbe's estimation, cannot be used to evaluate Paul since the textual comparison leans far too much on Luke–Acts.[221] In the end, these works have only confirmed what was already known, namely that Luke–Acts, Hebrews, James and 1 Peter are more stylized writings than those in the Pauline corpus.[222]

The question of a set of criteria for designating literature as 'popular' must also be addressed. Rydbeck demands that we proceed cautiously when (1) the papyri and the NT both exhibit a phenomenon which is absent from Attic Greek; and (2) 'the phenomenon in question deviates from the norm, especially because of its lack of occurrence in Attic Greek'.[223] These indices are often used to compress a wide range of literary achievement into a single category. What they actually reveal, however, are the two poles of language while remaining silent on what lies between. His work, inviting a gradation beyond Deissmann's, opens the

---

174. She adds in the same place that even Hermogenes uses a 'scientific style' to write a manual on rhetoric, suggesting that the writer chose to be 'informative rather than literary'.

[219] Browning, 'Apollonius Dyscolus', 86.

[220] Wifstrand ('Stylistic Problems', 170, 182) speaks of Paul's work as 'so highly coloured by his personality', and, 'as intensely individual'. The qualities that make Paul unique make him a difficult model for the later church to emulate.

[221] Malherbe, *Social Aspects*, 41.

[222] Alexander offers a more finely nuanced reading of the evidence in light of a deeper classical knowledge. She remarks that the scientific writers, while attaining to a higher level than much of the New Testament, would still not have been accepted as *literati* by those who made up the literary culture of that day. See her *Preface to Luke's Gospel*, chapter 8: 'The Social Matrix of Luke's Preface'. Should such an assessment be made of scientific writers and Luke's prefaces, it would be all the more indicative of the lowliness of Galatians, which lies beneath Luke's prefaces, and, in many ways, the remainder of Luke–Acts.

[223] Rydbeck, 'Linguistic Levels', 192–3.

door to, while not arguing for, the possibility that Paul's writings soar high above the lowest level of the papyri, despite rejection by the *literati*. Thus the indices merely help us distinguish the papyri from classical (at least Attic) literature, but fail to stratify the middle ground. Rydbeck then transcends these limits to contribute to our understanding of the 'intermediate level' of writing.[224]

This notion of a middle ground helps explain how von Wilamo-witz-Moellendorff could call Paul a great letter-writer[225] even as philologists such as Eduard Norden,[226] Franz Overbeck[227] and Paul Wendland[228] concluded that Paul came off badly when compared to rhetoricians and literary figures – or they simply deemed him too low for their attention.[229] Though all should acknowledge that Paul does not attain to great heights when judged by classical standards, or indeed when compared to other texts produced by well-educated professionals, even Eduard Norden insists that when evaluated according to the proper criteria (i.e. non-rhetorical ones), Paul stands up rather well in regard to style.[230] Edwin Judge similarly writes that 'the literary appraisal of Paul's own work ... would easily demonstrate that his style possesses a versatility and force, unconventional maybe by the standards of the professional rhetoricians, but so effective as to rank him as an orator and writer of rare distinction'.[231]

We have already mentioned Johannes Weiss and his respect for Paul's non-classical style. A fourth explanation for Paul's lan-guage level comes from Rudolf Bultmann, who, under Weiss' direction, invigorated the notion that Paul's letters partake of aspects of the diatribe, a form of discourse practised by popular philosophers in the Cynic-Stoic tradition. This represents more a

[224] Ibid., 193–7. See also Alexander's 'Greek Preface Writing', 48–74.

[225] Von Wilamowitz-Moellendorff, *Antigonos von Karystos*; see Dibelius (*An Philemon*) for a similar conclusion.

[226] Norden writes that Paul is totally 'unhellenic' (*Antike Kunstprosa*, 2: 499).

[227] Franz Overbeck maintained that the NT and the immediate post-apostolic era in many ways represented a unique sort of literature in that it was not of the classical mold, nor was it imitated in later, even patristic Christianity, the latter having reverted to Graeco-Roman forms: cf. *Über die Christlichkeit unserer heutigen Theologie*, 86. See Kümmel, *Investigation of Problems*, 204 and 435, n. 263.

[228] Wendland, *Handbuch zum Neuen Testament 2*, 354–6.

[229] Richards, *Secretary*, 211.

[230] Norden, *Antike Kunstprosa*, 2: 492–4; Wilder: 'early Christian literary arts were different from those that paganism produced, and ... Greek and traditional humanist categories are inadequate as measuring rods': cf. *Early Christian Rhetoric*, 44.

[231] Judge, 'Early Christians as Scholastic Community: II', 136.

lateral move than an advance from Deissmann's position since it too presupposes a popular rather than an artistic provenance for Paul's language. Bultmann establishes his own conception of the nature of Paul's letters with a comparison: 'Seneca's letters are literary works of art with a style based on the conscious intention of the author. The author *wanted* to write like this; whether he was in the habit of *usually* writing and speaking like this is another matter'.[232] Paul's letters are different: 'The letters of Paul, however, are real letters; each is entirely the result of a specific situation and mood. Paul did not reflect on their style, but wrote (moreover he was dictating!) as he always expressed himself, whether orally or in writing'.[233] Bultmann thus considered his letters close cousins to his preaching; and their style as that of the diatribe, the 'style of the Cynic-Stoic popular sermon'.[234] This style lacks 'artistic periods',[235] has few developed sentences, the sentences one does find 'often stand next to one another asyndectically',[236] and the logical relationships are not established by means of subordination but through various combinations of questions, answers, and imperatives.[237] The diatribe represents a less artistic alternative to the rhetoric of the handbooks.

A decade into this century, the evidence provided by Deissmann[238] was depended on to disparage Paul's style, against Deissmann's own conclusions, as haphazard and untidy – like the letters of the papyri.[239] Thus Bultmann proposed not to return to the limited options of the pre-Deissmann era, but to correct misdirected analyses of the 'common' language of the NT.[240] He sought to demonstrate that Paul's style exhibits features widely attested in the works of those popular philosophers who depended on the diatribe, suggesting, against contemporary opinion, that Paul should not be

---

[232] Bultmann, *Stil*, 3, my translation.
[233] Ibid.
[234] Ibid.
[235] Ibid., 14.
[236] Ibid.
[237] Ibid., 14–16.
[238] Scholarship by now had sufficient time to digest Adolf Deissmann's *Bibelstudien*.
[239] This is well documented in Kümmel, *Investigation of Problems*, 218–21.
[240] If, that is, 'common' can describe philosophers who run the gamut from the highly sophisticated (e.g. Dio Chrysostom), to the drop-outs of society. An aspect of Weiss' methodology which resembles Deissmann's is his attempt to show that aspects of Paul's language appear in the diatribe but not in the papyri: cf. *Neutestamentlichen Wissenschaft*, 10–11.

considered incompetent in matters of style. He had a particular model to follow, and even if that model was rather low, skilled conformity ought to be appreciated. Although his letters were not 'Kunstprodukte' like Seneca's, he did employ a recognized form.

Since our concern is not with the accuracy of the picture painted by Bultmann, or with the question of whether diatribe is a genre or a technique,[241] but rather with the way influential scholars have handled the intersection of Paul's literary level with his social background, we will not attempt to assess Bultmann's 'correctness'. We note only that adjustments to old ways of understanding diatribe have moved the discussion far from where Bultmann left it. The most significant critique by a NT scholar comes from Stanley Stowers,[242] who maintains that when the sources are read more critically than they were nearly a century ago, it becomes evident that diatribe was less a vagabond's means of reaching the crowds than the discourse of the classroom.[243] Stowers adds that the label 'popular philosophical' as used by Bultmann and others means no more than 'relatively non-technical', and that while it 'does not imply a specific pedagogical tradition . . . "diatribal" does'.[244] Thus even today, discussion concerning the diatribe supports our conclusion that Paul used a non-artistic mode of communication – now with the suggestion that it is not the language of the courts or the senate but the classroom.

A fifth explanation for the shape of Paul's communicative strategies is that proposed by, among others, E. Earle Ellis: Paul's 'mode of thought and speech' is the pattern established in the OT.[245] Even

---

[241] The trend has been against considering diatribe a genre. See Bonhöffer, *Epiktet und das Neue Testament*, 179; Capelle and Marrou, 'Diatribe'; Jocelyn, 'Diatribes and Sermons', 3–5; Schmidt, 'Diatribai' 2:1577–78; Rahn, *Morphologie der antiken Literatur*, 153–6; Stowers, *Diatribe*, 41–9. For a defence of the diatribe as genre see Gottschalk, 'Diatribe Again', 91–2; 'More on *DIATRIBAI*', 91–2; Lesky, *Geschichte der griechischen Literatur*, 179; Nock, 'Hermetic Writings', 126–37; Porter, 'Argument of Romans 5', 655–61.

[242] Stowers, *Diatribe*.

[243] Ibid., 54–78, especially 76–8. Stowers also demonstrates throughout his thesis that classicists were in the process of rejecting that understanding of the diatribe taken over by Bultmann even as he wrote, and they have continued to move the discussion in other directions. See pp. 26–39.

[244] Ibid., 78.

[245] Ellis, *Paul's Use of the Old Testament*, 38–82, 110; 'Midrash *Pesher* in Pauline Hermeneutics', 137–42; Longenecker, *Biblical Exegesis*. See McDonald (*Kerygma and Didache*) for a detailed study of patterns of discourse in Early Christianity. See also Wilder, *Early Christian Rhetoric*. Davies' now classic argument for reading Paul as a Jew rather than as dominated by Hellenism must be considered here: cf. *Paul and Rabbinic Judaism*.

'rhetorical studies' of Paul have concluded similarly. For example, style informs Campbell's rhetorical investigation of Romans,[246] but he arrives at the conviction that major Pauline devices derive from Hebrew poetry.[247] He thus enjoys the advantage of requiring no detailed educational or sociological discussion for style when defined primarily as the utilization of devices such as antithesis and paronomasia,[248] epanophora, parenthesis,[249] and isocolic reduplication.[250] Such features spring naturally from Paul's Jewish world.

Hengel writes that 'a study of the law such as Paul describes in Gal. 1.13 f. and Phil 3.5 was – precisely for the "diaspora" Pharisee – possible only in Jerusalem'.[251] Furthermore, the name Saul corresponds rather well with Paul's claim to be of the tribe of Benjamin (Rom. 11.1; Phil. 3.5),[252] a significant datum in that not every diaspora Jew had a Hebrew name, and many a Jew could not identify with a particular tribe. Thus Hengel supports the contention that Paul used Jewish forms by claiming for him a Jewish education. Even Nock, who gave much impetus to the suggestion that the diatribe is at play in Paul, can insist that the LXX is the greatest influence on Paul's style: moreover, 'Paul shows only the slightest acquaintance with pagan Greek literature, but he knew his Old Testament very well'.[253] And again: 'The style of Paul is the key to the understanding of his attitude to the world. He saw life in terms of the Septuagint and of Jewish apologetics, of the sermons which he heard at Tarsus as a boy'.[254] Nock further supports this suggestion of Jewish influence on Paul with these words:

> A great classical scholar, Eduard Norden, has remarked, 'Paul is a writer who I, at least, understand only with very great difficulty'. Probably all classical scholars would agree. The reason is that Paul's style is full of second-hand Semitisms which come from the Greek Bible. Paul must

[246] Campbell, *Rhetoric of Righteousness*, 77.
[247] Ibid., 85; speaking of antithesis. So also Lund, *Chiasmus*.
[248] Campbell, *Rhetoric of Righteousness*, 83–6.
[249] Ibid., 86–95.
[250] Ibid., 95–101.
[251] Kim's translation, *Origin*, 33–4, citing Hengel, 'Die Ursprünge der Christlichen Mission', 24.
[252] Kim, *Origin*, 32.
[253] Nock, *St Paul*, 235–6.
[254] Nock, 'The Vocabulary of the New Testament', 139. Cf. also Turner, *Grammar, III*; Berger, *Semitische Syntax in Neuen Testament*. See McKnight, 'New Testament and "Biblical" Greek', 36–42, for a different view.

have had some acquaintance with the Old Testament in Hebrew also and seems to see some of the original connotations which underlie the Greek as he quotes it; but the Greek version is the fact of importance.[255]

Nock concludes from his study of the 'stylistic phenomena' in Paul's epistles that his 'expression is externally Hellenic, but inwardly Jewish'.[256] Thus when one reconstructs Paul's background from data derived from his actual mode of expression, it often points more to Jewish than Graeco-Roman indicators. Certainly this data must be analysed alongside the evidence for Paul's *Hellenistic* Jewish background, but the balance seems weighted in favour of Judaism in terms of his discourse.

At first glance Judge's suggestion that Paul resembles a sophist seems to present a sixth alternative. He claims that Paul's rhetoric is learnt 'by hard experience rather than by training. It was as his own profession, that of rabbi, failed him (when ejected from the synagogues), that he took up the new one'.[257] But such a classification of Paul turns out to be a phantom: Judge means by 'sophist' nothing more than an itinerant teacher who tries to make a living along the way. He stresses that Paul was unlike those itinerants who could only 'repel people from the well-established circles in which Paul moved'.[258] Malherbe rejects significant aspects of Judge's reconstruction, showing that in major details Paul is quite unlike a sophist, and reminding us that Paul himself 'denounces his opponents as sophists and dissociates himself from their method'.[259] Perhaps Malherbe has poked holes in a straw man, for Judge himself counsels caution as he introduces the term 'sophist'.[260] Judge asks 'what other touring preacher established a set of corporate societies independent of himself and yet linked to him by a constant traffic of delegations?'[261] Furthermore, and with this he gives the very reason why he cannot consider Paul an orator:

---

[255] Nock, *St Paul*, 236.
[256] Ibid., 237.
[257] Judge, 'Early Christians as Scholastic Community', 127.
[258] Judge, 'St Paul and Classical Society', 32; though cf. Malherbe, *Social Aspects*, 49.
[259] Malherbe, ibid., 47–8. See the following interaction with Bruce Winter's argument. We might also add the difficult matter of whether Paul accepted money from those churches to which he spoke. Unwillingness to accept payment would render the designation 'sophist' unlikely.
[260] Judge, 'Early Christians as Scholastic Community', 127.
[261] Ibid.

we know from the fourth-century Fathers that he did not conform to all the complex rules of classical rhetoric. Moreover, he poured scorn on the rhetoric of his rivals, who one may assume followed the standard pattern. It is my belief that he deliberately refrained from the formal techniques of persuasion because he rejected the moral position one must adopt to employ them.[262]

Malherbe and Judge have therefore performed a valuable service by emphasizing that Paul *does not* share much with orators or those who so style themselves. In a brief *excursus* we present further evidence that Paul does not conform to what the crowd expects of an orator.

Excursus: the activities of the orator

Bruce Winter believes that alongside the style of Paul's writing one can place the apostle's activities as evidence of the distance between himself and classical orators. This argument enjoys the additional advantage of relying less on extra-Pauline texts,[263] and more on his own epistles. Of particular interest is the orator's entry into a city for the purpose of 'making disciples', that is, to establish a school for fee-paying students.[264] Winter demonstrates that these entries were expected to conform to the following set pattern. The sophist began with 'an oration about his own renown'[265] which needed to adhere to a prescribed form. The perils of deviation are illustrated in Philostratus' attack on Polemo, a well-known orator[266] who paraded his arrogance in Athens by abandoning convention: he neglected to speak of his own reputation,[267] which 'was simply not professional'.[268] Polemo comes under further criticism for omitting an encomium of Athens,[269] while Philagrus of Cilicia broke form by lamenting his wife who had died in Ionia.[270]

---

[262] Judge, 'Reaction against Classical Education', 11.
[263] I.e. the Book of Acts.
[264] See Winter, 'Entries', 55–74.
[265] Ibid., 58.
[266] Aristides attended his lectures in Smyrna. See comments by Behr in Aristides (LCL 1: vii; introduction and trans. C. A. Behr, 1973).
[267] Philostratus, *Lives of the Sophists* 535; cf. Winter, 'Entries', 58.
[268] Ibid., 58. Cf. Anderson, *Philostratus*, 45.
[269] Philostratus, *Lives of the Sophists* 535.
[270] Ibid., 579.

After this preliminary speech called the *dialexis*[271] came an original oration based upon topics suggested by the audience. Philostratus narrates an instance of deviation from the simple requirement of originality. The aforementioned Philagrus, fallen from favour because of his flawed first oration, was induced by the crowd to address a topic for which he had achieved fame elsewhere: 'The Uninvited'. When he began the speech pretending to be improvising, the audience read along from copies of the text which had reached Athens. 'Then the lecture became the scene of uproar and laughter, with Philagrus shouting and vociferating that it was an outrage on him not to be allowed to use what was his own; but he failed to win acquittal of the charge that was so fully proven'.[272]

D. A. Russell adds that such activities would have been conducted not in the common language but what he labels Demosthenic Greek.[273] This meant that for some a moment's reflection was needed before delivery. Aristides would wait until the following day – even when the emperor was in attendance. But his delay ought to be tolerated for he, as he himself claimed, belonged to those who 'do not vomit their speeches but try to make them perfect'.[274]

Against this background Winter argues that Paul in both 1 Corinthians and 1 Thessalonians rejects any suggestion that his entries follow the fixed pattern of the orators. To the Thessalonians Paul writes that he delivered no flattering encomium (1 Thess. 2.5a);[275] he did not use his entry as a means for personal gain but as a means to the advancement of the Thessalonians (2.6–8).[276] Paul further goes out of his way to deny any rhetorical deception (2.3).[277]

To the church in Corinth Paul makes similar statements. He denies coming to preach 'the mystery or testimony of God with superiority of rhetoric or wisdom'.[278] Winter suggests that this is

---

[271] Winter, 'Entries', 58; cf. Russell, *Declamation*, 77–8.

[272] Philostratus, *Lives of the Sophists* 579; cf. D. A. Russell, *Declamation*, 80–1.

[273] Philagrus is described by Philostratus as the most 'hot-tempered of the Sophists'. When arguing with Amphicles, the best student of Herodes, Amphicles challenged a statement with: 'In what classic is that word to be found?' Philagrus anwered: 'In Philagrus' (*Lives of the Sophists* 578). Only proper use protects even the best orators from abuse. Philagrus later was promoted to the chair of rhetoric at Rome: cf. *Lives*, 580.

[274] Philostratus, *Lives of the Sophists* 583; cf. Russell, *Declamation*, 79–80.

[275] Winter, 'Entries', 66.

[276] Ibid., 66–7.

[277] Ibid., 65.

[278] Ibid., 68–9.

because the topic had been determined by the preacher beforehand – he would not be expatiating on a topic shouted by the audience, but would instead address the topic of Jesus and his crucifixion.[279] Second, Paul's self-description reveals a less than dashing figure: his stage-manner betrays 'weakness and fear and much trembling'.[280]

Winter could have added that the text of Galatians also precludes the entry of an orator, for Paul's brief reminiscence of his entry into the region contains at least a hint of embarrassment. He recalls: 'you know that it was because of an illness of the flesh that I originally preached the gospel to you' (Gal. 4.13).[281] He felt his presence despicable,[282] hindered by a malady which, Longenecker suggests, 'would probably have been interpreted by them as demonic in nature'.[283] Yet he was accepted by a group quick to share its 'blessedness'[284] (4.14–15). Baasland proposes that the theme of persecution underpins the entire epistle, finding it in each major section: 1.13–14, 23; 3.4; 4.29; 5.11; and 'more or less all of' 6.12–18.[285] This is supported by Paul's closing assertion: 'for I bear in my body the *stigmata* of Jesus'. This self-description eliminates the possibility of an orator's triumphant entry; it also suggests that members of the Galatian congregations would not so regard Paul. They accept him none the less.

Language levels were steeply graduated

The preceding discussion suggests that (1) the ancient world had a steeply graduated hierarchy of 'literariness'; and (2) the mode of communication which we actually find Paul using is lower than the refined language which reveals the heights of ancient education. That is, Paul does not use the language of classical rhetoric.

We need to reckon with a hierarchy that is at once more steeply graduated than any experienced in the modern West, and also more determinative. At the top sit the classical giants; somewhere a good bit beneath them is the epistle to the Hebrews, then Luke's preface and similar technical literature; below that we find Paul, and

---

[279] Ibid., 69.
[280] Ibid.
[281] Betz, *Galatians*, 220 for translation (cf. also p. 224).
[282] Longenecker, *Galatians*, 191.
[283] Ibid.; cf. 2 Cor. 12.7.
[284] Longenecker, ibid., 192 for translation, though it is understood differently by Betz, *Galatians*, 227. Cf. Hauck and Bertram, 'μακάριος', 362–70.
[285] Baasland, 'Persecution', 142.

farther down, in some cases several steps beneath, lie the worst of the papyrus scraps – which sometimes reveal complete illiteracy.[286] Furthermore, all the evidence points to the conclusion that one cannot by simple imitation move more than a rung or two up the ladder.[287] Of course none of this precludes the possibility that Paul climbed down the ladder.[288] Reasons for this descent may be the presence of 'common people'[289] in his assembly, or Paul's own attitude towards rhetoric as the antithesis of 'true wisdom'. Thus Paul's texts may reveal his actual socio/literary level, or they may reflect the genius of a Martin Luther, who stepped outside the bounds of academic speech to accomplish his purposes through the 'vernacular'.[290] Paul may have had the ability of the orator, yet chose to employ a different sort of Greek: this need not lessen the effect of his letters, for they are indeed 'weighty'; it only lessens their overt artistry. He possesses the talent to win a hearing for his arguments even apart from the literate language of the orator. Hence we cannot with certainty ascertain his level of education, though at least some of the evidence suggests that he was rhetorically trained.[291] The best that we can do is establish a band that places him a fair distance above the bottom – with no discernible ceiling.

Can we be no more precise than to simply argue that Paul's language differs from the classical standard? Although it falls outside this work to put the entire NT into a hierarchy, we should recognize with Deissmann that 'One must be cautious in lumping together all of the biblical texts. They rather have to be studied separately'.[292] He argues that 'some writings use literary language,

---

[286] Turner, *Greek Papyri*, 82–8, 130 (p. 82 tells of an official who could only just manage his signature); Harris, *Ancient Literacy*.

[287] Cf. Wifstrand, 'Stylistic Problems', 176. So long as James conforms to his model he is safe. When he reaches for greater heights Semitisms begin to seep through.

[288] Hermogenes approaches the style of preface found in technical manuals in his rhetorical handbook. Alexander, *Contemporary Setting*, 136.

[289] Harris, *Ancient Literacy*, 141, estimates that between 20 and 30 per cent of a Hellenistic community would have had enough education to read and write. See pp. 116–46 for a discussion of the Hellenistic period. Cf. Hengel, *Judaism and Hellenism*, 58–106; Perry, *The Ancient Romances*, 63.

[290] Rydbeck, *Fachprosa*, 187, n. 2.

[291] Winter ('Entries') feels that evidence collected from the Corinthian and Thessalonian correspondence points in the direction of the non-use of possessed abilities. His assertion is that Paul would not so self-consciously deny using techniques of which he was not well-aware.

[292] Deissmann, 'Hellenistic Greek', 58.

or at least want to', and refers to the study done by Blass[293] which catalogues 'instances of hiatus in the Epistle to the Hebrews', describing his efforts as 'of immense importance . . . pedantic as they may appear'. He follows Blass' conclusion that Hebrews is the only text in the NT 'which in syntax and style reflects the care and skill of an artistic writer'.[294]

Paul's mode of discourse

Deissmann does not, however, stop there. He discusses the various types of writing found in the NT, then, by way of contrast, insists that the Pauline corpus consists of 'artifacts of colloquial language, even though Paul seems to have copied some from the rhetoricians'.[295] He remarks that Paul's wording was rife with terms considered taboo by the *literati*. 'For instance, no "author" who respects form would have written the magnificent γρηγορεῖτε στήκετε of 1 Cor. 16.13; both verbs are "quite vulgar", as Blass calls the latter'.[296] He nevertheless goes on to explain once again that Paul spoke and wrote the language of the 'common people' of Asia and Greece in a most dynamic and appealing way – providing one could tolerate the words which offend the Atticists.[297] The similarities between the papyri and Paul are not, to be sure, all encompassing, but Deissmann shows that regarding 'diction, style, and references to everyday life', the parallels are often striking.[298]

Paul's place on the continuum that divides the *literati* and the illiterate was widely acknowledged in the generation to follow Deissmann. Arthur Darby Nock wrote that Paul's non-use of a recognized structure to order his discussion displays his freedom from the requirements of rhetoric. 'He has his own scheme of the letter as then written; but within that scheme he passes from subject to subject, with an unrestrained use of vigorous parentheses.'[299] Nock again asserts that Paul stands outside the bounds of oratory, yet goes beyond the conclusions of Deissmann to designate Paul's

[293] Blass, *Grammatik des neutestamentlichen Griechisch*, 290–91.

[294] Deissmann, 'Hellenistic Greek', citing Blass, *Grammatik*, 290.

[295] Deissmann refers to Weiss, *Beiträge* at this point, and thus it is unclear whether he intends primarily stylistic 'rhetorical' elements, or aspects of Graeco-Roman rhetoric. We have briefly discussed the position of Weiss.

[296] Blass, *Grammatik des neutestamentlichen Griechisch*, 40.

[297] Deissmann, 'Hellenistic Greek', 58–9.

[298] Richards, *Secretary*, 211.

[299] Nock, *St Paul*, 234.

Greek a 'noteworthy phenomenon'. While it is subliterary and does not conform to 'proper' grammar, it does not sink to the depths of the papyri. 'There are no formal periods ... but there is a rhetorical movement and energy which express a powerful personality that did not shrink from coining bold phrases such as Gal. ii.7, "the Gospel of circumcision" '.[300]

So we do not, as stated repeatedly, deny that Paul was an eloquent speaker in his own right. Regarding this issue of competence, Robin Scroggs has been identified as a contributor to the debate with his article 'Paul as Rhetorician'.[301] It is worthwhile, then, to consider the evidence to determine how much Scroggs supports Paul's status as a rhetor.

He speaks to the competence of Paul, but does not attempt to describe Paul's academic achievements, and apart from one footnote,[302] he does not refer to Graeco-Roman rhetoric at all. He instead argues that Romans reveals the presence of *oral* material.[303] So when he writes that 'Paul can speak out of Hellenistic rhetorical practice as easily as he can support a point with the most subtle rabbinic hermeneutic',[304] his words when read in their context suggest only that Romans embodies homiletic material. He goes on then, rather than to support correspondence to classical orations, to present models for the two homilies he finds in Romans: but his evidence distances them from the handbooks. He writes concerning 'the exegetical homily' as found in Romans 1 to 4 and 9 to 11 that 'with its heavy use of Scripture as proof [it] obviously must have its roots in Judaism'.[305] The second model – the diatribe[306] – details the formal characteristics of Romans 5 to 8. Again we find a 'rhetorical' model that falls outside the concerns of the handbooks; and so, no matter how influential this form was, or how well NT writers resemble practitioners of the diatribe,[307] Scroggs' work does not bear direct weight on our discussion of classical rhetoric. We note only a peripheral point: that 'rhetoric', because it describes several levels of discourse, may be misleading when used to describe what Paul does in Romans. He may show signs of being a preacher,

---

[300] Nock, ibid., 235.
[301] Johanson, *To All The Brethren*, 34.
[302] Scroggs, 'Paul as Rhetorician', 274, n. 11.
[303] Ibid., 273–7.
[304] Ibid., 272.
[305] Ibid., 290.
[306] Scroggs relies heavily on Bultmann, *Stil*.
[307] If wandering Cynics should be so regarded. See Scroggs, ibid., 274.

but not a Graeco-Roman orator. In his single paragraph treating classical rhetoric, Scroggs says nothing that is inaccurate, but also nothing of direct relevance to even his own work on Romans as the embodiment of two homilies.

Another notion to be taken up under the umbrella of eloquence, or the competence of Paul, relates to the assertion that rhetoric was 'in the air' and thus the rules weighed upon all who attempted public communication. There was a time when a historian such as T. R. Glover could write that a Mediterranean boy heard constant argument, 'and the boy grew up with an instinct for argument, and a quickness to see reason and to trounce nonsense'.[308] This is precisely what one may no longer say, for even apart from the unattractiveness of lumping millions of people into the same categories and describing their character as combative, it is highly unlikely that every first-century Mediterranean male (at least) argued well by instinct and trounced all nonsense. Indeed one could cite more than a few studies of Paul that find some untrounced nonsense lurking in his letters – and Paul was not unusually slow to see reason. Surely such an important individual must not be sacrificed to the search for an ancient society.

But there is more than just common sense to direct at this position. Pliny laments the fact that 'mercenaries' are hired to applaud in court – but the din is so great that they do not know when to, and moreover, they do not understand the proceedings well enough even when they can hear. As a result they need a signal just to clap at the right place.[309] These hirelings, who, one may surmise, regularly frequent the courts, do not develop deep insight by their mere presence. More than simple exposure is needed.

Consider further that Marius Victorinus was considered the best rhetorician of his day but was also 'wholly incapable of giving clear expression to his thoughts'.[310] Any direct correlation between knowing the rules of rhetoric and being a successful communicator falters on this observation. Kennedy alludes to the lack of quality in Horace's theoretical work *The Art of Poetry* as compared to his superb *Odes*,[311] while Quintilian tells us that Quintus Hortensius was considered to be second only to Cicero among his contempor-

---

[308] Glover, *The Ancient World*, 27.
[309] Pliny, *Letters* 2.14.
[310] Bruce, 'Marius Victorinus and his Works', 223.
[311] Kennedy, *Classical Rhetoric*, 109.

aries, but when his texts are read they are unimpressive.[312]
Kennedy speaks of 'the gulf between practice and theory',[313] and
informs us that 'a number of successful speeches fail to persuade
readers in their written form; a number of great published works in
oratorical form were rhetorical failures when delivered'.[314] Cicero,
in a fictitious dialogue providing Antonius' comments concerning
Charmades, writes that 'not a single writer on rhetoric . . . had ever
been even remotely eloquent',[315] but that he could 'cite a countless
host of very eloquent men who had never learned the rules or been
at all anxious to make their acquaintance'.[316]

Eloquence does not depend on a particular form of education.
Demosthenes held that eloquence springs from instinct, as do skill
both in 'setting out how a deed was done' and in accomplishing
specific goals in the various parts of a speech.[317] Thus even if Paul
opted for a style of discourse heavily influenced by Jewish or other
non-rhetorical modes of communication, this would not automatically disqualify him from the ranks of the skilful communicator.
Deissmann describes Paul's idiom as 'the most brilliant example of
the artless though not inartistic colloquial prose of a travelled city-
resident of the Roman Empire, its wonderful flexibility making it
just the very Greek for use in a mission to the world'.[318]

Rhetoric and eloquence are not two sides of the same coin but
are discrete phenomena which, while sometimes existing side by
side, often do not; we need not discover classical rhetoric where it
is lacking – other rhetorics serve well enough. Thus, as we have
seen, biblical scholars, as well as the classicists who work on the
NT, often contribute considerably to defining a stratum for Paul.
Many, especially those who have paid closest attention to Paul's
writing strategy, have not been blind to the actual place of Paul's
writings. They thus oppose the notion that Paul uses rhetorical
technique.

Seyoon Kim argues against the likelihood that 'Paul had a

[312] Quintilian, *Institutio* 11.3.8.
[313] Kennedy, *Classical Rhetoric*, 109.
[314] Ibid., 252, n. 1 cites Demosthenes' *On the False Embassy* and Cicero's *Pro Murena*. Many of the examples in the above paragraph may reflect contrasts between *oral* and *written* speech.
[315] Also Quintilian, *Institutio* 8, prologue 3.
[316] Cicero, *De Oratore* 1.20.91. Cicero places no convincing alternative views in the mouth of someone who might follow a different line. It would thus appear that this is the author's position.
[317] Ibid., 1.20.90.
[318] Deissmann, *Light from the Ancient East*, 70.

formal education in Greek philosophy and rhetoric.[319] For beyond such popular elements of the Hellenistic culture as [Cynic-Stoic diatribe and "some popular Stoic concepts"] he does not show the kind of deep influence by Greek philosophy that we see in his contemporary, Philo of Alexandria'.[320] So the influences probably came from the (diaspora) Hellenistic Judaism within which Paul moved.[321]

Nils Dahl writes (with Acts 17 in view) that 'Despite their interest [the] Athenian philosophers did not accept Paul as a colleague or consider him their equal'. And 'Paul was not a philosopher, not even in the sense in which Philo . . . was a philosopher. Philo tried to prove that the Law of Moses embodied true philosophy. Paul deliberately rejected philosophical argumentation and rhetorical polish as vehicles of his message'.[322] Dahl adds that 'Paul's message does set him apart from the tradition of ancient philosophy and rhetoric. Yet if rhetoric is properly understood as the art of persuasion, Paul was himself a skilful rhetorician, at least when he wrote his letters'.[323] Dahl admittedly calls Paul's letters 'speeches', though he means not that they are Graeco-Roman rhetoric but that they reveal the stamp of orality.[324] He concludes: 'Paul was completely comfortable with the Greek language without feeling the constraint of the formal rules of literary style'.[325]

F. F. Bruce feels that 'there is no evidence that Paul ever received anything in the way of formal education from Greek teachers; the knowledge of Greek literature and culture that his letters reflect was part of the common stock of educated people in the Hellenistic world of the time, whether they were Jews or Gentiles'.[326] E. R. Richards in his major study of Paul's use of secretaries expresses doubt that he studied under a Hellenistic teacher of rhetoric, primarily because of his 'stylistic faults'.[327] Edwin Judge, writing as

[319] See also Hengel, *Pre-Christian Paul*, 3.
[320] Kim, *Origin*, 32.
[321] Ibid., 32–33.
[322] Dahl, *Missionary Theology*, 1.
[323] Ibid., 1–2, n. 1.
[324] Ibid., 7. See also his suggestion that Paul adopts a complex structure ('Two Notes on Romans 5').
[325] Dahl, *Studies in Paul*, 3.
[326] Bruce, *New Testament History*, 225. In his older work, Maurice Jones is clearly in awe of Paul's persuasive abilities – but he admits at the outset that Paul did not employ the expected techniques of the Greek teacher: cf. *St Paul the Orator*, 2.
[327] Richards, *Secretary*, 143. He cites Turner, *Grammar, III*:86, for Paul's stylistic deficiencies.

a social historian, concludes that '[Paul's] letters are overwhelming in their argumentative drive. They turn the mind with insistent logic or appealing metaphor, and compel assent with pleas or reproaches'. Paul, he suggests, 'deliberately refrained from the formal technique of persuasion' and explicitly desired to avoid 'persuasion' in 1 Corinthians 2.4,8.[328] Paul was a 'reluctant and unwelcome competitor in the field of professional sophistry'.[329]

So the quest for the nature of Paul's language begun by Deissmann has borne great fruit. Many scholars either adopt his conclusions as their starting point or find that their own work substantiates the result that Paul did not use the language of the classical *literati*. In the end all signposts point in the same direction: Paul did not employ the language of rhetoric.

Conclusions

One must move cautiously from skilful communication to classical training in rhetoric.[330] We know so little of first-century Palestinian Judaism and Pharisaism that it is tempting to grab hold of whatever presents itself, but to leap from the structure of Galatians to Paul's education to education of Pharisees in Jerusalem is dangerous; yet even the claim that Paul reveals the skills of a professional orator is not unknown.[331]

Galatians does not sound like a classical oration. This is the considered opinion of the fathers and Christianity's earliest opponents,[332] and is, moreover, to be inferred from the existence of works by classicists, patristic scholars and others who attempt to classify the language of the NT. Paul simply did not use the language – meaning patterns of speech related to word choice and form – that protected an orator from abuse and scorn.[333] A rhetorical fiction would, it seems, have exposed Paul to even greater

---

[328] Judge, 'Reaction against Classical Education', 11.

[329] Judge, 'Paul's Boasting', 37–50. For the role of rhetoric in Corinth see Munck, *Paul and Salvation*, 148–54, especially 153. For the notion of competition among 'missionaries' of various persuasions in the days of the early church see Georgi, *Opponents of Paul in Second Corinthians*, 151–5. On Christian preachers distancing themselves from sophists, see Munck (ibid., 153) who refers to Nock, *St Paul*, 149.

[330] Especially in light of the argument that NT writers were almost universally admitted to lack classical eloquence.

[331] Smit, 'Deliberative Speech', 24; Barrett, *Freedom and Obligation*, 31–2.

[332] If we may extend their assessment of Scripture in general to Galatians. They certainly do not seem to have distinguished Galatians from the rest.

[333] Roberts, *Greek Rhetoric and Literary Criticism*, 54.

ridicule than would a straightforward delivery. And while the Galatians presumably could not imitate an oration any better than Paul, all could instinctively identify the appropriate register.[334]

Furthermore, to argue that Paul did not know that he needed to use an elevated language, or that he failed in the effort, cannot stand. The first of these arguments is doomed by its self-contradiction. If Paul possessed the mental agility to learn the art of rhetoric on the street corner he would at least be aware that it employs its own language. If he failed to observe the need for the right language, can we attribute to him the ability to master the discipline? As for the second argument, one cannot maintain that Paul in Galatians tried, but failed, to imitate the language appropriate to oratory unless one also argues that all the Pauline correspondences are failed attempts to employ this language, for we find no paradigmatic language differences among the various epistles held to be Pauline. In fact, when certain epistles are held to be of a different style, the normal response is not to posit premeditated differences in stylistic intention, but rather different authorship.[335] The uniformity of the major Pauline epistles in matters of style undermines this argument.[336] One gains the impression from Lucian, after adjusting for exaggeration, that it would be relatively easy for an educated person to masquerade as an orator – especially before a simple audience: 'cull from some source fifteen, or not more than twenty, Attic words, drill yourself carefully in them, and have them ready at the tip of your tongue, and the crowd will look up to you and think you amazing'.[337] This Paul never attempts to do.

We are left to conclude that Paul did not, in writing Galatians, employ the language appropriate to oratory. This conclusion motivated various modern scholars to propose alternative modes and rhetorics to account for Paul's style. The epistle could no more have been accepted by his contemporaries as a piece of Graeco-Roman rhetoric than by these writers, nor does it seem that Paul would have so hoped.

[334] Cicero asserts that the public and the critic agree on oratory, and that differences in ranking the best would merely reflect taste, not knowledge: cf. *Brutus* 49.186–189.

[335] See for instance the NT letters which tradition attributes to Peter.

[336] Though obviously we may allow for minor stylistic variations.

[337] Lucian, *A Professor of Public Speaking*, 16 (LCL 4).

8

CONCLUSIONS

By defining rhetoric's various levels of discourse and exploring its relationship to that specific form of rhetoric described in the handbooks, it has been argued that classical handbook rhetoric is a quite focused and even venue-driven activity which is not found in the epistle to the Galatians.

This leaves us to explain how a rhetorical reading of Galatians has become so widely accepted. The orientation of any comparison must be divided between subject and objects (i.e. between the objects of comparison and the one doing the comparing), suggesting that only rigid conformity to strictly defined criteria can begin to approach an acceptable level of 'objectivity'. Frank Kermode observes of another sphere:

> There must be supra-literary forces, cultural pressures, which tend to make us seek narrative coherence, just as we expect a conundrum to have an answer, and a joke a point. Our whole practice of reading is founded on such expectations, and of course, the existence of genres such as the pointless joke and the deviant conundrum depends upon the prior existence of the normal sort.[1]

It is this sense of expectation which robs us of true objectivity, for if readers supply the missing pieces of a text based on expectations (regardless of their source) then they will sometimes create parallels between types of texts when the mind performs its inevitable and often unconscious task of bending the data to fit the categories. Likewise, 'perception (and reading is an instance of perception) always occurs within a set of assumptions that precon-

[1] Kermode, *Genesis of Secrecy*, 53. He is indebted for certain ideas to Shklovsky, 'La construction de la nouvelle et du roman', 170–96. Shklovsky writes that we provide needed items – such as endings – even when they are absent. See *Genesis of Secrecy*, 65 and 153, n. 18.

strains what could possibly be perceived (or heard, or tasted, or touched)'.[2] Once Galatians is expected to look like an example of classical rhetoric, it does not seem to matter how far the text deviates from the handbook descriptions – the designation 'rhetoric' is still accepted. I contend that for a genre label to inspire confidence it must be predictive. That is, confidence in designations of literary types depends on the ability to form hypotheses during preliminary exposure which are confirmed only as they successfully predict what follows. To find similarities alone is dangerous, for the mind adeptly smooths over obstacles and fills in blanks. We have seen that regarding Galatians, some have gone beyond smoothing obstacles to trying to explain wide deviation from the standard, all the while maintaining that Galatians is part of the genre and species to which they think it conforms.

Paul, however, would not have been well served by classical rhetoric.

> [T]here is no room for ethical and rhetorical standards in the sense of the ancients ... Surely the New Testament writings are extremely effective; the tradition of the prophets and the Psalms is alive in them, and in some of them – those written by authors of more or less pronounced Hellenistic culture – we can trace the use of Greek figures of speech. But the spirit of rhetoric ... could not extend its dominion to them for the simple reason that their subject would not fit into any of the known genres.[3]

Immediacy of purpose transcends the stylistic concerns and subject restrictions of classical oratory. Such differences imply apostolic Christianity's radical discontinuity with certain aspects of its surrounding culture. While these breaks with the environment are admittedly particular rather than universal, wrongly identifying important aspects of Paul's social and intellectual world will lead us down the wrong path, for 'In the last analysis the differences in style between the writings of antiquity and early Christianity are conditioned by the fact that they were composed from a different point of view and for different people'.[4]

Paul wrote Galatians independently of the rules of Graeco-

[2] Fish, *Doing What Comes Naturally*, 83.
[3] Auerbach, *Mimesis*, 45.
[4] Ibid., 46.

Roman rhetoric, which ought to discourage analysis based on the handbooks. If one argues that the handbooks can interpret texts written independently of them, we respond that Galatians matches so poorly their treatment of level 4 rhetoric that such undertakings are of little value. Furthermore, since the handbooks were never intended as a basis for analysing texts, and are not very helpful when used to analyse non-classical rhetorical texts, they should not be used for that purpose.

Summary

Several scholars argue that Galatians is nothing more than a speech with an epistolary wrapper. Others have been less bold, merely suggesting that Galatians closely conforms to the recommendations of the handbooks. We have seen that a great deal of evidence opposes the notion that Galatians is crafted to resemble a classical speech.

First, although the handbooks say much about the shape and order of a speech, few have read them critically since Betz so thoroughly compared their dictates with Galatians. Our investigation has, however, turned up data which suggest that the epistle does not conform to the descriptions as well as some suppose.

Second, when the discussion shifts from the question of structure to the species of Galatians we find that very few 'rhetorical critics' show any interest in the frame of the speech. Although Betz allows it to inform his conclusion that Galatians is appropriate to a courtroom, subsequent writers rarely give much weight to the fact that deliberative speeches are for the assembly and epideictic primarily for festivals and celebrations. Once rhetoric is more broadly defined as universal persuasive discourse, it is unclear that the handbooks are relevant to the analysis – for they discuss level 4, not universal rhetoric.

Third, Paul's level of language also reveals the inappropriateness of relating the epistle to classical oratory. First, patristic attitudes toward Paul's writing oppose the notion that 'rhetorical analysis' of Galatians is a traditional and recently rediscovered way of reading, for both Christians and their opponents found Paul to be no sophisticated author. Second, attempts to explain the 'unique' language of the NT, or at least to provide a social and literary milieu for what are clearly non-classical texts, highlight the fact that Paul did not use the language of the *literati*. Since oratory was the domain of the elite and demanded a particular level of language, Paul's writings should not be so identified.

It is possible to view Galatians as more than one type of 'rhetoric'. The first position, held by Betz, Smit and only a few others, is that Galatians is a speech. While this outlook presents the most interesting options, it is unlikely. Galatians simply does not conform to the handbooks or to extant speeches, and was reckoned to be something else by early Christian rhetoricians; they in fact took Paul's rejection of rhetoric's value system seriously (1 Cor. 1–3). The other extreme – widely held by recent students of Galatians – is that the epistle, like all texts, can be explained with the help of the handbooks. While this may be true in some limited sense, such a claim overlooks the exclusivity of the handbooks' purpose, and requires a methodological defence which to this point has been lacking.

Implications and significance

If we extricate Paul's method of communication from the realm of rhetoric, we thereby eliminate a ground for questioning the historical reliability of Galatians' biographical details. The argument that Paul sacrificed accuracy for the sake of his purpose stems from an assumed conformity to the handbook, and thus, upon rhetoric's dismissal, should be evaluated on other grounds. Although it does not necessarily follow that the more common position is correct – that Paul's own report is more reliable than Luke's due to the latter's tendentiousness – at least one insufficient argument is swept aside.

The discarding of rhetoric also frees us from illegitimate restraints imposed by the notion that Paul exhibited an advanced rhetorical education.[5] Other avenues remain open to those in search of Paul's social status, wealth and education, but classical rhetoric turns out to be a cul-de-sac.

Finally, we have seen that to the early Christian readers of Paul, his non-use of rhetoric had theological implications. If we are to understand Paul's attitude toward Christian communication we must not superimpose an alien rhetoric over Paul's own. Only when Paul is allowed to speak on his own terms can we begin to see what

---

[5] This does not require that he lacked this education, but that his epistles do not demonstrate it: it must be defended on other grounds.

it means to identify Christ as the logos and the Spirit as the persuader.

Further study

Further study in several spheres is warranted by the conclusions of this thesis. We will mention just three.

First, the world of Paul is receiving ever more attention as its study by social historians produces significant results. Attempts to describe his background will receive new life with the removal of inapplicable forms of rhetoric from the discussion.

Second, a major component of Paul's social milieu is the rhetoric which he creates by merging various communicative techniques. Having rejected a restrictive rhetoric in favour of an attempt to describe Paul's own discourse strategy, we can consider (1) his 'commonplaces'; (2) methods of (and motives for) using devices such as examples, irony, allegory, etc.; and (3) how the shape of the epistle carries communicative force. Such a venture may teach us more about the apostle's values and cultural outlook than will allowing them to be determined from outside.

An aspect of Paul's rhetoric which has been too much neglected in this thesis and in rhetorical analysis of Galatians in general is proofs. In other contexts the emphasis has shifted from the structure of arguments to their logic[6] – and in ours it would be valuable to isolate the premises on which Paul constructs his syllogisms or ask whether he displays a discernible consistency when basing arguments on weakness,[7] power,[8] dependence and independence, examples, Scriptural authority, tradition, and so on.

More attention also needs to be paid to the narrative of Galatians as a functional *story*. Narrative theory may offer much to the reader who wishes to explore the impact of Galatians 1–2 not as first-century oratory but as a living text.[9]

Such clarification would then help explain the relationship between the various parts of the epistle. As it stands, the rhetorical explanation fails to provide for a linear, cumulative analysis of the

---

[6] Investigations which move generally in this direction include Johanson, *To All the Brethren*; Siegert, *Argumentation*.

[7] A work which combines several of these elements is Plank, *Irony of Affliction*.

[8] See, for example, Castelli, *Imitating Paul*; 'Interpretations of Power'; Schütz, *Paul and Apostolic Authority*.

[9] A standard is Chatman, *Story and Discourse*.

epistle – but this must be our goal. We need to discover how the epistle creates expectations and then satisfies them (or leaves them unsatisfied), how it creates momentum until some end has been achieved.

Furthermore, few in biblical studies have noticed that rhetoric underwent changes once it became the property of Christian writers. Indeed this very transition, and the difficulties it presents, has led to a criticism of Kennedy by classicists: in a review of *Greek Rhetoric Under Christian Emperors*, we read that in his discussion of the sub-apostolic era, Kennedy appears 'to be attempting to extend the concept of rhetoric beyond its proper application'.[10] Rhetoric was reshaped, creating the opportunity to introduce methods of communication with links to the needs and purposes of the new community, once the church became a powerful social institution. Thus an examination of rhetoric's evolution in the hands of Christians might tell us much about their view of Scripture and Paul's rhetoric.

Finally, Galatians itself is ripe for analysis based on recently developed approaches to rhetoric. We still have a great deal to learn about Paul's passionate response to opponents and the way his message spoke then and continues to speak today. When a new rhetoric – one which accounts for developments in disciplines such as psychology, pragmatics and sociology of knowledge – can be utilized alongside methods as diverse as discourse analysis and reader response criticism, we will be able to make genuine gains in our understanding of Galatians.

[10] Frendo, 'Review of *Greek Rhetoric*', 204.

SELECT BIBLIOGRAPHY

Ancient sources

Anaximines *Rhetorica ad Alexandrum*, Trans. H. Rackham, LCL 317 (in Aristotle, vol. 16), Cambridge, MA: Harvard University Press, 1937.

Aristophanes *The Birds*, trans. B. B. Rogers, LCL 179, London: Heinemann, 1979.

Aristotle *The 'Art' of Rhetoric*, trans. J. H. Freese, LCL 193, London: Heinemann, 1926.

The Poetics, trans. W. H. Fyfe, LCL 199, London: Heinemann, 1927.

Arnobius *The Seven Books of Arnobius Against the Heathen, ANF* 6: 413–539.

Augustine *Augustine on Romans: Propositions from the Epistle to the Romans* and *Unfinished Commentary on the Epistle to the Romans*, ed. and trans. Paula Fredriksen, Texts and Translations 23; Early Christian Literature Series 6, Chico: Scholars Press, 1982.

Confessions, trans. W. Watts (1631), LCL, London: Heinemann, 1912.

De Doctrina Christiana, NPNF, First Series 2, 519–97.

Basil *Letters, NPNF*, Second Series 8, 109–327.

Chrysostom *Commentary on the Epistle to the Galatians*, Library of the Fathers of the Holy Catholic Church Anterior to the Division of the East and West 6, Oxford: John Henry Parker, 1948.

Homilies on First Corinthians, NPNF, First Series 12, 1–269.

Homily on Galatians, NPNF, First Series 12, 1–48.

On the Priesthood, trans. T. Allen Moxon, Early Christian Classics, London: SPCK, 1907.

On the Priesthood, NPNF, First Series 9, 33–83.

Cicero *Brutus*, trans. G. L. Hendrickson, LCL 342, London: Heinemann, 1939.

De Inventione, trans. H. M. Hubbell, LCL 386, London: Heinemann, 1949.

De Oratore (2 vols.), vol. 1 E. W. Sutton and H. Rackham; vol. 2 H. Rackham, LCL 348–9, London: Heinemann, 1942.

De Partitione Oratorie, H. Rackham, LCL 349, London: Heinemann, 1942.

Orator, trans. H. M. Hubbell, LCL 342, London: Heinemann, 1962.

Topica, trans. H. M. Hubbell, LCL 386, London: Heinemann, 1949.

Demetrius *On Style*, trans. W. R. Roberts, LCL 199 (in Aristotle, vol. 23), London: Heinemann, 1927.

Demosthenes *The Public Orations of Demosthenes* (2 vols.), trans. Arthur Wallace Pickard, Oxford: Clarendon Press, 1912.

Dio (Chrysostom) *Discourses* (5 vols.), trans. J. W. Cohoon and H. L. Crosby, LCL, London: Heinemann, 1932–51.

Dionysius of Halicarnassus *On Literary Composition*, trans. W. R. Roberts, rev. S. Usher, in *The Critical Essays* 5, LCL 466, London: Heinemann, 1985.

Hermogenes *On Stases* in 'Hermogenes' *On Stases*: A Translation with an Introduction and Notes', R. Nadeau, *The Speech Teacher* 31 (1964) 361–424.

   'On Types', in *Ancient Literary Criticism: The Principal Texts in New Translations*, ed. D. A. Russell and M. Winterbottom, Oxford: Clarendon, 1972, 561–79.

Hock, R. F. and E. N. O'Neil (eds.) *The Chreia in Ancient Rhetoric: 1. The Progymnasmata*, Texts and Translations 27; Graeco-Roman Religion Series 9, Atlanta: Scholars Press, 1986.

Jerome *Apology for Himself Against the Book of Rufinus*, *NPNF*, Second Series 3, 482–541.

   Letters, *NPNF*, Second Series 6, 1–295.

   The Perpetual Virginity of the Virgin Mary, *NPNF*, Second Series 6, 334–46.

Josephus *Against Apion*, trans. H. St. J. Thackeray, LCL, London: Heinemann, 1926.

Lactantius *Divine Institutes*, *ANF* 7, 9–223.

Lake, Kirsopp *The Apostolic Fathers* (2 vols.), LCL, London: Heinemann, 1912–13.

Leo the Great *Letters*, *NPNF*, Second Series 12, 1–114.

Longinus *On the Sublime*, trans. W. H. Fyfe, LCL 199 (in Aristotle, vol. 23), London: Heinemann, 1927.

Menander Rhetor ed. and trans. Donald A. Russell and N. G. Wilson, Oxford: Clarendon Press, 1981.

Origen *Contra Celsum*, trans. H. Chadwick, Cambridge: Cambridge University Press, 1953.

Philodemus 'Art of Rhetoric', in 'The *Rhetorica* of Philodemus', trans. H. M. Hubbell, *Transactions of the Connecticus Academy of the Arts and Sciences* 23 (1920) 243–382.

Philostratus *Life of Apollonius* (2 vols.), trans. F. C. Conybeare, LCL 16–17, London: Heinemann, 1912.

Plato *Gorgias*, trans. W. Hamilton, London: Penguin, 1971.

   Gorgias, trans. W. R. Lamb, LCL 166, London: Heinemann, 1983.

   Phaedrus, trans. H. N. Fowler; introduction W. R. Lamb, LCL 36, London: Heinemann, 1914.

Pseudo-Cicero *Rhetorica ad Herennium*, trans. Harry Caplan, LCL 403 (Cicero, *Rhetorica ad Herennium*), London: Heinemann, 1954.

Quasten, Johannes *Patrology, 3: The Golden Age of Patristic Literature*, Westminster, MD: Newman, 1960.

Quintilian *Institutio Oratoria* (4 vols.), trans. H. E. Butler, LCL 124–7, London: Heinemann, 1920–2.

Spengel, L. (ed.) *Rhetores Graeci* (3 vols.), Leipzig: Teubner, 1853–6, repr. Frankfurt: Minerva, 1966.

Stein, James Aloysius *Encomium of Saint Gregory, Bishop of Nyssa, On His Brother Saint Basil: Commentary With Annotated Text, Introduction and Translation*, Patristic Studies 17, Washington: Catholic University of America Press, 1928.

Strabo *Geography* (8 vols.), trans. H. L. Jones, LCL, London: Heinemann, 1929.

Tacitus *A Dialogue on Oratory*, trans. W. Peterson, rev. M. Winterbottom, LCL 35, London: Heinemann, 1970.

Tatian *Address of Tatian to the Greeks, ANF* 2, 59–83.

Tertullian *On Prescription Against Heretics, ANF* 3, 243–65.

Theodore 'Commentary of Galatians 4.22–31', trans. K. Froehlich, in *Biblical Interpretation in the Early Church*, 95–103.

Theophilus of Antioch *Ad Autolycum*, text and trans. Robert M. Grant, Oxford: Clarendon Press, 1970.

Walz, Christian (ed.) *Rhetores Graeci* (9 vols.), Stuttgart/Tübingen: Cottae, 1832–6, repr. Osnabrück: Otto Zeller, 1968.

General bibliography

Achtemeier, Paul J. '"Some Things in Them Hard to Understand": Reflections on an Approach to Paul', *Interpretation* 38 (1984) 254–67.

Albright, W. F. 'From the Patriarchs to Moses: I. From Abraham to Joseph', *Biblical Archaeologist* 36 (1973) 5–33.

'From the Patriarchs to Moses: II. Moses out of Egypt', *Biblical Archaeologist* 36 (1973) 48–76.

Aletti, Jean-Noël 'La présence d'un modèle rhétorique en Romains: Son rôle et son importance', *Biblica* 71 (1990) 1–24.

'La *Dispositio* Rhétorique dans les Épîtres Pauliniennes: Propositions de Méthode', *New Testament Studies* 38 (1992) 385–401.

Alexander, Loveday 'Luke–Acts in its Contemporary Setting With Special Reference to the Prefaces (Luke 1:1–4 and Acts 1:1)', DPhil. thesis, Oxford University, 1977.

'Luke's Preface in the Context of Greek Preface Writing', *Novum Testamentum* 28 (1986) 48–74.

'The Living Voice: Scepticism Towards the Written Word in Early Christianity and in Graeco-Roman Texts', in *The Bible in Three Dimensions: Essays in Celebration of Forty Years of Biblical Studies in the University of Sheffield*, JSOTS 87, ed. D. J. A. Clines, S. E. Fowl, S. E. Porter, Sheffield: JSOT Press, 1990, 221–47.

The Preface to Luke's Gospel: Literary Convention and Social Context in Luke 1.1–4 and Acts 1.1, SNTSMS 78, Cambridge: Cambridge University Press, 1993.

Alonso-Schökel, L. *The Inspired Word: Scripture in the Light of Language and Literature*, New York: Herder, 1965.

Alter, Robert *The Art of Biblical Narrative*, New York: Basic Books, 1981.

The Art of Biblical Poetry, New York: Basic Books, 1985.

Amergen, Thomas *Stylistic Influence of the Second Sophistic on the*

Panegyrical Sermons of St. John Chrysostom: A Study in Greek Rhetoric. Patristic Studies 5; Washington DC: Catholic University Press of America, 1921.

Anderson, B. W. 'The New Frontier of Rhetorical Criticism' in *Rhetorical Criticism – Essays in Honor of James Muilenburg*, ed. J. J. Jackson and M. Kessler, Pittsburgh: Pickwick Press, 1974, ix–xviii.

Anderson, Bernhard 'From Analysis to Synthesis: The Interpretation of Genesis 1–11', *Journal of Biblical Literature* 97 (1978) 23–39.

Anderson, G. *Philostratus*, London: Croom Helm, 1986.

Arnhart, Larry *Aristotle on Political Reasoning: A Commentary on the Rhetoric*, Dekalb, IL: Northern Illinois University Press, 1981.

Atkins, J. W. H. *Literary Criticism in Antiquity: A Sketch of its Development* (2 vols.), Cambridge: Cambridge University Press, 1934.

English Literary Criticism II: The Renascence, London: Methuen & Co., 1947.

Attridge, Harold *A Commentary on the Epistle to the Hebrews*, Philadelphia: Fortress, 1989.

Auerbach, Erich *Mimesis: The Representation of Reality in Western Literature*, ET, Princeton: Princeton University Press, 1953.

Aune, David E. 'Review of H. D. Betz's *Galatians*', *Religious Studies Review* 7 (1981) 323–8.

The New Testament in its Literary Environment, Philadelphia: Westminster, 1987.

'Romans as a *Logos Protreptikos* in the Context of Ancient Religious and Philosophical Propaganda', in *Paulus und das Antike Judentum*, ed. M. Hengel and U. Heckel, Tübingen: J. C. B. Mohr, 1991, 91–124.

Baasland, Ernst 'Persecution: A Neglected Theme in the Letter to the Galatians', *Studia Theologica* 38 (1984) 135–50.

Bachmann, Michael *Sünder oder Übertreter: Studien zur Argumentation in Gal. 2,15ff*, Wissenschaftliche Untersuchungen zum Neuen Testament 59, Tübingen: J. C. B. Mohr, 1992.

Bahr, G. J. 'Paul and Letter Writing in the First Century', *Catholic Biblical Quarterly* 28 (1966) 465–77.

Bailey, James L. and Vander Broek, Lyle D. *Literary Forms in the New Testament*, London: SPCK, 1992.

Baldwin, Charles S. *Ancient Rhetoric and Poetic*, New York: Macmillan, 1924.

Medieval Rhetoric and Poetic, New York: Macmillan, 1928.

Ball, Ivan J. 'The Rhetorical Shape of Zephaniah', in *Perspectives on Language and Text: Essays and Poems in Honor of Francis I. Andersen's Sixtieth Birthday; July 28, 1985*, ed. E. W. Conrad and E. G. Newing, Winona Lake, IN: Eisenbrauns, 1987, 155–65.

Bammel, Ernst 'Gottes ΔΙΑΘΗΚΗ (Gal. III. 15–17) und das Jüdische Rechtsdenken', *New Testament Studies* 6 (1960) 313–19.

Barclay, John M. G. *Obeying the Truth: A Study of Paul's Ethics in Galatians*, Edinburgh: T. & T. Clark, 1988.

Barclay, William 'The New Testament and the Papyri', in *The New Testament in Historical and Contemporary Perspective: Essays in*

Memory of G. H. C. Macgregor, ed. H. Anderson and W. Barclay, Oxford: Oxford University Press, 1965, 57–81.

Bardy, Gustave 'L'église et l'enseignement pendant les trois premiers siècles', *Revue des Sciences religieuses* 12 (1932) 1–28.

Barnes, Timothy David *Tertullian: A Historical and Literary Study*, Oxford: Clarendon Press, 1971.

Barrett, Charles Kingsley *Freedom and Obligation: A Study of the Epistle to the Galatians*, Philadelphia: Westminster, 1985.

'Galatians as an Apologetic Letter', *Interpretation* 34 (1980) 414–17.

Bauer, Chrysostomus *John Chrysostom and his Time* (2 vols.), Westminster, MD: Newman, 1959–60.

Beaudean, John William *Paul's Theology of Preaching*, National Association of Baptist Professors of Religion Dissertation Series 6, Macon, GA: Mercer University Press, 1988.

Becker, Jürgen *Paul: Apostle to the Gentiles*, ET, Louisville: Westminster/John Knox, 1993.

Beker, J. Christiaan *Der Sieg Gottes: Eine Untersuchung zur Struktur des paulinischen Denkens*, Stuttgart: Katholisches Bibelwerk, 1988.

Bender, John and Wellbery, David E. 'Rhetoricality: On the Modernist Return of Rhetoric', in *The Ends of Rhetoric: History, Theory and Practice*, ed. J. Bender and D. E. Wellbery, Stanford: Stanford University Press, 1990, 3–39.

Bengel, Johann *Gnomon of the New Testament* (2 vols.), ET, Philadelphia: Perkins, Line & Higgins, 1860–2 (1742).

Benko, Stephen 'Pagan Criticism of Christianity During the First Two Centuries AD', *Aufstieg und Niedergang der Römischen Welt* 2.23.2, Berlin: De Gruyter, 1980, 1055–1118.

Benz, E. *Marius Victorinus und die Entwicklung der Abendländischen Metaphysik*, Forschung zur Kirchen- und Geistgeschichte, Stuttgart: Kohlhammer, 1932.

Berchman, Robert M. 'Galatians (1:1–5): Paul and Greco-Roman Rhetoric', in *Judaic and Christian Interpretation of Texts*, ed. J. Neusner and E. Frerichs, London: University Press of America, 1987, 1–15.

Berger, Klaus *Semitische Syntax in Neuen Testament*, Göttingen: Vandenhoeck & Ruprecht, 1962.

'Apostelbrief und Apostolische Rede/Zum Formular Frühchristlicher Briefe', *Zeitschrift für die Neutestamentliche Wissenschaft* 65 (1974) 190–231.

Exegese des Neuen Testaments, Uni-Taschenbücher 658, Heidelberg: Quelle & Meyer, 1977.

'Hellenistische Gattungen im Neuen Testament', *Aufstieg und Niedergang der Römischen Welt* 2.25.2, Berlin: De Gruyter, 1984, 1031–1432.

Berlin, Adele *Poetics and Interpretation of Biblical Narrative*, Sheffield: Almond, 1983.

Bernard, Robert W. 'The Rhetoric of God in the Figurative Exegesis of Augustine', in *Biblical Hermeneutics in Historical Perspective: Studies in Honor of Karlfried Froehlich on His Sixtieth Birthday*, ed. M. S. Burrows and P. Rorem, Grand Rapids: Eerdmans, 1991, 88–99.

Betz, Hans Dieter *Der Apostel Paulus und die Sokratische Tradition: Eine exegetische Untersuchung zu seiner 'Apologie' 2 Kor 10–13*, Beiträge zur historischen Theologie 45, Tübingen: J. C. B. Mohr, 1972.

'The Literary Composition and Function of Paul's Letter to the Galatians', *New Testament Studies* 21 (1975) 354–79.

'In Defense of the Spirit: Paul's Letter to the Galatians as a Document of Early Christian Apologetics', in *Aspects of Religious Propaganda in Judaism and Early Christianity*, ed. E. Schüssler, Fiorenza, Notre Dame: University of Notre Dame Press, 1976, 99–114.

Galatians: A Commentary on Paul's Letter to the Churches in Galatia, Hermeneia, Philadelphia: Fortress, 1979.

2 Corinthians 8 and 9: A Commentary on the Administrative Letters of the Apostle Paul, Hermeneia, Philadelphia: Fortress, 1985.

'Hellenismus', *Theologische Realenzyklopädie* 15, Berlin: De Gruyter, 1986, 19–35.

'The Problem of Rhetoric and Theology According to the Apostle Paul', in *L'Apôtre Paul: personnalité, style, et conception du ministère*, ed. A. Van Hoye, BETL 73, Leuven: Leuven University Press, 1986, 16–48.

Der Galaterbrief: Ein Kommentar zum Brief des Apostels Paulus an die Gemeinden in Galatien, München: Kaiser, 1988.

Bitzer, Lloyd 'The Rhetorical Situation', *Philosophy and Rhetoric* 1 (1968) 1–14.

Black, C. Clifton 'Keeping Up with Recent Studies XVI: Rhetorical Criticism and Biblical Interpretation', *Expository Times* 100 (1989) 252–8.

'Rhetorical Questions: The New Testament, Classical Rhetoric, and Current Interpretation', *Dialog* (Minnesota) 29 (1990) 62–70.

Black, Edwin *Rhetorical Criticism: A Study in Method*, New York: Macmillan, 1965.

Black, Matthew 'The Biblical Languages', in *The Cambridge History of the Bible, vol. 1: From the Beginning to Jerome*, ed. P. Ackroyd and C. F. Evans (Cambridge: Cambridge University Press, 1970) 1–11.

Blair, Hugh *Lectures on Rhetoric and Belles Lettres*, 1783.

Blass, F. *Grammatik des Neutestamentlichen Griechisch*, Göttingen: Vandenhoeck & Ruprecht, 1896.

Bligh, John *Galatians: A Discussion of St Paul's Epistle*, Householder Commentaries 1, London: St Paul Publications, 1969.

Blommerde, M. 'Is There an Ellipsis Between Gal. 2:3 and 2:4?' *Biblica* 56 (1975) 100–2.

Boice, James Montgomery 'Galatians', in *Expositor's Bible Commentary*, vol. 10, Grand Rapids: Zondervan, 1976, 407–508.

Bonhöffer, A. *Epiktet und das Neue Testament*, Religionsgeschichte Versuche und Vorarbeiten, Geissen: Töpelmann, 1911.

Bonnard, Pierre *L'Épitre de Saint Paul aux Galates*, Commentaire du Nouveau Testament 9; Neuchâtel: Delachaux et Niestlé Éditeurs, ²1972.

Booth, Wayne C. 'How Not to Use Aristotle: The *Poetics*', in *Now Don't Try to Reason With Me: Essays and Ironies for a Credulous Age*, Chicago: University of Chicago Press, 1970.

A Rhetoric of Irony, Chicago: University of Chicago Press, 1974.

The Rhetoric of Fiction, Chicago: University of Chicago Press, [2]1982.

Borch-Jacobsen, Mikkel 'Analytic Speech: From Restricted to General Rhetoric', in *The Ends of Rhetoric: History, Theory and Practice*, ed. J. Bender and D. E. Wellbery, Stanford: Stanford University Press, 1990, 127–39.

Bornkamm, Günther *Paul*, Stuttgart: Kohlhammer, 1969.

Botha, J. E. 'On the "Reinvention" of Rhetoric', *Scriptura* 31 (1989) 14–31.

Jesus and the Samaritan Woman: A Speech-Act Reading of John 4.1–42, Leiden: Brill, 1991.

'Style in the New Testament: The Need for Serious Reconsideration', *Journal for the Study of the New Testament* 43 (1991) 71–87.

Botha, P. J. 'Greco-Roman Literacy as Setting for New Testament Writings', *Neotestamentica* 26 (1992) 195–225.

Bouwman, A. Gijs. 'Die Hagar-und Sara-Perikope (Gal. 4,21–31): Exemplarische Interpretation zum Schriftbeweis bei Paulus', in *Aufstieg und Niedergang der Römischen Welt* 2.25.4, Berlin: De Gruyter, 1987, 3135–55.

'De Twee Testamenten. Een Exegese van Gal. 4,12–31', *Tijdschrift voor Filosofie en Theologie* 48 (1987) 259–76.

Bowersock, Glen W. *Greek Sophists in the Roman Empire*, Oxford: Oxford University Press, 1973.

Brandt, William J. *Rhetoric of Argumentation*, Indianapolis: Bobbs-Merrill, 1970.

Brinsmead, Bernard Hungerford *Galatians: Dialogical Response to Opponents*, SBLDS 65, Chico: Scholars Press, 1982.

Brinton, Alan 'Situation in the Theory of Rhetoric', *Philosophy and Rhetoric* 14 (1981) 234–48.

Brooks, Cleanth 'Irony as a Principle of Structure', in *Literary Opinion in America*, ed. M. D. Zable, New York: Harper & Brothers, 1951, 729–41.

Broshi, M. 'La Population de l'ancienne Jérusalem', *Revue Biblique* 82 (1975) 5–14.

Broughton, T. R. S. 'Roman Asia', in *An Economic Survey of Ancient Rome; iv: Africa, Syria, Greece, Asia Minor*, Baltimore: Johns Hopkins Press, 1938.

Browning, Robert *Medieval and Modern Greek*, London: Hutchinson University Library, 1969.

'Apollonius Dyscolus', [2]*OCD*, 86.

Bruce, F. F. *New Testament History*, New York: Doubleday, 1971.

The Epistle to the Galatians: A Commentary on the Greek Text, New International Greek Testament Commentary, Exeter: Paternoster, 1982.

The Acts of the Apostles: The Greek Text with Introduction and Commentary, Grand Rapids: Eerdmans, [3]1990.

'Marius Victorinus and his Works', in *A Mind for What Matters: Collected Essays*, Grand Rapids: Eerdmans, 1990, 213–32.

Buckley, Thomas W. *Apostle to the Nations: The Life and Letters of St Paul*, Boston: St Paul Editions, 1981.

Bullinger, Ethelbert W. *Figures of Speech Used in the Bible: Explained and Illustrated*, London: Eyre & Spottiswoode, 1898.

Bultmann, Rudolf *Der Stil der paulinischen Predigt und die Kynisch-Stoische Diatribe*, Göttingen: Vandenhoeck & Ruprecht, 1910.

'Paulus', [2]*Religion in Geschichte und Gegenwart*, 5: cols. 1020–45.

The History of the Synoptic Tradition, ET, Oxford: Blackwell, [2]1972.

Bünker, Michael *Briefformular und rhetorische Dispositio im 1 Korintherbrief*, Göttinger Theologische Arbeiten 28, Göttingen: Vandenhoeck & Ruprecht, 1984.

Burgess, Theodore C. *Epideictic Literature*, repr. Studies in Classical Philosophy 3; University of Chicago Press, 1902, New York: Garland, 1987.

Burke, Kenneth *A Grammar of Motives* (1st edn 1945), Berkeley: University of California Press, 1969.

A Rhetoric of Motives (1st edn 1950), Berkeley: University of California Press, 1969.

The Rhetoric of Religion: Studies in Logology, Berkeley: University of California Press, 1970.

Burkitt, F. C. *Christian Beginnings*, London: University of London, 1924.

Burney, C. F. *The Aramaic Origin of the Fourth Gospel*, Oxford: Clarendon Press, 1922.

The Poetry of Our Lord: An Examination of the Formal Elements of Hebrew Poetry in the Discourses of Jesus Christ, Oxford: Clarendon Press, 1925.

Burridge, Richard A. *What are the Gospels? A Comparison with Graeco-Roman Biography*, SNTSMS 70, Cambridge: Cambridge University Press, 1992.

Burrows, M. 'The Johannine Prologue as Aramaic Verse', *Journal of Biblical Literature* 45 (1926) 57–69.

Burton, Ernest De Witt *A Critical and Exegetical Commentary on the Epistle to the Galatians*, International Critical Commentary, Edinburgh: T&T Clark, 1921.

Caird, G. B. *The Language and Imagery of the Bible*, London: Duckworth, 1980.

Callaway, J. S. 'Paul's Letter to the Galatians and Plato's *Lysias*', *Journal of Biblical Literature* 67 (1948) 353–6.

Calvin, John *Commentaries on the Epistle of Paul the Apostle to the Romans*, ET, John Owen, Grand Rapids: Eerdmans, 1947.

Cameron, Averil *Christianity and the Rhetoric of Empire: The Development of Christian Discourse*, Berkeley: University of California Press, 1991.

Campbell, Douglas S. *Rhetoric of Righteousness in Romans 3.21–26*, JSNTS 65, Sheffield: JSOT Press, 1992.

Campbell, George *Philosophy of Rhetoric, A Facsimile Reproduction of the 1841 edition (Originally 1776), with an Introduction by Charlotte Downey*, American Linguistics 1700–1900: Scholars' Facsimiles & Reprints 460, Delmar, NY: Scholars' Facsimiles & Reprints, 1992.

Campbell, James *The Influence of the Second Sophistic on the Style of the Sermons of Saint Basil the Great*, Patristic Studies 2, Washington, DC: Catholic University of America Press, 1922.

Capelle, W. and Marrou, H. I. 'Diatribe', in *Reallexicon für Antike und*

Christentum, ed. T. Klanser *et al.*, Stuttgart: Anton Hiersemann, 1948, 3: 998.

Carson, Donald A. 'Understanding Misunderstanding in the Fourth Gospel', *Tyndale Bulletin* 33 (1982) 59–91.

Carter, Robert E. 'The Chronology of St John Chrysostom's Early Life', *Traditio* 18 (1962) 357–64.

Cassuto, Umberto *Genesis I, From Adam to Noah*, Jerusalem: Magnes, 1961. *Genesis II, From Noah to Abraham*, Jerusalem: Magnes, 1964.

Castelli, Elizabeth A. *Imitating Paul: A Discourse of Power*, Louisville: Westminster/John Knox, 1991.
'Interpretations of Power in 1 Corinthians', *Semeia* 54 (1991) 197–222.

Charles, R. H. *A Critical and Exegetical Commentary on the Revelation of St. John*, Edinburgh: T&T Clark, 1920.

Chatman, Seymour *Story and Discourse: Narrative Structure in Fiction and Film*, Ithaca, NY: Cornell University Press, 1978.

Church, F. 'Rhetorical Structure and Design in Paul's Letter to Philemon', *Harvard Theological Review* 71 (1978) 17–33.

Clark, Donald Leman *Rhetoric in Greco-Roman Education*, New York: Columbia University Press, 1957.

Clark, Mary T. 'The NeoPlatonism of Marius Victorinus the Christian', in *Neo-Platonism and Early Christian Thought: Essays in Honour of A. H. Armstrong*, ed. H. J. Blumenthal and R. A. Markus, London: Variorum, 1981, 153–9.

Clarke, Andrew *Secular and Christian Leadership in Corinth: A Socio-Historical and Exegetical Study of 1 Corinthians 1–6*, Leiden: Brill, 1993.

Clarke, M. L. *Rhetoric at Rome: A Historical Survey*, London: Cohen & West, 1953.
'Quintilian on Education', in *Empire and Aftermath: Silver Latin II*, ed. T. A. Dorey, London: Routledge & Kegan Paul, 1975, 98–118.

Classen, C. Joachim 'Paulus und die Antike Rhetorik', *Zeitschrift für die neutestamentliche Wissenschaft* 82 (1991) 1–33.
'St Paul's Epistles and Ancient Greek and Roman Rhetoric', in *Rhetoric and The New Testament: Essays from the 1992 Heidelberg Conference*, ed. S. Porter and T. H. Olbricht, JSNTS 90, Sheffield: JSOT Press, 1994, 265–91.

Clifford, Richard J. 'Rhetorical Criticism in the Exegesis of Hebrew Poetry', in SBL Seminar Papers 1980 (Scholars Press) 17–28.

Clines, David J. A. *The Theme of the Pentateuch*, JSOTS 10, Sheffield: JSOT Press, 1978.

Clines, David J. A. and Exum, J. Cheryl 'The New Literary Criticism', in *The New Literary Criticism and the Hebrew Bible*, JSOTS 143, Sheffield: Sheffield Academic Press, 1993, 11–25.

Coggan, Donald *Paul: Portrait of a Revolutionary*, London: Hodder & Stoughton, 1984.

Cole, Thomas *The Origins of Rhetoric in Ancient Greece*, Johns Hopkins University Press: Baltimore, 1991.

Colson, F. H. 'μετεσχημάτισα in 1 Cor. vi.6', *Journal of Theological Studies* 17 (1915–16) 379–84.

Colwell, E. C. 'The Greek Language', in *The Interpreter's Dictionary of the Bible*, Nashville: Abingdon, 1962, 2: 479–87.

Consigny, Scott 'Rhetoric and its Situations', *Philosophy and Rhetoric* 7 (1974) 175–86.

Conzelmann, Hans *A Commentary on the First Epistle to the Corinthians*, Philadelphia: Fortress, 1975.

Cook, David 'The Prescript as Programme in Galatians', *Journal of Theological Studies* 43 (1992) 511–19.

Corbett, Edward P. J. *Classical Rhetoric for the Modern Student*, New York: Oxford University Press, ³1990.

Cosgrove, Charles *The Cross and the Spirit: A Study in the Argument and Theology of Galatians*, Macon, GA: Mercer University Press, 1988.

Cousar, Charles B. *Galatians*, Interpretation, Louisville: John Knox, 1982.

Crafton, Jeffrey A. *The Agency of the Apostle: A Dramatic Analysis of Paul's Response to Conflict in 2 Corinthians*, JSNTS 51, Sheffield: JSOT Press, 1991.

Cremer, Hermann *Biblico-Theological Dictionary of the New Testament Greek Idioms*, ET, Edinburgh: T&T Clark, ³1883.

Cronjé, J. V. W. 'Defamiliarization in the Letter to the Galatians', in *A South African Perspective on the New Testament*, ed. J. H. Petzer and P. J. Hartin, Leiden: Brill, 1986, 214–27.

Crook, J. A. *Law and Life of Rome: 90 BC to AD 212*, Ithaca, NY: Cornell University Press, 1984.

Crosby, M. R. 'Paul's Persuasive Language in Romans 5', in *Persuasive Artistry: Studies in New Testament Rhetoric in Honor of George A. Kennedy*, ed. D. Watson, JSNTS 50, Sheffield: JSOT Press, 1991, 209–26.

Crutwell, Charles Thomas *A Literary History of Early Christianity Including the Fathers and the Chief Heretical Writers of the Ante-Nicene Period* (2 vols.), London: Charles Griffin & Co., 1893.

Culler, Jonathan *The Pursuit of Signs: Semiotics, Literature, Deconstruction*, Ithaca, NY: Cornell University Press, 1981.

Dahl, Nils A. 'Two Notes on Romans 5', *Studia Theologica* 5 (1951), 37–48.

'Letter', in *The Interpreter's Dictionary of the Bible*, Supplement Volume, Nashville: Abingdon, 1976, 538–41.

'The Missionary Theology in the Epistle to the Romans', in *Studies in Paul*, Minneapolis: Augsburg, 1977, 70–94.

Dalman, G. *The Words of Jesus Considered in the Light of Post-Biblical Jewish Writings and the Aramaic Language*, Edinburgh: T&T Clark, 1902.

Daube, David 'Rabbinic Methods of Interpretation and Hellenistic Rhetoric', *Hebrew Union College Annual* 22 (1948) 239–64.

Davies, W. D. *Paul and Rabbinic Judaism: Some Rabbinic Elements in Pauline Theology*, Philadelphia: Fortress, ⁴1980.

'Review of H. D. Betz's *Galatians*', *Religious Studies Review* 7 (1981) 310–18.

Deissmann, Adolf *Bible Studies: Contributions Mostly from Papyri and Inscriptions to the History of the Language, the Literature, and the*

Religion of Hellenistic Judaism and of Primitive Christianity, ET, Edinburgh: T&T Clark, 1901.

Light from the Ancient East: The New Testament Illustrated by Recently Discovered Texts of the Graeco-Roman World, ET, London: Hodder & Stoughton, [4]1927.

'Hellenistic Greek With Special Consideration of the Greek Bible', ET, in The Language of the New Testament, ed. S. Porter, JSNTS 60, Sheffield: Sheffield Academic Press, 1991, 39–59.

DeMan, Paul 'Semiology and Rhetoric', in Allegories of Reading: Figured Language in Rousseau, Nietzsche, Rilke and Proust, New Haven, CT: Yale University Press, 1979.

Dewey, Arthur J. 'Review of Frank Witt Hughes's Early Christian Rhetoric and 2 Thessalonians', in Critical Review of Books in Religion (1991) 203–5.

Dewey, J. Markan Public Debate: Literary Techniques, Concentric Structure, and Theology in Mark 2:1–3:6 (SBLDS 48), Missoula, MT: Scholars Press, 1980.

Dibelius, Martin From Tradition to Gospel, ET, London: Ivor Nicholson & Watson, 1934.

Paul (ed. and completed W. G. Kümmel), ET, London: Longmans, Green and Co., 1953.

An Philemon, Herders Theologischer Kommentar Zum Neuen Testament, Tübingen: Mohr, [3]1953.

Dixon, P. Rhetoric, London: Methuen, 1971.

Dockery, David S. Biblical Interpretation Then and Now: Contemporary Hermeneutics in the Light of the Early Church, Grand Rapids: Baker, 1992.

Dorey, T. A. Erasmus, Albuquerque: University of New Mexico Press, 1970.

Doty, W. G. 'The Classification of Epistolary Literature', Catholic Biblical Quarterly 31 (1969) 183–99.

'The Concept of Genre in Literary Analysis', in SBL Proceedings 1972: Book of Seminar Papers for 108th Annual Meeting (2 vols.), ed. Lane C. McGaughy, 2: 413–48.

Letters in Primitive Christianity, Philadelphia: Fortress, 1973.

Downing, F. G. 'A Bas Les Aristos: The Relevance of Higher Literature for the Understanding of the Earliest Christian Writings', Novum Testamentum 30 (1988) 212–230.

Duke, Paul D. Irony in the Fourth Gospel, Atlanta: Scholars Press, 1985.

Duncan, George S. The Epistle of Paul to the Galatians, Moffat New Testament Commentary, London: Hodder & Stoughton, 1934.

Dunn, James D. G. Galatians, Black's New Testament Commentary 9, Peabody, MA: Hendrickson, 1993.

'Paul's Epistle to the Romans: An Analysis of Structure and Argument', Aufstieg und Niedergang der Römischen Welt 2.25.4, Berlin: De Gruyter, 1987, 2842–90.

Ebeling, Gerhard The Truth of the Gospel: An Exposition of Galatians, ET, Philadelphia: Fortress, 1985.

Eissfeldt, O. M. The Old Testament: An Introduction, New York: Harper & Row, 1965.

Elliott, Neil *The Rhetoric of Romans: Argumentative Constraint and Strategy and Paul's Dialogue with Judaism*, JSNTS 45, Sheffield: JSOT Press, 1990.

Ellis, E. Earle 'Midrash *Pesher* in Pauline Hermeneutics', in *Grace Upon Grace: Festschrift for L. Kuyper*, ed. J. I. Cook, Grand Rapids: Eerdmans, 1975, 137–42.

Paul's Use of the Old Testament, Grand Rapids: Baker, ²1981.

Ellspermann, Gerald L. *The Attitude of the Early Christian Latin Writers Toward Pagan Literature and Learning*, Catholic University of America Patristic Studies 82, Cleveland: John T. Zubal, 1984.

Erasmus *Paraphrases on Romans* (*In epistolam Pauli Apostoli ad Romanos paraphrasis*), in *Collected Works of Erasmus* vol. 42, ed. Robert D. Sider, Toronto: University of Toronto Press, 1984.

Paraphrases on Galatians (*In epistolam Pauli Apostoli ad Galatas paraphrasis*), in *Collected Works of Erasmus* vol. 42, ed. Robert D. Sider, Toronto: University of Toronto Press, 1984.

Ernesti, J. C. T. *Lexicon Technologiae Graecorum*, Leipzig, 1795 (repr. Hildesheim: Olms, 1962).

Evans, G. R. *The Language and Logic of the Bible: The Earlier Middle Ages*, Cambridge: Cambridge University Press, 1984.

Fantham, Elaine 'The Growth of Literature and Criticism at Rome', in *Cambridge History of Literary Criticism 1: Classical Criticism*, Cambridge: Cambridge University Press, 1989, 220–44.

'Latin Criticism of the Early Empire', in *Cambridge History of Literary Criticism 1: Classical Criticism*, Cambridge: Cambridge University Press, 1989, 274–96.

Farenga, Vincent 'Periphrasis on the Origin of Rhetoric', *Modern Language Notes* 94 (1980) 1033–55.

Farrar, F. N. *The Life and Work of St Paul*, London: Cassell & Co., 1904.

Feldman, Louis H. 'Flavius Josephus Revisited: The Man, His Writings, and His Significance', in *Aufstieg und Niedergang der Römischen Welt* 2.21.2, Berlin: De Gruyter, 1984, 763–862.

Ferguson, Everett J. *Backgrounds of Early Christianity*, Grand Rapids: Eerdmans, ²1993.

Finley, M. I. *Politics in the Ancient World*, Cambridge: Cambridge University Press, 1983.

Fish, Stanley *Doing What Comes Naturally: Change, Rhetoric, and the Practice of Theory in Literary and Legal Studies*, Durham, NC: Duke University Press, 1989.

Fitzgerald, John T. 'Paul, the Ancient Epistolary Theorists, and 2 Corinthians 10–13', in *Greeks, Romans, and Christians: Essays in Honor of Abraham J. Malherbe*, ed. D. L. Balch, E. Ferguson and W. Meeks, Minneapolis: Fortress, 1990, 190–200.

Fleming, Joy Lynn Elasky 'A Rhetorical Analysis of Genesis 2–3: With Implications for a Theology of Man and Woman', unpublished thesis, Université des Sciences Humaines de Strasbourg, 1987.

Fokkelman, J. P. *Narrative Art in Genesis: Specimens of Stylistic and Structural Analysis*, Amsterdam: Van Gorcum, Assen, 1975.

Forbes, Christopher 'Comparison, Self-Praise and Irony: Paul's Boasting and the Conventions of Hellenistic Rhetoric', *New Testament Studies* 32 (1986) 1–30.

Fortin, Ernest L. 'Augustine and the Problem of Christian Rhetoric', *Augustinian Studies* 5 (1974) 85–100.

Fox, Mary M. *The Life and Times of Saint Basil the Great as Revealed in his Works*, Patristic Studies 57; Washington, DC: Catholic University of America Press, 1939.

Frei, Hans *The Eclipse of Biblical Narrative: A Study in Eighteenth and Nineteenth Century Hermeneutics*, New Haven, CT: Yale University Press, 1974.

Frend, W. H. C. *The Rise of Christianity*, London: Darton, Longman & Todd, 1984.

Frendo, J. D. 'Review of Kennedy's *Greek Rhetoric under Christian Emperors*', *The Classical Review* NS 34 (1984) 204–5.

Frye, Northrop *Anatomy of Criticism: Four Essays*, Princeton: Princeton University Press, 1957.

Fung, Ronald Y. K. *The Epistle to the Galatians*, New International Commentary on the New Testament, Grand Rapids: Eerdmans, 1988.

Funk, Robert *Language, Hermeneutics, and Word of God: The Problem of Language in the New Testament and Contemporary Theology*, New York: Harper & Row, 1966.

Gadamer, Hans Georg 'Rhetoric, Hermeneutics, and the Critique of Ideology', ET, in *The Hermeneutics Reader*, ed. K. Mueller-Vollmer, New York, Continuum, 1989, 278–86.

Gammie, John G. 'Paraenetic Literature: Toward the Morphology of a Secondary Genre', *Semeia* 50 (1990) 41–77.

Garnsey, Peter *Social Status and Legal Privilege in the Roman Empire*, Oxford: Oxford University Press, 1970.

Gaventa, Beverly R. 'Galatians 1 and 2: Autobiography as Paradigm', *Novum Testamentum* 28 (1986) 309–26.

Gempf, Conrad H. *Historical and Literary Appropriateness in the Mission Speeches of Paul in Acts*, unpublished PhD thesis, University of Aberdeen, 1988.
  'Public Speaking and Published Accounts', in *The Book of Acts in its First Century Setting, v. 1: Ancient Literary Setting*, ed. Bruce W. Winter and Andrew D. Clarke, Grand Rapids: Eerdmans, 1993, 259–303.

Georgi, Dieter *The Opponents of Paul in Second Corinthians*, Philadelphia: Fortress, 1986.

Getty, M. *A Commentary on Galatians and Romans*, New York: Image Books, 1982.

Gill, Jerry H. 'Jesus, Irony and the New Quest', *Encounters* 41 (1980) 139–51.

Glover, Terrot Reaveley *The Conflict of Religions in the Early Roman Empire*, London: Methuen, [9]1920.
  The Ancient World: A Beginning (previously published by Cambridge University Press, 1935), Harmondsworth: Penguin Books, 1944.

Goldstein, Jonathon A. *The Letters of Demosthenes*, New York: Columbia University Press, 1968.

Gottschalk, H. B. 'Diatribe Again', *Liverpool Classical Monthly* 7 (1982) 91–2.
'More on *DIATRIBAI*', *Liverpool Classical Monthly* 8 (1983) 91–2.
Grabbe, Lester 'Josephus', in *Dictionary of Biblical Interpretation*, ed. R. J. Coggins and J. L. Houlden, London: SCM, 1990, 365–8.
Grassi, Ernesto *Rhetoric as Philosophy: The Humanist Tradition*, University Park: Pennsylvania State University Press, 1980.
Gray, G. B. *Sacrifice in the Old Testament: Its Theory and Practice*, Oxford: Clarendon Press, 1925.
Greenwood, David 'Rhetorical Criticism and Formgeschichte: Some Methodological Considerations', *Journal of Biblical Literature* 89 (1970) 418–26.
Griffin, Miriam 'Cicero and Rome', in *The Oxford History of the Classical World*, ed. John Boardman et al., Oxford: Oxford University Press, 1988, 76–100.
Guthrie. W. K. C. *The Sophists*, Cambridge: Cambridge University Press, 1971.
Hadot, P. *Porphyre et Victorinus*, Paris: Études Augustiniennes, 1968.
Haenchen, Ernst *The Acts of the Apostles*, Oxford: Blackwell, 1971.
Hagendahl, Harald 'Piscatorie et non Aristotelice: Zu Einem Schlagwort bei den Kirchenvätern', *Septentionalia et Orientalia: Studia B. Karlgren Dedicata*, Kungliga Vitterhets Historie och Antikvitets Akademiens Londlingan 91, Stockholm, 1959, 184–93.
Augustine and the Latin Classics, vol. 2: Augustine's Attitude, Göteborg: Almqvist & Wiksell, 1967.
Hall, Robert G. 'The Rhetorical Outline of Galatians: A Reconsideration', *Journal of Biblical Literature* 106 (1987) 277–87.
'Historical Inference and Rhetorical Effect: Another Look at Galatians 1 and 2', in *Persuasive Artistry: Studies in New Testament Rhetoric in Honor of George A. Kennedy*, ed. D. F. Watson; JSNTS 50, Sheffield: JSOT Press, 1991, 308–20.
Hansen, Walter G. *Abraham in Galatians: Epistolary and Rhetorical Contexts*, JSNTS 29, Sheffield: JSOT Press, 1989.
Hanson, A. Y. *Studies in Paul's Technique and Theology*, Grand Rapids: Eerdmans, 1974.
Hanson, R. P. C. *Allegory and Event: A Study of the Sources and Significance of Origen's Interpretation of Scripture*, London: SCM, 1959.
Harmon, A. M. 'The Poet κατ' Εξοχην', *Classical Philology* 18 (1923) 35–47.
Harnisch, Wolfgang 'Einübung des neuen Seins: Paulinsiche Paränese am Beispiel des Galaterbriefs', *Zeitschrift für Theologie und Kirche* 84 (1987) 279–96.
Harris, William V. *Ancient Literacy*, Cambridge, MA: Harvard University Press, 1989.
Hatch, Edwin *Essays in Biblical Greek*, Oxford: Clarendon Press, 1889.
The Influence of Greek Ideas on Christianity, New York: Harper, ²1957.
Hauck, F. and Bertram, G. 'μακάριος', in *Theological Dictionary of the New Testament* 4: 362–70.

Hausamann, Suzi 'Die Rhetorik im Dienst der reformatorischen Schrift-
    sauslegung', in *Kerygma und Dogma* 20 (1974) 305–14.
Hays, Richard B. 'Recent Books on Galatians', *Quarterly Review* 5 (1985)
    95–102.
    *The Faith of Jesus Christ: An Investigation of the Narrative Substructure
    of Galatians 3:1–4:11.* Chico: Scholars Press, 1988.
Heinrici, Carl F. G. *Der erste Brief an die Korinther*, Meyer Kommentar 7,
    Göttingen: Vandenhoeck & Ruprecht, [8]1896.
    *Der Zweite Brief an die Korinther, mit einem Anhang: zum Hellenismus
    des Paulus*, Meyer Kommentar 6, Göttingen: Vandenhoeck & Ru-
    precht, [8]1900.
Hengel, Martin 'Die Ursprünge der Christlichen Mission', *New Testament
    Studies* 18 (1971) 15–38.
    *Judaism and Hellenism: Studies in their Encounter in Palestine During the
    Early Hellenistic Period*, ET, Philadelphia: Fortress, 1974.
    Property and Riches in the Early Church, ET, London: SCM, 1974.
    The Pre-Christian Paul, ET, London: SCM, 1991.
Henry, Paul 'Augustine and Plotinus', *Journal of Theological Studies* 38
    (1937) 1–23.
Hester, James 'Placing the Blame: The Presence of Epideictic in Galatians
    1–2', in *Persuasive Artistry: Studies in New Testament Rhetoric in
    Honor of George A. Kennedy*, ed. D. F. Watson, JSNTS 50, Sheffield:
    JSOT Press, 1991, 281–307.
    'The Rhetorical Structure of Galatians 1:11–2:14', *Journal of Biblical
    Literature* 103 (1984) 223–33.
    'The Use and Influence of Rhetoric in Galatians 2:1–14', *Theologische
    Zeitschrift* 42 (1986) 386–408.
Hinks, D. A. G. 'Tria Genera Causarum', *Classical Quarterly* 30 (1936)
    170–6.
Hock, Ronald F. 'Paul's Tentmaking and the Problem of his Social Class',
    Journal of Biblical Literature 94 (1978) 555–64.
Hock, Ronald F. and O'Neil, Edward N. *The Chreia in Ancient Rhetoric
    vol.1: The Progymnasmata*, Atlanta: Scholars Press, 1986.
Hommel, Hilderbrecht 'Rhetorik', in *Kleine Pauly*, München: Alfred
    Druckenmüller, 1972, 4: 1403.
Horsley, G. H. R. 'The Fiction of Jewish Greek', in *New Testament
    Documents Illustrating Early Christianity, 5: Linguistic Essays*, ed.
    G. H. R. Horsley, Sydney: Ancient History Document Research
    Centre, Macquarie University, 1989, 5–40.
    '*Koine* or Atticism – A Misleading Dichotomy', in *New Testament
    Documents Illustrating Early Christianity, 5: Linguistic Essays*, ed.
    G. H. R. Horsley, Sydney: Ancient History Document Research
    Centre, Macquarie University, 1989, 41–8.
House, Paul R. 'The Rise and Current Status of Literary Criticism of
    the Old Testament', in *Beyond Form Criticism: Essays in Old
    Testament Literary Criticism*, Winona Lake, IN: Eisenbrauns, 1992,
    3–22.
Howard, George *Paul: Crisis in Galatia: A Study in Early Christian
    Theology*, Cambridge: Cambridge University Press, 1979.

Howell, E. B. 'St Paul and the Greek World', *Expository Times* 71 (1960) 328–32.

Hübner, Hans 'Der Galaterbrief und das Verhältnis von antiker Rhetorik und Epistolographie', *Theologische Literaturzeitung* 4 (1984) 241–50.

'Galaterbrief', *Theologische Realenzyklopädie* XII, Berlin: De Gruyter, 1984, 5–14.

Hudson, H. Hoyt 'The Field of Rhetoric', in *Historical Studies of Rhetoric and Rhetoricians*, ed. R. F. Howes, Ithaca, NY: Cornell University Press, 1961, 3–15.

Hughes, Frank Witt *Early Christian Rhetoric and 2 Thessalonians*, JSNTS 30, Sheffield: JSOT Press, 1989.

'The Rhetoric of 1 Thessalonians', in *The Thessalonian Correspondence*, BETL 87, Leuven: University of Leuven Press, 1990, 99–113.

'Review of Duane Watson's *Invention, Arrangement and Style: Rhetorical Criticism of Jude and 2 Peter*', *Biblica* 71 (1990) 273–6.

Hull, W. E. 'A Teaching Outline of Galatians', *Review and Expositor* 69 (1972) 429–30.

Huppé, Bernard *Doctrine and Poetry: Augustine's Influence on Old English Poetry*, New York, 1959.

Iser, Wolfgang *The Act of Reading: A Theory of Aesthetic Response*, Baltimore: Johns Hopkins University Press, 1978.

Jacks, Leo V. *St Basil and Greek Literature*, Patristic Studies 1, Washington, DC: University of America Press, 1922.

Jackson, J. J. and Kessler, M. *Rhetorical Criticism: Essays in Honor of James Muilenburg*, Pittsburgh: Pickwick Press, 1974.

Jannaris, Antonius N. *An Historical Greek Grammar Chiefly of the Attic Dialect as Written and Spoken From Classical Antiquity Down to the Present Time: Founded Upon the Ancient Texts, Inscriptions, Papyri and Present Popular Greek*, repr. Hildesheim: Georg Olms Verlag, ²1987.

An Historical Greek Grammar: Chiefly of the Attic Dialect as Written and Spoken From Classical Antiquity Down to the Present Time, London: Macmillan & Co., 1897.

Jasper, David 'In the Sermon I have Just Completed, Wherever I said Aristotle, I Meant Saint Paul', in *The Bible as Rhetoric: Studies in Biblical Persuasion and Credibility*, Warwick Studies in Philosophy and Literature, ed. Martin Warner, New York: Routledge, 1990, 133–52.

Jewett, Robert *The Thessalonian Correspondence: Pauline Rhetoric and Millenarian Piety*, Philadelphia: Fortress, 1986.

'The Rhetorical Function of Numerical Sequences in Romans', in *Persuasive Artistry: Studies in New Testament Rhetoric in Honor of George A. Kennedy*, ed. D. F. Watson, JSNTS 50, Sheffield: JSOT Press, 1991, 227–45.

Jocelyn, H. D. 'Diatribes and Sermons', *Liverpool Classical Monthly* 7 (1982) 3–7.

'"Diatribes" and the Greek Book-Title Διατριβαί', *Liverpool Classical Monthly* 8 (1983) 89–91.

Johanson, Bruce *To All the Brethren: A Text-Linguistic and Rhetorical*

Approach to I Thessalonians, Coniectanea Biblica NT Series 16, Stockholm: Almqvist & Wiksell International, 1987.

Johnstone, C. L. 'An Aristotelian Trilogy: Ethics, Rhetoric, Politics, and the Search for Truth', *Philosophy and Rhetoric* 13 (1980) 1–24.

Jolowicz, H. F. and Nicholas, B. *Historical Introduction to the Study of Roman Law*, Cambridge: Cambridge University Press, ³1972.

Jones, A. H. M. 'St John Chrysostom's Parentage and Education', *Harvard Theological Review* 46 (1953) 171–3.

'The Social Background of the Struggle between Paganism and Christianity', in *The Conflict Between Paganism and Christianity in the Fourth Century*, ed. Arnaldo Momigliano, Oxford: Clarendon Press, 1963, 17–37.

Jones, C. P. *The Roman World of Dio Chrysostom*, London: Harvard University Press, 1978.

Jones, Maurice *St Paul the Orator: A Critical, Historical, and Explanatory Commentary on the Speeches of St Paul*, London: Hodder & Stoughton, 1910.

Jordan, Mark D. 'Ancient Philosophical Protreptic and the Problem of Persuasive Genres', *Rhetorica* 4 (1986) 309–33.

Judge, Edwin A. *The Social Pattern of Christian Groups in the First Century: Some Prolegomena to the Study of the New Testament Ideas of Social Obligation*, London: Tyndale Press, 1960.

'The Early Christians as a Scholastic Community' (2 parts), *Journal of Religious History* 1 (1960–1) 4–15, 125–37.

'Paul's Boasting in the Light of Contemporary Rhetorical Practice', *Australian Biblical Review* 16 (1969) 37–50.

'St Paul and Classical Society', in *Jahrbuch für Antike und Christentum* 15 (1972) 19–36.

'Antike und Christentum: Some Recent Work From Cologne', *Prudentia* 5.1 (1973) 1–13.

Rank and Status in the World of St Paul, The Broadhead Memorial Lecture, University of Canterbury, 1981.

'The Reaction against Classical Education in the New Testament', *Journal of Christian Education*, paper 77 (July, 1983) 7–14.

Karris, Robert 'The Occasion of Romans: A Response to Professor Donfried', in *The Romans Debate*, T&T Clark, ²1991, 125–27.

Kehnscherper, G. 'Der Apostel Paulus als römischer Bürger', *Studia Evangelica 2: Papers presented to the Second International Congress on New Testament Studies held at Christ Church, Oxford, 1961, part 1: The New Testament Scriptures*, ed. F. L. Cross, Berlin: Akademie Verlag, 1964, 411–40.

Kennedy, George A. 'The Earliest Rhetorical Handbooks', *American Journal of Philology* 80 (1959) 169–78.

'An Estimate of Quintilian', *American Journal of Philology* 83 (1962) 130–46.

The Art of Persuasion in Greece, Princeton: Princeton University Press, 1963.

Art of Rhetoric in the Roman World, Princeton: Princeton University Press, 1972.

Classical Rhetoric and its Christian and Secular Tradition from Ancient to Modern Times, London: Croom Helm, 1980.

Greek Rhetoric under Christian Emperors, Princeton: Princeton University Press, 1983.

'An Introduction to the Rhetoric of the Gospels', *Rhetorica* 1 (1983) 17–31.

New Testament Interpretation Through Rhetorical Criticism, Chapel Hill: University of North Carolina Press, 1984.

'Christianity and Criticism', in *The Cambridge History of Literary Criticism vol 1, Classical Criticism*, ed. G. A. Kennedy, Cambridge: Cambridge University Press, 1989, 330–46.

'The Evolution of a Theory of Artistic Prose', in *The Cambridge History of Literary Criticism, vol. 1, Classical Criticism*, ed. G. A. Kennedy, Cambridge: Cambridge University Press, 1989, 184–99.

'Hellenistic Literary and Philosophical Scholarship', in *The Cambridge History of Literary Criticism vol. 1, Classical Criticism*, ed. G. A. Kennedy, Cambridge: Cambridge University Press, 1989, 200–19.

'"Truth" and "Rhetoric" in the Pauline Epistles', in *The Bible as Rhetoric: Studies in Biblical Persuasion and Credibility*, Warwick Studies in Philosophy and Literature, ed. M. Warner, London/New York: Routledge, 1990, 195–202.

Kenney, E. J. 'Small Writing and Less Reading', *Classical Review* 41 (1991) 168–9.

Kepple, R. J. 'An Analysis of Antiochene Exegesis of Galatians 4, 24–26', *Westminster Theological Journal* 39 (1977) 239–49.

Kermode, Frank *The Genesis of Secrecy*, Cambridge, MA: Harvard University Press, 1979.

Kessler, Martin 'A Methodological Setting for Rhetorical Criticism', *Semitics* 4 (1974) 22–36; repr. in *Art and Meaning: Rhetoric in Biblical Literature*, ed. D. J. A. Clines, D. M. Gunn and A. J. Hauser, JSOTS 19, Sheffield: JSOT Press, 1982, 1–19.

Kikiwada, Isaac M. 'The Shape of Genesis 11:1–9', in *Rhetorical Criticism: Essays in Honor of James Muilenburg*, ed. J. J. Jackson and M. Kessler, Pittsburgh Theological Monograph Series 1, Pittsburgh: Pickwick Press, 1974, 18–32.

'Some Proposals for the Definition of Rhetorical Criticism', *Semitics* 5 (1977) 67–91.

'Genesis on Three Levels', *Annual of the Japanese Biblical Institute* 7 (1981) 3–15.

'A Quantitative Analysis of The "Adam and Eve," "Cain and Abel," and "Noah" Stories,' in *Perspectives on Language and Text: Essays and Poems in Honor of Francis I. Andersen's Sixtieth Birthday, July 28, 1985*, ed. Edgar W. Conrad and Edward G. Newing, Winona Lake, IN: Eisenbrauns, 1987, 195–203.

Kilpatrick, G. D. 'Atticism and the Text of the New Testament', in *Neutestamentliche Aufsätze: Festschrift für Prof. Josef Schmid zum 70. Geburtstag*, ed. J. Blinzler, O. Kuss and F. Mußner, Regensburg: Friedrich Pustet, 1963, 125–37.

'Some Thoughts on Modern Textual Criticism and the Synoptic Gospels', *Novum Testamentum* 19 (1977) 275–92.

Kim, Seyoon *The Origin of Paul's Gospel*, Wissenschaftliche Untersuchungen zum Neuen Testament 2.4, Tübingen: J. C. B. Mohr, ²1984.

Kinneavy, James L. *A Theory of Discourse*, New York: W. W. Norton, 1980.

Klauck, Hans-Josef 'Hellenistische Rhetorik im Diasporajudentum: Das Exordium des Vierten Makkabäerbuchs (4 Makk 1.1–12)', *New Testament Studies* 35 (1989) 451–65.

Klemm, D. E. 'Toward a Rhetoric of Postmodern Theology: Through Barth and Heidegger', *Journal of the American Academy of Religion* 55 (1987) 443–69.

Kloppenborg, John S. *The Formation of Q: Trajectories in Ancient Wisdom Collections*, Studies in Antiquity and Christianity, Philadelphia: Fortress, 1987.

Knott, Betty I. *Introduction to Dialogus Ciceronianus (The Ciceronian: A Dialogue on the Ideal Latin Style* [1528]), trans. and annotated Betty I. Knott, in *The Collected Works of Erasmus*, vol. 28, ed. A. H. T. Levi, Toronto: University of Toronto Press, 1986.

Koester, Helmut 'I Thessalonians: Experiment in Christian Writing', in *Continuity and Discontinuity in Church History*, ed. F. F. Church and T. George, Leiden: Brill, 1979, 33–44.

Introduction to the New Testament, 2, History and Literature of Early Christianity, ET, Philadelphia: Fortress, 1982.

König, Eduard *Stilistik, Rhetorik, Poetik in Bezug auf die Biblische Literatur*, Leipzig: T. Weicher, 1900.

Koptak, Paul E. 'Rhetorical Identification in Paul's Autobiographical Narrative: Galatians 1.13–2.14', *Journal for the Study of the New Testament* 40 (1990) 97–113.

Köster, Friedrich 'Did Paul Model his Language after that of Demosthenes?', *Bibliotheca Sacra* 18 (1854) 514–27.

Kraftchick, Steven J. 'Ethos and Pathos in Galatians Five and Six: A Rhetorical Analysis', unpublished PhD dissertation, Emory University, 1985.

Kroll, W. 'Rhetorik' *Pauly's Realencyclopädie der classischen Altertumswissenschaft*, Supplement 8, Stuttgart: Metzler, 1940, 1039–1138.

Kümmel, Werner Georg *The New Testament: The History of the Investigation of its Problems*, ET, London: SCM, 1973.

Kurz, William S. 'Hellenistic Rhetoric in the Christological Proofs of Luke–Acts', *Catholic Biblical Quarterly* 42 (1980) 171–95.

Kustas, George L. 'Saint Basil and the Rhetorical Tradition', in *Basil of Caesarea: Christian, Humanist, Ascetic*, ed. P. J. Fedwick, Toronto: Pontifical Institute of Mediaeval Studies, 1981, 221–79.

Lagrange, M.-J. *Saint Paul, Epître aux Galates*, Paris: Gabalda, ²1925.

Lakoff, Robin Tolmach *Talking Power: The Politics of Language*, New York: Harper Collins, 1990.

Lambrecht, Jan 'Rhetorical Criticism and the New Testament', *Bijdragen, Tijdschrift voor Filosofie en Theologie* 50 (1989) 239–53.

LaPiana, G. 'The Roman Church at the End of the Second Century', *Harvard Theological Review* 18 (1925) 201–77.

Lategan, Bernard 'Is Paul Defending his Apostleship in Galatians?: The Function of Galatians 1.11–12 and 2.19–20', *New Testament Studies* 34 (1988) 411–30.

'Levels of Reader Instruction in the Text of Galatians', *Semeia* 48 (1989) 171–84.

Lausberg, Heinrich *Handbuch der Literarischen Rhetorik: Eine Grundlegung der Literaturwissenschaft* (2 vols.), Stuttgart: Franz Steiner, [2]1973.

Elemente der literarischen Rhetorik, München: Hüber, [8]1984.

Lee, J. A. L. 'Some Figures of Speech of Jesus in Mark's Gospel', *Novum Testamentum* 27 (1985) 1–26.

Leech, Jeffrey *Principles of Pragmatics*, Linguistics Library Series; London: Longman, 1983.

Leeman, Anton D. 'The Variety of Classical Rhetoric' in *Rhetoric Revalued: Papers from the International Society for the History of Rhetoric*, Medieval and Renaissance Texts and Studies 19, ed. B. Vickers, Binghamton, NY: Center for Medieval and Early Renaissance Studies, 1982, 41–46.

Lentz, John C. *Luke's Portrait of Paul*, SNTSMS 77, Cambridge: Cambridge University Press, 1993.

Lesky, A. *Geschichte der griechischen Literatur*, Bern: Francke, [2]1963.

Levinson, John R. 'Did the Spirit Inspire Rhetoric?: An Exploration of George Kennedy's Definition of Early Christian Rhetoric', in *Persuasive Artistry: Studies in New Testament Rhetoric in Honor of George A. Kennedy*, ed. D. Watson, JSNTS 50, Sheffield: JSOT Press, 1991, 25–40.

Levinson, Stephen C. *Pragmatics*, Cambridge: Cambridge University Press, 1983.

Lietzmann, Hans *The Beginnings of the Christian Church*, ET London: Lutterworth Press, [3]1953.

Lightfoot, Joseph Barber 'On the Style and Character of the Epistle to the Galatians', *Journal of Classical and Sacred Philology* 3 (1857) 289–327.

Saint Paul's Epistle to the Galatians: A Revised Text with Introduction, Notes and Dissertations, London: Macmillan, [10]1896.

Lim, Timothy H. 'Not in Persuasive Words of Wisdom, but in the Demonstration of the Spirit and Power', *Novum Testamentum* 29 (1987) 137–49.

Litfin, Duane *St Paul's Theology of Proclamation: 1 Corinthians 1–4 and Greco-Roman Rhetoric*, SNTSMS 79, Cambridge: Cambridge University Press, 1994.

Llewelyn, S. R. 'The Revocation of Wills and Gal. 3.15', *New Documents Illustrating Early Christianity* 6, ed. S. R. Llewelyn, Sydney: Ancient History Document Research Centre: Macquarie University, 1992, 41–7.

Long, William R. 'The *Paulusbild* in the Trial of Paul in Acts', in *Society of Biblical Literature Seminar Papers* 22 (1983) 87–105.

Longenecker, Richard *The Ministry and Message of Paul*, Grand Rapids: Zondervan, 1971.

   Biblical Exegesis in the Apostolic Period, Grand Rapids: Eerdmans, 1975.

   Galatians, Word Bible Commentary, Dallas: Word Books, 1990.

Lösch, Stephen 'Die Dankesrede des Tertulles: Apostelgeschichte 24,1–4', *Theologische Quartalschrift* 112 (1931) 259–319.

Lüdemann, Gerd *Early Christianity According to the Traditions in Acts: A Commentary*, ET, London: SCM, 1984.

   Paul, Apostle to the Gentiles: Studies in Chronology, ET, London: SCM, 1984.

Lührmann, Dieter *Galatians*, Minneapolis: Fortress, 1992.

Lund, Nils Wilhelm *Chiasmus in the New Testament* (1st edn. Chapel Hill: University of North Carolina Press, 1942), Peabody, MA: Hendriksen, 1992.

Lundblom, J. R. *Jeremiah: A Study in Ancient Hebrew Rhetoric*, Missoula: Scholars Press, 1975.

Lyons, George *Pauline Autobiography: Toward a New Understanding*, SBLDS 73, Atlanta: Scholars Press, 1985.

McDonald, J. I. H. *Kerygma and Didache: The Articulation and Structure of the Earliest Christian Message*, Cambridge: Cambridge University Press, 1980.

   'Rhetorical Criticism', in *A Dictionary of Biblical Interpretation*, London: SCM, 1990, 599–600.

   'Synchronic Exegesis', in *A Dictionary of Biblical Interpretation*, London: SCM, 1990, 657–8.

McDonald, P. M. 'Romans 5.1–11 as a Rhetorical Bridge', *Journal for the Study of the New Testament* 40 (1990) 81–96.

McGuire, M. 'The Structural Study of Speech', in *Festschrift für D. Ehninger*, ed. R. E. McKerrow, Glenview, IL: Foresmen, 1982, 1–22.

McKnight, Edgar V. 'Is the New Testament Written in "Holy Ghost" Greek?', *The Bible Translator* 16 (1965) 87–93.

   'The New Testament and "Biblical" Greek', *Journal of Bible and Religion* 34 (1966) 36–42

   Post-Modern Use of the Bible: The Emergence of Reader-Oriented Criticism, Nashville: Abingdon Press, 1988.

McLean, Bradley H. 'Galatians 2.7–9 and the Recognition of Paul's Apostolic Status at the Jerusalem Conference: A Critique of G. Luedemann's Solution', *New Testament Studies* 37 (1991) 67–76.

McLuhan, H. M. 'Edgar Poe's Tradition', *The Sewanee Review* 52 (1944) 25–8.

Mack, Burton L. 'Decoding the Scripture: Philo and the Rules of Rhetoric', in *Nourished With Peace: Studies in Hellenistic Judaism in Memory of Samuel Sandmel*, ed F. E. Greenspahn, E. Hilgert and B. L. Mack, Chico: Scholars Press, 1984, 81–115.

   Anecdotes and Arguments: The Chreia in Antiquity and Early Christianity, Occasional Papers 10, Claremont, CA: Institute for Antiquity and Christianity, 1987.

   Rhetoric and the New Testament, Minneapolis: Fortress, 1990.

Mack, Burton L. and Robbins, Vernon K. *Patterns of Persuasion in the Gospels*, Sonoma, CA: Polebridge Press, 1989.

MacMullen, Ramsay *Christianizing the Roman Empire*, New Haven, CT: Yale University Press, 1984.

Malherbe, Abraham J. 'The Beasts at Ephesus', *Journal of Biblical Literature* 87 (1968) 71–80.

'"Gentle as a Nurse": The Cynic Background of 1 Thessalonians', *Novum Testamentum* 12 (1970) 203–17.

'Ancient Epistolary Theorists', *Ohio Journal of Religious Studies* 5 (1977) 3–77.

The Social Aspects of Early Christianity, Baton Rouge: Louisiana State University, 1977 (rev. Philadelphia: Fortress, [2]1983).

'μη γενοιτο in the Diatribe and Paul', *Harvard Theological Review* 73 (1980) 231–40.

'Exhortation in First Thessalonians', *Novum Testamentum* 25 (1983) 235–56.

Paul and the Popular Philosophers, Minneapolis: Fortress, 1989.

Malina, Bruce *Christian Origins and Cultural Anthropology: Practical Modes for Biblical Interpretation*, Atlanta: John Knox Press, 1986.

Mann, Friedhelm 'Gregor, Rhetor et Pastor: Interpretation des Proömiums der Schrift Gregor von Nyssa "De infantibus praemature abreptis"', *Vigiliae Christianae* 31 (1976) 126–47.

Manson, T. W. 'The Problem of the Epistle to the Galatians', in *Studies in the Gospels and the Epistles*, ed. M. Black, Manchester: Manchester University Press, 1962, 168–89.

Marrou, Henri *A History of Education in Antiquity*, ET, London: Sheed & Ward, 1956.

St Augustine and His Influence Through the Ages, ET, London: Longmans, no date.

Marshall, I. Howard *Acts*, Tyndale NT Commentaries, Grand Rapids: Eerdmans, 1980.

Marshall, Peter 'Invective: Paul and His Enemies in Corinth', in *Perspectives on Language and Text: Essays and Poems in Honor of Francis I. Andersen's Sixtieth Birthday, July 28, 1985*, ed Edgar W. Conrad and Edward G. Newing, Winona Lake, IN: Eisenbrauns, 1987, 359–373.

Martin, Josef *Antike Rhetorik: Technik und Methode*, Handbuch der Altertumswissenschaft II, 3; München: Beck, 1974.

Martyn, J. Louis 'Apocalyptic Antinomies in Paul's Letter to the Galatians', *New Testament Studies* 31 (1985) 412–20.

Matera, Frank J. 'The Culmination of Paul's Argument to the Galatians: Gal. 5.1–6.17', *Journal for the Study of the New Testament* 32 (1988) 79–91.

Galatians, Sacra Pagina Series 9, Collegeville, MN: Liturgical Press, 1992.

Meeks, Wayne 'Review of H. D. Betz's *Galatians*', *Journal of Biblical Literature* 100 (1981) 304–7.

First Urban Christians: The Social World of the Apostle Paul, New Haven, CT: Yale University Press, 1983.

Meinardus, Otto F. A. *St Paul in Ephesus and the Cities of Galatia and Cyprus*, New York: Caratzas Publishing Company, 1979.

Melanchthon, Philip *Paul's Letter to the Colossians*, ed. and ET D. C. Parker, Sheffield: Almond Press, 1989.

Commentary on Romans, ET, Fred Kramer, St Louis: Concordia Publishing House, 1992.

Melugin, R. A. *The Formation of Isaiah 40–55*, Beihefte zur Zeitschrift für die alttestamentliche Wissenschaft 141, New York: De Gruyter, 1976.

Merk, Otto 'Der Beginn der Paränese im Galaterbrief', *ZNW* 60 (1969) 83–104.

Metzger, Bruce M. 'The Language of the New Testament', *The Interpreter's Bible*, ed. George Arthur Buttrick, Nashville: Abingdon Press, 1951, 7: 43–69.

The Text of the New Testament: Its Transmission, Corruption, and Restoration, Oxford: Oxford University Press, ³1992.

Meyer, Paul W. 'Review of H. D. Betz's *Galatians*', *Religious Studies Review* 7 (1981) 318–23.

Minn, H. R. 'Classical Reminiscence in St Paul', *Prudentia* 6.2 (1974) 93–8.

'Effective Techniques in Pauline Diction', *Prudentia* 7.2 (1975) 89–93.

Mitchell, Margaret M. *Paul and the Rhetoric of Reconciliation: An Exegetical Investigation of the Language and Composition of 1 Corinthians*, Louisville: Westminster/John Knox, 1992.

Montgomery, J. B. 'Galatians', *Expositor's Bible Commentary*, Grand Rapids: Zondervan, 1976.

Morgenthaler, Robert *Lukas und Quintilian: Rhetorik als Erzählkunst*, Zürich: Gotthelf, 1993.

Morton, A. Q. and McLeman, James *Paul, the Man and the Myth: A Study in the Authorship of Greek Prose*, London: Hodder & Stoughton, 1966.

Moss, Jean Dietz 'Galileo's *Letter to Christiana*: Some Rhetorical Considerations', *Renaissance Quarterly* 36 (1983) 547–76.

Moule, Charles F. D. *An Idiom Book of New Testament Greek*, Cambridge: Cambridge University Press, ²1959.

Moulton, James Hope, *A Grammar of New Testament Greek, 1: Prolegomena*, Edinburgh: T&T Clark, ³1908.

Moulton, James Hope Howard, Wilbert Francis *A Grammar of New Testament Greek, 2: Accidence and Word-Formation*, Edinburgh: T&T Clark, 1929.

Moulton, James Hope and Milligan, George *The Vocabulary of the Greek New Testament Illustrated From the Papyri and Other Non-Literary Sources*, London: Hodder & Stoughton, 1930.

Muilenberg, James 'Literary Form in the Fourth Gospel', *Journal of Biblical Literature* 51 (1932) 40–53.

'The Literary Character of Isaiah 34', *Journal of Biblical Literature* 59 (1940) 339–65.

'Form Criticism and Beyond', *Journal of Biblical Literature* 88 (1969): 1–18; repr. in *Beyond Form Criticism: Essays in Old Testament Literary Criticism*, ed. P. R. House, *Sources for Biblical and Theological Study* 2, Winona Lake, IN: Eisenbrauns, 1992, 46–69.

Mukarosky, J. 'Standard Language and Poetic Language', ET, in *A Prague School Reader on Esthetics, Literary Structure, and Style*, Washington, DC: Georgetown University Press, 1964, 17–30.

Mullins, Terence Y. 'Formulas in New Testament Epistles', *Journal of Biblical Literature* 91 (1972) 385.

Munck, Johannes *Paul and the Salvation of Mankind*, ET, London: SCM, 1959.

Munier, Charles 'Carthage', *Encyclopedia of the Early Church* (2 vols.), ed. Angelo Di Berardino, ET, Cambridge: James Clarke, 1992, 1: 147–8.

Murphy, James J. 'Saint Augustine and the Debate about a Christian Rhetoric', *Quarterly Journal of Speech* 46 (1960) 400–10.

Rhetoric in the Middle Ages, Berkeley: University of California Press, 1974.

Mußner, Franz *Der Galaterbrief*, Herders Theologischer Kommentar Zum Neuen Testament 9; Freiburg/ Basel: Herder, [2]1974.

Nagy, Gregory 'The Crisis of Performance', in *The Ends of Rhetoric: History, Theory, Practice*, ed. J. Bender and D. Wellbery, Stanford: Stanford University Press, 1990, 43–59.

Neill, Stephen and Wright, Tom *The Interpretation of The New Testament: 1861–1986*, Oxford: Oxford University Press, [2]1988.

Neyrey, Jerome H. 'The Forensic Defense Speech and Paul's Trial Speeches in Acts 22–26: Form and Function', in *Luke–Acts: New Perspectives From the SBL Seminar*, ed. C. H. Talbert, New York: Crossroads, 1984, 210–24.

Paul in Other Words: A Cultural Reading of His Letters, Louisville: Westminster/John Knox Press, 1990.

Niederstrasser, Heinz *Kerygma und Paideia: Zum Problem der erziehenden Gnade*, Stuttgart: Evangeliches Verlagswerk Stuttgart, 1967.

Nock, Arthur Darby 'A New Edition of the Hermetic Writings', *Journal of Egyptian Archaeology* 11 (1925) 126–37.

'The Vocabulary of the New Testament', *Journal of Biblical Literature* 52 (1933) 131–9.

St Paul, New York: Harper & Row, 1938.

Early Gentile Christianity and its Hellenistic Background, The Cloister Library, New York: Harper Torchbooks, 1964.

Norden, Eduard 'Über die Anfänge der patristischen Literatur', *Historische Zeitschrift* 48 (1882) 417–72.

Die Antike Kunstprosa vom VI Jahrhundert vor Christus bis in die Zeit der Renaissance (2 vols.), Stuttgart: Teubner, [9]1983.

Oepke, Albrecht *Der Brief des Paulus an die Galater*, Theologischer Handkommentar zum Neuen Testament 9, Berlin: Evangelische Verlagsanstalt, [3]1973.

Olbricht, Thomas H. 'An Aristotelian Rhetorical Analysis of 1 Thessalonians', in *Greeks, Romans, and Christians: Essays in Honor of Abraham J. Malherbe*, ed. D. Balch, E. Ferguson and W. A. Meeks, Minneapolis: Fortress, 1990, 216–36.

Orchard, Bernard 'The Ellipse between Galatians 2,3 and 2,4', *Biblica* 54 (1973) 469–81.

Oroz, J. *La retórica augustiniana: Clasicismo y Cristianismo*, Texte und Untersuchungen zur Geschichte der Altchristlichen Literatur 81; Berlin: Akademie Verlag, 1962.

Osiek, C. *Galatians*, Wilmington, DE: Michael Glazier, 1981.

Overbeck, Franz *Über die Christlichkeit unserer heutigen Theologie, Zweite, um eine Einleitung und ein Nachwort vermehrte Auflage*, Leipzig: Teubner, 1903.

Über die Anfänge der patristischen Literatur, Darmstadt: Wissenschaftliche Buchgesellschaft, ²1966.

Owen, E. C. E. 'St Gregory of Nyssa: Grammar, Vocabulary, and Style', *Journal of Theological Studies* 26 (1925) 64–71.

Palmer, Leonard R. *The Greek Language*, London: Faber & Faber, 1980.

Parker, T. H. L. *Calvin's New Testament Commentaries*, London: SCM, 1971.

Commentaries on The Epistle to the Romans: 1532–1542, Edinburgh: T&T Clark, 1986.

Patte, Daniel *What is Structural Exegesis?*, Philadelphia: Fortress, 1976.

Pelletier, A. *Flavius Josèphe, adaptateur de la lettre d'Aristé: Une réaction atticisante contre la koinè*, Paris: Études et Commentaires 45, 1962.

Pelser, G. M. M., DuToit, A. B., Kruger, M. A., Lemmer, H. R. and Roberts, J. H. 'Discourse Analysis of Galatians', Addendum to *Neotestamentica* 26 (1992) 1–41.

Perelman, Chaim *The New Rhetoric and the Humanities: Essays on Rhetoric and its Applications*, ET, Synthese Library 140, Dordrecht: D. Reidel, 1979.

The Realm of Rhetoric, ET, Notre Dame: University of Notre Dame Press, 1982.

Perelman, Chaim and Olbrechts-Tyteca, L. *The New Rhetoric: A Treatise on Argumentation*, ET, Notre Dame: University of Notre Dame Press, 1969.

Perry, B. E. *The Ancient Romances*, Sather Classical Lectures; Berkeley: University of California Press, 1967.

Petersen, Norman R. *Literary Criticism for New Testament Critics*, Philadelphia: Fortress, 1978.

Rediscovering Paul: Philemon and the Sociology of Paul's Narrative World, Philadelphia: Fortress, 1985.

Pilch, J. 'The Epistle to the Galatians', *Collegeville Bible Commentary*, Collegeville, MN: Sacra Pagina, 1983.

Pitta, Antonio *Disposizione e Messaggio Della Lettera Ai Galati: Analisi retorico-letteraria*, Analecta Biblica 131, Roma: Editrice Pontificio Instituto Biblico, 1992.

Plank, Karl A. *Paul and the Irony of Affliction*, Society of Biblical Literature Semeia Studies, Atlanta: Scholars Press, 1987.

Pleket, H. W. 'Urban Elites and Business in the Greek Part of the Roman Empire', in *Trade in the Ancient Economy*, ed. Peter Garnsey, Keith Hopkins and C. R. Whittaker, London: The Hogarth Press, 1983, 131–44.

Pogoloff, Stephen Mark 'Isocrates and Contemporary Hermeneutics', in *Persuasive Artistry: Studies in New Testament Rhetoric in Honor of*

George A. *Kennedy*, ed. D. Watson, JSNTS 50, Sheffield: JSOT Press, 1991, 338–62.

Poland, Lynn 'The Bible and the Rhetorical Sublime', in *The Bible as Rhetoric: Studies in Biblical Persuasion and Credibility*, Warwick Studies in Philosophy and Literature, ed. M. Warner, London/New York: Routledge, 1990, 29–47.

Porter, Calvin 'Romans 1.18–32: Its Role in the Developing Argument', *New Testament Studies* 40 (1994) 210–28.

Porter, Stanley E. *Verbal Aspect in the Greek of the New Testament, with Reference to Tense and Mood*, Frankfurt: Peter Lang, 1989.

The Language of the New Testament: Classic Essays, Sheffield: JSOT, 1991.

'The Argument of Romans 5: Can a Rhetorical Question Make a Difference?', *Journal of Biblical Literature* 110 (1991) 655–77.

'The Theoretical Justification for Application of Rhetorical Categories to Pauline Epistolary Literature', in *Rhetoric and the New Testament: Essays from the 1992 Heidelberg Conference*, ed. S. E. Porter and T. H. Olbricht, JSNTS 90, Sheffield: JSOT Press, 1993, 100–122.

Powell, Mark Allan *What is Narrative Criticism?*, Minneapolis: Fortress, 1990.

Probst, Hermann *Paulus und der Brief: Die Rhetorik des antiken Briefes als Form der Paulinischen Korintherkorrespondenz (1 Kor 8–10)*, Wissenschaftliche Untersuchungen zum Neuen Testament 2.45, Tübingen: J. C. B. Mohr, 1991.

Quacquarelli, A. 'Rhetoric', *Encyclopedia of the Early Church* (2 vols.), ed. Angelo Di Berardino, ET, Cambridge: James Clarke, 1992, 2: 735–36.

Radermacher, Ludwig *Neutestamentliche Grammatik: das Griechisch des Neuen Testaments im Zussamenhang mit der Volkssprache*, Tübingen: J. C. B. Mohr, [2]1925.

Rahn, H. *Morphologie der antiken Literatur: Eine Einführung*, Darmstadt: Wissenschaftliche Buchgesellschaft, 1969.

Ramsay, William *The Cities of St Paul: Their Influence on his Life and Thought*, The Dale Memorial Lectures 1907, London: Hodder & Stoughton, 1907.

St Paul the Traveller and the Roman Citizen, Grand Rapids: Baker, [2]1972.

Rand, E. K. 'The Latin Literature of the West from the Antonines to Constantine', in *Cambridge Ancient History v. 12: The Imperial Crisis and Recovery*. A.D.193–324, Cambridge: Cambridge University Press, 1939, 571–610.

Rauber, D. F. 'Literary Values in the Book of Ruth', *Journal of Biblical Literature* 89 (1970) 27–37.

Reardon, B. P. *The Form of Greek Romance*, Princeton: Princeton University Press, 1991.

Reed, Jeffrey T. 'Using Ancient Rhetorical Categories to Interpret Paul's Letters: A Question of Genre', in *Rhetoric and the New Testament: Essays from the 1992 Heidelberg Conference*, ed. S. E. Porter and T. H. Olbricht, JSNTS 90, Sheffield: JSOT Press, 1993, 292–324.

Reinmuth, Eckart '"Nicht Vergeblich" Bei Paulus und Pseudo-Philo, Liber Antiquitato im Biblicarum', *Novum Testamentum* 33 (1991) 97–124.

Renehan, R. 'Classical Greek Quotations in the New Testament', in *The Heritage of the Early Church: Essays in Honor of G. V. Florovsky on the Occasion of His Eightieth Birthday*, Orientalia Christiana Analecta 195, ed. D. Neiman and M. Schatkin, Rome: Pontifical Institute of Oriental Studies, 1973, 17–46.

Rhoads, Donald and Michie, David *Mark as Story*, Philadelphia: Fortress, 1982.

Richards, I. A. *The Philosophy of Rhetoric*, New York/London: Oxford University Press, 1936.

Richards, E. Randolph *The Secretary in the Letters of Paul*, Wissenschaftliche Untersuchungen zum Neuen Testament, 2.42, Tubingen: J. C. B. Mohr, 1991.

Ricoeur, Paul 'The Hermeneutical Function of Distanciation', *Philosophy Today* 17 (1973) 121–39.

Interpretation Theory: Discourse and the Surplus of Meaning, Fort Worth: Texas Christian University Press, 1976.

Robbins, Vernon K. *Jesus the Teacher: A Socio-Rhetorical Interpretation of Mark*, Philadelphia: Fortress, 1984.

Robbins, Vernon K. and Patton, John H. 'Rhetoric and Biblical Criticism', *Quarterly Journal of Speech* 66 (1980) 327–50.

Roberts, William Rhys *Greek Rhetoric and Literary Criticism*, New York: Longmans, Green, 1928.

Robertson, A. T. *A Grammar of the Greek New Testament in the Light of Historical Research*, New York: Hodder & Stoughton, [4]1923.

Rohde, J. *Der Brief des Paulus an die Galater*, Berlin: Evangelische Verlagsanstalt, 1989.

Rolland, P. 'La Structure littéraire et l'unité de l'Épître aux Philippiens', *Revue des sciences Réligieuses* 64 (1990) 213–16.

Rosenfield, L. W. 'The Practical Celebration of Epideictic', in *Rhetoric in Transition: Studies in the Nature and Uses of Rhetoric*, ed. E. E. White, University Park: University of Pennsylvania Press, 1980, 131–55.

Russell, Donald A. 'Rhetoric, Greek', *Oxford Classical Dictionary*, ed. N. G. L. Hammond and H. H. Scullard, Oxford: Clarendon Press, [2]1970.

Criticism in Antiquity, London: Duckworth, 1981.

Greek Declamation, Cambridge: Cambridge University Press, 1983.

'Greek Criticism of the Empire', in *The Cambridge History of Literary Criticism vol. 1: Classical Criticism*, ed. G. A. Kennedy, Cambridge: Cambridge University Press, 1989, 297–329.

Russell, Walter B. III 'Rhetorical Analysis of the Book of Galatians, Part 1', *Bibliotheca Sacra* 150 (1993) 341–58.

'Rhetorical Analysis of the Book of Galatians, Part 2', *Bibliotheca Sacra* 150 (1993) 416–39.

Rydbeck, Lars *Fachprosa, Vermeintliche Volkssprache und Neues Testament*, Uppsala: Acta University Upsal, 1967.

'On the Question of Linguistic Levels', ET, in *The Language of the New*

Testament, JSNTS 60, ed. S. Porter, Sheffield: Sheffield Academic Press, 1991, 191–204.

Sampley, J. Paul '"Before God, I Do Not Lie" (Gal. 1.20): Paul's Self-Defence in the Light of Roman Legal Praxis', *New Testament Studies* 23 (1977) 477–82.

Sanders, Jack T. 'Paul's "Autobiographical" Statements in Galatians 1–2', *Journal of Biblical Literature* 85 (1966) 335–43.

Saunders, A. N. W. *Greek Political Oratory*, London: Penguin Books, 1970.

Scheible, Heinz 'Melanchthon', *Theologische Realenzyklopädie* XII, Berlin: De Gruyter, 1992, 371–410.

Schenke, Hans-Martin 'Four Problems in the Life of Paul Reconsidered', in *The Future of Early Christianity: Essays in Honor of Helmut Koester*, ed. B. A. Pearson, Minneapolis: Fortress, 319–28.

Schlatter, Adolf *Die Briefe an die Galater, Epheser, Kolosser und Philemon*, Schlatters Erläuterungen zum Neuen Testament 7, Stuttgart: Calwer, no date.

Schlier, Heinrich *Der Brief an die Galater*, Kritisch-Exegetischer Kommentar über das Neue Testament Begründet von Heinrich August Wilhelm Meyer 7, Vandenhoeck & Ruprecht: Göttingen, [12]1962.

Schmid, W. *Der Atticismus in Seinen Hauptvertretern von Dionysius von Halicarnass bis auf den Zweiten Philostratus* (5 vols.), 1887–97, repr. Hildesheim: Olms, 1964.

Schmidt, W. 'Diatribai', Der Kleine Pauly, ed. K. Ziegler and W. Sontheimer, 5 vols., Stuttgart: Druckenmüller, 1964–75, 2: 1577–8.

Schoeps, Hans Joachim *Paul: the Theology of the Apostle in the Light of Jewish Religious History*, ET, Philadelphia: Westminster, 1961.

Schüssler-Fiorenza, Elizabeth 'Rhetorical Situation and Historical Reconstruction in 1 Corinthians', *New Testament Studies* 33 (1987) 386–403.

Schütz, John Howard *Paul and the Anatomy of Apostolic Authority*, SNTSMS 26, Cambridge: Cambridge University Press, 1975.

Scott, John A. *Homer and his Influence*, London: George G. Harrap, 1925.

Scroggs, Robin 'Paul as Rhetorician: Two Homilies in Romans 1–11', in *Jews, Greeks and Christians: Religious Cultures in Late Antiquity: Essays in Honor of William David Davies*, ed. R. Hamerton-Kelly and R. Scroggs, Leiden: Brill, 1976, 271–98.

Seeley, David 'Review of Charles A. Wanamaker, *The Epistle to the Thessalonians*', *Catholic Biblical Quarterly* 54 (1992) 183–84.

Selb, Walter 'Διαθήκη im Neuen Testament: Randbemerkungen eines Juristen zu einem Theologenstreit', *Journal of Jewish Studies* 25 (1974) 183–96.

Sherwin-White, A. N. *Roman Society and Roman Law in the New Testament*, Oxford: Clarendon Press, 1963.

Shklovsky, Viktor 'Art as Device', ET, in *Russian Formalist Criticism: Four Essays*, ed. L. Lemon and M. Reis, Lincoln, NE: University of Nebraska Press, 1965, 5–24.

'La construction de la nouvelle et du roman', in *Théories de la littérature: Textes des Formalistes russes*, ed. T. Todorov, Paris: Seuil, 1965, 170–96.

Sider, Robert D. 'Approaches to Tertullian: A Study of Recent Scholarship', *Second Century* 2 (1982) 228–60.

The Gospel and its Proclamation, Message of the Fathers of the Church 10, ed. Thomas Halton, Wilmington, DE: Michael Glazier, 1983, 60–4.

Siegert, Folker *Argumentation bei Paulus, gezeigt an Röm 9–11*, Wissenschaftliche Untersuchungen zum Neuen Testament 34, Tübingen: J. C. B. Mohr, 1985.

Silva, Moises 'Semantic Borrowing in the New Testament', *New Testament Studies* 22 (1976) 104–10.

'New Lexical Semitisms', *Zeitschrift für die neutestamentliche Wissenschaft* 29 (1978) 253–7.

Skinner, B. F. *Beyond Freedom and Dignity*, New York: Alfred A. Knopf, 1971.

Sloan, Thomas O. 'Restoration of Rhetoric to Literary Study', *The Speech Teacher* 16 (1967) 91–7.

'Rhetoric', in *Encyclopaedia Britannica* 28 (1979) 802–3.

Sloan, T. O. and Perelman, Chaim 'Rhetoric', in *Encyclopaedia Britannica Macropedia* 15 (1979) 798–805.

Smiles, Vincent Michael 'The Gospel and the Law in Galatia: Paul's Response to Jewish-Christian Separatism and the Threat of Galatian Apostasy', unpublished PhD dissertation, Fordham University, 1989.

Smit, Joop 'The Letter of Paul to the Galatians: A Deliberative Speech', *New Testament Studies* 35 (1989) 1–26.

'The Genre of 1 Corinthians 13 in the Light of Classical Rhetoric', *Novum Testamentum* 33 (1991) 193–216.

Smith, James H. and Parks, Edward W. (eds.) *The Great Critics: An Anthology of Literary Criticism*, New York: W. W. Norton & Co., 1951.

Snyman, Andreas H. 'Style and Meaning in Romans 8:31–39', *Neotestamentica* 18 (1984) 94–103.

'On Studying the Figures (*Schemata*) in the New Testament', *Biblica* 69 (1988) 93–107.

'Style and the Rhetorical Situation of Romans 8.31–39', *New Testament Studies* 34 (1988) 218–31.

Snyman, A. H. and Cronjé, J. V. W. 'Toward a New Classification of the Figures (ΣΧΗΜΑΤΑ) in the Greek New Testament', *New Testament Studies* 32 (1986) 113–21.

Solmsen, F. 'Drei Rekonstruktionen zur Antiken Rhetorik und Poetik', *Hermes* 67 (1932) 133–54.

'The Aristotelian Tradition in Ancient Rhetoric', *American Journal of Philology* 62 (1941) 35–50, 169–90.

Souter, Alexander *The Earliest Latin Commentaries on the Epistles of Paul*, Oxford: Clarendon Press, 1927.

Spencer, Aida Besançon 'The Wise Fool (and the Foolish Wise): A Study of Irony in Paul', *Novum Testamentum* 23 (1981) 349–60.

Paul's Literary Style: A Stylistic and Historical Comparison of II Corinthians 11:16–12:13, Romans 8:9–39, and Philippians 3:2–4:13, Evangelical Theological Society Monograph Series Jackson: ETS, 1984.

Sperber, Dan and Wilson, Deirdre 'Rhetoric and Relevance', in *The Ends of Rhetoric: History, Theory, Practice*, ed. J. Bender and D. E. Wellbery, Stanford: Stanford University Press, 1990, 140–155.

Staats, Reinhart 'Chrysostomus über die Rhetorik des Apostels Paulus: Makarianische Kontexte', *Vigiliae Christianae* 46 (1992) 225–40.

Stambaugh, John and Balch, David *The Social World of the First Christians*, London: SPCK, 1986.

Standaert, Beno 'La rhétorique antique et l'épître aux Galates', *Foi et Vie* 84 (1985) 33–40.

'La rhétorique ancienne dans Saint Paul', in *L'Apôtre Paul: Personnalité, style et conception du ministère*, ed. A. Vanhoye, Bibliotheca ephemeridum theologicarum lovaniensium 73, Leuven: Leuven University Press, 1986, 78–92.

Stanley, Christopher D. *Paul and the Language of Scripture: Citation Technique in the Pauline Epistles and Contemporary Literature*, Cambridge: Cambridge University Press, 1992.

'"Under a Curse": A Fresh Reading of Galatians 3.10–14', *New Testament Studies* 36 (1990) 481–511.

Stegemann, Wolfgang 'War der Apostel Paulus ein römischer Bürger?', *Zeitschrift für die neutestamentliche Wissenschaft* 78 (1987) 200–29.

Stevens, P. T. 'Aristotle and the Koine – Notes on the Prepositions', *The Classical Quarterly* 30 (1936) 204–17.

Stowers, Stanley Kent *The Diatribe and Paul's Letter to the Romans*, SBLDS 57, Missoula: Scholars Press, 1981.

'Social Status, Public Speaking and Private Teaching: The Circumstances of Paul's Preaching Activity', *Novum Testamentum* 26 (1984) 59–82.

Letter Writing in Greco-Roman Antiquity, Library of Early Christianity 5, Philadelphia: Westminster, 1986.

Strauss, Gerhard *Schriftgebrauch, Schriftauslegung, und Schriftbeweis bei Augustin*, Beiträge zur Geschichte der biblischen Hermeneutik, Tübingen: J. C. B. Mohr, 1959.

Sumney, J. L. 'The Bearing of a Pauline Rhetorical Pattern on the Integrity of 2 Thessalonians', *Zeitschrift für die Neutestamentliche Wissenschaft* 81 (1990) 192–204.

Suhl, Alfred 'Der Galaterbrief – Situation and Argumentation', in *Aufstieg und Niedergang der Römischen Welt* 2.25.4, Berlin: De Gruyter, 1987, 3067–134.

Swetnam, J. 'Review of H. D. Betz's *Galatians*', *Biblica* 62 (1981) 594–7.

Tajra, Harry W. *The Trial of St Paul: A Juridical Exegesis of the Second Half of the Acts of the Apostles*, Wissenschaftliche Untersuchungen zum Neuen Testament 2: 35, Tübingen: J. C. B. Mohr, 1989.

Tannehill, R. C. *The Sword of His Mouth*, Semeia Supplements 1, Philadelphia: Fortress, 1975.

Taylor, A.E. 'Review of E. Benz's *Marius Victorinus und die Entwicklung der abenländischer Metaphysik*', *Classical Review* 47 (1933) 86.

Taylor, Nicholas *Paul, Antioch and Jerusalem: A Study in Relationships and Authority in Earliest Christianity*, JSNTS 66, Sheffield: JSOT Press, 1992.

Teuffel, W. S. *Geschichte der Römischen Literatur*, Leipzig: Teubner, 1890.

Thackeray, Henry St. John *A Grammar of the Old Testament in Greek According to the Septuagint*, Cambridge: Cambridge University Press, 1909.
  Josephus the Man and the Historian, New York: Jewish Institute of Religion Press, 1929.
Thompson, M. B. 'Teaching/Paraenesis', in *Dictionary of Paul and his Letters*, Downers Grove: IVP, 1993, 922–23.
Thonssen, Lester and Baird, A. Craig *Speech Criticism: The Developments of Standards for Rhetorical Appraisal*, New York: Krieger, ²1970.
Thurén, Lauri *The Rhetorical Strategy of 1 Peter: With Special Regard to Ambiguous Expressions*, Åbo: Åbo Akademis Förlag, 1990.
Townsend, John T. 'Ancient Education in the Time of the Early Roman Empire', in *Early Church History: The Roman Empire as the Setting of Primitive Christianity*, ed. S. Benko and J. J. O'Rourke (US edn. 1971: *The Catacombs and the Colosseum*), London: Oliphants, 1972, 139–63.
Trible, Phyllis *God and the Rhetoric of Sexuality*, Philadelphia: Fortress, 1978.
Trites, Allison A. 'The Importance of Legal Scenes and Language in the Book of Acts', *Novum Testamentum* 16 (1974) 278–84.
Trudgill, Peter *Sociolinguistics: An Introduction to Language and Society*, London: Penguin Books, 1983.
  Introducing Language and Society, London: Penguin Books, 1992.
Turner, E. G. *Greek Papyri: An Introduction*, Oxford: Clarendon Press, 1968.
Turner, Nigel *Grammar of the Greek New Testament, III: Syntax*, Edinburgh: T.&T. Clark, 1963.
  Grammatical Insights into the New Testament, Edinburgh: T&T Clark, 1965.
  'The Literary Character of New Testament Greek', *New Testament Studies* 20 (1974) 107–14.
Tyrell, Robert Yelverton *Cicero in his Letters*, London: Macmillan & Co., 1956.
Van Unnik, W. C. *Sparsa Collecta: The Collected Essays of W. C. Van Unnik; 1: Evangelia, Paulina, Acta*, Novum Testamentum Supplement 29, Leiden: Brill, 1973.
Veltman, Fred 'Defense Speeches of Paul in Acts', in *Perspectives on Luke–Acts*, ed. C. H. Talbert, Edinburgh: T&T Clark, 1975, 243–56.
Verseput, D. J. 'Paul's Gentile Mission and the Jewish Christian Community: A Study of the Narrative in Galatians 1 and 2', *New Testament Studies* 39 (1993) 36–58.
Via, Dan O. Jr. *The Parables: Their Literary and Existential Dimension*, Philadelphia: Fortress, 1967.
Viard, A. 'Paul. Epître aux Galates', *Dictionnaire de la Bible*, Supplement 7 (1966) 211–26.
Vischer, Lukas 'Die Rechtfertigung der Schriftstellerei in der Alten Kirche', *Theologische Zeitschrift* 12 (1956) 320–36.
Vitti, A. M. 'L'Eloquenza di S. Paolo nelle sue Lettere', *Biblica* 21 (1940) 413–25.
Voelz, James W. 'The Language of the New Testament', in *Aufstieg und*

Niedergang der Romischen Welt 2.25.2, Berlin: DeGruyter, 1984, 893–977.

Vogels, Walter 'Diachronic and Synchronic Studies of Hosea 1–3', *Biblische Zeitschrift* 28 (1984) 94–8, and *Revue des sciences religieuses* 57 (1983) 249–60.

Volkmann, Richard *Die Rhetorik der Griechen und Römer in systematischer Übersicht*, Leipzig: T. Weicher, 1885.

Von Campenhausen, Hans *The Fathers of the Latin Church* (formerly published in the US as *Men Who Shaped the Western Church*), Stanford: Stanford University Press, 1969.

Votaw, Clyde Weber *The Gospels and Contemporary Biographies in the Greco-Roman World* (First printed as 'The Gospels and Contemporary Biographies', in *American Journal of Theology* 19 (1915) 45–73, 217–49), Philadelphia: Fortress, 1970.

Vouga, François 'La construction de l'histoire en Galates 3–4', *Zeitschrift für die neutestamentliche Wissenschaft* 75 (1984) 259–69.

'Zur rhetorischen Gattung des Galaterbriefes', *Zeitschrift für die neutestamentliche Wissenschaft* 79 (1988) 291–2.

Walker, William O. Jr. 'Why Paul Went to Jerusalem: The Interpretation of Galatians 2:1–5', *Catholic Biblical Quarterly* 54 (1992) 503–10.

Watson, Duane Frederick *Invention, Arrangement and Style: Rhetorical Criticism of Jude and 2 Peter*, SBLDS 104, Atlanta: Scholars Press, 1988.

'A Rhetorical Analysis of Philippians, and its Implications for the Unity Question', *Novum Testamentum* 30 (1988) 57–88.

'1 Corinthians 10:23–11:1 in the Light of Greco-Roman Rhetoric: The Role of Rhetorical Questions', *Journal of Biblical Literature* 108 (1989) 301–18.

'A Rhetorical Analysis of 2 John According to Greco-Roman Convention', *New Testament Studies* 35 (1989) 104–30.

'Diatribe', in *Dictionary of Paul and his Letters*, Downers Grove, IL: InterVarsity, 1993, 213.

'Rhetorical Criticism of the New Testament', in *Rhetorical Criticism of the Bible: A Comprehensive Bibliography with Notes on History and Method*, Leiden: Brill, 1994, 101–206.

Weiss, Johannes 'Beiträge zur paulinischen Rhetorik', in *Theologische Studien: Festschriften für Bernard Weiss*, ed. C. R. Gregory *et al.*, Göttingen: Vandenhoeck & Ruprecht, 1897, 165–247.

Die Aufgaben der neutestamentlichen Wissenschaft, Göttingen: Vandenhoeck & Ruprecht, 1910.

Der erste Korintherbrief, Meyer Kommentar 7, Göttingen: Vandenhoeck & Ruprecht, [9]1910.

Earliest Christianity: A History of the Period AD 30–150 (2 vols.), ET, New York: Harper & Brothers, 1959.

Wellek, R. and Warren, A. *Theory of Literature*, London: Penguin Books, [3]1963.

Wendland, Hans *Die Briefe an die Korinther*, Das NT Deutsch, Göttingen: Vandenhoeck & Ruprecht, [10]1964.

Wendland, Paul *Handbuch zum Neuen Testament 2 and 3; Teil 2: Die hellenistisch-römische Kultur in ihrem Beziehungen zu Judentum und Christentum; Teil 3: Die Urchristlichen Literaturformen*, Tübingen: J. C. B. Mohr, 1912.

Werbeck, W. 'Galaterbrief', *Religion in Geschichte und Gegenwart* (1958) 2: 1187–90.

Wessels, G. F. 'The Call to Responsible Freedom in Paul's Persuasive Strategy: Galatians 5:13–6:10', *Neotestamentica* 26 (1992) 461–84.

Westcott, B. F. *The Epistle to the Hebrews*, Grand Rapids: Eerdmans, 1984.

Westermann, Claus 'Sprache und Struktur der Prophetie Deuterojesajas', in *Forschung im Alten Testament*, Theologische Bücherei 24, Munchen: Kaiser, 1964, 92–164.

Westlake, H. D. 'The Setting of Thucydidean Speeches', in *The Speeches in Thucydides: A Collection of Original Studies With a Bibliography*, ed. Philip A. Stadter, Chapel Hill, NC: University of North Carolina Press, 1973, 90–108.

Whately, Richard *Elements of Rhetoric*, repr. of 1832 edn. ed. D. Ehninger; Carbondale, IL: Southern Illinois University Press, ³1963. (See also facsimile reproduction with introductions by Charlotte Downey and Howard Coughlin, Delmar, NY: Scholars' Facsimiles and Reprints, 1991.)

White, John L. 'Introductory Formulae in the Body of the Pauline Letter', *Journal of Biblical Literature* 90 (1971) 91–7.

The Form and Function of the Body of the Greek Letter: A Study of the Letter-Body in the Non-literary Papyri and in Paul the Apostle, SBLDS 2, Missoula, MT: University of Montana, 1972.

'New Testament Epistolary Literature in the Framework of Ancient Epistolography', *Aufstieg und Niedergang der Römischen Welt* 2.25.2, Berlin: De Gruyter, 1984, 1730–56.

Light from Ancient Letters, Foundations and Facets, Philadelphia: Fortress, 1986.

'Apostolic Mission and Apostolic Message: Congruence in Paul's Epistolary Rhetoric, Structure and Imagery', in *Origins and Method: Towards a New Understanding of Judaism and Christianity: Essays in Honour of John C. Hurd*, ed. B. H. McLean, JSNTS 86, Sheffield: JSOT Press, 1993, 145–61.

Wibbing, Siegfried *Die Tugend- und Lasterkataloge im Neuen Testament, und ihre Traditionsgeschichte unter besonderer Berücksichtigung der Qumran-Texte*, Berlin: Alfred Töpelmann, 1959.

Wichelns, Herbert A. 'Some Differences Between Literary Criticism and Rhetorical Criticism', in *Historical Studies of Rhetoric and Rhetoricians*, ed. R. F. Howes, Ithaca, NY: Cornell University Press, 1961, 217–24.

Wifstrand, Albert 'Stylistic Problems in James and Peter', *Studia Theologica* 1 (1948) 170–82.

'Det grekiska Prosaspråket. Ev historisk översikt', *Eranos* 50 (1952) 149–54.

Wilamowitz-Moellendorff, Ulrich von *Antigonos von Karystos*, Philologische Untersuchungen 4, Berlin: Weidmann, 1881.

History of Classical Scholarship, ET, Baltimore: Johns Hopkins University Press, 1982.

Wilder, Amos N. *The New Voice: Religion, Literature, Hermeneutics*, New York: Herder & Herder, 1969.

Early Christian Rhetoric: The Language of the Gospel, Cambridge MA: Harvard University Press, 1971.

Theopoetic: Theology and the Religious Imagination, Philadelphia: Fortress, 1976.

The Bible and the Literary Critic, Philadelphia: Fortress, 1991.

Wilkinson, J. 'Ancient Jerusalem: Its Water Supply and Population', *Palestinean Excavation Quarterly* 106 (1974) 33–51.

Wilson, N. G. *Saint Basil on the Value of Greek Literature*, London: Duckworth, 1975.

Wilson, Robert R. *Sociological Approaches to the Old Testament*, Philadelphia: Fortress, 1984.

Wilson, Thomas *St Paul and Paganism*, Edinburgh: T&T Clark, 1926.

Wimsatt, W. K. and Brooks, C. *Literary Criticism: A Short History I: Classical and Neo-Classical Criticism*, Chicago: University of Chicago Press, 1957.

Winer, Georg Benedict *Grammatik des Neutestamentlichen Sprachidioms als sichere Grundlage der neutestamentlichen Exegese*, Leipzig, [6]1855.

Winter, Bruce 'The Importance of the *Captatio Benevolentiae* In the Speeches of Tertullus and Paul in Acts 24:1–21', *Journal of Theological Studies* 42 (1991) 505–31.

'Official Proceedings and the Forensic Speeches in Acts 24–26', in *The Book of Acts in its First Century Setting, vol. 1: Ancient Literary Setting*, ed. B. W. Winter and A. D. Clarke, Grand Rapids: Eerdmans, 1993, 305–36.

'The Entries and Ethics of Orators and Paul (1 Thessalonians 2:1–12)', *Tyndale Bulletin* 44 (1993) 55–74.

Winterbottom, Michael 'Quintilian and the *Vir Bonus*', *Journal of Roman Studies* 54 (1964) 90–7.

'Quintilian and Rhetoric', in *Empire and Aftermath: Silver Latin II*, ed. T. A. Dorey, London: Routledge & Kegan Paul, 1975, 79–97.

'School and Courtroom', in *Rhetoric Revalued: Papers from the International Society for the History of Rhetoric*, ed. B. Vickers, Medieval & Renaissance Texts and Studies 19, Binghamton, New York: Center for Medieval & Early Renaissance Studies, 1982, 59–70.

Winterowd, W. Ross *Rhetoric: A Synthesis*, New York: Holt, Rinehart & Winston, 1968.

Wire, Antoinette Clark *The Corinthian Women Prophets: A Reconstruction Through Paul's Rhetoric*, Minneapolis: Fortress, 1990.

'Prophecy and the Women Prophets in Corinth', in *Gospel Origins and Christian Beginnings: In Honor of James M. Robinson*, ed. H. Goehring and J. T. Sanders, Sonoma, CA: Polebridge Press, 1990, 134–50.

Worthington, Ian 'The Canon of the Ten Attic Orators', in *Persuasion: Greek Rhetoric in Action*, ed. Ian Worthington, London: Routledge, 1994, 244–63.

Wright, Dale S. 'The Discourse of Awakening: Rhetorical Practice in

Classical Ch'an Buddhism', *Journal of the American Academy of Religion* 61 (1993) 23–40.

Wuellner, Wilhelm 'Topusforschung und Torahinterpretation bei Paulus und Jesus', *New Testament Studies* 24 (1978) 463–83.

'Greek Rhetoric and Pauline Argumentation', in *Early Christian Literature and the Classical Intellectual Tradition: in Honorem Robert M. Grant*, eds. W. R. Schoedel and R. L. Wilken, Théologie Historique 54, Paris: Etudes Beauchesne, 1979, 177–88.

'Paul as Pastor, the Function of Rhetorical Questions in First Corinthians', in *L'Apôtre Paul. Personnalité, Style, et Conception du Ministère*, BETL 73, ed. A Vanhoye, Leuven: Leuven University Press, 1986, 49–77.

'Where is Rhetorical Criticism Taking Us?', *Catholic Biblical Quarterly* 49 (1987) 448–63.

Zmijewski, Josef *Der Stil der paulinischen 'Narrenrede': Analyse der Sprachgestaltung in 2 Kor 11, 1–12,10 als Beitrag zur Methodik von Stiluntersuchungen neutestamentlicher Texte*, Bonner Biblische Beiträge 52, Köln/Bonn: Peter Hanstein, 1978.

INDEX OF SUBJECTS

Abraham 109, 112
Acts 9.11, 213; 22.3, 211; 23.15, 206; 24, 204–7; 24.1–9, 30; 24.10, 205; 24.11–22, 205–6; 24.21, 205; 24.26, 215
Agricola, R. 199, 200
Alburtius 13
Alexandria 24, 211
Ambrose 168, 190
Amphicles 246
analysis 12, 19, 22, 26–9, 148, 169, 190, 198, 224; literature 26–7, 29; texts 19, 169
analytical method 150
Anaximenes 120
ancient education, see *paideia*
anthropological crit. 5
Antioch 188
Antiochus IV Epiphanes 212
Antipater 20
Antiphon 97
Apollonius 218–19, 212, 238
apologetic 53, 145
apologetic letter 33, 54, 55
Apuleius 219
Archigenes 218–19
argumentation 68
Aristarchus 24
Aristides 245–6
Ariston 13
Aristophanes 24, 225
Aristotelian analysis 42, 79, 123, 146–8, 158
Aristotle 8, 12–13, 29, 43, 111, 125, 132, 137, 199, 200, 210
   Ars Rhetorica 13, 39, 41–2, 125, 154, 159; *Constitution of Athens* 232
   in modern studies 68, 80–1, 121, 122–3, 127, 137, 140–1, 147–8, 150–1, 159, 162, 198–9

Politics 125; rhetorical theory 12–13, 37, 41, 42, 63–4, 122–3, 127, 128–9, 148, 151
Arnobius 168, 184–6
arrangement *see* structure
Asconius Pedianus 28
Asianism 43
assembly 33, 35, 125, 154
Asterius of Cappadocia 196
Athanasius 190
Athens 8, 181, 212, 219, 229, 245
Attic revival 222; date of 222–3, 229–30, 238
Atticism 43, 218, 223–4, 229–30, 238
   Paul's use of 217
Atticists 249
audience 161, 210–11
Augustine 127, 168, 190–6, 203; *Confessions* 190–1; *De Doctrina Christiana* 190–1, 192–6
Augustus 212
Averroes 199

Bacchylides 232
baptismal liturgy 109
Basil 175–6, 178
Betz, H. D. 35, 39–40, 64, 156, 160, 168–9
   method of rhetorical criticism 14, 29, 32, 49, 52–60, 70, 80, 86, 89, 153–4, 156, 165, 201, 259
   species of Galatians 35, 132–41, 146–7, 156, 162, 201
   structure of Galatians 90–2
Blair, Hugh 151

Calvin, J. 168
Calvus 223
Celsus 167, 171–2, 174, 217
Ch'an Buddhism 10–12

Chrysostom 99, 104–5, 176–81, 200
Cicero 12, 16, 28, 37, 42–3, 49, 52, 125,
    132, 199, 220, 223–4, 252
    Brutus 33, 39; church fathers 188, 189,
        193; *De Inventione* 19, 39, 41, 67,
        107, 108; *De Oratore* 16, 39, 43,
        223; in modern studies 39–40, 78,
        81, 94–5, 98, 100–1, 116, 137;
        Institutio Oratoria 18, 39; rhetorical
        theory 16–17, 19, 25–6, 34–5, 37,
        67, 98, 121, 125, 128, 155–6, 220,
        224
    Topica 37, 39
civic oratory 37
classroom 111, 242
classroom discourse 242
Clement of Alexandria 51
conclusio 114
1 Cor. 1–2, 195; 1.10–17, 177; 2.4–5,
    172, 254; 10.23–11.1, 142; 16.13,
    249
2 Cor. 6.2–10, 192
council 8, 12, 16–17, 33
courts 8, 12, 13, 16–19, 34, 38, 59, 86,
    94, 122, 125, 133, 148, 156, 180,
    184, 190, 201, 204–8, 220, 242, 251,
    258
Cremer, H. 231
Cynic-Stoic popular sermon 241
Cyprian 168, 183–4

Damascus 213
deliberative 33, 35, 54, 56–8, 120–1, 122,
    125–6, 130, 141, 153, 160–1, 165
    function of 162–3, 165
delivery 15, 28, 148
Demetrius 23, 26
Demosthenes 15, 28, 33, 97, 152–3, 178,
    182, 252
    De Corona 33; *Epistle 1* 33; *On the
        Peace* 56, 152–3
device, *see* rhetorical device
diachronic 56, 76–9, 87, 156–8
dialectic 13
diatribe 12, 14, 30, 110–11, 167–8,
    241–2, 250
Dio Chrysostom 211
Diogenes of Halicarnassus 223–4
Dionysius of Halicarnassus 23, 26, 28–9,
    222
Dioscurides 237
dispositio see structure
domain 207
Domitian 221

Domitius Afer 124

education, early Christian 123, 197
encomium 246
enthymeme 197
enumeratio 119
epideictic 35, 59, 121–3, 125–9, 140,
    162–4, 180
    effect of 125; function of 125–6,
        162–3; style 128
Epimenides *De oraculis* 217
Epiphanus of Salamis 197
epistles 49, 51; analysis 133; conventions
    2, 14, 21, 31, 36, 51, 95–7, 163–4;
    structure 2, 31, 119, 156; style 2;
    theorists 164; theory 163–4
Erasmus 203
ethics 13, 147
ethos 8, 149
example 109, 142–4, 157
exhoratio 152–3
exhortation 153, 161
exordium 36, 93, 99, 107, 109, 117, 132,
    201, 206; of Galatians 93–9, 178–9,
    201

Felix 204–5, 215
Festus 189
figures 27, 77, 83, 191
forensic, *see* judicial
form criticism 1, 49
forum *see* senate
frame 122, 141, 144, 150, 156, 161, 165,
    208, 258

Galatians 1–2, 36, 54, 92–109, 135–6,
    145; 1.1–13, 178–9; 1.10, 180–1;
    1.6–2.21, 201; 1.10–2.21, 104, 179;
    1.12–2.14, 152; 1.22–4, 180; 1.22,
    214; 1.6–9, 94; 2.3–5, 226–7;
    2.6–10, 227–8; 2.7, 250; 3–4,
    109–12, 132; 3.15, 112; 3.1, 180,
    201; 4.10–20, 192; 4.12–20, 160;
    4.13–15, 247; 4.12–6.10, 160; 4.24,
    180; 5–6, 61; 5.12, 156; 5.13, 179;
    5.13–6.10, 54, 179; 5.7–12, 155;
    6.11–18, 118, 138, 247
Galen 218, 221
Gamaliel 188, 213, 214
genre 55, 58
genre theory 144
genus didacticum 64, 201–2
Gischala 212
government 148

Graeco-Roman society 160
Greek literature 199, 222, 243
Greek: Attic 43, 205, 208, 210, 218, 222, 229–30
  koinē 224–7, 229–30; Semitic 236–7
Gregory of Nazianus 170, 184
Gregory of Nyssa 181

handbooks 1, 3, 7, 12, 14, 16–17, 27, 39–43, 56–7, 65, 76, 85, 89, 92, 97, 113, 116, 132, 143, 149, 156, 210, 258
Hebrews 247–8
Hegesippus 221
Hermagoras 26, 42
Hermogenes 19
Herodotus 30
Hilary 168
historical-critical method 76
Homer 30, 195, 217
Horace 189, 251

indignatio 154–5
intent 1, 162
intrinsic analysis 47
invention 27–8
Isaeus 225
Isocrates 178; *Antidosis* 32

Jerome 168, 188–90, 212
Jerusalem 214, 227; population 214
Jesus: education 172
John of Antioch 196
Josephus 51, 222, 225, 235; style 225, 235
judge and jury 101–2, 134, 148, 156, 207
judicial 13, 14, 35, 53, 57–8, 120, 122, 125, 130, 131–6, 137, 147, 154, 156, 160, 162, 165, 180–1, 206–8
  purpose 122, 162–3
Juvenal 182

Kennedy, G. 18, 29, 53, 56, 64, 148, 154, 156, 158–9, 161, 177, 182, 186, 205–6, 261
  ancient literary criticism 22–4, 25–9, 32–3, 42, 170, 198, 251
  method of rhetorical criticism 3, 14, 27, 29–30, 33–4, 39, 53–4, 61–3, 80–2, 86–9, 136–7, 140, 146–50, 158, 165, 261
  species of Galatians 21, 35, 53, 136–40, 150, 154, 156, 160
  structure of Galatians 91

Lactanius 168, 186–8
Leo the Great 196
Leontius 179
letter-writing 14, 30–1
levels of rhetoric 2, 7, 9, 14, 18–22, 51, 57
literacy 248
literary criticism 69, 77, 83–4; ancient 24–34; modern 47
literature 149
logos 8, 149
Longenecker, R.: method of rhetorical criticism 17, 56, 79–80, 88, 158–61
  species of Galatians 32, 160; structure of Galatians 90, 92
Longinus 23, 26
Luke–Acts 247
Luke's *tendenz* 213–14
Luther, M. 168, 248
Lysias 97, 225

Marius Victorinus 251
Martial 221
meaning 26, 81
Melanchthon 64, 168, 199–202
memory 28
Menander, *Thais* 217
Minucius Felix 168
Muretus 124

narratio 36, 97–107, 152–3, 179, 201
  beginning 101–2; of Galatians 99–105; purpose of 102–5; type 99–100
narrative 104–5, 109, 137, 144, 152–3, 201, 204
Neoptolemus 152
'new rhetoric' 146, 164
NT: style 1, 51, 173, 177–8, 230, 248–9; vocabulary 173, 177, 230
Nichomachus 237
non-rational persuasion 8, 9

Oecolampadius 200
orator: activities 245–7; entry 245–6
Origen 170–5
OT: criticism 44–9, 75

paideia 2, 19, 23, 25, 111, 123, 203, 209, 218–19, 220–3, 229–30
papyri 95, 232–3, 248
paraenesis 112–14, 119, 132, 138–40
partitio (enumeratio) 106–7
pathos 8, 149

Paul: Atticisms 217–18; background
  2–3, 5–6, 55, 181, 209, 211, 243,
  259; citizenship 211–13; education
  2–3, 76, 209, 213–15, 248, 253–4,
  259; financial circumstances 2, 209,
  215; Jerusalem 213–14; language 5,
  177–8, 189, 196, 203, 210, 217,
  224–7, 228, 232, 247; Pharisee
  213–14; social status 2, 6, 76, 209;
  secretaries 253; style 26, 51–2, 55,
  58, 167, 170, 177–8, 189, 192,
  216–17, 228, 244; Tarsus 211–13,
  215; trade 221
Paul of Samosata 169
peroratio 36, 114–15, 117
persuasion 8, 36, 57, 66, 69, 174–9, 181,
  254
persuasive strategy 66, 80
Philagrus of Cilicia 246
Philip of Macedon 152–3
Philo 253
philosophy 19–20, 111, 147
Philostratus 211, 218, 245; *Life of
  Apollonius* 212
Plato 13, 19, 32, 95, 105, 174, 178, 182;
  Defense of Socrates at his Trial 95;
  Dialectic 13; *Gorgias* 19; *Letter 7*
  32; *Menexenus* 140; *Republic* 105
Platonism 182
Pliny 251
Plutarch 105, 222
Polemo 245
political oratory 13–14
politics 13, 17, 19, 125, 147, 184
Pompey 212
preaching 123, 198
primary rhetoric 81
Priscian 239
probatio 36, 103–4, 106, 109, 132
propositio 36, 102, 105–9, 179
  Galatians 102; purpose of 105–8, 117,
  105–9, 201
Pseudo-Demetrius 2, 112
Pseudo-Libanius 2–3
Pseudo-Lysias 140
Ptolemaeus 237

Quintilian 12–13, 34, 39, 103–3, 124,
  132, 137, 151, 179, 201, 219–20
  in modern studies 40–1, 52, 65–7, 78,
  98–9, 102–3, 107, 109, 149
  rhetorical theory 13, 16–18, 20, 25, 28,
  42–3, 98–9, 108, 112, 115–16, 142,
  151, 251–2

Quintus Hortensius 251

rationality 73
register 2, 206–8
rhetoric: Christian 51, 83, 109, 152, 184
  content 18–21; definitions 12–13, 41;
  Galatians 52–6; historical crit.
  69–77; history 19, 53, 120, 124–5,
  232; Jewish 55, 61–2, 66, 165, 198,
  243–4; literary criticism 25–6, 72–6;
  NT study 44–56; OT study 44–9, 78;
  persuasion 66–9, 78, 161; preaching
  123, 198; public speech 15–16;
  universal 7–8, 23, 71, 83, 147–9, 159
Rhetorica ad Alexandrum 14–15, 39, 103,
  126, 154, 156
Rhetorica ad Herennium 15, 40–1, 93,
  104, 106, 123, 127, 129
rhetorical device 65, 83, 95, 176, 210,
  243
rhetorical situation 75–6, 130
Rhodian style 43
Romans 201–2, 250–1; 1.20, 173; 5.3–5
  191; 8.28–9 192
Rome 41, 213, 215, 223

schools: Greek 3; philosophical 2
secondary rhetoric 81–2
secretaries 222, 253
senate 13–14, 59, 122, 140, 242
Seneca 20, 241–2
Septuagint 66, 177, 225–6, 243
Servius 28
Sitz-im-Leben 49, 130–1, 145
social history 75
sociology 1
sophists 180, 222, 245–6
Sophocles 222
species 5, 27, 34–5, 57, 59, 83, 113,
  139–40, 144, 146–7, 150, 152, 154,
  161, 201, 206, 257–8
speeches 161; delivery 15, 28, 148;
  orality 14–15, 22–3, 28, 161
stance 1
Stoicism 182
Strabo 211
structure 27, 30, 33, 35–6, 42, 57, 60, 68,
  83, 90, 119, 144–5, 153, 170, 177–8,
  184, 205–6, 249, 258
style 20, 25, 26–7, 32, 43, 68, 82–3, 149,
  167–9, 173, 184, 191, 243, 249; *see
  also under* Paul
stylistics 83
synchronic 56, 67, 76–80, 87, 156–9, 161

syntax 249
Syria 231

Tacitus 17, 182
Tarsus 212–13, 215, 243
Tatian 171–2, 196
taxis, see structure
teachers 244
teaching, *see paideia*
Tertullian 168, 182–3, 184
Tertullus 205–6
Theodoret of Chyrrhus 198
Theodorus of Gadara 13
Theophilos of Antioch 171

Thomas of Chobham 198–9
Thucydides 29–30, 178, 222
time 192
Titus 227
topoi 37–8, 110, 180

venues 13, 16–17, 19, 33, 38, 111
  court 8, 12–13, 15–16, 19, 21, 35, 38,
    59, 111, 124–5, 156, 204–5, 207
  political assembly 12, 14, 18, 21, 33–5,
    111
Virgil 189, 195

Whately (Bishop) 15

INDEX OF MODERN AUTHORS

Albright, W. 46
Alexander, L. 218, 220
Alonso-Schökel, L. 68
Alter, R. 68
Amergen, T. 169
Aune, D. 2, 21, 99, 111

Baasland, E. 247
Ball, I. 48
Barclay, J. 109
Barrett, C. K. 2, 90, 113
Becker, J. 104
Berlin, A. 68
Betz, H. D. 4–5, 14, 29, 32, 35, 39–40,
    49, 52–9, 64, 70, 80, 86–8, 90,
    92–111, 113–18, 131–41, 145–6,
    154, 156, 159–62, 165, 168, 179,
    186, 201, 228, 258–9
Black, C. C. 49–50, 66, 69, 74
Black, E. 60, 63
Black, M. 231
Blair, H. 123, 151
Bligh, J. 114, 228
Booth, W. 37, 67
Bornkamm, G. 213
Botha, J. E. 84
Brandt, W. 22
Brinsmead, B. 35, 55–6, 91
Browning, R. 229–30, 238
Bruce, F. F. 206, 253
Bultmann, R. 44, 130, 168, 214, 240–2
Burke, K. 8–9, 20, 38, 67, 190
Burkitt, F. C. 227
Burney, C. F. 236
Burton, E. 118

Campbell, D. 4, 40, 64–6, 84, 190, 243
Cassuto, U. 46
Castelli, E. 73
Charles, R. H. 236

Clarke, M. L. 41
Classen, C. J. 64, 74, 195, 201
Clines, D. 47, 72
Corbett, E. 22, 32
Cosgrove, C. 106
Cremer, H. 231
Cronjé, J. V. W. 84–5

Dahl, N. 109, 253
Dalman, G. 236
Deissmann, A. 216, 233–7, 239, 241,
    248–9, 252, 254
Doty, W. 36, 144
Duncan, G. 227
Dunn, J. 114

Ellis, E. 242
Exum, C. 47, 72

Feldman, L. H. 222
Fitzgerald, J. 2
Fleming, J. 72
Fokkelman, J. P. 72, 75
Forbes, C. 3, 59
Frye, N. 46
Frye, R. M. 80
Funk, R. 58

Gadamer, H. G. 67
Gehman, H. 231
Gitay, Y. 49
Glover, T. R. 171, 251

Haenchen, E. 207, 214
Hagendahl, H. 195
Hall, R. 4, 91, 101, 104, 141
Hansen, G. W. 56, 112, 156–9, 161
Hays, R. 54–5
Heinrici, C. F. G. 44, 216
Hengel, M. 217, 221, 243

Hester, J. 35, 58, 92, 101, 163–4
Hudson, H. 20
Hughes, F. W. 33, 40

Jewett, R. 49
Johanson, B. 61, 122, 147, 151
Judge, E. 64, 70, 198, 214, 240, 244–5, 253

Kennedy, G. 3, 14, 18, 21, 23–30, 33, 39, 42, 53–4, 56, 61–4, 80–2, 86–8, 91, 105, 113, 117, 130, 136–41, 144, 146, 148–50, 152, 154, 156–61, 165, 170, 176–8, 182, 186, 197–8, 205–6, 251–2, 261
Kermode, F. 256
Kessler, M. 77–9, 159
Kikiwada, I. M. 46
Kilpatrick, G. D. 222
Kim, S. 214, 252
Koester, H. 151, 213
Koptak, P. 69
Kümmel, W. G. 231
Kurz, W. 204

Lambrecht, J. 22
Lategan, B. 83
Lausberg, H. 40
Lightfoot, J. B. 5, 105, 115, 118, 228
Litfin, D. 5, 71
Longenecker, R. 17, 32, 56, 79, 88–9, 92, 96–7, 105, 135, 156–61, 165, 247
Lüdemann, G. 4, 213
Lund, N. 197

Mack, B. 3–4, 17, 45, 59, 150, 168
Malherbe, A. 64–5, 203, 232, 239, 244–5
Malina, B. 5
Manson, T. W. 227
Marrou, H. 111, 182, 195
Martin, J. 40
Matera, F. 114
McDonald, J. I. H. 86–7
Meeks, W. 53
Merk, O. 113, 132
Meyer, P. 110
Michie, D. 68
Minn, H. R. 217
Mitchell, M. 57, 59, 69–71, 74
Moulton, J. H. 228
Muilenburg, J. 44–9, 53–5, 68, 74–5, 78, 86
Mukarosky, J. 85

Neyrey, J. 5
Nock, A. D. 243–5, 249
Norden, E. 216, 233, 240, 243

Olbrechts-Tyteca, L. 8, 15
Olbricht, T. 40, 146–7, 150, 198
Overbeck, F. 216, 240

Palmer, L. 223
Parker, T. H. L. 199–201
Patte, D. 69
Patton, J. 68
Pelletier, A. 223
Perelman, C. 8–9, 15, 67, 70, 73, 127, 163
Petersen, N. 29
Plank, K. 69
Pogoloff, S. M. 67–8
Porter, S. 20, 32, 81–3

Quacquarelli, A. 203

Radermacher, L. 236
Ramsay, W. 212
Rauber, D. F. 46
Rhoads, D. 68
Richards, E. R. 253
Robbins, V. K. 68
Roberts, W. R. 238
Robertson, A. T. 236
Ropes, J. H. 113
Russell, D. A. 246
Russell, W. III 92, 141
Rydbeck, L. 221, 237–9

Saunders, A. 128
Schenke, H.-M. 213
Scroggs, R. 250
Shklovsky, V. 85
Siegert, F. 69
Sloan, T. O. 31
Smit, J. 2, 35, 40, 57–8, 91, 113, 153–6, 165, 259
Snyman, A. H. 84
Standaert, B. 91
Stanley, C. 141
Stegemann, W. 213
Stowers, S. 113, 242

Thackeray, H. 222, 236
Thurén, L. 73–4
Turner, N. 227, 231, 236

Veltman, F. 203

Vogels, W. 78
Volkman, R. 40
Von Campenhausen 195
Vouga, F. 56, 58, 151–2, 156

Watson, D. 62–3, 141–3, 146
Weiss, J. 44, 216, 240
Wendland, H. 44
Wendland, P. 216, 240
Westcott, B. F. 225

White, J. L. 35–6, 95, 97, 162–3, 165
Wifstrand, A. 237–9
Wilamowitz-Moellendorff, U. von
    240
Wilder, A. 50–2, 78, 151
Wilson, T. 217
Winter, B. 5, 206, 245–7
Winterowd, W. R. 77
Wright, D. S. 10–1
Wuellner, W. 87, 199

Society for New Testament Studies

MONOGRAPH SERIES

Recent titles in the series:

75.   Covenant and Sacrifice in the Letter to the Hebrews
      JOHN DUNNILL
      0 521 43158 1

76.   The Plan of God in Luke–Acts
      JOHN T. SQUIRES
      0 521 43175 1

77.   Luke's Portrait of Paul
      JOHN C. LENTZ, JR
      0 521 43316 9

78.   The Preface to Luke's Gospel
      LOVEDAY ALEXANDER
      0 521 43444 0

79.   St Paul's Theology of Proclamation
      DUANE LITFIN
      0 521 45178 7

80.   Discipleship and Family Ties in Mark and Matthew
      STEPHEN C. BARTON
      0 521 46530 3

81.   Romans and the Apologetic Tradition
      ANTHONY J. GUERRA
      0 521 47126 5

82.   Wrestling with Rationality in Paul
      JOHN D. MOORES
      0 521 47223 7

83.   Paul on Marriage and Celibacy
      WILL DEMING
      0 521 47284 9

84.   The Faith of Jesus Christ in Early Christian Traditions
      IAN G. WALLIS
      0 521 47352 7

85.   Feasting and Social Rhetoric in Luke 14
      WILLI BRAUN
      0 521 49553 9

86. Power Through Weakness
   TIMOTHY B. SAVAGE
   0 521 49640 3

87. The Paradox of Salvation: Luke's Theology of the Cross
   PETER DOBLE
   0 521 55212 5

88. Apocalyptic Eschatology in the Gospel of Matthew
   DAVID C. SIM
   0 521 55365 2

89. The Character and Purpose of Luke's Christology
   H. DOUGLAS BUCKWALTER
   0 521 56180 9

90. Matthew's Emmanuel
   DAVID D. KUPP
   0 521 57007 7

91. The Zion Traditions and the Aims of Jesus
   KIM HUAT TAN
   0 521 58006 4

92. Paul's Gift from Philippi
   G. W. PETERMAN
   0 521 57220 7

93. The Pastoral Letters as Composite Documents
   JAMES D. MILLER
   0 521 56048 9

94. Christology and the Synoptic Problem
   PETER M. HEAD
   0 521 58488 4

95. Jesus and the Angels
   PETER R. CARRELL
   0 521 59011 6

96. Philo and Paul among the Sophists
   BRUCE W. WINTER
   0 521 59108 2

97. Eschatology in the Making
   VICKY BALABANSKI
   0 521 59137 6

98. Endurance in Suffering
   N. CLAYTON CROY
   0 521 59305 0

99. Jesus und der Täufer
   PETER BÖHLEMANN
   0 521 59421 9
100. Pontius Pilate in History and Interpretation
   HELEN K. BOND
   0 521 63114 9
101. Rhetoric and Galatians
   PHILIP H. KERN
   0 521 63117 3